Lesser Feasts and Fasts • 2024

Lesser Feasts and Fasts • 2024

Conforming to The General Convention 2024

Church
PUBLISHING

Church Publishing
19 East 34th Street
New York, NY 10016

ISBN 978-1-64065-808-0 (hardcover)

ISBN 978-1-64065-809-7 (ebook)

Contents

Preface

Christians have since ancient times honored people whose lives represent heroic commitment to Christ and who have borne witness to their faith even at the cost of their lives. Such witnesses, by the grace of God, live in every age. The criteria used in the selection of those to be commemorated in the Episcopal Church are set out below ("Principles of Revision," pages 623-624) and represent a growing consensus among provinces of the Anglican Communion also engaged in enriching their calendars.

What we celebrate in the lives of the saints is the presence of Christ expressing itself in and through particular lives lived in the midst of specific historical circumstances. In the saints we are not dealing with absolutes of perfection but human lives, in all their diversity, open to the movement of the Holy Spirit. Many a holy life, when carefully examined, will reveal flaws or the bias of a particular moment in history or ecclesial perspective. It should encourage us to realize that the saints, like us, are first and foremost redeemed sinners in whom the risen Christ's words to St. Paul come to fulfillment, "My grace is sufficient for you, for my power is made perfect in weakness."

This volume includes all feasts of our Lord and other major feasts, titled in **BOLD** letters. Other commemorations ("lesser feasts") are in capital/lowercase letters. Lesser feasts authorized for trial use by the General Convention are enclosed in [brackets].

The lesser feasts provide opportunities for optional observance. They are not intended to replace the fundamental celebration of Sunday and major Holy Days.

Historically, commemorations have originated in the local community, and the Principles of Revision (pages 623-624) expect that significant commemoration exists at the local level before a person is added to the Calendar of the Book of Common Prayer. This volume includes guidance for crafting local commemorations (pages 625-627) affirmed by the 81st General Convention. Communities may develop their own collects and readings for these commemorations, or select them from the Common of Saints (pages 593-607) or the New Commons for Various Occasions (pages 611-622).

As the Standing Commission on Liturgy and Music and the General Convention add or delete names from the calendar, successive editions of this volume will be published, each edition bearing in the title the date of the General Convention to which it is a response.

The Calendar of the Church Year

The Calendar of the Church Year

The Church Year consists of two cycles of feasts and holy days: one is dependent upon the movable date of the Sunday of the Resurrection or Easter Day; the other, upon the fixed date of December 25, the Feast of our Lord's Nativity or Christmas Day.

Easter Day is always the first Sunday after the full moon that falls on or after March 21. It cannot occur before March 22 or after April 25.

The sequence of all Sundays of the Church Year depends upon the date of Easter Day. But the Sundays of Advent are always the four Sundays before Christmas Day, whether it occurs on a Sunday or a weekday. The date of Easter also determines the beginning of Lent on Ash Wednesday, and the feast of the Ascension on a Thursday forty days after Easter Day.

1. Principal Feasts

The Principal Feasts observed in this Church are the following:

Easter Day
Ascension Day
The Day of Pentecost
Trinity Sunday
All Saints' Day, *November 1*
Christmas Day, *December 25*
The Epiphany, *January 6*

These feasts take precedence of any other day or observance. All Saints' Day may always be observed on the Sunday following November 1, in addition to its observance on the fixed date.

2. Sundays

All Sundays of the year are feasts of our Lord Jesus Christ. In addition to the dated days listed above, only the following feasts, appointed on fixed days, take precedence of a Sunday:

The Holy Name
The Presentation
The Transfiguration

The feast of the Dedication of a Church, and the feast of its patron or title, may be observed on, or be transferred to, a Sunday, except in the seasons of Advent, Lent, and Easter.

All other Feasts of our Lord, and all other Major Feasts appointed on fixed days in the Calendar, when they occur on a Sunday, are normally transferred to the first convenient open day within the week. When desired, however, the Collect, Preface, and one or more of the Lessons appointed for the Feast may be substituted for those of the Sunday, but not from the Last Sunday after Pentecost through the First Sunday after the Epiphany, or from the Last Sunday after the Epiphany through Trinity Sunday.

With the express permission of the bishop, and for urgent and sufficient reason, some other special occasion may be observed on a Sunday.

3. Holy Days

The following Holy Days are regularly observed throughout the year. Unless otherwise ordered in the preceding rules concerning Sundays, they have precedence over all other days of commemoration or of special observance:

Other Feasts of our Lord

The Holy Name
The Presentation
The Annunciation
The Visitation
Saint John the Baptist
The Transfiguration
Holy Cross Day

Other Major Feasts

All feasts of Apostles
All feasts of Evangelists
Saint Stephen
The Holy Innocents
Saint Joseph
Saint Mary Magdalene
Saint Mary the Virgin
Saint Michael and All Angels
Saint James of Jerusalem
Independence Day
Thanksgiving Day

Fasts

Ash Wednesday
Good Friday

Feasts appointed on fixed days in the Calendar are not observed on the days of Holy Week or of Easter Week. Major Feasts falling in these weeks are transferred to the week following the Second Sunday of Easter, in the order of their occurrence.

Feasts appointed on fixed days in the Calendar do not take precedence over Ash Wednesday.

Feasts of our Lord and other Major Feasts appointed on fixed days, which fall upon or are transferred to a weekday, may be observed on any open day within the week. This provision does not apply to Christmas Day, the Epiphany, and All Saints' Day.

4. Days of Special Devotion

The following days are observed by special acts of discipline and self-denial:

Ash Wednesday and the other weekdays of Lent and of Holy Week, except the feast of the Annunciation.

Good Friday and all other Fridays of the year, in commemoration of the Lord's crucifixion, except for Fridays in the Christmas and Easter seasons, and any Feasts of our Lord which occur on a Friday.

5. Days of Optional Observance

Subject to the rules of precedence governing Principal Feasts, Sundays, and Holy Days, the following may be observed with the Collects, Psalms, and Lessons duly authorized by this Church:

Commemorations listed in the Calendar
Other Commemorations, using the Common of Saints
The Ember Days, traditionally observed on the Wednesdays, Fridays, and Saturdays after the First Sunday in Lent, the Day of Pentecost, Holy Cross Day, and December 13
The Rogation Days, traditionally observed on Monday, Tuesday, and Wednesday before Ascension Day
Various Occasions

Provided that there is no celebration of the Eucharist for any such occasion on Ash Wednesday, Maundy Thursday, Good Friday, and Holy Saturday; and provided further, that none of the Propers appointed for Various Occasions is used as a substitute for, or as an addition to, the Proper appointed for the Principal Feasts.

MARCH

1 David of Wales, *Bishop,* c. 544
2 Chad of Lichfield, *Bishop,* 672
3 John and Charles Wesley, *Priests,* 1791, 1788
4
5
6
7 Perpetua and Felicity, *Martyrs,* 202
8
9 Gregory of Nyssa, *Bishop and Theologian,* c. 394
10 Harriet Ross Tubman, *Social Reformer,* 1913
11
12 Gregory the Great, *Bishop and Theologian,* 604
13 James Theodore Holly, *Bishop,* 1911
14
15 Vincent de Paul, *Priest,* and Louise de Marillac, *Vowed Religious, Workers of Charity,* 1660
16
17 Patrick of Ireland, *Bishop and Missionary,* 461
18 Cyril of Jerusalem, *Bishop and Theologian,* 386
19 **Saint Joseph**
20 Cuthbert, *Bishop,* 687
21 Thomas Ken, *Bishop,* 1711
22 James De Koven, *Priest,* 1879
23 Gregory the Illuminator, *Bishop and Missionary,* c. 332
24 Óscar Romero, *Archbishop and Martyr,* 1980, and the Martyrs of El Salvador
25 **The Annunciation of Our Lord Jesus Christ to the Blessed Virgin Mary**
26 Harriet Monsell, *Monastic,* 1883
27 Charles Henry Brent, *Bishop,* 1929
28 James Solomon Russell, *Priest,* 1935
29 John Keble, *Priest and Poet,* 1866
30 Mary of Egypt, *Monastic,* c. 421
31 John Donne, *Priest and Poet,* 1631

APRIL

1 Frederick Denison Maurice, *Priest,* 1872
2 James Lloyd Breck, *Priest,* 1876
3 Richard of Chichester, *Bishop,* 1253
4 Martin Luther King, Jr., *Pastor and Martyr,* 1968
5 Harriet Starr Cannon, *Monastic,* 1896
6
7 Tikhon, *Bishop and Ecumenist,* 1925
8 William Augustus Muhlenberg, *Priest,* 1877
9 Dietrich Bonhoeffer, *Pastor and Theologian,* 1945
10 William Law, *Priest,* 1761
11 George Augustus Selwyn, *Bishop,* 1878
12
13
14 Zenaida, Philonella, and Hermione, *Unmercenary Physicians,* c. 100, c. 117
15 Damien, *Priest,* 1889, and Marianne Cope, *Monastic,* 1918, of Hawai'i
16 Peter Williams Cassey, *Deacon,* 1917, and Anna Besant Cassey, 1875
17 Kateri Tekakwitha, *Lay Contemplative,* 1680
18 Juana Inés de la Cruz, *Monastic and Theologian,* 1695
19 Alphege, *Archbishop of Canterbury and Martyr,* 1012
20
21 Anselm, *Archbishop of Canterbury and Theologian,* 1109
22 Hadewijch of Brabant, *Poet and Mystic,* thirteenth century
23 Toyohiko Kagawa, *Social Reformer,* 1960
24
25 **Saint Mark the Evangelist**
26
27 Zita of Tuscany, *Worker of Charity,* 1271
28
29 Catherine of Siena, *Mystic and Prophetic Witness,* 1380
30

MAY

1 **The Apostles Saint Philip and Saint James**
2 Athanasius of Alexandria, *Bishop and Theologian,* 373
3 Elisabeth Cruciger, *Poet and Hymnographer,* 1535
4 Monica, *Mother of Augustine of Hippo,* 387
5 Martyrs of the Reformation Era
6 [George of Lydda, *Soldier and Martyr,* c. 304]
7
8 Julian of Norwich, *Mystic and Theologian,* c. 1417
9 Gregory of Nazianzus, *Bishop and Theologian,* 389
10
11 Johann Arndt and Jacob Boehme, *Mystics,* 1621 and 1624
12
13 Frances Perkins, *Social Reformer,* 1965
14
15 Pachomius of Tabenissi, *Monastic,* 348
16
17 Thurgood Marshall, *Public Servant,* 1993
18
19 Dunstan, *Archbishop of Canterbury,* 988
20 Alcuin of York, *Deacon,* 804
21 Lydia of Thyatira, *Coworker of the Apostle Paul*
22 Helena of Constantinople, *Protector of the Holy Places,* 330
23
24 Jackson Kemper, *Bishop and Missionary,* 1870
25 Bede, *Priest and Historian,* 735
26 Augustine, *First Archbishop of Canterbury,* 605
27
28 Mechthild of Magdeburg, *Mystic,* c. 1282
29
30
31 **The Visitation of the Blessed Virgin Mary**

JUNE

1 Justin, *Martyr,* 167
2 Blandina and Her Companions, the Martyrs of Lyons, 177
3 The Martyrs of Uganda, 1886
4 John XXIII (Angelo Giuseppe Roncalli), *Bishop,* 1963
5 Boniface, *Bishop and Missionary,* 754
6
7
8 Melania the Elder, *Monastic,* 410
9 Columba of Iona, *Monastic,* 597
10 Ephrem of Nisibis, *Deacon and Poet,* 373
11 **Saint Barnabas the Apostle**
12 Enmegahbowh, *Priest and Missionary,* 1902
13 The First Book of Common Prayer, 1549
14 Basil of Caesarea, *Bishop and Theologian,* 379
15 Evelyn Underhill, *Mystic and Writer,* 1941
16 Joseph Butler, *Bishop and Theologian,* 1752
17 Marina the Monk, *Monastic,* fifth century
18 Bernard Mizeki, *Martyr,* 1896
19 Adelaide Teague Case, *Educator,* 1948
20
21
22 Alban, *Martyr,* c. 304
23
24 **The Nativity of Saint John the Baptist**
25
26 Isabel Florence Hapgood, *Ecumenist,* 1928
27
28 Irenaeus of Lyons, *Bishop and Theologian,* c. 202
29 **The Apostles Saint Peter and Saint Paul**
30

JULY

1 Pauli Murray, *Priest,* 1985
2 Moses the Black, *Monastic and Martyr,* c. 400
3
4 **Independence Day** (United States)
5
6 Eva Lee Matthews, *Monastic,* 1928
7
8 Priscilla and Aquila, *Coworkers of the Apostle Paul*
9
10
11 Benedict of Nursia, *Monastic,* c. 543
12
13
14 Argula von Grumbach, *Scholar and Church Reformer,* c. 1554
15
16
17 William White, *Bishop,* 1836
18
19 Macrina of Caesarea, *Monastic and Teacher,* 379
20 Elizabeth Cady Stanton, Amelia Bloomer, and Sojourner Truth, *Social Reformers,* 1902, 1894, and 1883
21 Maria Skobtsova, *Monastic and Martyr,* 1945
22 **Saint Mary Magdalene**
23 John Cassian, *Monastic and Theologian,* 435
24 Thomas à Kempis, *Priest and Mystic,* 1471
25 **Saint James the Apostle**
26 The Parents of the Blessed Virgin Mary
27 William Reed Huntington, *Priest,* 1909
28 Johann Sebastian Bach, *Composer,* 1750
29 [The Ordination of the Philadelphia Eleven]
Mary and Martha of Bethany
30 William Wilberforce, *Social Reformer,* 1833
31 Ignatius of Loyola, *Priest and Spiritual Writer,* 1556

AUGUST

1 Joseph of Arimathea
2
3 Joanna, Mary, and Salome, *Myrrh-Bearing Women*
4
5
6 **The Transfiguration of Our Lord Jesus Christ**
7 John Mason Neale, *Priest and Hymnographer,* 1866
8 Dominic, *Priest and Friar,* 1221
9 Edith Stein (Teresa Benedicta of the Cross), *Philosopher, Monastic, and Martyr,* 1942
10 Laurence of Rome, *Deacon and Martyr,* 258
11 Clare of Assisi, *Monastic,* 1253
12 Florence Nightingale, *Nurse,* 1910
13 Jeremy Taylor, *Bishop and Theologian,* 1667
14 Jonathan Myrick Daniels, *Martyr,* 1965
15 **Saint Mary the Virgin, Mother of Our Lord Jesus Christ**
16
17
18
19
20 Bernard of Clairvaux, *Monastic and Theologian,* 1153
21
22
23
24 **Saint Bartholomew the Apostle**
25 Louis, *King,* 1270
26 Simeon Bachos the Ethiopian Eunuch
27 Thomas Gallaudet and Henry Winter Syle, *Priests,* 1902 and 1890
28 Augustine of Hippo, *Bishop and Theologian,* 430
29 The Beheading of Saint John the Baptist
30 Margaret Ward, Margaret Clitherow, and Anne Line, *Martyrs,* 1588, 1586, and 1601
31 Aidan of Lindisfarne, *Bishop,* 651

SEPTEMBER

1 David Pendleton Oakerhater, *Deacon,* 1931
2 The Martyrs of New Guinea, 1942
3 Phoebe, *Deacon*
4 Paul Jones, *Bishop,* 1941
5 Katharina Zell, *Church Reformer and Writer,* 1562
6 Hannah More, *Religious Writer and Philanthropist,* 1833
7 [Élie Naud]
Kassiani, *Poet and Hymnographer,* 865
8 The Nativity of the Blessed Virgin Mary
9 Constance, Thecla, Ruth, Frances, Charles Parsons, and Louis Schuyler, *Martyrs,* 1878
10 Alexander Crummell, *Priest,* 1898
11
12 John Henry Hobart, *Bishop,* 1830
13 Cyprian of Carthage, *Bishop and Martyr,* 258
14 **Holy Cross Day**
15 Catherine of Genoa, *Mystic and Nurse,* 1510
16 Ninian, *Bishop,* c. 430
17 Hildegard of Bingen, *Mystic and Scholar,* 1179
18 Edward Bouverie Pusey, *Priest,* 1882
19 Theodore of Tarsus, *Archbishop of Canterbury,* 690
20 John Coleridge Patteson, *Bishop,* and his Companions, *Martyrs,* 1871
21 **Saint Matthew, Apostle and Evangelist**
22 Philander Chase, *Bishop,* 1852
23 Thecla of Iconium, *Proto-Martyr Among Women,* c. 70
24 Anna Ellison Butler Alexander, *Deaconess and Teacher,* 1947
25 Sergius of Radonezh, *Monastic,* 1392
26 Lancelot Andrewes, *Bishop,* 1626
27 Euphrosyne/Smaragdus of Alexandria, *Monastic,* fifth century
28 Paula and Eustochium of Rome, *Monastics and Scholars,* 404 and c. 419
29 **Saint Michael and All Angels**
30 Jerome, *Priest and Scholar,* 420

OCTOBER

1 Thérèse of Lisieux, *Monastic,* 1897
2 Remigius of Rheims, *Bishop,* c. 530
3 John Raleigh Mott, *Ecumenist and Missionary,* 1955
4 Francis of Assisi, *Friar and Deacon,* 1226
5
6 William Tyndale, *Priest,* 1536
7 Birgitta of Sweden, *Mystic,* 1373
8
9 Robert Grosseteste, *Bishop,* 1253
10 Vida Dutton Scudder, *Educator,* 1954
11 Philip, *Deacon and Evangelist*
12 Edith Cavell, *Nurse,* 1915
13
14 Samuel Isaac Joseph Schereschewsky, *Bishop and Missionary,* 1906
15 Teresa of Avila, *Mystic and Monastic Reformer,* 1582
16 Hugh Latimer and Nicholas Ridley, *Bishops and Martyrs,* 1555, and Thomas Cranmer, *Archbishop of Canterbury,* 1556
17 Ignatius of Antioch, *Bishop and Martyr,* c. 115
18 **Saint Luke the Evangelist**
19 Henry Martyn, *Priest and Missionary,* 1812
20 Cornelius the Centurion
21
22
23 **Saint James of Jerusalem, Brother of Our Lord Jesus Christ and Martyr,** c. 62
24
25 Tabitha (Dorcas) of Joppa
26 Alfred, *King,* 899
27
28 **Saint Simon and Saint Jude, Apostles**
29 James Hannington, *Bishop,* and his Companions, *Martyrs,* 1885
30 Maryam of Qidun, *Monastic,* fourth century
31

NOVEMBER

1 **All Saints**
2 All Souls / All the Faithful Departed
3 Richard Hooker, *Priest and Theologian,* 1600
4 [Adeline Blanchard Tyler and her Companions]
5
6 William Temple, *Archbishop of Canterbury,* 1944
7 Willibrord, *Bishop and Missionary,* 739
8 Ammonius, *Hermit,* c. 403
9 Richard Rolle, Walter Hilton, and Margery Kempe, *Mystics,* 1349, 1396, and c. 1440
10 Leo of Rome, *Bishop,* 461
11 Martin of Tours, *Bishop,* 397
12 Charles Simeon, *Priest,* 1836
13
14 The Consecration of Samuel Seabury, 1784
15 Herman of Alaska, *Missionary,* 1837
16 Margaret of Scotland, *Queen,* 1093
17 Hugh of Lincoln, *Bishop,* 1200
18 Hilda of Whitby, *Abbess,* 680
19 Elizabeth of Hungary, *Princess,* 1231
20 Edmund, *King,* 870
21 Mechthilde of Hackeborn and Gertrude the Great, *Mystics and Theologians,* 1298 and 1302
22 Clive Staples Lewis, *Apologist and Spiritual Writer,* 1963
23 Clement of Rome, *Bishop,* c. 100
24 Catherine of Alexandria, Barbara of Nicomedia, and Margaret of Antioch, *Martyrs,* c. 305
25 James Otis Sargent Huntington, *Monastic and Priest,* 1935
26
27
28 Kamehameha and Emma of Hawai'i, *King and Queen,* 1863 and 1885
29
30 **Saint Andrew the Apostle**

DECEMBER

1 Charles de Foucauld, *Monastic and Martyr,* 1916
2 Channing Moore Williams, *Bishop and Missionary,* 1910
3 Francis Xavier, *Priest and Missionary,* 1552
4 John of Damascus, *Priest and Theologian,* c. 760
5 Clement of Alexandria, *Priest and Theologian,* c. 210
6 Nicholas of Myra, *Bishop,* c. 342
7 Ambrose of Milan, *Bishop and Theologian,* 397
8 Nicholas Ferrar, *Deacon,* 1637
9
10
11 Frederick Howden, Jr., *Priest and Chaplain of the Armed Forces,* 1941
12 Francis de Sales, Bishop, and Jane de Chantal, *Vowed Religious,* 1622 and 1641
13 Lucy of Syracuse, *Martyr,* 304
14 John of the Cross, *Mystic and Monastic Reformer,* 1591
15 Nino of Georgia, *Missionary,* c. 332
16
17 Dorothy L. Sayers, *Apologist and Spiritual Writer,* 1957
18
19
20 Katharina von Bora, *Church Reformer,* 1552
21 **Saint Thomas the Apostle**
22
23
24
25 **The Nativity of Our Lord Jesus Christ**
26 **Saint Stephen, Deacon and Martyr**
27 **Saint John, Apostle and Evangelist**
28 **Holy Innocents**
29 Thomas Becket, *Archbishop of Canterbury and Martyr,* 1170
30
31 Frances Joseph Gaudet, *Educator and Social Reformer,* 1934

The Proper for the Lesser Feasts

Concerning the Proper for the Lesser Feasts

Proper Collects, Lessons, and Psalms are provided for each of the Lesser Feasts.

On occasion an appropriate selection may be made from the Common of Saints (pages 593-607) or the New Commons for Various Occasions (pages 609-622).

Any of the Readings may be lengthened at discretion. The selections from the Psalter may be lengthened or shortened.

The Preface of the Season (when there is one) may always be substituted for the Preface indicated in the Proper for the Lesser Feasts.

The Book of Common Prayer provides three Prefaces "Of a Saint" that may be used at discretion on certain of the Lesser Feasts. This book indicates the most appropriate of those Prefaces by the use of numerals in parentheses: (1), (2), or (3).

An appropriate Collect, Psalm, and Lessons from the Common of Saints or the New Commons for Various Occasions may always be substituted for those assigned to a Lesser Feast.

The designation of this day as the Feast of the Holy Name was new to the 1979 revision of the Book of Common Prayer. Previous Anglican Prayer Books called it the Feast of the Circumcision. January 1 is, of course, the eighth day after Christmas Day, and the Gospel according to Luke records that eight days after his birth the child was circumcised and given the name Jesus.

The liturgical commemoration of the Circumcision is of Gallican origin, and a Council in Tours in 567 enacted that the day was to be kept as a fast day to counteract pagan festivities connected with the beginning of the new year. In the Roman tradition, January 1 was observed as the octave day of Christmas, and it was particularly devoted to the Virgin Mary.

The early preachers of the Gospel lay stress on the name as showing that Jesus was a man of flesh and blood, though also the Son of God, who died a human death, and whom God raised from death (Acts 2:32, 4:12). The name "Jesus" was given to him, as the angel explained to Joseph, because he would "save his people from their sins" (Matthew 1:21), as the name means "Savior" or "Deliverer" in Hebrew.

Then, as now, people longed to be freed from evils: political, social, and spiritual. The name of Jesus calls to mind the true freedom that is ours through Jesus Christ.

The Holy Name of Our Lord Jesus Christ

I Eternal Father, who didst give to thine incarnate Son the holy name of Jesus to be the sign of our salvation: Plant in every heart, we beseech thee, the love of him who is the Savior of the world, even our Lord Jesus Christ; who liveth and reigneth with thee and the Holy Ghost, one God, in glory everlasting. *Amen.*

II Eternal Father, who gave to your incarnate Son the holy name of Jesus to be the sign of our salvation: Plant in every heart, we pray, the love of him who is the Savior of the world, our Lord Jesus Christ; who lives and reigns with you and the Holy Spirit, one God, in glory everlasting. *Amen.*

Lessons and Psalm

Numbers 6:22-27
Psalm 8
Galatians 4:4-7 *or* Philippians 2:5-11
Luke 2:15-21

Preface of the Incarnation

Elizabeth Ann Seton was the founder of the Sisters of Charity, the first community of sisters established in the United States.

Elizabeth was born in New York City on August 28, 1774, and was raised as an Episcopalian. She endured a turbulent childhood and suffered severe bouts of depression, but persevered by immersing herself in poetry, piano lessons, and devoted participation in the Episcopal Church. From a young age, she desired to help the sick and poor. In 1795 she married William Seton, and their family came to include five children. During this time, she also founded the Society for the Relief of Poor Widows with Small Children.

In 1801, however, the family business went bankrupt. In 1803, her husband developed symptoms of tuberculosis, and they set sail for Italy in the hopes that the warm climate might cure his disease. The Italian authorities, fearing yellow fever, quarantined them in a cold stone hospital for the dying. William soon died and left Elizabeth a young widow with five children and few resources. While struggling with these losses, she was befriended by Roman Catholics and, as a result, was drawn to the Catholic Church.

Returning to New York, she encountered bitter opposition from her Episcopalian family for her new religious leanings. With five children to support, she found herself alone and in financial straits. She turned to Catholic clergy for support and, in 1805, she formally became a member of the Catholic Church.

In 1806, she met Father Louis Dubourg, who wanted to start a congregation of women religious, patterned after the French Daughters of Charity of Saint Vincent de Paul. In 1809 Elizabeth took vows and became "Mother Seton" to a small community of seven women, known as the Sisters of Charity of Saint Joseph, who were dedicated to teaching. The sisters were given land in rural Maryland and, in 1810, they opened Saint Joseph's Free School to educate needy girls. The sisters intertwined social ministry, education, and religious formation in all of their varied works. Out of the pioneering work of Elizabeth Seton, five independent communities of the Sisters of Charity now exist, offering ministry and care for the most vulnerable.

Elizabeth Ann Seton remained the superior of the Sisters of Charity until her death on January 4, 1821.

The legacy of the Sisters of Charity has left a lasting impact on the Episcopal Church as well as on the Catholic Church. The earliest Anglican religious orders for women used the rule of the Sisters of Charity as the basis for their own rules, and there have been Sisters of Charity in the Anglican Communion since 1869.

Elizabeth Ann Seton

Vowed Religious and Educator, 1821

I Give us grace, O God, to love thee in all things and above all things; that, following the example of thy servant Elizabeth Ann Seton, we might express our love for thee in the service of others. Through Jesus Christ our Lord, who liveth and reigneth with thee and the Holy Ghost, one God, in glory everlasting. *Amen.*

II Give us grace, O God, to love you in all things and above all things; that, following the example of your servant Elizabeth Ann Seton, we might express our love for you in the service of others. Through Jesus Christ our Lord, who lives and reigns with you and the Holy Spirit, one God, in glory everlasting. *Amen.*

Lessons and Psalm

2 Esdras 2:15-24
Psalm 119:105-112
Romans 16:17-20
Luke 14:15-23

Preface of the Incarnation

Sarah, Theodora, and Syncletica are the three desert mothers, or *ammas,* whose sayings are included in the fifth-century *Apophthegmata Patrum,* the sayings of the desert fathers. The collections include a total of forty-seven sayings attributed to these three women.

The sayings relate that Amma Sarah lived beside a beautiful river for sixty years, yet never lifted her eyes in distraction from prayer to look at it. She often said, "If I prayed to God that all people should approve of my conduct, I should find myself a penitent at the door of each one, but I shall rather pray that my heart may be pure towards all." Many people came to visit her seeking spiritual advice. On one occasion some monks came to her claiming to be from the highly regarded community of Scetis and she offered them a basket of fruit from which they took the rotten fruit and left the good fruit for others to eat. She then said to them, "You are true monks of Scetis." At another time, some elderly monks, considered to be great anchorites, came to see her hoping to humiliate her and shame her. They came to her and said, "Be careful not to become conceited because we great anchorites are coming to see you, a mere woman!" Amma Sarah only replied, "According to nature I am a woman, but not according to my thoughts. It is I who am a man and you who are women."

Amma Theodora was the wife of a Roman tribune, but after his death she retired to the desert to live an ascetic life. She was consulted by many people for her wisdom on prayer. According to one of her teachings, those who set their minds to pray are often overcome with distraction, depression, faintheartedness, or headaches. But she relates the story of how a certain monk, every time he felt too ill to pray, declared: "Clearly I am very near death, and so I should get up and pray right now before I die!" In this way, he resisted temptation. Yet Amma Theodora also stressed that temptations can only be overcome through humility rather than through asceticism, for even the demons fast and keep vigil and live in deserted places, but they do not have humility.

Amma Syncletica lived a life of asceticism in a tomb in Alexandria. She wrote, "if you find yourself in a place, do not forsake it to go to another place, for that will harm you a great deal. Just as a bird who abandons the eggs that she was sitting on prevents them from hatching, so too a monastic grows cold and her faith dies when she wanders from one place to another." She also taught that it was possible to live a spiritual life within secular society, not only as a monk or a nun. "There are many who live in the desert yet behave as though they were in town, and they are wasting their time. It is possible to be a monastic in one's mind while living in a crowd, and it is also possible for a monastic to live in a crowd amidst her own thoughts."

Sarah, Theodora, and Syncletica of Egypt

Desert Mothers, fourth–fifth century

I Fix our hearts on thee, O God, in pure devotion, that aided by the example of thy servants Sarah, Theodora, and Syncletica, the vain pursuits of this world may have no hold upon us, and that by the consuming fire of thy Spirit, we may be changed into the image and likeness of thy Son, Jesus Christ our Lord; to whom with thee and the same Spirit be all honor and glory, now and for ever. *Amen.*

II Fix our hearts on You, O God, in pure devotion, that aided by the example of your servants Sarah, Theodora, and Syncletica, the vain pursuits of this world may have no hold upon us, and that by the consuming fire of your Spirit, we may be changed into the image and likeness of your Son, Jesus Christ our Lord; to whom with you and the same Spirit be all honor and glory, now and for ever. *Amen.*

Lessons and Psalm

Proverbs 9:1-6
Psalm 119:65-72
James 4:1-10
Mark 12:18-27

Preface of the Incarnation

The name "Epiphany" is derived from a Greek word meaning "manifestation" or "appearing." Anglican Prayer Books interpret the word as, "The Manifestation of Christ to the Gentiles." The last phrase, of course, is a reference to the story of the Magi from the East.

A Christian observance on January 6 is found as early as the end of the second century in Egypt. The feast combined commemorations of three events that were considered manifestations of the Incarnate Lord: the visit of the Magi, led by the star of Bethlehem; the Baptism of Jesus in the waters of the Jordan River; and Jesus' first recorded miracle, the changing of water into wine at the wedding of Cana.

Epiphany is still the primary Feast of the Incarnation in Eastern churches, and the three-fold emphasis is still prominent. In the West, however, including Anglican churches, the story of the Magi has tended to overshadow the other two events. Modern lectionary reform, reflected in the 1979 Prayer Book, has recovered the primitive trilogy by setting the event of Christ's Baptism as the theme of the First Sunday after the Epiphany in all three years, and by providing the story of the Miracle at Cana as the Gospel for the Second Sunday after the Epiphany in Year C.

It is a practice in some communities to bless chalk on Epiphany so that people may use it to bless their homes. Traditionally, the chalking is done above the lintel and takes this form: 20+C+M+B+18, in which "18" is replaced by the current year. The letters are the abbreviation for the Latin phrase "Christus mansionem benedicat"—"Christ bless this house." (A second meaning and mnemonic device is "Caspar, Melchior, and Balthazar," the traditional names for the Magi.) The + signs represent the cross, and 20-18 is the year.

The following prayer is traditionally used for the blessing of chalk:

> Loving God, bless this chalk which you have created, that it may be helpful to your people; and grant through the invocation of your most Holy Name that we who use it in faith to write upon the door of our home the names of your holy ones Caspar, Melchior, and Balthazar, may receive health of body and protection of soul for all who dwell in or visit our home; through Jesus Christ our Lord. *Amen.*

The Epiphany of Our Lord Jesus Christ

I O God, who by the leading of a star didst manifest thy only-begotten Son to the peoples of the earth: Lead us, who know thee now by faith, to thy presence, where we may behold thy glory face to face; through the same Jesus Christ our Lord, who liveth and reigneth with thee and the Holy Ghost, one God, now and for ever. *Amen.*

II O God, by the leading of a star you manifested your only Son to the peoples of the earth: Lead us, who know you now by faith, to your presence, where we may see your glory face to face; through Jesus Christ our Lord, who lives and reigns with you and the Holy Spirit, one God, now and for ever. *Amen.*

Lessons and Psalm

Isaiah 60:1-6
Psalm 72:1-7, 10-14
Ephesians 3:1-12
Matthew 2:1-12

Preface of the Epiphany

Harriet Bedell was born in Buffalo, New York, on March 19, 1875. Inspired by an Episcopal missionary, she enrolled as a student at the New York Training School for Deaconesses, where she was instructed in religion, missions, teaching, and health. She then became a missionary-teacher among the Cheyenne at the Whirlwind Mission in Oklahoma.

In 1916, Bedell was sent to Stevens Village, Alaska, where she was set apart as a deaconess in 1922. She also served as a teacher and nurse at St. John's in the Wilderness at Allakaket, just 40 miles south of the Arctic Circle, from which she sometimes traveled by dogsled to remote villages. During her last years in Alaska, Bedell opened a boarding school.

In 1932, hearing about the plight of the Seminoles in Florida, Bedell used her own salary to reopen a mission among the Mikasuki Indians. There, she worked to revive some of their traditional crafts: doll-making, basket-weaving, and intricate patchwork designs. The arts and crafts store that they established to sell their handicrafts improved the economy of the Blades Cross Mission. Though officially forced to retire at age 63, Bedell continued her ministry of health care, education, and economic empowerment until 1960 when Hurricane Donna wiped out her mission.

Active into her eighties, Deaconess Bedell drove an average of 20,000 miles per year during her ministry. She was one of the most popular writers in the Episcopal mission periodical, *The Spirit of Missions*. Bedell won the respect of indigenous people through her compassion and respect for their way of life and beliefs. While active in ministry among the Cheyenne, she was eventually adopted into the tribe and given the name "Bird Woman." The Diocese of Southwest Florida has long celebrated Harriet Bedell Day on January 8, the anniversary of her death in 1969.

Harriet Bedell

Deaconess and Missionary, 1969

I Holy God, fill us with compassion and respect for all people, and empower us for the work of ministry whether near or far away; that like thy servant Harriet Bedell, we may show forth thy praise, not only with our lips, but in our lives, and by giving up ourselves to thy service. Through Jesus Christ our Lord, who liveth and reigneth with thee and the Holy Ghost, one God, for ever and ever. *Amen.*

II Holy God, fill us with compassion and respect for all people, and empower us for the work of ministry whether near or far away; that like your servant Harriet Bedell, we may show forth your praise, not only with our lips, but in our lives, and by giving up ourselves to your service. Through Jesus Christ our Lord, who lives and reigns with you and the Holy Spirit, one God, for ever and ever. *Amen.*

Lessons and Psalm

Exodus 2:1-10
Psalm 96:1-7
1 Corinthians 1:4-9
Matthew 5:1-12

Preface of Apostles and Ordinations

Julia Chester Emery was born in Dorchester, Massachusetts, on September 24, 1852. In 1876 she succeeded her sister, Mary, as Secretary of the Woman's Auxiliary of the Board of Missions, which had been established by the General Convention in 1871.

During the forty years that she served as Secretary, Julia helped the Episcopal Church to recognize its call to proclaim the gospel both at home and overseas. Her faith, her courage, her spirit of adventure, and her ability to inspire others combined to make her a leader respected and valued by the whole church.

She visited every diocese and missionary district within the United States, encouraging and expanding the work of the Woman's Auxiliary, and in 1908 she served as a delegate to the Pan-Anglican Congress in London. From there she traveled around the world, visiting missions in remote areas of China, Japan, Hong Kong, the Philippines, Hawai'i, and then all the dioceses on the Pacific Coast before returning to New York. Although travel was not easy in those days, she wrote that she went forth "with hope for enlargement of vision, opening up new occasions for service, acceptance of new tasks."

Through her leadership a network of branches of the Woman's Auxiliary was established, which shared a vision of and a commitment to the church's mission. An emphasis on educational programs, a growing recognition of social issues, development of leadership among women, and the creation of the United Thank Offering are further parts of the legacy Julia left to the church when she retired in 1916.

In 1921, a year before she died on January 9, 1922, the following appeared in the periodical *The Spirit of Missions*: "In all these enterprises of the church, no single agency has done so much in the last half-century to further the church's mission as the Woman's Auxiliary." Much of that accomplishment was due to the creative spirit of its secretary for forty of those fifty years, Julia Chester Emery.

Julia Chester Emery

Lay Leader and Missionary, 1922

I God of all creation, who dost call us to make disciples of all nations and to proclaim thy mercy and love: Grant that we, after the example of thy servant Julia Chester Emery, might have vision and courage in proclaiming the Gospel to the ends of the earth; through Jesus Christ, our light and our salvation, who liveth and reigneth with thee and the Holy Ghost, ever one God, for ever and ever. *Amen.*

II God of all creation, who calls us to make disciples of all nations and to proclaim your mercy and love: Grant that we, after the example of your servant Julia Chester Emery, might have vision and courage in proclaiming the Gospel to the ends of the earth; through Jesus Christ, our light and our salvation, who lives and reigns with you and the Holy Spirit, one God, for ever and ever. *Amen.*

Lessons and Psalm

Ecclesiasticus 3:30—4:6
Psalm 67
Romans 12:6-13
Mark 10:42-45

Preface of a Saint (2)

William Laud was born in 1573 and became Archbishop of Canterbury in 1633, having been Charles I's principal ecclesiastical adviser for several years before. He was the most prominent of a new generation of church leaders who disliked many of the more Protestant ritual practices that had developed during the reign of Elizabeth I, and who were bitterly opposed by the Puritans.

Laud believed that the Church of England was in direct continuity with the medieval church, and he stressed the unity of church and state, exalting the role of the monarch as the supreme governor of the church. He emphasized the centrality of the priesthood and the sacraments, particularly the Eucharist, and he caused consternation by insisting on reverencing the altar, returning it to its pre-Reformation position against the eastern wall of the church and hedging it about with rails.

As head of the courts of High Commission and Star Chamber, Laud was abhorred for the harsh sentencing of prominent Puritans. His identification with the unpopular policies of King Charles, his support of the war against Scotland in 1640, and his efforts to make the church independent of Parliament all made him widely disliked. He was impeached for treason by the Long Parliament in 1640, and finally beheaded on January 10, 1645.

Laud's reputation has remained controversial to this day. Honored as a martyr and condemned as an intolerant bigot, he was compassionate in his defense of the rights of the common people against the landowners. He was honest, devout, and loyal to the king and to the rights and privileges of the Church of England. He tried to reform and protect the church in accordance with his sincere convictions. But in many ways he was out of step with the views of the majority of people in his day, especially about the "Divine Right of Kings."

Laud made a noble end, praying on the scaffold: "The Lord receive my soul and have mercy upon me, and bless this kingdom with peace and charity, that there may not be this effusion of Christian blood amongst them."

William Laud

Archbishop of Canterbury, 1645

I Keep us, O Lord, constant in faith and zealous in witness; that, like thy servant William Laud, we may live in thy fear, die in thy favor, and rest in thy peace; for the sake of Jesus Christ thy Son our Lord, who liveth and reigneth with thee and the Holy Ghost, one God, for ever and ever. *Amen.*

II Keep us, O Lord, constant in faith and zealous in witness; that, like your servant William Laud, we may live in your fear, die in your favor, and rest in your peace; for the sake of Jesus Christ your Son our Lord, who lives and reigns with you and the Holy Spirit, one God, for ever and ever. *Amen.*

Lessons and Psalm

Wisdom 1:6-15
Psalm 73:24-29
Hebrews 12:5-14
Matthew 10:32-39

Preface of a Saint (2)

Aelred was born in 1109, into a family who had long been the treasurers of the shrine of Cuthbert of Lindisfarne at Durham Cathedral. While still a youth, he was sent for education in upper-class life to the court of King David of Scotland, son of Queen Margaret. The king's stepsons, Simon and Waldef, were his models and intimate friends. But after intense disillusionment and inner struggle, Aelred went to Yorkshire, where he became a Cistercian monk at the abbey of Rievaulx in 1133.

Aelred soon became a major figure in English church life. Sent to Rome on diocesan affairs by Archbishop William of York, he returned by way of Clairvaux. Here he made a deep impression on Bernard, who encouraged the young monk to write his first work, *The Mirror of Charity,* on Christian perfection. In 1143, Aelred led the founding of a new Cistercian house at Revesby. Four years later, he was appointed abbot of Rievaulx. By the time of his death in 1167, the abbey had more than 600 monks, including Aelred's biographer and friend, Walter Daniel. During this period, Aelred wrote his best-known work, *Spiritual Friendship.*

Friendship, Aelred teaches, is both a gift from God and a creation of human effort. While love should be universal and freely given to all, friendship is a particular love between individuals, of which the example is Jesus and John the Beloved Disciple. As abbot, Aelred allowed his monks to hold hands and give other expressions of friendship. In the spirit of Anselm of Canterbury and Bernard of Clairvaux, Aelred writes:

"There are four qualities that characterize a friend: Loyalty, right intention, discretion, and patience. Right intention seeks for nothing other than God and natural good. Discretion brings understanding of what is done on a friend's behalf, and ability to know when to correct faults. Patience enables one to be justly rebuked, or to bear adversity on another's behalf. Loyalty guards and protects friendship, in good or bitter times."

Aelred died in the year 1167.

Aelred of Rievaulx

Monastic and Theologian, 1167

I Grant to thy people, Almighty God, a spirit of mutual affection; that, following the example of thy servant Aelred of Rievaulx, we might know the love of Christ in loving one another; through the same Jesus Christ our Lord, who liveth and reigneth with thee and the Holy Ghost, one God, now and for ever. *Amen.*

II Grant to your people, Almighty God, a spirit of mutual affection; that, following the example of your servant Aelred of Rivaulx, we might know the love of Christ in loving one another; through the same Jesus Christ our Lord, who lives and reigns with you and the Holy Spirit, one God, now and for ever. *Amen.*

Lessons and Psalm

Ecclesiasticus 6:5-17
Psalm 36:5-10
Philippians 2:1-4
John 15:9-17

Preface of a Saint (2)

Hilary, Bishop of Poitiers, was a prolific writer on scripture and doctrine, an orator, and a poet to whom some of the earliest Latin hymns have been attributed. Augustine called him "the illustrious doctor of the churches." Jerome considered him "the trumpet of the Latins against the Arians."

Hilary was born in Poitiers, in Gaul, about 315, into a pagan family of wealth and power. In his writings, he describes the stages of the spiritual journey that led him to the Christian faith. He was baptized when he was about thirty.

In 350, Hilary was made Bishop of Poitiers. Although he demurred, he was finally persuaded by popular acclamation. He proved to be a bishop of skill and courage. His orthodoxy was shown when, in 355, the Emperor Constantius ordered all bishops to sign a condemnation of Athanasius, under pain of exile. Hilary wrote to Constantius, pleading for peace and unity. His plea accomplished nothing, and, when he dissociated himself from three Arian bishops in the West, Constantius ordered Julian (later surnamed the Apostate) to exile him to Phrygia. There he remained for three years without complaining, writing biblical commentaries and his principal work, *On the Trinity.*

Hilary was then invited by a party of "semi-Arians," who hoped for his support, to a Council at Seleucia in Asia, largely attended by Arians. With remarkable courage, in the midst of a hostile gathering, Hilary defended the Council of Nicaea and the Nicene doctrine of the Trinity. He wrote again to Constantius, offering to debate Saturninus, the Western bishop largely responsible for his exile. The Arians feared the results of such an encounter and persuaded Constantius to simply return Hilary to Poitiers.

In 360, Hilary was welcomed back to his see with great demonstrations of joy and affection. He continued his battle against Arianism, but he never neglected the needs of his people. While fierce in controversy with heretical bishops, he was always a loving and compassionate pastor to the people of his diocese. He died in Poitiers in 367. Among his disciples was Martin, later Bishop of Tours, whom Hilary encouraged in his endeavors to promote the monastic life.

The hymn "Hail this day's joyful return" (*The Hymnal 1982*, #223; #224) is attributed to Hilary.

Hilary of Poitiers

Bishop, 367

I Keep us steadfast, Lord God, in that true faith that we professed at our baptism; that, like thy servant Hilary of Poitiers, we may rejoice in having thee for our Father, and may abide in thy Son, in the fellowship of the Holy Ghost; for thou livest and reignest for ever and ever as one God in Trinity of Persons. *Amen.*

II Keep us steadfast, Lord God, in that true faith that we professed at our baptism; that, like your servant Hilary of Poitiers, we may rejoice in having you for our Father, and may abide in your Son, in the fellowship of the Holy Spirit; for you live and reign for ever and ever as one God in Trinity of Persons. *Amen.*

Lessons and Psalm

Zechariah 6:9-15
Psalm 119:97-104
1 John 2:18-25
Luke 15:1-7

Preface of Trinity Sunday

Richard Meux Benson and Charles Gore are remembered for their role in the revival of Anglican monasticism in the nineteenth century.

Richard Meux Benson was born in London in 1824. He was educated at home until he went to Christ Church, Oxford, where he studied under Edward Bouverie Pusey. He was subsequently ordained as a priest and served as vicar of the village of Cowley, not far from Oxford. In 1858 Fr. Benson conducted the first of many silent retreats for priests for which he later became well known. Also around this time, he established a church dedicated to St. John the Evangelist in Cowley, and made plans to travel to India to gather a community of missionaries to live with him in poverty. His bishop, however, urged him to stay in England, where the Oxford Movement was spreading.

At this time, although there were several Anglican monastic communities for women, there were not yet any communities for men. Therefore, in 1865, Fr. Benson and Fr. S. W. O'Neill established a community that was both contemplative and externally focused, which they called the Mission Priests of St. John the Evangelist. It was the first religious order for men in the Church of England since the Reformation. Fr. Benson was named Superior, and as such, developed the Society's Rule of Life and Constitution. The brothers recited the Daily Office together, were urged to spend at least an hour in contemplation each day, and continued their priestly ministry outside of the monastery. In the late 1800s the Society spread to the United States, India, and South Africa. Fr. Benson himself visited the community in Cambridge, Massachusetts, and remained there for a number of years before returning to England, where he died in 1915.

Charles Gore was born in 1853 in Wimbledon and was educated mainly at Oxford. He was ordained in 1876 and served in positions at Cuddesdon and Pusey House, Oxford, both of which were focused upon theological education and the formation of clergy. While at Pusey House, Gore founded the Community of the Resurrection, a community for men that sought to combine the rich traditions of the religious life with a lively concern for the demands of ministry in the modern world.

Gore, a prolific writer and noted theologian, was a principal progenitor of liberal Anglo-Catholicism in late nineteenth- and early twentieth-century Anglicanism. He was concerned to make the critical scholarship of the age available to the church, particularly with respect to the Bible. A second but no less important concern was to prick the conscience of the church and plead for its engagement in the work of social justice for all. Between 1902 and 1919, Gore served successively as bishop of the dioceses of Worcester, Birmingham, and Oxford, seamlessly uniting his vocations of bishop, monastic, and theologian. He died in 1932.

Richard Meux Benson

Priest and Vowed Religious, 1915

and Charles Gore

Bishop and Vowed Religious, 1932

I Gracious God, who didst kindle in thy servants Richard Meux Benson and Charles Gore the grace to lead a revival of monastic life: Grant us also the resolve to serve thee faithfully in contemplation and prayer, ministering to the world that thou hast made, through Jesus Christ our Lord, who liveth and reigneth with thee and the Holy Ghost, ever one God, in glory everlasting. *Amen.*

II Gracious God, who kindled in your servants Richard Meux Benson and Charles Gore the grace to lead a revival of monastic life: Grant us also the resolve to serve you faithfully in contemplation and prayer, ministering to the world that you have made, through Jesus Christ our Lord, who lives and reigns with you and the Holy Spirit, ever one God, in glory everlasting. *Amen.*

Lessons and Psalm

1 Kings 19:9-18
Psalm 27:5-11
1 John 4:7-12
John 17:6-11

Preface of a Saint (2)

In the third century, many Christians turned away from the corrupt and decadent society of the time and went to live in deserts or on mountains, in solitude, fasting, and prayer. Antony of Egypt was an outstanding example of this early monastic movement, but he was not merely a recluse. He is traditionally regarded as the founder of Christian monasticism because of his role as an inspirational teacher and guide, which spread the popularity of the new monastic movement considerably.

Antony's parents were Christians, and he grew up to be thoughtful, devout, and introspective. When his parents died, he and his younger sister were left alone to care for a sizable estate. Six months later, while attending church, he heard the reading about the rich young man whom Christ directed to sell all that he had and give to the poor. Hearing his own call from God through this scripture, Antony at once gave his land to the villagers and sold most of his goods, giving the proceeds to the poor.

Later, after meditating on Christ's exhortation, "Do not be anxious about tomorrow," he sold what remained of his possessions, placed his sister in a "house of virgins," and became an anchorite (solitary ascetic). The vocational path taken by Antony's sister is one of many indications that, although Antony has traditionally been known as the founder of monasticism, some forms of urban monastic life (particularly for women) existed even before his call to undertake a monastic vocation in the solitude of the desert.

Athanasius, whose work *The Life of Antony* quickly spread Antony's fame far beyond Egypt, writes that Antony spent his days praying, reading, and doing manual labor. For a time, he was tormented by temptations and demons in various guises, but he resisted, and the demons fled. Moving to the mountains across the Nile from his village, Antony dwelt alone for twenty years. In 305, he left his cave and founded an early form of monastic communal life—a collection of cells inhabited by ascetics living under his guidance. Athanasius writes of such colonies: "Their cells, like tents, were filled with singing, fasting, praying, and working so that they might give alms, and they had love and peace with one another."

Athanasius further said of Antony: "He was like a physician given by God to Egypt. For who met him grieving and did not go away rejoicing? Who came full of anger and was not turned to kindness? . . . What monk who had grown slack was not strengthened by coming to him? Who came troubled by doubts and failed to gain peace of mind?" Antony died in 356.

Antony of Egypt

Monastic, 356

I O God, as thou by thy Holy Ghost didst enable thy servant Antony to withstand the temptations of the world, the flesh, and the devil; so give us grace to follow thee with pure hearts and minds; through Jesus Christ our Lord, who liveth and reigneth with thee and the same Holy Ghost, one God, for ever and ever. *Amen.*

II O God, as you by your Holy Spirit enabled your servant Antony to withstand the temptations of the world, the flesh, and the devil; so give us grace to follow you with pure hearts and minds, through Jesus Christ our Lord, who lives and reigns with you and the Holy Spirit, one God, for ever and ever. *Amen.*

Lessons and Psalm

Ecclesiastes 6:1-12
Psalm 91
James 1:9-11
Mark 10:17-22

Preface of a Saint (2)

When Jesus' disciple Simon confessed, "You are the Christ," Jesus responded, "You are Peter, and on this rock I will build my church." This fisherman and his brother Andrew were the first disciples called by Jesus. Peter figures prominently in the Gospels, often stumbling, impetuous, intense, and uncouth.

It was Peter who attempted to walk on the sea, and began to sink; it was Peter who impulsively wished to build three tabernacles on the mountain of the Transfiguration; it was Peter who, just before the crucifixion, three times denied knowing his Lord.

But it was also Peter who, after Pentecost, risked his life to do the Lord's work, speaking boldly of his belief in Jesus. It was also Peter, the Rock, whose strength and courage helped the young church in its questioning about the mission beyond the Jewish community. Opposed at first to the baptism of Gentiles, he had the humility to admit a change of heart, and to baptize the Roman centurion Cornelius and his household. Even after this, Peter had a continuing struggle with his conservatism, for Paul, writing to the Galatians, rebukes him for giving way to the demands of Jewish Christians to dissociate himself from table-fellowship with Gentiles.

Though the New Testament makes no mention of it, the tradition connecting Peter with Rome is early and credible. According to a legend based on that tradition, Peter fled from Rome during the persecution under Nero. On the Appian Way, he met Christ, and asked him, "Domine, quo vadis?" ("Lord, where are you going?") Jesus answered, "I am coming to be crucified again." Peter thereupon retraced his steps, and was shortly thereafter crucified, head downwards. "I am not worthy to be crucified as my Lord was," he is supposed to have said.

As we watch Peter struggle with himself, often stumble, love his Lord and deny him, speak rashly and act impetuously, his life reminds us that our Lord did not come to save the godly and strong but to save the weak and the sinful. Simon, an ordinary human being, was transformed by the Holy Spirit into the "Rock," and became the leader of the Church.

Since 1908, the eight days between the feast of the Confession of Saint Peter and the feast of the Conversion of Saint Paul have been observed ecumenically as the Week of Prayer for Christian Unity.

The Confession of Saint Peter the Apostle

I Almighty Father, who didst inspire Simon Peter, first among the apostles, to confess Jesus as Messiah and Son of the living God: Keep thy Church steadfast upon the rock of this faith, that in unity and peace we may proclaim the one truth and follow the one Lord, our Savior Jesus Christ; who liveth and reigneth with thee and the Holy Ghost, one God, now and for ever. *Amen.*

II Almighty Father, who inspired Simon Peter, first among the apostles, to confess Jesus as Messiah and Son of the living God: Keep your Church steadfast upon the rock of this faith, so that in unity and peace we may proclaim the one truth and follow the one Lord, our Savior Jesus Christ; who lives and reigns with you and the Holy Spirit, one God, now and for ever. *Amen.*

Lessons and Psalm

Acts 4:8-13
Psalm 23
1 Peter 5:1-4
Matthew 16:13-20

Preface of Apostles and Ordinations

Wulfstan was one of the few Anglo-Saxon bishops to retain his see after the Norman Conquest of England in 1066. Beloved by all classes of society for his humility, charity, and courage, he was born in Warwickshire about 1008, and educated in the Benedictine abbeys of Evesham and Peterborough. He spent most of his life in the cathedral monastery of Worcester as monk, prior, and then as bishop of the see from 1062 until his death on January 18, 1095. He accepted the episcopate with extreme reluctance, but having resigned himself to it, he administered the diocese with great effectiveness. As bishop, he rapidly became famous for his continued monastic asceticism and personal sanctity.

Even though Wulfstan had been sympathetic to King Harold of Wessex, he was among those who submitted to William the Conqueror at Berkhamstead in 1066. He therefore was allowed to retain his see. At first, the Normans tended to disparage him for his lack of learning and his inability to speak French, but he became one of William's most trusted advisers and administrators, and remained loyal in support of William I and William II in their work of reform and orderly government. He assisted in the compilation of the Domesday Book and supported William I against the rebellious barons in 1075. William came to respect a loyalty based on principle and not on self-seeking. Archbishop Lanfranc also recognized the strength of Wulfstan's character, and the two men worked together to end the practice at Bristol of kidnaping Englishmen and selling them as slaves in Ireland.

Because he was the most respected prelate of the Anglo-Saxon Church, Wulfstan's profession of canonical obedience to Lanfranc, William the Conqueror's Archbishop of Canterbury, proved to be a key factor in the transition from Anglo-Saxon to Anglo-Norman Christianity. William's policy, however, was to appoint his own fellow Normans to the English episcopate and by the time of William's death in 1087, Wulfstan was the only English-born bishop still living.

Wulfstan of Worcester

Bishop, 1095

I Almighty God, whose only-begotten Son led captivity captive and gave gifts to thy people: Multiply among us faithful pastors, who, like thy holy bishop Wulfstan, will give courage to those who are oppressed and held in bondage; and bring us all, we pray, into the true freedom of thy kingdom; through Jesus Christ our Lord, who liveth and reigneth with thee and the Holy Ghost, one God, for ever and ever. *Amen.*

II Almighty God, whose only-begotten Son led captivity captive and gave gifts to your people: Multiply among us faithful pastors, who, like your holy bishop Wulfstan, will give courage to those who are oppressed and held in bondage; and bring us all, we pray, into the true freedom of your kingdom; through Jesus Christ our Lord, who lives and reigns with you and the Holy Spirit, one God, for ever and ever. *Amen.*

Lessons and Psalm

Genesis 12:1-9
Psalm 84:7-12
1 Corinthians 4:1-5
John 15:5-16

Preface of Baptism

In 236, an assembly was held at Rome to elect a pope as successor to Antherus. In the throng was Fabian, a layman from the countryside of another part of Italy. Suddenly, according to the historian Eusebius, a dove flew over the crowd and lighted on Fabian's head. In spite of the fact that he was both a total stranger and not even a candidate for election, the people unanimously chose Fabian to be pope, shouting, "He is worthy! He is worthy!" Fabian was ordained to the episcopate without opposition.

During his fourteen years as pontiff, Fabian made numerous administrative reforms. He developed the parochial structure of the Church in Rome, and established the custom of venerating martyrs at their shrines in the catacombs. He also appointed seven deacons and seven sub-deacons to write the lives of the martyrs, so that their deeds would not be forgotten in times to come.

In the year 250, the Emperor Decius ordered everyone within the Roman Empire to offer sacrifices to the Roman gods and for the welfare of the emperor. The refusal of many Christians to do this resulted in a number of them being executed. As the head of his community, Fabian was one of the earliest to be martyred, setting a courageous example for the rest of the church to emulate.

Cyprian of Carthage, in a letter to Fabian's successor Cornelius, wrote that Fabian was an incomparable man. "The glory of his death," Cyprian commented, "befitted the purity and holiness of his life."

Fabian was buried in the catacombs of Rome, where his grave marker still exists. It is in fragments, but the words "Fabian . . . bishop . . . martyr" remain dimly visible.

Fabian

Bishop and Martyr, 250

I Grant, Almighty God, that in all times of trial and persecution, we might remain steadfast in faith and endurance, according to the example of thy servant Fabian, who was faithful even unto death. We ask this for the sake of him who laid down his life for us all, Jesus Christ our Savior; who livest and reignest with thee and the Holy Spirit, one God, for ever and ever. *Amen.*

II Grant, Almighty God, that in all times of trial and persecution, we might remain steadfast in faith and endurance, according to the example of your servant Fabian, who was faithful even unto death. We ask this for the sake of him who laid down his life for us all, Jesus Christ our Savior; who lives and reigns with you and the Holy Spirit, one God, for ever and ever. *Amen.*

Lessons and Psalm

2 Esdras 2:42-48
Psalm 126
1 Corinthians 15:35-44
Matthew 10:24-30

Preface of a Saint (3)

Agnes and Cecilia are two of the most venerated early Christian martyrs, and were both killed during persecutions in Rome.

As a young girl around twelve or thirteen years of age, Agnes was denounced as a Christian when she rejected propositions from men who wanted to marry her. She refused to change her mind or to sacrifice to the Roman gods, and so she was tortured and executed. The early fathers of the church praised her courage and chastity and drew upon parallels with her name, which means "pure" in Greek and "lamb" in Latin.

Pilgrims still visit Agnes' tomb and the catacomb surrounding it, beneath the basilica named for her on the Via Nomentana in Rome that Pope Honorius I (625–638) built in her honor to replace an older shrine erected by the Emperor Constantine. On her feast day at the basilica, two lambs are blessed, whose wool is woven into a scarf called the pallium, with which the Pope invests archbishops. Pope Gregory the Great sent such a pallium in 601 to Augustine, the first Archbishop of Canterbury. A representation of the pallium appears on the coat of arms of Archbishops of Canterbury to this day.

Cecilia is the patron saint of singers, organ builders, musicians, and poets. According to fifth-century sources, Cecilia was of noble birth and was betrothed to a pagan named Valerian. Cecilia's witness resulted in the conversion of both Valerian and his brother, Tiburtius. Because of their conversion, the brothers were martyred and, while Cecilia was burying them, she too was arrested. After several failed attempts to put her to death, she died from injuries sustained by the ordeal. The date of her martyrdom is generally believed to be 230.

Remembered for the passion with which she sang the praises of God, Cecilia was first depicted in Christian art as a martyr, but, since the fourteenth century, she has often been shown playing the organ, a theme picked up by Raphael in his famous altarpiece for San Giovanni in Monte, Bologna, painted around 1516. Her story has inspired centuries of artistic representations in paintings, sculptures, mosaics, and stained glass. Composers such as Handel, Purcell, Howells, and Britten have written choral works and mass settings in her honor. Many music schools, choral societies, and concert series bear her name.

Agnes and Cecilia of Rome

Martyrs, 304 and c. 230

I Almighty and everlasting God, who dost choose those whom the world deemeth powerless to put the powerful to shame: Grant us so to cherish the memory of thy youthful martyrs Agnes and Cecilia, that we might share their pure and steadfast faith in thee; through Jesus Christ our Lord, who liveth and reigneth with thee and the Holy Ghost, one God for ever and ever. *Amen.*

II Almighty and everlasting God, who chooses those whom the world deems powerless to put the powerful to shame: Grant us so to cherish the memory of your youthful martyrs Agnes and Cecilia, that we might share their pure and steadfast faith in you; through Jesus Christ our Lord, who lives and reigns with you and the Holy Spirit, one God for ever and ever. *Amen.*

Lessons and Psalm

Song of Songs 2:10-13
Psalm 45:11-16
2 Corinthians 6:16-18
Matthew 18:1-6

Preface of a Saint (3)

Vincent was a native of Huesca, in northeastern Spain, and was ordained as a deacon by Valerius, Bishop of Saragossa, who commissioned him to preach throughout his diocese. In the early years of the fourth century, the fervent Christian community in Spain fell victim to a persecution ordered by the Roman emperors Diocletian and Maximian. Dacian, governor of Spain, arrested both Valerius and his deacon Vincent, and had them imprisoned at Valencia.

According to one account, Valerius had a speech impediment, and so Vincent was often called upon to preach for him. When the two prisoners were challenged to renounce their faith, amid threats of torture and death, Vincent said to his bishop, "Father, if you order me, I will speak." Valerius is said to have replied, "Son, as I committed you to dispense the word of God, so I now charge you to answer in vindication of the faith which we defend."

The young deacon then told the governor that he and his bishop had no intention of betraying the one true God. The vehemence and enthusiasm of Vincent's defense showed no caution in his defiance of the judges, and Dacian's fury was increased by this exuberance in Christian witness. Valerius was exiled, but the angry Dacian ordered that Vincent be tortured.

Although the accounts of his martyrdom have been heavily embellished, Augustine of Hippo writes that Vincent's unshakable faith enabled him to endure grotesque punishments and, finally, death. Vincent's cult spread rapidly throughout the early church, and he was venerated as a bold and outspoken preacher and witness to the truth of the living Christ. He remains an important model for the ministry of deacons not only in doing works of justice and mercy, but also in proclaiming and teaching the truths of the Christian faith to the church and to the world.

Vincent of Saragossa

Deacon and Martyr, 304

I Almighty God, whose deacon Vincent, upheld by thee, was neither terrified by threats nor overcome by torments: Strengthen us, we beseech thee, to endure all adversity with invincible and steadfast faith; through Jesus Christ our Lord, who liveth and reigneth with thee and the Holy Ghost, one God, for ever and ever. *Amen.*

II Almighty God, whose deacon Vincent, upheld by you, was neither terrified by threats nor overcome by torments: Strengthen us to endure all adversity with invincible and steadfast faith; through Jesus Christ our Lord, who lives and reigns with you and the Holy Spirit, one God, for ever and ever. *Amen.*

Lessons and Psalm

Jeremiah 26:12-15
Psalm 31:1-5
Revelation 7:13-17
Luke 12:4-12

Preface of a Saint (3)

Writing about Phillips Brooks in 1930, William Lawrence, who had known him as a young man, began, "Phillips Brooks was a leader of youth . . . His was the spirit of adventure, in thought, life, and faith." To many who know him only as the author of "O little town of Bethlehem," this part of Brooks' life and influence is little known.

Born in Boston in 1835, Phillips Brooks graduated from Harvard University and began his career as a teacher at Boston Latin School. He was soon fired, however, and grappled with despair over finding his true vocation. He wrote: "I do not know what will become of me and I do not care much . . . I wish I were fifteen years old again. I believed I might become a stunning man, but somehow or other I do not seem in the way to come to much now." This vocational struggle ultimately led him to offer himself for ordained ministry, and he went to study for the priesthood at Virginia Theological Seminary.

Brooks began his ordained ministry in Philadelphia, where his impressive personality and his eloquence immediately attracted attention. After ten years in Philadelphia, he returned to Boston as rector of Trinity Church, which was destroyed in the Boston fire three years later. It is a tribute to Brooks' preaching, character, and leadership that in four years of worshiping in temporary and bare surroundings, the congregation grew and flourished. The new Trinity Church was a daring architectural enterprise for its day, with its altar placed in the center of the chancel, "a symbol of unity; God and man and all God's creation."

Brooks was regarded as one of the greatest preachers of his generation, and many of his sermons have continued to stand the test of time. These have passages that still grasp the reader, even though they cannot convey the warmth and vitality which so impressed his hearers. James Bryce wrote, "There was no sign of art about his preaching, no touch of self-consciousness. He spoke to his audience as a man might speak to his friend, pouring forth with swift, yet quiet and seldom impassioned earnestness, the thoughts of his singularly pure and lofty spirit."

Brooks died in Boston on January 23, 1893.

Phillips Brooks

Bishop, 1893

I Everlasting God, who dost implant thy living Word in the minds and on the lips of all who proclaim thy truth: Grant that we, like thy pastor and preacher Phillips Brooks, might proclaim thy Gospel in our own generation with grace and power. Through Jesus Christ our Lord, who livest and reignest with thee and the Holy Ghost, ever one God, now and for ever. *Amen.*

II Everlasting God, who implants your living Word in the minds and on the lips of all who proclaim your truth: Grant that we, like your pastor and preacher Phillips Brooks, might proclaim your Gospel in our own generation with grace and power. Through Jesus Christ our Lord, who lives and reigns with you and the Holy Spirit, ever one God, now and for ever. *Amen.*

Lessons and Psalm

Jonah 3:1-10
Psalm 84:7-12
Ephesians 3:14-21
Matthew 24:24-27

Preface of a Saint (3)

Florence Li Tim-Oi was the first woman ordained as a priest in the Anglican Communion. Named by her father "much beloved daughter," Li Tim-Oi was born in Hong Kong in 1907. When she was baptized as a student, she chose the name of Florence in honor of Florence Nightingale. Florence studied at Union Theological College in Guangzhou (Canton). In 1938, upon graduation, she served as a lay worker, first in Kowloon and then in nearby Macao.

In May 1941 Florence was ordained as a deaconess. Some months later, Hong Kong fell to Japanese invaders, and priests could not travel to Macao to celebrate the Eucharist. Despite this setback, Florence continued her ministry. Her work came to the attention of Bishop Ronald Hall of Hong Kong, who decided that "God's work would reap better results if she had the proper title" of priest. On January 25, 1944, the Feast of the Conversion of St. Paul, Bishop Hall ordained her as a priest.

When World War II came to an end, Florence Li Tim-Oi's ordination became the subject of much controversy. She made the personal decision not to exercise her priesthood until it was acknowledged by the wider Anglican Communion. Undeterred, she continued to minister with great faithfulness, and in 1947 was appointed rector of St. Barnabas Church in Hepu where, on Bishop Hall's instructions, she was still to be called priest.

When the Communists came to power in China in 1949, Florence undertook theological studies in Beijing to further understand the implications of the Three-Self Movement (self-rule, self-support, and self-propagation) which now determined the life of the churches. She then moved to Guangzhou to teach and to serve at the Cathedral of Our Savior. However, for sixteen years during the Cultural Revolution, from 1958 onwards, all churches were closed. Florence was forced to work first on a farm and then in a factory. Accused of counterrevolutionary activity, she was required to undergo political reeducation. Finally, in 1974, she was allowed to retire from her work in the factory.

In 1979 the churches reopened, and Florence resumed her public ministry. Then, two years later, she was allowed to visit family members living in Canada. While there, to her great joy, she was licensed as a priest in the Diocese of Montreal and later in the Diocese of Toronto, where she finally settled until her death on February 26, 1992.

Florence Li Tim-Oi

Priest, 1992

I Almighty God, who dost pour out thy Spirit upon thy sons and daughters: Grant that we, following the example of thy servant Florence Li Tim-Oi, chosen priest in thy church, may with faithfulness, patience, and tenacity proclaim thy holy gospel to all the nations, through Jesus Christ our Lord, who liveth and reigneth with thee and the Holy Ghost, one God, in glory everlasting. *Amen.*

II Almighty God, who pours out your Spirit upon your sons and daughters: Grant that we, following the example of your servant Florence Li Tim-Oi, chosen priest in your church, may with faithfulness, patience, and tenacity proclaim your holy gospel to all the nations, through Jesus Christ our Lord, who lives and reigns with you and the Holy Spirit, one God, in glory everlasting. *Amen.*

Lessons and Psalm

Joel 2:28-32
Psalm 116:1-12
Galatians 3:23-29
Luke 5:1-11

Preface of a Saint (2)

Paul, or Saul as he was known until he became a Christian, was a Roman citizen, born at Tarsus, in present-day Turkey. He was brought up as an observant Jew, studying in Jerusalem for a time under Gamaliel, the most famous rabbi of the day. Describing himself, he said, "I am an Israelite, a descendant of Abraham, a member of the tribe of Benjamin" (Romans 11:1).

A few years after the death of Jesus, Saul came in contact with the new Christian movement, and became one of the most fanatical of those who were determined to stamp out this "dangerous heresy." Saul witnessed the stoning of Stephen and approved of it. He was on the way to Damascus to lead in further persecution of the Christians when his dramatic conversion took place.

From that day, Paul devoted his life totally to Christ, and especially to the conversion of Gentiles. The Acts of the Apostles describes the courage and determination with which he planted Christian congregations over a large area of the land bordering the eastern Mediterranean.

His letters, which are the earliest Christian writings, established him as one of the early founders of Christian theology. He writes, "I have been crucified with Christ; it is no longer I who live, but Christ who lives in me; and the life I now live in the flesh I live by faith in the Son of God, who loved me and gave himself for me" (Galatians 2:20).

Paul describes himself as small and insignificant in appearance: "His letters are weighty and strong," it was said of him, "but his bodily presence is weak, and his speech of no account" (2 Corinthians 10:10). He writes of having a disability or affliction which he had prayed God to remove from him, and quotes the Lord's reply, "My grace is sufficient for you, for my power is made perfect in weakness." Therefore, Paul went on to say, "I will all the more gladly boast of my weaknesses, that the power of Christ may rest upon me" (2 Corinthians 12:9).

Paul is believed to have been martyred at Rome in the year 64 under Nero.

The feast of the Conversion of Saint Paul marks the end of the Week of Prayer for Christian Unity.

The Conversion of Saint Paul the Apostle

I O God, who, by the preaching of thine apostle Paul, hast caused the light of the Gospel to shine throughout the world: Grant, we beseech thee, that we, having his wonderful conversion in remembrance, may show forth our thankfulness unto thee for the same by following the holy doctrine which he taught; through Jesus Christ our Lord, who liveth and reigneth with thee, in the unity of the Holy Ghost, one God, now and for ever. *Amen.*

II O God, who by the preaching of your apostle Paul has caused the light of the Gospel to shine throughout the world: Grant, we pray, that we, having his wonderful conversion in remembrance, may show ourselves thankful to you by following his holy teaching; through Jesus Christ our Lord, who lives and reigns with you, in the unity of the Holy Spirit, one God, now and for ever. *Amen.*

Lessons and Psalm

Acts 26:9-21
Psalm 67
Galatians 1:11-24
Matthew 10:16-22

Preface of Apostles and Ordinations

Timothy was a native of Lystra in Asia Minor, the son of a Greek father and a Jewish mother who was a believer. We learn from the Acts of the Apostles that "he was well spoken of by the brethren at Lystra and Iconium. Paul wanted Timothy to accompany him; and he took him and circumcised him because of the Jews who were in those places, for they all knew that his father was a Greek" (Acts 16:1-3). In addition to being a devoted companion of Paul, Timothy was entrusted with missions to the Thessalonians, to encourage them under persecution, and to the Corinthians, to strengthen the converts in the faith. Timothy became Paul's representative at Ephesus, and, according to Eusebius, the first bishop of that city.

Titus was, like Timothy, a companion of Paul, who calls him "my true child in the common faith" (Titus 1:4). Titus, a Greek, accompanied Paul and Barnabas from Antioch to Jerusalem at the time of the apostolic council. During Paul's third missionary journey, Titus was sent on urgent missions to Corinth. Paul writes, "And besides our own comfort we rejoice still more at the joy of Titus because his mind has been set at rest by you all . . . And his heart goes out all the more to you, as he remembers the obedience of you all and the fear and trembling with which you received him" (2 Corinthians 7:13, 15).

Later, Titus was entrusted with the organization of the Church in Crete, where Eusebius reports he was the first bishop. Paul writes, "This is why I left you in Crete, that you might amend what was defective and appoint presbyters in every town as I directed you" (Titus 1:5).

As companions of Paul, Timothy and Titus are commemorated together close to the feast of Paul's conversion. Paul several times mentions their youth, while entrusting them with great responsibilities in administration and in the proclaiming of the Gospel, a reminder that not age but faithfulness, care, and the love of Christ are the important qualities for Christian leadership.

Timothy and Titus

Companions of Saint Paul

I Almighty God, who didst call Timothy and Titus to do the work of evangelists and teachers, and didst make them strong to endure hardship: Strengthen us to stand fast in adversity, and to live godly and righteous lives in this present time, that with sure confidence we may look for our blessed hope, the glorious appearing of our great God and Savior Jesus Christ; who liveth and reigneth with thee and the Holy Ghost, one God, now and for ever. *Amen.*

II Almighty God, who called Timothy and Titus to be evangelists and teachers, and made them strong to endure hardship: Strengthen us to stand fast in adversity, and to live godly and righteous lives in this present time, that with sure confidence we may look for our blessed hope, the glorious appearing of our great God and Savior Jesus Christ; who lives and reigns with you and the Holy Spirit, one God, now and for ever. *Amen.*

Lessons and Psalm

Isaiah 42:1-7
Psalm 112:1-9
2 Timothy 1:1-8 *or* Titus 1:1-5
John 10:1-10

Preface of Pentecost

John Chrysostom was born around 354 in Antioch, Syria. As a young man, he first responded to the call of desert monasticism until his health was impaired. He then returned to Antioch after six years as a monk and was ordained a priest. In 397, he became Bishop of Constantinople.

John, called "Chrysostom," which means "the golden-mouthed," is regarded as one of the greatest preachers in Christian history. People flocked to hear him. His eloquence was accompanied by an acute sensitivity to the needs of people. He saw preaching as an integral part of pastoral care, and as a medium of teaching. He warned that if a priest had no talent for preaching the Word of God, the souls of those in his charge "will fare no better than ships tossed in the storm."

Chrysostom is renowned to this day for his Easter sermon, which continues to be read from pulpits around the world. It reads in part: "Hell is angry because it has been thwarted! Hell is angry because it has been mocked! Hell is angry because it has been destroyed! It is angry because it has been abolished! It is angry because it has been taken captive! Hell seized a body but it discovered God. It seized earth and it encountered heaven. It seized what it saw and was vanquished by what it did not see. O death, where is thy sting? O hell, where is thy victory?"

Chrysostom describes the Christian eucharistic liturgy as a glorious experience, in which all of heaven and earth join together in the worship of God. His treatise remains a classic manual on the priestly vocation and its demands. The priest, he wrote, must be "dignified, but not haughty; awe-inspiring, but kind; affable in his authority; impartial, but courteous; humble, but not servile, strong but gentle . . ."

Chrysostom was particularly eloquent concerning the Christian obligation to care for the poor, saying: "If you cannot remember everything, instead of everything, I beg you, remember this without fail, that not to share our own wealth with the poor is stealing from the poor and deprivation of their means of life, for we do not possess our own wealth but theirs. If we have this attitude, we will certainly offer our money; and by nourishing Christ in poverty here and laying up great profit hereafter, we will be able to attain to the good things that are to come."

While he was extolled as a preacher and pastor, his fiery temperament was poorly suited to the subtle politics demanded by his ministry as a bishop, and his episcopate was short but tumultuous. He was twice exiled, and he died during the second period of banishment, on September 14, 407. Thirty-one years later, his remains were brought back to Constantinople, and were buried on January 27, which thus became the traditional date of his commemoration.

John Chrysostom

Bishop and Theologian, 407

I O God, who didst give thy servant John Chrysostom grace eloquently to proclaim thy righteousness in the great congregation, and fearlessly to bear reproach for the honor of thy Name: Mercifully grant to all who proclaim thy word such excellence in preaching that all thy people may be made partakers of the glory that shall be revealed; through Jesus Christ our Lord, who liveth and reigneth with thee and the Holy Ghost, one God for ever and ever. *Amen.*

II O God, who gave your servant John Chrysostom grace eloquently to proclaim your righteousness in the great congregation, and fearlessly to bear reproach for the honor of your Name: Mercifully grant to all who proclaim your word such excellence in preaching, that all your people may be made partakers of the glory that shall be revealed; through Jesus Christ our Lord, who lives and reigns with you and the Holy Spirit, one God for ever and ever. *Amen.*

Lessons and Psalm

Jeremiah 1:4-10
Psalm 49:1-8
1 Corinthians 12:31—13:7
Luke 21:12-15

Preface of a Saint (2)

Thomas Aquinas is one of the most influential theologians in the history of Western Christianity. Born into a noble Italian family, probably in 1225, he entered the new Dominican Order of Preachers as a young man, and soon became an outstanding teacher in an age of intellectual ferment.

Perceiving the challenges that the recent rediscovery of Aristotle's works might entail for traditional Christian doctrine, especially in their emphasis upon empirical knowledge derived from reason and sense perception independent of faith and revelation, Thomas asserted that reason and revelation are in basic harmony. "Grace," he said, "is not the denial of nature, but the perfection of it." This synthesis Thomas accomplished in his greatest works, the *Summa Theologiae* and the *Summa Contra Gentiles,* which even today continue to exercise profound influence on Christian thought and philosophy. Although his theology is now considered to be conventional by many Christians, especially among Roman Catholics, in his own day Thomas was considered a bold thinker, even a "radical," and certain aspects of his thought were condemned by the ecclesiastical authorities. His canonization on July 18, 1323, vindicated him.

Thomas understood God's disclosure of his Name, in Exodus 3:14, "I Am Who I Am," to mean that God is Being, the Ultimate Reality from which everything else derives its being. The difference between God and the world is that God's essence is to exist, whereas all other beings derive their being from him by the act of creation. Although God and the world are distinct, there is, nevertheless, an analogy of being between God and the world, since the Creator is reflected in his creation. It is therefore possible to have a limited knowledge of God by analogy from the created world. On this basis, human reason can demonstrate that God exists; that he created the world; and that he contains in himself, as their cause, all the perfections that exist in his creation. The distinctive truths of Christian faith, however, such as the Trinity and the Incarnation, are known only by revelation.

In December 1273, after decades of churning out theological writings at an astonishing pace, Thomas suddenly stopped, leaving his great *Summa* unfinished. When pressed as to why, he could only say that he had experienced a mystical encounter so profound that all of his former words seemed empty to him now. "All that I have written seems to me like so much straw compared to what I have seen and what has been revealed to me!"

Thomas died in 1274, just under fifty years of age. In 1369, on January 28, his remains were transferred to Toulouse. In addition to his many theological writings, he composed several eucharistic hymns. They include "O saving Victim" (*The Hymnal 1982,* #310; #311) and "Now, my tongue, the mystery telling" (*The Hymnal 1982,* #329; #330; #331).

Thomas Aquinas

Friar and Theologian, 1274

I Almighty God, who hast enriched thy church with the singular learning and holiness of thy servant Thomas Aquinas: Enlighten us more and more, we pray, by the disciplined thinking and teaching of Christian scholars, and deepen our devotion by the example of saintly lives; through Jesus Christ our Lord, who liveth and reigneth with thee and the Holy Ghost, one God, for ever and ever. *Amen.*

II Almighty God, who has enriched your church with the singular learning and holiness of your servant Thomas Aquinas: Enlighten us more and more, we pray, by the disciplined thinking and teaching of Christian scholars, and deepen our devotion by the example of saintly lives; through Jesus Christ our Lord, who lives and reigns with you and the Holy Spirit, one God, for ever and ever. *Amen.*

Lessons and Psalm

Wisdom 7:7-14
Psalm 119:97-104
1 Corinthians 11:23-26
Matthew 13:24-30

Preface of Trinity Sunday

Queen Lili'uokalani was persistent advocate for justice and nonviolence. She recognized the "Beloved Community" in her own day and refused to sanction the use of force or to encourage her people to respond violently when faced by heavily armed forces from the United States Navy acting in support of a band of insurrectionists (largely from the United States and Europe) as her government was illegally overthrown on January 17, 1893. In doing so, she prevented the undue bloodshed of her people against overwhelming force. Appealing to President Grover Cleveland, she surrendered her throne to the American government and pleaded with her subjects to respect her decision. As a result, she was forcefully removed from her throne and subsequently imprisoned for her witness in opposition to American imperialism. Her model of grace left a powerful symbol of God's love that continues to be at the center of the Native Hawaiian community and thus a gift to the entire Church.

Queen Lili'uokalani was also a respected musician and composer. Among her most well-known compositions is the Queen's Prayer, Ke Aloha o Ka Haku, sung most Sundays at parishes in Hawai'i. It is based upon her reading of the only two books allowed to her during her imprisonment, the Holy Bible and the Book of Common Prayer. As a neighbor to St. Andrew's Cathedral, she received refuge during the counterrevolution with the Anglican Sisters at St. Andrew's Priory School for Girls. Together with the Bishop, the Right Reverend Alfred Willis, they would minister and visit her during her imprisonment and these deeds of charity would influence Her Majesty to become a member of our Church. The lyrics reflect her faith in the face of adversity:

A 'o Kou 'oia i'o, he hemolelo ho'i	Your truth, so perfect.
Ko'u noho mihi 'ana, a pa'ahao 'ia	I live in sorrow, imprisoned.
'O 'oe ku'u lama, kou nani, ko'u ko'o	You are my light, your glory my support
Mai nânâ 'ino'ino, nâ hewa o kânaka	Behold not with malevolence, the sins of man,
Akä e huikala, a ma'ema'e nô	But forgive, and forgive.
No laila e ka Haku, ma lalo o kou 'êheu	And so, O Lord, beneath your wings,
Kô mâkou maluhia, a mau loa aku nô	Be our peace, forever more.

Queen Lili'uokalani died on November 11, 1917, and is buried at the Mauna 'Ala Royal Mausoleum in Honolulu, Hawai'i.

The traditional date of this commemoration is November 11, the date of Queen Lili'uokalani's death and may be so observed. Because that day is both the commemoration of Veteran's Day in the United States and the commemoration of Martin of Tours in the churchwide calendar, the date recommended here, January 29, is the date of Lili'uokalani's coronation as Queen of the Hawaiian Kingdom.

[Liliʻuokalani of Hawaiʻi]

I Almighty God, who called thy daughter Liliʻuokalani to an earthly throne that she might advance thy heavenly kingdom, and endowed her with gift of song and love for her people: Grant that we may imitate her perseverance in adversity, her commitment to peace, and her capacity for forgiveness. All this we ask in the name of thy Son Jesus Christ, who liveth and reigneth with thee and the Holy Ghost, one God, for ever and ever. *Amen.*

II Almighty God, who called your daughter Liliʻuokalani to an earthly throne that she might advance your heavenly kingdom, and endowed her with gift of song and love for her people: Grant that we may imitate her perseverance in adversity, her commitment to peace, and her capacity for forgiveness. All this we ask in the name of your Son Jesus Christ, who liveth and reigneth with thee and the Holy Ghost, one God, for ever and ever. *Amen.*

Lessons and Psalm

Isaiah 26:1-8
Psalm 57:7-11
Colossians 3:12-15
Matthew 5:38-45

Preface of a Saint (1)

"How much virtue and ability, how much holiness and purity I found in her," said Jerome of Marcella, "I am afraid to say, lest I may exceed the bounds of men's belief." Marcella was born in Rome in 325 to Albina, a noblewoman noted for her piety and learning. When Marcella was a child, her mother invited Athanasius of Alexandria to sojourn in her home during his exile. At his feet, Marcella studied the lives of the holy monastics of the Thebaid, and Athanasius gave her a copy of his *Life of Antony*.

After being widowed as a young woman, Marcella devoted herself to the asceticism of Antony. Trading her costly array for a simple brown dress, she made her home into a house of prayer and refuge. Her example inspired other women to form a community, sometimes called the Brown Dress Society, that was devoted to chastity, poverty, fasting, prayer, studying the scriptures, and serving the poor and needy. Together with Paula (September 28), Marcella is one of the mothers of Roman monasticism.

In 382, Pope Damasus invited Jerome to Rome, where he lodged in Marcella's Aventine Hill estate. During those three years a friendship developed between Marcella, Paula, and Jerome, without which Jerome's Latin translation of the scriptures (later called the Vulgate) would not have been written. Marcella and Paula were both remarkably erudite; Jerome found in them not only friends but colleagues with whom to discuss the challenges of interpreting and translating the scriptures. After the death of Damasus, Jerome, joined by Paula and her daughter Eustochium, left for Jerusalem; although they urged Marcella to join them, she was determined to remain in Rome. She and Jerome corresponded for the remainder of her life. After his departure, scholars came to her to seek her insight on obscure matters in the Greek and Hebrew scriptures.

In 410 the Visigoths invaded Rome. Alaric's soldiers pillaged Marcella's home in search of wealth. They scourged the eighty-five-year-old woman, demanding that she surrender her hidden treasures, all of which she had long since spent in charity. She only pleaded with the soldiers not to harm her protégé Principia. They were both eventually taken to St. Paul's Church, which had been designated a sanctuary. The following day, Marcella died in Principia's arms.

Marcella of Rome

Monastic and Scholar, 410

I O God, who dost satisfy the longing soul and fillest the hungry with good things: Grant that we, like thy servant Marcella, may hunger and thirst after thee above the vain pomp and glory of the world, and delight in thy word above all manner of riches; through Jesus Christ our Lord, who liveth and reigneth with thee and the Holy Spirit, one God now and for ever. *Amen.*

II O God, who satisfies the longing soul and fills the hungry with good things: Grant that we, like your servant Marcella, may hunger and thirst after you above the vain pomp and glory of the world, and delight in your word above all manner of riches; through Jesus Christ our Lord, who lives and reigns with you and the Holy Spirit, one God, now and for ever. *Amen.*

Lessons and Psalm

1 Kings 17:8-16
Psalm 124
Colossians 3:1-4
Mark 12:41-44

Preface of a Saint (2)

Along with Patrick, Brigid is one of the most beloved Irish saints. She was born into slavery in the middle of the fifth century, the daughter of a local chieftain and one of his slaves. Her father, Dubhthach, was the poet laureate of King Loeghaire and a pagan, but her mother, Brocca, was a Christian.

Even as a young girl, Brigid was notorious for giving away all of the family's food and goods in order to feed and assist the poor. Enraged, her father tried to sell her to the king of Leinster, but even while the two men were negotiating her price, she took her father's jeweled sword and gave it to a beggar so that he could sell it to feed his family. The king was impressed with her compassion and resourcefulness, and offered Dubhthach his own jeweled sword as a replacement, telling him to give his daughter her freedom.

Gathering a group of women around her, Brigid founded a monastery in 470 at Kildare, a place whose name meant "Church of the Oak." This was the first monastic community for women in Ireland. To secure the sacraments, Brigid persuaded the anchorite Conlaed to receive ordination as a bishop and to bring his community of monks to Kildare, thus establishing a double monastery for both men and women. She also founded a renowned scriptorium and center for manuscript illumination at the monastic community.

Brigid actively participated in leadership and in policy-making decisions, not only within her own monastic federation but also within the councils and synods of the Irish church. She died around 523 at Kildare. Her remains are said to have been re-interred with those of Patrick at Downpatrick in the ninth century.

Brigid of Kildare

Monastic, c. 523

I O God, whose servant Brigid, kindled with the flame of thy love, became a shining light in thy church: Grant that we also may be aflame with the spirit of love and discipline, and walk before thee as children of light; through Jesus Christ our Lord, who liveth and reigneth with thee, in the unity of the Holy Ghost, one God, now and for ever. *Amen.*

II O God, whose servant Brigid, kindled with the flame of your love, became a shining light in your church: Grant that we also may be aflame with the spirit of love and discipline, and walk before you as children of light; through Jesus Christ our Lord, who lives and reigns with you, in the unity of the Holy Spirit, one God, now and for ever. *Amen.*

Lessons and Psalm

Tobit 2:9-14
Psalm 138
1 Corinthians 1:26-31
Matthew 6:19-24

Preface of a Saint (2)

Today's feast is sometimes known as the Purification of Saint Mary the Virgin, and also as Candlemas. In the Orthodox Church it has also been called the Meeting of Christ with Simeon. Such a variety of names is ample testimony to the wealth of spiritual meaning that generations of Christians have discovered in this small incident.

The title "The Presentation" reminds us of the Jewish law (Exodus 13:2; 22:29) that every firstborn son had to be dedicated to God in memory of the Israelites' deliverance from Egypt, when the firstborn sons of the Egyptians died and those of Israel were spared.

When Mary placed her infant son into the arms of Simeon, it was the meeting of the Old and New Dispensations. The old sacrifices, the burnt offerings and oblations, were done away; a new and perfect offering had come into the temple. God had provided himself a lamb for the burnt offering (Genesis 22:8), his only Son. The offering was to be made once for all on the cross. At every Eucharist, those who are in Christ recall that sinless offering and unite "themselves, their souls and bodies" with the self-oblation of their Lord and Savior.

It is traditional that candles are blessed on this day, for use throughout the rest of the year, which is why the feast is also sometimes known as "Candlemas."

The Presentation of Our Lord Jesus Christ in the Temple

I Almighty and everliving God, we humbly beseech thee that, as thy only-begotten Son was this day presented in the temple, so we may be presented unto thee with pure and clean hearts by the same thy Son Jesus Christ our Lord; who liveth and reigneth with thee and the Holy Ghost, one God, now and for ever. *Amen.*

II Almighty and everliving God, we humbly pray that, as your only-begotten Son was this day presented in the temple, so we may be presented to you with pure and clean hearts by Jesus Christ our Lord; who lives and reigns with you and the Holy Spirit, one God, now and for ever. *Amen.*

Lessons and Psalm

Malachi 3:1-4
Psalm 84 *or* 24:7-10
Hebrews 2:14-18
Luke 2:22-40

Preface of the Epiphany

Anskar was one of those valiant Christians of whom it might be said, "These shall plant the seed, but others shall reap the harvest." As Archbishop of Hamburg, he was papal legate for missionary work among the Scandinavians. The immediate result of his devoted and perilous labors was minimal: two churches established on the border of Denmark and one priest settled in Sweden. He also participated in the consecration of Gotbert, first bishop in Sweden. Nevertheless, it was the seed from which a fruitful mission would later grow.

Anskar was born in the Somme region of France in 801, and educated in the outstanding monastic school in nearby Corbie Abbey. His teaching skill led him to be chosen to be sent out by Corbie as master of a new monastery school in Saxon Germany. His strongest call, however, was to be a missionary.

He was stirred, his biographer Rimbert says, by a prolonged vision, in which a voice said, "Go and return to me crowned with martyrdom." When King Harald of Denmark sought missionaries for that country in 826, Anskar was one of those selected. Rimbert notes that Anskar's missionary purpose caused astonishment. Why should he wish to leave his brothers to deal with "unknown and barbarous folk?" Some of the brethren tried to deter him; others mocked him.

Steadfast in his resolve, Anskar established a school and mission in Denmark, working conscientiously but unsuccessfully to convert and evangelize. He was not totally discouraged. Another vision appeared, with a voice saying, "Go and declare the work of God to the nations." Shortly afterward, about 829, he was called to Sweden and eagerly accepted the invitation. Yet meager aid both from the monastery and the emperor frustrated his efforts.

While still a young man, Anskar was consecrated as Archbishop of Hamburg in 831. He continued his work among the Scandinavians until 848, when he retired to the See of Bremen and died in 865.

The seeds of his efforts were not to bear fruit until over one hundred years later, when Viking devastation, weakness in the Frankish Church, and the lowest ebb of missionary enthusiasm came to an end. The rich harvest of conversion was three generations away. Nevertheless, Anskar is now looked upon by Scandinavians as their apostle.

Anskar

Bishop and Missionary, 865

I Keep thy church from discouragement in the day of small things, O God, in the knowledge that when thou hast begun a good work, thou shalt bring it to a fruitful conclusion, just as thou didst for thy servant Anskar; through Jesus Christ our Lord, who liveth and reigneth with thee and the Holy Ghost, one God, for ever and ever. *Amen.*

II Keep your church from discouragement in the day of small things, O God, in the knowledge that when you have begun a good work, you will bring it to a fruitful conclusion, just as you did for your servant Anskar; through Jesus Christ our Lord, who lives and reigns with you and the Holy Spirit, one God, for ever and ever. *Amen.*

Lessons and Psalm

Genesis 11:1-9
Psalm 13
Acts 1:1-9
Mark 6:7-13

Preface of Apostles and Ordinations

It is believed that Manche Masemola was born around 1913, in Marishane, South Africa. She grew up with her parents, two older brothers, a younger sister named Mabule, and a cousin named Lucia. She was not sent to school, but worked with her family on their farm. Her family was not Christian, but rather followed traditional local religious practices. The Christian community in their region was very small, and was looked upon by most people with much suspicion.

In 1919 Fr. Augustine Moeka of the Anglican Community of the Resurrection established a mission at Marishane. Manche Masemola and her cousin Lucia first heard Moeka preach as a result. She was eager to learn more, and began to attend worship services and classes at the mission twice a week.

Soon she expressed a desire to be baptized, but her parents tried to forbid her. When their prohibitions failed to dissuade her, she was beaten. On a number of occasions, Manche Masemola remarked to Lucia and Moeka that she would die at her parents' hands and be baptized in her own blood. Then, on or near February 4, 1928, her mother and father took her away to an isolated place and killed her, and buried her by a granite rock on a remote hillside. She was about fifteen years old.

Although she was not yet baptized, the church has historically recognized catechumens who died before they could be baptized as being baptized by their desire for baptism. In 1935 a small group of Christians first made a pilgrimage to her grave. Larger groups followed in 1941 and 1949. Now, hundreds visit the site every August. In 1975 her name was added to the calendar of the Church of the Province of Southern Africa.

Manche Masemola is one of the twentieth-century martyrs whose statues are displayed at Westminster Abbey. More than 40 years after her daughter's murder, her mother was also baptized into the church in 1969.

Manche Masemola

Martyr, 1928

I Almighty and Everlasting God, who didst kindle the flame of thy love in the heart of thy faithful martyr Manche Masemola: Grant unto us thy servants, a like faith and power of love, that we who rejoice in her triumph may profit by her example; through Jesus Christ our Lord, who liveth and reigneth with thee and the Holy Ghost, one God, for ever and ever. *Amen.*

II Almighty and Everlasting God, who kindled the flame of your love in the heart of your faithful martyr Manche Masemola: Grant to us your servants, a like faith and power of love, that we who rejoice in her triumph may profit by her example; through Jesus Christ our Lord, who lives and reigns with you and the Holy Spirit, one God, for ever and ever. *Amen.*

Lessons and Psalm

Ruth 1:8-18
Psalm 118:8-14
James 5:7-11
Matthew 19:13-15

Preface of a Saint (3)

Agatha of Sicily was one of the most highly venerated virgin martyrs from the early church. It is believed that she was born around 231 to a rich and noble family. From a very young age, she chose to dedicate her life to God as a consecrated virgin, but this did not stop men from making unwanted advances toward her.

One of those men was Quitianus, the local Roman prefect, who thought that he could use his status and power to compel her to give up her vow. He tried to blackmail her by threatening to expose her as a Christian, but she would not yield to him. Because she consistently spurned his advances, he denounced her as a Christian during the Decian persecution. When she came to the trial, she learned that he was both her accuser and her judge.

In spite of this, Agatha refused to change her mind, and so Quitianus sentenced her to be imprisoned in a brothel. While she remained confined there for a month, she never wavered in her resolve that she would never willingly give herself to him or to any other man.

Eventually Quitianus grew impatient with her fortitude and sentenced her to be tortured to death. She was killed in the year 251. Counted as a virgin martyr because of her refusal to consent, she is regarded as the patron of all those who are subjected to sexual harassment or assault. Because of her popularity, she was one of the very few saints who were retained on the calendar of the 1662 Book of Common Prayer after the Reformation.

Agatha of Sicily

Martyr, c. 251

I Almighty and everlasting God, who didst strengthen thy martyr Agatha with constancy and courage: Grant us for the love of thee to make no peace with oppression, to fear no adversity, and to have no tolerance for those who wouldst use their power to abuse or exploit; Through Jesus Christ our Lord, to whom with thee and the Holy Ghost be all honor and glory, now and for ever. *Amen.*

II Almighty and everlasting God, who strengthened your martyr Agatha with constancy and courage: Grant us for the love of you to make no peace with oppression, to fear no adversity, and to have no tolerance for those who would use their power to abuse or exploit; Through Jesus Christ our Lord, to whom with you and the Holy Spirit be all honor and glory, now and for ever. *Amen.*

Lessons and Psalm

Judith 9:1-4, (5-9), 10-14
Psalm 125
Romans 8:31-39
Mark 9:42-50

Preface of a Saint (1)

The introduction of Christianity into Japan in the sixteenth century, first by the Jesuits under Francis Xavier, and then by the Franciscans, has left records of heroism and self-sacrifice in the annals of Christian witness. It has been estimated that by the end of that century there were about 300,000 baptized believers in Japan.

Unfortunately, these initial successes were compromised by rivalries among the religious orders, and the interplay of colonial politics, both within Japan and between Japan and the Spanish and Portuguese, aroused suspicion about Western intentions of conquest. After a period of ambiguous support by shoguns Nobunaga and Hideyoshi in the last half of the century, the Christian enterprise began to suffer cruel persecution and suppression, culminating in nationwide edicts banning Christianity under the Tokugawa shogunate at the beginning of the Edo era in 1603.

The first victims were six Franciscan friars and twenty of their converts, who were crucified at Nagasaki, February 5, 1597. In his powerful novel *Silence,* based on the event, Shusaku Endo writes:

> They were martyred. But what a martyrdom! I had long read about martyrdom in the lives of the saints—how the souls of the martyrs had gone home to Heaven, how they had been filled with glory in Paradise, how the angels had blown trumpets. This was the splendid martyrdom I had often seen in my dreams. But the martyrdom of the Japanese Christians I now describe to you was no such glorious thing. What a miserable and painful business it was! The rain falls unceasingly on the sea. And the sea which killed them surges on uncannily—in silence.

By 1630, what was left of Christianity in Japan was driven underground. Yet it is remarkable that two hundred and fifty years later there were found many men and women, without priests or sacraments, who had preserved through the generations a vestige of Christian faith.

The Martyrs of Japan

1597

I O God our Father, who didst bring the holy martyrs of Japan through the suffering of the cross to the joys of eternal life: Grant that we, encouraged by their example, may hold fast to the faith we profess, even unto death itself; through Jesus Christ our Lord, who liveth and reigneth with thee and the Holy Ghost, one God, now and for ever. *Amen.*

II O God our Father, who brought the holy martyrs of Japan through the suffering of the cross to the joys of eternal life: Grant that we, encouraged by their example, may hold fast to the faith we profess, even unto death itself; through Jesus Christ our Lord, who lives and reigns with you and the Holy Spirit, one God, now and for ever. *Amen.*

Lessons and Psalm

Lamentations 3:52-60
Psalm 39:5-8
Galatians 2:19-3:6
Mark 8:34-38

Preface of Holy Week

Josephine Margaret Bakhita was born in Olgossa in the Darfur region of southern Sudan. At the age of seven, she was kidnapped and sold into slavery. The girl was so traumatized by the experience that she was unable to remember her name. Bakhita means "fortunate one"—a name given to her by the same slave raiders who forcefully removed her from her family and village. Even as a child, she said that she experienced God in her heart without ever having been evangelized. She said, "Seeing the sun, the moon and the stars, I said to myself: Who could be the Master of these beautiful things? And I felt a great desire to see him, to know him and to pay him homage."

Although technically illegal, the entire Sudan region in the late nineteenth century was a raiding ground for various groups of armed slave traders. Enslaved for twelve years, she endured untold hardship and suffering. She was resold several times, finally in 1883 to the Italian consul in Khartoum, Sudan. After he gave her to his friend Augusto Michieli, she went with him and his family to Italy, where she worked as a nanny for their young daughter, Mimmina. Accompanying the girl to Venice's Institute of the Catechumens, Josephine found herself drawn to Christianity. She was baptized as Josephine in 1890.

The hardships in her life meant that Josephine did not easily express her joy. But she often expressed the joy she experienced through Christ at the font where she was baptized, kissing it and saying: "Here I became one of the daughters of God!"

Josephine entered religious life in 1896 as a Canossian Daughter of Charity. In 1902, she went to the city of Schio (northeast of Verona), where she served her religious community. She soon became well loved by the children attending the sisters' school and by the local citizens. By the end of her life, Josephine was renowned across Italy for her loving, spiritual wisdom.

Josephine knew the reality of being a slave, an immigrant, and a spiritual seeker. Even today, countless children, women, and men continue to be victimized and trafficked into slavery. Josephine serves as an inspiration to those who work to free girls and women from oppression and violence, and to return them to their dignity in the full exercise of their rights. Not only is she a model of resistance, Josephine also reminds us of our obligation to strive against the evil and injustice of human trafficking and uphold the dignity of every human person.

Bakhita (Josephine Margaret Bakhita)

Monastic, 1947

I O God of Love, who didst deliver thy servant Josephine Margaret Bakhita from the bondage of slavery to the true freedom of thy service; Grant to the wounded thy healing grace in mind, body, and spirit and to thy church the zeal to combat exploitation and slavery in all its forms; through Jesus Christ our Lord. *Amen.*

II O God of Love, who delivered your servant Josephine Margaret Bakhita from the bondage of slavery to the true freedom of your service; Grant to the wounded your healing grace in mind, body, and spirit and to your church the zeal to combat exploitation and slavery in all its forms; through Jesus Christ our Lord. *Amen.*

Lessons and Psalm

Amos 8:4-12
Psalm 3
James 2:1-7
Luke 3:1-9

Preface of a Saint (3)

The twin sister of Benedict of Nursia, founder of the Benedictine order, Scholastica is the patron saint of nuns, having dedicated herself to God in her youth.

What we know about her we owe to the *Dialogues* of Gregory the Great. Although tradition has it that she lived in a large religious community in Plumbariola, there is no evidence that a convent existed there at that time. It is now speculated that she lived in a small hermitage with a few other religious women. Plumbariola was convenient to her brother's monastery at Monte Cassino, and Benedict regularly visited his sister to discuss the scriptures and spiritual matters.

On one such visit, late in her life, Scholastica—perhaps knowing that her time was short—begged her brother to remain overnight. Benedict refused, as this would violate his own monastic rule. Scholastica then prayed for God's intervention, and the weather, which was already threatening, turned violent, so that Benedict was trapped. (Ironically, Scholastica is often invoked against heavy rain!) When he reproved his sister, she replied, "See, I asked you, and you would not listen to me. So I asked my Lord, and he has listened to me." Gregory writes, "It is no wonder that the woman who had desired to see her brother that day proved at the same time that she was more powerful than he was."

Three days later, after he had returned to his monastery, Benedict saw his sister's soul, in the form of a dove, ascending to heaven. He had her buried in his own tomb, and when he died he was buried with her.

Scholastica of Nursia

Monastic, 543

I Assist us, O God, to love one another as sisters and brothers, and to balance discipline with love and rules with compassion, according to the example shown by thy servant Scholastica; for the sake of thy Son Jesus Christ our Lord, to whom with thee and the Holy Ghost be all honor and glory, now and for ever. *Amen.*

II Assist us, O God, to love one another as sisters and brothers, and to balance discipline with love and rules with compassion, according to the example shown by your servant Scholastica; for the sake of your Son Jesus Christ our Lord, to whom with you and the Holy Spirit be all honor and glory, now and for ever. *Amen.*

Lessons and Psalm

Ecclesiastes 12:1-18
Psalm 4:1-5
Acts 4:32-35
Matthew 6:5-8

Preface of a Saint (1)

Barbara Clementine Harris was born in Philadelphia, Pennsylvania, on June 12, 1930. She was active in the civil rights struggles of the 1960s and continued as a powerful advocate for the civil enfranchisement of all people in the United States. Ordained as a priest in 1980, her ministry was in both the parish and the public square. She continued to address issues of civil injustice while also offering a prophetic critique of the Episcopal Church for its homophobia, racism, and sexism.

Although General Convention included the provision for electing and consecrating women to be bishops in 1976, no woman became a bishop until Barbara Harris was elected as bishop suffragan for the Diocese of Massachusetts on September 24, 1988. Her election and subsequent consecration were not without controversy, including threats on her life by those opposed to the inclusion of women in the House of Bishops. Despite these threats, she was consecrated bishop on February 11, 1989. Sixty bishops served as co-consecrators before a congregation of eight thousand people.

As a bishop, Harris shaped a generation of leaders through her powerful preaching as chief pastor at the Cathedral Church of St. Paul in Boston; her witnessing, preaching, and teaching in the Diocese of Massachusetts and beyond; her advocacy for, in her words, "the least, the last, and the lost"; and her joy in sharing her faith, especially through hymns. She said of her work as a bishop, "I certainly don't want to be one of the boys. I want to offer my peculiar gifts as a black woman . . . a sensitivity and an awareness that comes out of more than a passing acquaintance with oppression."

Bishop Harris served the people of the Diocese of Massachusetts as their suffragan bishop for thirteen years, until her retirement in 2002. After her retirement, she served from 2003 to 2007 as an assisting bishop in the Diocese of Washington, D.C. and she continued to be in demand worldwide as a preacher until the end of her life.

The first woman ordained as a bishop in the Episcopal Church and the worldwide Anglican Communion, Barbara Harris has been joined by more than fifty women in the episcopate. She died on March 13, 2020.

The Consecration of Barbara Clementine Harris

First Woman Bishop in the Anglican Communion, 1989

I God of the prophets, we give thee thanks for calling Barbara Clementine Harris to the office of bishop. Open our eyes to behold the wondrous works thou hast prepared for thy church in calling women to share in the ministry of the episcopate. May we, inspired by their example as faithful shepherds, wise teachers, courageous prophets, and guardians of the faith, proclaim the Good News and carry out the works of Jesus Christ in the world; who with thee and the Holy Ghost liveth and reigneth for ever and ever. *Amen.*

II God of the prophets, we give you thanks for calling Barbara Clementine Harris to the office of bishop. Open our eyes to behold the wondrous works you have prepared for your church in calling women to share in the ministry of the episcopate. May we, inspired by their example as faithful shepherds, wise teachers, courageous prophets, and guardians of the faith, proclaim the Good News and carry out the works of Jesus Christ in the world; who with you and the Holy Spirit lives and reigns for ever and ever. *Amen.*

Lessons and Psalm

Isaiah 58:6-12
Psalm 33:18-22
Philippians 4:1-9
Luke 18:1-8

Preface of Apostles and Ordinations

Theodora was a ninth-century Byzantine empress who has long been commemorated as a saint in the Orthodox Churches for her role in the restoration of icons following the iconoclastic controversy. Although in theory that conflict had been settled in favor of the veneration of icons at the Seventh Ecumenical Council in 787, in practice disagreements remained strong, and the iconoclastic party included many prominent members of society, including within the imperial family.

A young noblewoman of Armenian descent, Theodora was married to the young emperor Theophilos in the year 830. Although both were sincere Christians, the couple had strong disagreements about religious matters. Theophilos was an iconoclast and believed that the veneration of icons was idolatry. Theodora, however, maintained her own practice of venerating images in spite of her husband's opposition. On one occasion, when a servant reported to Theophilos that his wife had been seen venerating icons, she sweetly informed him that she had merely been "playing with dolls." Two of her icons are kept in a monastery on Mount Athos to this day, where they are referred to as "Theodora's dolls."

In spite of this theological conflict, the couple seem to have had a largely happy marriage, and had five daughters and two sons. Theophilos, however, died very young at the age of 29, and Theodora's life changed considerably. Her young son Michael was only a toddler and was too young to assume leadership, and so she ruled the Byzantine empire as his regent from 842 until 855.

One of Theodora's first acts as regent was to summon a synod of bishops to revisit the question of icons and iconoclasm. The practice of icon veneration was restored, and the synod ended in a procession that carried icons back into the Hagia Sophia.

Despite this victory, however, Theodora was noted for the particular gentleness with which she treated her theological opponents. She negotiated strongly with the church to ensure that her late husband would not be condemned as a heretic, and pursued a moderate policy of accommodation with clergy who had been iconoclasts. This was strongly opposed by more extreme factions within the church who wanted to see them denounced and punished as heretics, but Theodora remained firm in her attitude of respect for those who had held differing opinions. This ultimately led most of the iconoclastic party to gradually accept the majority view and to remain within the church.

Theodora is therefore remembered not only for her role in restoring the veneration of icons to the church but for her firm and diplomatic insistence upon reconciliation with those who had held opposing views, which made this one theological controversy that ended in reconciliation rather than in schism.

Theodora ruled as regent until her son came of age in 855. In 857 she retired to the monastery of Gastria, and seems to have died there some time after 867.

Theodora

Empress, c. 867

I O God, who didst call thy servant Theodora to an earthly throne that she might advance thy heavenly kingdom and who didst give her the wisdom to establish unity where there had been division; Create in thy church such godly union and concord that we might proclaim the Gospel of the Prince of Peace, not only in correct theology but in right actions; through the same Jesus Christ our Lord, who liveth and reigneth with thee and the Holy Ghost, one God, for ever and ever. *Amen.*

II O God, who called your servant Theodora to an earthly throne that she might advance your heavenly kingdom and who gave her the wisdom to establish unity where there had been division; Create in your church such godly union and concord that we might proclaim the Gospel of the Prince of Peace, not only in correct theology but in right actions; through the same Jesus Christ our Lord, who lives and reigns with you and the Holy Spirit, one God, for ever and ever. *Amen.*

Lessons and Psalm

1 Samuel 25:2-3, 23-31
Psalm 100
Colossians 1:15-20
Luke 17:1-10

Preface of a Saint (3)

Absalom Jones was born enslaved to Abraham Wynkoop, a wealthy Anglican planter, in 1746 in Delaware. He was working in the fields when Abraham recognized that he was an intelligent child and ordered that he be trained to work in the house. Absalom eagerly accepted instruction in reading. He also saved money he was given and bought books (among them a primer, a spelling book, and a bible). Abraham Wynkoop died in 1753, and by 1755 his younger son Benjamin had inherited the plantation. When Absalom was sixteen, Benjamin Wynkoop sold the plantation and Absalom's mother, sister, and five brothers. Wynkoop brought Absalom to Philadelphia, where he opened a store and joined St. Peter's Church. In Philadelphia, Benjamin Wynkoop permitted Absalom to attend a night school for Black people operated by Quakers following the tradition established by abolitionist teacher Anthony Benezet.

At twenty, with the permission of their masters, Absalom married Mary Thomas, who was enslaved to Sarah King, who also worshipped at St. Peter's. The Rev. Jacob Duche performed the wedding at Christ Church. Absalom and his father-in-law, John Thomas, used their savings and sought donations and loans primarily from prominent Quakers, in order to purchase Mary's freedom. Absalom and Mary worked very hard to repay the money borrowed to buy her freedom. They saved enough money to purchase property and to buy Absalom's freedom. Although he repeatedly asked Benjamin Wynkoop to allow him to buy his freedom, Wynkoop refused. Absalom persisted because as long as he was enslaved, Wynkoop could take his property and his money. Finally, in 1784 Benjamin Wynkoop freed Absalom by granting him a manumission. Absalom continued to work in Wynkoop's store as a paid employee.

Absalom left St. Peter's Church and began worshipping at St. George's Methodist Episcopal Church. He met Richard Allen, who had been engaged to preach at St. George's, and the two became lifelong friends. Together, in 1787, they founded the Free African Society, a mutual aid benevolent organization that was the first of its kind organized by and for Black people. Members of the Society paid monthly dues for the benefit of those in need. At St. George's, Absalom and Richard served as lay ministers for the Black membership. The active evangelism of Jones and Allen significantly increased Black membership at St. George's. The Black members worked hard to raise money to build an upstairs gallery intended to enlarge the church. The church leadership decided to segregate the Black worshippers in the gallery without notifying them. During a Sunday morning service, a dispute arose over the seats Black members had been instructed to take in the gallery. The ushers attempted to physically remove them by first accosting Absalom Jones. Most of the Black members present indignantly walked out of St. George's in a body.

Prior to the incident at St. George's, the Free African Society had initiated religious services. Some of these services were presided over by the Rev. Joseph Pilmore, an assistant at St. Paul's Episcopal Church. The Society established communication with similar Black groups in other cities. In 1792 the Society began to build the African Church of Philadelphia. The church membership took a denominational vote and decided to affiliate with the Episcopal Church. Richard Allen withdrew from the effort as he favored affiliation with the Methodist Church. Absalom Jones was asked to provide pastoral leadership, and after prayer and reflection, he accepted the call.

The African Church was dedicated on July 17, 1794. The Rev. Dr. Samuel Magaw, rector of St. Paul's Church, preached the dedicatory address. Dr. Magaw was assisted at the service by the Rev. James Abercrombie, assistant minister at Christ Church. Soon thereafter, the congregation applied for membership in the Episcopal Diocese of Pennsylvania on the following conditions: 1) that they would be received as an organized body; 2) that they would have control over their local affairs; 3) that Absalom Jones would be licensed as lay reader, and, if qualified, be ordained as a minister. In October 1794, it was admitted as the African Episcopal Church of St. Thomas. The church was incorporated under the laws of the Commonwealth of Pennsylvania in 1796. Bishop William White ordained Jones as deacon in 1795 and as priest on September 21, 1802.

Jones was an earnest preacher. He denounced slavery and warned the oppressors to "clean their hands of slaves." To him, God was the Father, who always acted on "behalf of the oppressed and distressed." But it was his constant visiting and mild manner that made him beloved by his congregation and by the community. St. Thomas Church grew to over 500 members during its first year. The congregants formed a day school and were active in moral uplift, self-empowerment, and anti-slavery activities. Known as "the Black Bishop of the Episcopal Church," Jones was an example of persistent faith in God and in the Church as God's instrument. Jones died on this day in 1818.

Absalom Jones

Priest, 1818

I Set us free, O heavenly Father, from every bond of prejudice and fear; that, honoring the steadfast courage of thy servant Absalom Jones, we may show forth in our lives the reconciling love and true freedom of the children of God, which thou hast given us in thy Son our Savior Jesus Christ; who liveth and reigneth with thee and the Holy Ghost, one God, now and for ever. *Amen.*

II Set us free, heavenly Father, from every bond of prejudice and fear; that, honoring the steadfast courage of your servant Absalom Jones, we may show forth in our lives the reconciling love and true freedom of the children of God, which you have given us in your Son our Savior Jesus Christ; who lives and reigns with you and the Holy Spirit, one God, now and for ever. *Amen.*

Lessons and Psalm

Isaiah 42:5-9
Psalm 126
Galatians 5:1-5
John 15:12-15

Preface of a Saint (1)

Cyril and Methodius, brothers born in Thessalonika, are honored as apostles to the southern Slavs and as the founders of Slavic literary culture. Cyril was a philosopher and a deacon who eventually became a monastic missionary. Methodius was first the governor of a Slavic colony who subsequently turned to the monastic life, and later served as both abbot and bishop.

In 862, the King of Moravia asked for missionaries who would teach his people in their native language. Since both Cyril and Methodius knew Slavonic, and both were learned men—Cyril was known as "the Philosopher"—the Patriarch chose them to lead the mission.

As part of his task among the Moravians, Cyril invented an alphabet to transcribe the native tongue, probably the "Glagolitic," in which Slavo-Roman liturgical books in Russian and Serbian are still written. The "Cyrillic" alphabet is thought to have been originated by Cyril's followers.

Pressures by the German clergy, who opposed the brothers' teaching, preaching, and writing in Slavonic, and the lack of a bishop to ordain new priests for their people, caused the two brothers to seek foreign help. They found a warm welcome at Rome from Pope Adrian II, who determined to ordain both men bishops and approved the Slavonic liturgy. Cyril, however, died in 869 at Rome and was buried there. Methodius, now a bishop, returned to Moravia as Metropolitan of Sirmium.

Methodius, still harassed by German bishops, was imprisoned at their behest. Eventually, he was released by Pope John VIII, on the condition that Slavonic, "a barbarous language," be used only for preaching. Later, the enmity of the Moravian prince caused Methodius to be recalled to Rome on charges of heresy. Papal support again allowed him to return to Moravia and to use Slavonic in the liturgy.

Methodius completed a Slavonic translation of the Bible and of Byzantine ecclesiastical law, while continuing his missionary activities. He is believed to have died in 885 in what is now Slovakia. At his funeral, celebrated in Greek, Latin, and Slavonic, "the people came together in huge numbers . . . for Methodius had been all things to all people that he might lead them all to heaven."

Cyril and Methodius

Missionaries, 869, 885

I Almighty and everlasting God, who by the power of the Holy Spirit didst move thy servants Cyril and Methodius to bring the light of the Gospel to a hostile and divided people: Overcome, we pray thee, by the love of Christ, all bitterness and contention among us, and make us one united family under the banner of the Prince of Peace; who liveth and reigneth with thee and the same Spirit, one God, now and for ever. *Amen.*

II Almighty and everlasting God, who by the power of the Holy Spirit moved your servants Cyril and Methodius to bring the light of the Gospel to a hostile and divided people: Overcome all bitterness and strife among us by the love of Christ, and make us one united family under the banner of the Prince of Peace; who lives and reigns with you and the Holy Spirit, one God, now and for ever. *Amen.*

Lessons and Psalm

Ecclesiastes 4:7-12
Psalm 29
Philippians 1:15-26
Mark 16:15-20

Preface of Apostles and Ordinations

Thomas Bray was born at Marton, in Shropshire, England, in 1656. After graduating from Oxford and being ordained as a priest, he became a country parson in Warwickshire. In 1696 he was invited by the Bishop of London to be responsible for the oversight of church work in the colony of Maryland. Three years later, as the Bishop's Commissary, he sailed to the American colonies for his first, and only, visitation.

Though he spent only two and a half months in Maryland, Bray was deeply concerned about the neglected state of the American churches, and the great need for the education of clergy, laity, and children. At a general visitation of the clergy at Annapolis, before his return to England, he emphasized the need for the instruction of children, and insisted that no clergyman be given a charge unless he had a good report from the ship in which he crossed the Atlantic, "whether . . . he gave no matter of scandal, and whether he did constantly read prayers twice a day and catechize and preach on Sundays, which, notwithstanding the common excuses, I know can be done by a minister of any zeal for religion." His understanding of, and concern for, Native Americans and African Americans were far ahead of his time. He founded thirty-nine lending libraries in America, as well as numerous schools. He raised money for missionary work and influenced young English priests to go to America.

Bray tried hard to have a bishop consecrated for the American colonies, but failed. His greatest contributions were the founding of the Society for Promoting Christian Knowledge and the Society for the Propagation of the Gospel, both of which are still effectively in operation after two and a half centuries of work all over the world.

From 1706 to 1730, Bray was the rector of St. Botolph Without Aldgate in London, where, until his death there on February 15, 1730, at the age of 72, he served with energy and devotion, while continuing his efforts on behalf of Black slaves in America and in the founding of parochial libraries.

When the deplorable condition of English prisons was brought to Bray's attention, he set to work to influence public opinion and to raise funds to alleviate the misery of the inmates. He organized Sunday "Beef and Beer" dinners in prisons, and advanced proposals for prison reform. It was Thomas Bray who first suggested to General Oglethorpe the idea of founding a humanitarian colony for the relief of honest debtors, but he died before the Georgia colony became a reality.

Thomas Bray

Priest and Missionary, 1730

I O God of compassion, who didst open the heart of thy servant Thomas Bray to answer the needs of the church in the New World: Make thy church diligent at all times to propagate the Gospel and to promote the spread of Christian knowledge; through Jesus Christ our Lord, who liveth and reigneth with thee and the Holy Ghost, one God, for ever and ever. *Amen.*

II O God of compassion, who opened the heart of your servant Thomas Bray to answer the needs of the church in the New World: Make your church diligent at all times to propagate the Gospel, and to promote the spread of Christian knowledge; through Jesus Christ our Lord, who lives and reigns with you and the Holy Spirit, one God, for ever and ever. *Amen.*

Lessons and Psalm

Jonah 4:1-11
Psalm 85:7-13
Philippians 2:5-11
Luke 5:27-32

Preface of Pentecost

Janani Luwum was born in 1922 to Acholi parents in Mucwini, Uganda, near the Sudanese border. After his early years as a teacher and lay reader in Gulu, he was sent to St. Augustine's College, Canterbury. He was ordained as a priest in 1956 and returned to Uganda to assume responsibility for twenty-four congregations. After several years of service that included work at a local theological college, Luwum returned to England on scholarship for further study at the London College of Divinity.

In 1969, Luwum became Bishop of Northern Uganda, where he was a faithful visitor to his parishes as well as a growing influence at international gatherings of the Anglican Communion. In 1974, he was elected Archbishop of the Church of Uganda, Rwanda, Burundi, and Boga-Zaire.

Luwum's new position brought him into direct contact and eventual confrontation with the Ugandan military dictator, Idi Amin, as the archbishop sought to protect his people from the brutality of Amin's regime. In August of 1976, Makerere University was sacked by government troops. With Archbishop Luwum as their chair, the Christian leaders of the country drafted a strong memorandum of protest against officially sanctioned rape and murder.

In early February 1977, the archbishop's residence was searched for arms by government security forces. On February 16, President Amin summoned Luwum to his palace. He went there, accompanied by the other Anglican bishops and by the Roman Catholic cardinal archbishop and a senior leader of the Muslim community. After being accused of complicity in a plot to murder the President, most of the clerics were allowed to leave. However, Archbishop Luwum was ordered to remain behind. As his companions departed, Luwum said, "They are going to kill me. I am not afraid." He was never seen alive again. The following day the government announced that he had been killed in an automobile accident while resisting arrest. Only after some weeks had passed was his bullet-riddled body released to his family for burial.

Early in his confrontation with the Ugandan government, Archbishop Luwum answered one of his critics by saying, "I do not know how long I shall occupy this chair. I live as though there will be no tomorrow . . . While the opportunity is there, I preach the gospel with all my might, and my conscience is clear before God."

Janani Luwum

Archbishop and Martyr, 1977

I O God, whose Son the Good Shepherd laid down his life for his sheep: We give thee thanks for thy faithful shepherd, Janani Luwum, who after his Savior's example gave up his life for the sake of his flock. Grant us to be so inspired by his witness that we make no peace with oppression, but live as those who are sealed with the cross of Christ, who died and rose again, and now liveth and reigneth with thee and the Holy Ghost, one God, for ever and ever. *Amen.*

II O God, whose Son the Good Shepherd laid down his life for his sheep: We give you thanks for your faithful shepherd, Janani Luwum, who after his Savior's example gave up his life for the sake of his flock. Grant us to be so inspired by his witness that we make no peace with oppression, but live as those who are sealed with the cross of Christ, who died and rose again, and now lives and reigns with you and the Holy Spirit, one God, for ever and ever. *Amen.*

Lessons and Psalm

Ecclesiasticus 4:20-28
Psalm 119:129-136
2 Corinthians 6:1-10
John 12:24-32

Preface of Holy Week

Martin Luther was born November 10, 1483, at Eisleben, in Germany. His intellectual abilities were evident early, and his father planned a career for him in law. Luther's real calling lay elsewhere, however, and in 1505, he entered the local Augustinian monastery. He was ordained as a priest on April 3, 1507.

In October 1512, Luther received his doctorate in theology, and shortly afterward he was installed as a professor of biblical studies at the University of Wittenberg. His lectures on the Bible were popular, and within a few years he made the university a center for biblical humanism. As a result of his theological and biblical studies, he called into question the practice of selling indulgences. On the eve of All Saints' Day, October 31, 1517, he posted on the door of the castle church in Wittenberg the notice of an academic debate on indulgences, listing 95 theses for discussion. As the effects of the theses became evident, the pope called upon the Augustinian order to discipline their member. After a series of meetings, political maneuvers, and attempts at reconciliation, Luther, at a meeting with the papal legate in 1518, refused to recant.

Luther was excommunicated on January 3, 1521. The Emperor Charles V summoned him to the meeting of the Imperial Diet at Worms. There Luther resisted all efforts to make him recant, insisting that he had to be proved in error on the basis of Scripture. The Diet passed an edict calling for the arrest of Luther. Luther's own prince, the Elector Frederick of Saxony, however, had him spirited away and placed for safekeeping in his castle.

There Luther translated the New Testament into German and began the translation of the Old Testament. He then turned his attention to the organization of worship and education. He introduced congregational singing of hymns, composing many himself, and issued model orders of services. He published his large and small catechisms for instruction in the faith. During the years from 1522 to his death, Luther wrote a prodigious quantity of books, letters, sermons, and tracts. Luther died at Eisleben on February 18, 1546.

Martin Luther

Pastor and Reformer, 1546

I O God, our refuge and our strength, who didst raise up thy servant Martin Luther to reform and renew thy church in the light of thy word: Defend and purify the church in our own day and grant that, through faith, we may boldly proclaim the riches of thy grace, which thou hast made known in Jesus Christ our Savior, who with thee and the Holy Ghost, liveth and reigneth, one God, now and for ever. *Amen.*

II O God, our refuge and our strength, who raised up your servant Martin Luther to reform and renew your church in the light of your word: Defend and purify the church in our own day and grant that, through faith, we may boldly proclaim the riches of your grace, which you have made known in Jesus Christ our Savior, who with you and the Holy Spirit, lives and reigns, one God, now and for ever. *Amen.*

Lessons and Psalm

Isaiah 55:6-11
Psalm 46
Romans 3:21-28
John 15:1-11

Preface of Trinity Sunday

Agnes Tsao Kou Ying, Agatha Lin Zhao, and Lucy Yi Zhenmei were three lay catechists who were martyred in China in the mid-nineteenth century for refusing to renounce the Christian faith. Although Christians were persecuted at this time in large part because of the association between the Christian religion and imperial colonialism, all three of these women were raised within Chinese Christian families, and saw no conflict between their identity as Christians and their identity as Chinese women. All three were canonized by the Roman Catholic Church on October 1, 2000.

Agnes Tsao Kou Ying was born in the small village of Wujiazhai in Guizhou Province in 1821. She was orphaned at a young age, and had to work to support herself. She married at age 18, but was treated poorly by her in-laws because they disapproved of her Christian faith. After only two years of marriage, her husband died, and she took shelter with an elderly Christian widow who taught her more about the faith. In 1852, the missionary priest Fr. Auguste Chapdelaine heard of her education in the scriptures and in Christian doctrine, and he invited her to accompany him to the province of Guangxi in order to catechize women and children there. After four years of this work, however, they were both arrested and tortured to death. Agnes Tsao Kou Ying died on January 22, 1856.

Agatha Lin Zhao was born in 1817, the only child of Christian parents. She had many suitors, and her parents had arranged an advantageous marriage for her. However, when she was 18 she asked to be released from the betrothal, and to dedicate herself to work in the church as a single laywoman instead. This was a considerable sacrifice for her parents since it would end their family line, but they agreed to her wish. She earned a university degree, and then returned to her home to run a school for girls. She was arrested in 1857, although she defended herself by protesting that she had been preparing the girls to be good wives since she was teaching them traditional Chinese culture and manners. When she refused to renounce her Christian faith, however, she was executed on January 28, 1858.

Lucy Yi Zhenmei was born to a Catholic family in Sichuan on December 9, 1815. Keenly interested in theological and historical studies, she began university studies but her health and family circumstances did not permit her to continue. Instead, after the death of her father, she lived at home with her mother and brother and worked to support her family. She assisted in the parish by teaching at the local school and by catechizing women and children. Although the church offered to pay her for her work, she insisted upon working for free in order to give something back to the church. In 1862 she accompanied Fr. Wen Nair to open a new Christian mission, but this effort was received poorly by the local authorities. They and three other Christian leaders were arrested and sentenced to death without a formal trial. Lucy Yi Zhenmei was executed by beheading on February 19, 1862.

Agnes Tsao Kou Ying, Agatha Lin Zhao, and Lucy Yi Zhenmei

Catechists and Martyrs, 1856, 1858, 1862

I Lord Jesus Christ, who willingly walked the way of the cross: Strengthen thy church through the witness of thy servants Agnes Tsao Kou Ying, Agatha Lin Zhao, and Lucy Yi Zhenmei to hold fast to the path of discipleship even unto death; for with the Father and Holy Ghost thou livest and reignest, one God, for ever and ever. *Amen.*

II Lord Jesus Christ, who willingly walked the way of the cross: Strengthen your church through the witness of your servants Agnes Tsao Kou Ying, Agatha Lin Zhao, and Lucy Yi Zhenmei to hold fast to the path of discipleship even unto death; for with the Father and Holy Spirit you live and reign, one God, for ever and ever. *Amen.*

Lessons and Psalm

Exodus 23:1-9
Psalm 25
2 Corinthians 6:16-18
Matthew 25:1-13

Preface of a Saint (3)

Born a slave in February 1818, Frederick Douglass was separated from his mother at the age of eight and given by his new owner, Thomas Auld, to his brother and sister-in-law, Hugh and Sophia Auld. Sophia attempted to teach Frederick to read, along with her son, but her husband put a stop to this, claiming that "it would forever unfit him to be a slave." Frederick learned to read in secret, earning small amounts of money when he could and paying neighbors to teach him.

In 1838, Frederick Bailey (as he was then known) escaped and changed his name to Frederick Douglass. At the age of 14, he had experienced a conversion to Christ in the African Methodist Episcopal Church, and his recollection of that tradition's spiritual music sustained him in his struggle for freedom: "Those songs still follow me, to deepen my hatred of slavery, and quicken my sympathies for my brethren in bonds."

An outstanding orator, Douglass was sent on speaking tours in the Northern States sponsored by the American Anti-Slavery Society. The more renowned he became, the more he had to worry about recapture. In 1845, he went to England on a speaking tour. His friends in America raised enough money to buy out his master's legal claim to him, so that he could return to the United States in safety. Douglass eventually moved to New York and edited the pro-abolition journal *North Star,* named for the fleeing slave's nighttime guide.

Douglass was highly critical of churches that did not disassociate themselves from slavery. Challenging those churches, he quoted Jesus' denunciation of the Pharisees: "They bind heavy burdens and grievous to be borne, and lay them on men's shoulders; but they themselves will not move them with one of their fingers" (Matthew 23:4).

A strong advocate of racial integration, Douglass disavowed Black separatism and wanted to be counted as equal among his white peers. When he met Abraham Lincoln in the White House, he noted that the President treated him as a kindred spirit without one trace of condescension. Douglass died in 1895.

Frederick Douglass

Social Reformer, 1895

I Almighty God, we bless thy Name for the witness of Frederick Douglass, whose impassioned and reasonable speech moved the hearts of people to a deeper obedience to Christ: Strengthen us also to speak on behalf of those in captivity and tribulation, continuing in the way of Jesus Christ our Liberator; who with thee and the Holy Ghost dwelleth in glory everlasting. *Amen.*

II Almighty God, we bless your Name for the witness of Frederick Douglass, whose impassioned and reasonable speech moved the hearts of people to a deeper obedience to Christ: Strengthen us also to speak on behalf of those in captivity and tribulation, continuing in the way of Jesus Christ our Liberator; who with you and the Holy Spirit dwells in glory everlasting. *Amen.*

Lessons and Psalm

Isaiah 32:11-18
Psalm 35:23-28
Hebrews 2:10-13
Luke 4:14-21

Preface of a Saint (2)

Margaret's story is one that raises questions at each of the many turns it took. She was born into a farming family outside the village of Laviano, near Perugia. Her mother died when she was a child and after her father remarried, there was enough tension in her home that she ran away. The various accounts of her life remark on her beauty and suggest it might have been jealousy that created ill feelings in her stepmother. With the burden of grief and discomfort in her home, it is not surprising that she turned outside her home for affection from those attracted to her for her beauty.

At some point, she left her home and native village and took a position as a servant in a wealthy man's home. When he took her as his mistress, it was with a promise that he would marry her. She bore him a son, and despite that obligation, he still held back from the unlikely marriage of a nobleman with a farm girl. She continued to live with him in apparent luxury, though without the stability and respect that marriage would have provided. Where previous perspectives might have seen a loose, if not scheming woman, it is perhaps just as obvious that this was a young woman seeking a place of acceptance and safety whose trust was misplaced in the man with whom she sought to build a life.

That all came to an end at his death. He had been away, either on a journey or out hunting, and his dog returned without him. The dog led Margaret to the place where her child's father was buried, the victim of murder. In her grief, Margaret decided to return to her father's house. He refused to admit her, and her native village turned its back on her. In grief and abandonment, she took her son and sought refuge with the Franciscans. They found her a home with devout women who provided a home for such cases. After three years of probation, she became a Tertiary of the Franciscans and her son eventually became a Friar. She spent the balance of her life following a strict pattern of life and an intense spiritual life dedicated to the Passion of Christ and his Presence in the Eucharist.

Her own experience led her to establish a hospital and home for those in need, and she gathered a group of women to live together in the religious life and to serve as nurses. She also took an active role in public life, twice challenging the Bishop of Arezzo for his warlike and extravagant lifestyle. She died on February 22, 1297.

While in prayer, Margaret heard the words, "What is your wish, poverella (little poor one)?" and she replied, "I neither seek nor desire for anything but You, my Lord Jesus."

Margaret of Cortona

Monastic, 1297

I Grant, O God, to all thy people, as to thy servant Margaret of Cortona, the spirit of repentance and supplication, that we might seek and desire nothing in this transitory life above thee; through Jesus Christ our Lord. *Amen.*

II Grant, O God, to all your people, as to your servant Margaret of Cortona, the spirit of repentance and supplication, that we might seek and desire nothing in this transitory life above you; through Jesus Christ our Lord. *Amen.*

Lessons and Psalm

Zephaniah 3:7-13
Psalm 30:6-13
James 5:1-6
Luke 7:36-50

Preface of a Saint (2)

Polycarp, born in the year 69, was one of the leaders of the church who carried on the tradition of the apostles through the troubled controversies around Gnosticism in the second century. According to Irenaeus, who had known him in his early youth, Polycarp was a pupil of John, "the disciple of the Lord," and had been appointed a bishop by "apostles in Asia."

We possess a letter from Polycarp to the Church in Philippi. It reveals his firm adherence to the faith, and his pastoral concern for fellow Christians in trouble.

An early account of the martyrdom of Polycarp on February 23 is also preserved. It probably occurred in the year 156. The account tells of Polycarp's courageous witness in the amphitheater at Smyrna. When the proconsul asked him to curse Christ, Polycarp said, "Eighty-six years I have served him, and he never did me any wrong. How can I blaspheme my King who saved me?" The account reports that the magistrate was reluctant to kill the gentle and harmless old man, but his hand was forced by the mob, who clamored that he be thrown to wild beasts, as was the fate of other Christians on that day.

Instead, Polycarp was burned at the stake. Before his ordeal, he is reported to have looked up to heaven, and to have prayed: "Lord God Almighty, Father of your beloved and blessed child Jesus Christ, through whom we have received knowledge of you, God of angels and hosts and all creation, and of the whole race of the upright who live in your presence, I bless you that you have thought me worthy of this day and hour, to be numbered among the martyrs and share in the cup of Christ, for resurrection to eternal life, for soul and body in the incorruptibility of the Holy Spirit. Among them may I be accepted before you today, as a rich and acceptable sacrifice just as you, the faithful and true God, have prepared and foreshown and brought about. For this reason and for all things I praise you, I bless you, I glorify you, through the eternal heavenly high priest Jesus Christ, your beloved child, through whom be glory to you, with him and the Holy Spirit, now and for the ages to come. *Amen.*"

Polycarp of Smyrna

Bishop and Martyr, 156

I O God, the maker of heaven and earth, who didst give thy venerable servant, the holy and gentle Polycarp, the boldness to confess Jesus Christ as King and Savior and the steadfastness to die for that faith: Give us grace, following his example, to share the cup of Christ and to rise to eternal life; through Jesus Christ our Lord, who liveth and reigneth with thee and the Holy Ghost, one God, now and for ever. *Amen.*

II O God, the maker of heaven and earth, you gave your venerable servant, the holy and gentle Polycarp, the boldness to confess Jesus Christ as King and Savior and the steadfastness to die for his faith: Give us grace, following his example, to share the cup of Christ and to rise to eternal life; through Jesus Christ our Lord, who lives and reigns with you and the Holy Spirit, one God, now and for ever. *Amen.*

Lessons and Psalm

Numbers 23:5-12
Psalm 199:9-16
Revelation 2:8-11
Matthew 20:20-28

Preface of a Saint (3)

In the nine days of waiting between Jesus' Ascension and the Day of Pentecost, the disciples remained together in prayer. During this time, Peter reminded them that the defection and death of Judas had left the fellowship of the Twelve with a vacancy. The Acts of the Apostles records Peter's proposal that "one of the men who have accompanied us during all the time that the Lord Jesus went in and out among us, beginning from the baptism of John until the day when he was taken up from us—one of these must become a witness with us to his resurrection" (Acts 1:21-22). Two men were nominated, Joseph called Barsabbas who was surnamed Justus, and Matthias. After prayer, the disciples cast lots, and the lot fell to Matthias, who was then enrolled with the eleven.

Scripture does not relate anything further about Matthias, but gives him as an example to Christians of one whose faithful companionship with Jesus qualifies him to be a suitable witness to the resurrection, and whose service is unheralded and unsung.

There are, however, several non-biblical early Christian accounts of his mission and ministry, such as the second-century text *The Acts of Andrew and Matthias in Cannibal City*. According to this account, immediately after the selection of Matthias, the apostles cast lots to determine which of them would take responsibility for which part of the world, and the unlucky Matthias was dispatched to a city of cannibals! Although an unabashedly fictionalized account, it is nevertheless an inspiring tale that shows Matthias being dealt the worst possible lot, and yet nevertheless responding to his call with equanimity, competence, and grace, which are the same qualities we see reflected in the canonical account that is given by Scripture.

Saint Matthias the Apostle

I O Almighty God, who into the place of Judas didst choose thy faithful servant Matthias to be of the number of the Twelve: Grant that thy Church, being delivered from false apostles, may always be ordered and guided by faithful and true pastors; through Jesus Christ our Lord, who liveth and reigneth with thee, in the unity of the Holy Ghost, one God, now and for ever. *Amen.*

II Almighty God, who in the place of Judas chose your faithful servant Matthias to be numbered among the Twelve: Grant that your Church, being delivered from false apostles, may always be guided and governed by faithful and true pastors; through Jesus Christ our Lord, who lives and reigns with you, in the unity of the Holy Spirit, one God, now and for ever. *Amen.*

Lessons and Psalm

Acts 1:15-26
Psalm 15
Philippians 3:13b-21
John 15:1, 6-16

Preface of Apostles and Ordinations

Emily Malbone Morgan, with the support of Harriet Hastings, was the founder of the Society of the Companions of the Holy Cross (SCHC), in 1884. Begun as a community of Episcopal laywomen rooted in disciplined devotion, the society became both a faithful community of discipleship and prayer, and a strong force for social justice reform during the social gospel era around the turn of the twentieth century.

Emily Malbone Morgan was born on December 10, 1862, in Hartford, Connecticut. Her family were prominent Hartford citizens and their Anglican roots ran deep on both sides of her family.

A primary inspiration for Morgan was her friendship with Adelyn Howard. Howard was homebound and because of her confinement sought Morgan's support for both spiritual companionship and as a means by which she could offer intercessory prayer for others. In response to her friend's need, Morgan called together a small group of women for prayer and companionship. From that beginning, the Society of the Companions of the Holy Cross came into being.

Morgan had a particular concern for working women who were tired, restless, and who had little hope for a vacation. In response, Morgan, with the help of a growing number of her Companions, developed summer vacation houses across the Northeast where working women and their daughters could have some time away for physical and spiritual renewal and refreshment.

In 1901, the Society established a permanent home in Byfield, Massachusetts. With the construction of new facilities on the site in 1915, it took the name Adelynrood, which continues to exist as the headquarters and retreat center of the Society.

Morgan never married; she and her sisters in the Society of the Companions of the Holy Cross lived a life of prayer, contemplation, and social justice, particularly for women. She died on February 27, 1937.

Emily Malbone Morgan

Lay Leader and Contemplative, 1937

I Inspire us, Gracious God, with that same spirit of devotion that animated thy servant Emily Malbone Morgan; that, like her, we might dedicate our lives to thy service and to the welfare of others; through Jesus Christ our Lord, who liveth and reigneth with thee, in the unity of the Holy Ghost, one God, now and for ever. *Amen.*

II Inspire us, Gracious God, with that same spirit of devotion that animated your servant Emily Malbone Morgan; that, like her, we might dedicate our lives to your service and to the welfare of others; through Jesus Christ our Lord, who lives and reigns with you, in the unity of the Holy Spirit, one God, now and for ever. *Amen.*

Lessons and Psalm

2 Samuel 14:12-17
Psalm 119:137-144
Romans 16:1-6
Luke 10:38-42

Preface of God the Holy Spirit

When Jesus passed through Samaria (John 4:3-42) he stopped at Jacob's Well in Sychar, a well that the patriarch Jacob had left to his son Joseph. Sitting by the well to rest, the Lord asked a Samaritan woman who came to the well to draw water to give him a drink. The request violated cultural taboos—a man speaking privately with a woman, and a Jew speaking to a Samaritan—anticipating the theological insight of Galatians 3:28. Their brief encounter is one of notable theological depth in which Jesus makes the first of several important "I am" statements in John's Gospel. The Samaritan woman had been married five times and was living with a man to whom she was not married. Whether this was through her own fault or due to unfortunate circumstances beyond her control the text does not indicate. However, she has the distinct honor of being the first person to whom Jesus reveals his Messianic title and the first person to preach the gospel that Jesus is the Christ.

While unnamed in the Johannine text, Orthodox Christian tradition has it that the woman was baptized by the Apostles on the first Pentecost and given the name Photini, "the enlightened one" (Svetlana, in the Russian Church). Celebrated in the Orthodox Church as an Evangelist, "Equal to the Apostles," a significant hagiography developed around her. She, her sisters, and her children are said to have been cruelly tortured and martyred at the command of the emperor Nero.

Over the centuries many churches have been built at the site of Jacob's Well, where Jesus held discourse with the Samaritan woman; the present church building within Bir Ya'qub Monastery was built in 1893 by order of the Greek Orthodox Patriarch of Jerusalem and consecrated to St. Photini.

Photini

The Samaritan Woman, c. 67

I O Almighty God, whose most blessed Son didst reveal to the Samaritan woman that He is indeed the Christ, the Savior of the World; Grant us to drink of the well that springeth up to everlasting life that we may worship Thee in spirit and in truth through thy Son, Jesus Christ our Lord. *Amen.*

II O Almighty God, whose most blessed Son revealed to the Samaritan woman that He is indeed the Christ, the Savior of the World; Grant us to drink of the well that springs up to everlasting life that we may worship you in spirit and in truth through your Son, Jesus Christ our Lord. *Amen.*

Lessons and Psalm

Genesis 24:12-20
Psalm 119:33-40
Colossians 2:16-23
John 4:4-26

Preface of Apostles and Ordinations

George Herbert is famous for his poems and for his prose work, *A Priest to the Temple, or, The Country Parson.* He described his poems as "a picture of the many spiritual conflicts that have passed betwixt God and my soul, before I could submit mine to the will of Jesus my Master; in whose service I have found perfect freedom."

Herbert was born in Montgomery, Wales, on April 3, 1593, a cousin of the Earl of Pembroke. Through his official position as Public Orator of Cambridge, he was brought into contact with the Court of King James I and Prince (later King) Charles. Whatever hopes he may have had as a courtier were dimmed, however, because of his associations with persons who were out of favor with King Charles I—principally John Williams, Bishop of Lincoln. Herbert had begun studying divinity in his early twenties, and, in 1626, he was ordained as a priest. In 1630, King Charles provided him with a living as rector of the parishes of Fugglestone and Bemerton. His collection of poems, *The Temple,* was given to his friend Nicholas Ferrar and published posthumously. Two of his poems are well-known hymns: "Teach me, my God and King" (*The Hymnal 1982,* #592) and "Let all the world in every corner sing" (*The Hymnal 1982,* #402; #403). Their grace, strength, and metaphysical imagery influenced later poets, including Henry Vaughan and Samuel Taylor Coleridge.

Lines from his poem "Love 3" have moved many readers:

Love bade me welcome: yet my soul drew back,
    Guilty of dust and sin.
But quick-eyed Love, observing me grow slack
    From my first entrance in,
Drew nearer to me, sweetly questioning
    If I lacked anything.

"A guest," I answered, "worthy to be here":
    Love said, "You shall be he."
"I, the unkind, ungrateful? Ah, my dear,
    I cannot look on thee."
Love took my hand, and smiling did reply,
    "Who made the eyes but I?"

"Truth, Lord; but I have marred them; let my shame
    Go where it doth deserve."
"And know you not," says Love, "who bore the blame?"
    "My dear, then I will serve."
"You must sit down," says Love, "and taste my meat."
    So I did sit and eat.

Herbert was unselfish in his devotion and service to others. His words, "Nothing is little in God's service," have reminded Christians again and again that everything in daily life, small or great, may be a means of serving and worshiping God.

George Herbert

Priest and Poet, 1633

I Almighty God, who didst call thy servant George Herbert from the pursuit of worldly honors to be a poet and a pastor of souls: Give us grace, we pray, joyfully to dedicate all our powers to thy service; through Jesus Christ our Lord, who liveth and reigneth with thee and the Holy Ghost, one God, for ever and ever. *Amen.*

II Almighty God, who called your servant George Herbert from the pursuit of worldly honors to be a poet and a pastor of souls: Give us grace, we pray, joyfully to dedicate all our powers to your service; through Jesus Christ our Lord, who lives and reigns with you and the Holy Spirit, one God, for ever and ever. *Amen.*

Lessons and Psalm

Ecclesiastes 4:13-5:7
Psalm 23
2 Corinthians 4:16-18
Mark 9:2-8

Preface of a Saint (1)

Anna Julia Haywood Cooper was born on August 10, 1858, in Raleigh, North Carolina, to an enslaved Black woman, Hannah Stanley, and a white man, presumably her mother's owner. Two years after the Civil War ended, she attended St. Augustine Normal School and Collegiate Institute, which had been founded by the Episcopal Church to educate African American teachers and clergy. There she became an Episcopalian and married George Cooper, one of her instructors, who was one of the first African American Episcopal priests in North Carolina.

Following the death of her husband, Cooper studied mathematics at Oberlin College, and moved to Washington, D.C., to teach at Washington Colored High School. She was an active member of St. Luke's Church in Washington, D.C., while Alexander Crummell served as its rector.

Cooper emphasized the importance of equal education for African Americans. An advocate for African American women, Cooper assisted in organizing the Colored Women's League and the first Colored Settlement House in Washington, D.C. In 1892, her book *A View from the South* was published, in which she challenged the Episcopal Church to offer more direct support for the African American members of its church in their quest for advancement and improvement in a segregated society. She wrote, "religion (ought to be if it isn't) a great deal more than mere gratification of the instinct for worship linked with the straight-teaching of irreproachable credos. Religion must be life made true; and life is action, growth, development—begun now and ending never."

On April 3, 1925, at the age of 67, Cooper became the fourth African American woman to complete a doctorate, granted by the Sorbonne in Paris. From 1930 to 1942, she served as President of Frelinghuysen University in Washington, D.C. She died on February 27, 1964, at the age of 105.

Anna Julia Haywood Cooper

Educator, 1964

I Almighty God, who didst inspire thy servant Anna Julia Haywood Cooper with the love of learning and the skill of teaching: Enlighten us more and more through the discipline of learning, and deepen our commitment to the education of all thy children; through Jesus Christ our Lord, who liveth and reigneth with thee and the Holy Ghost, one God, for ever and ever. *Amen.*

II Almighty God, who inspired your servant Anna Julia Haywood Cooper with the love of learning and the skill of teaching: Enlighten us more and more through the discipline of learning, and deepen our commitment to the education of all your children; through Jesus Christ our Lord, who lives and reigns with you and the Holy Spirit, one God, for ever and ever. *Amen.*

Lessons and Psalm

Proverbs 9:7-12
Psalm 10:15-19
1 Timothy 4:6-16
Luke 4:14-21

Preface of a Saint (3)

Despite the overwhelming victory of the pagan Angles, Saxons, and Jutes in the fifth century, one part of Britain continued in the ways of Christianity—Wales, the land west of the Wye River.

David was born around the year 500 in Menevia. Little is known of his early life, but, while still fairly young, he founded a monastery near Menevia and became its abbot. He is said to have been strict in governing of his own monastery, yet loving in his treatment and correction of wrongdoers. He required monks to pull ploughs themselves rather than relying on animal labor, and to spend every evening in spiritual reading and writing. No personal possessions were permitted, and to even say "my book" or "my robe" were offenses, since monks had only the use of those things, not the possession of them. One of his nicknames, "the Waterman," may indicate that he allowed the monks in his care to drink only water at meals instead of the customary wine or mead.

David's strongest desire was to study and meditate in the quiet of his monastery, but he was virtually dragged to an assembly of bishops called to combat the heresy of Pelagianism. Once there, David proved to be so eloquent and learned that Archbishop Dubricius chose him as his own successor as Primate of Wales. In time, David founded eleven other monasteries in Wales and made a pilgrimage to Jerusalem.

A scholar, a competent administrator, and a man of moderation, David filled the offices he held with distinction. He became a leader and guardian of the Christian faith in Wales. Eventually, he moved the center of episcopal government to Menevia, which is still an episcopal city, now called Ty-Dewi (House of David).

David of Wales

Bishop, c. 544

I Almighty God, who didst call thy servant David to be a faithful and wise steward of thy mysteries for the people of Wales: Mercifully grant that, following his purity of life and zeal for the Gospel of Christ, we may, with him, praise thee both here on earth and also in thy everlasting kingdom; through Jesus Christ our Lord, who liveth and reigneth with thee and the Holy Ghost, one God, for ever and ever. *Amen.*

II Almighty God, who called your servant David to be a faithful and wise steward of your mysteries for the people of Wales: Mercifully grant that, following his purity of life and zeal for the Gospel of Christ, we may, with him, praise you both here on earth and also in your everlasting kingdom; through Jesus Christ our Lord, who lives and reigns with you and the Holy Spirit, one God, for ever and ever. *Amen.*

Lessons and Psalm

Proverbs 15:14-21
Psalm 135:13-21
1 Thessalonians 2:7b-12
Mark 4:26-29

Preface of Apostles and Ordinations

Chad was born in Northern England around 634, one of four brothers dedicated to service in the church. Chad was trained by Aidan of Lindisfarne as a follower of the Celtic tradition in ritual. His elder brother Cedd had built a monastery at Lastingham, where he governed as abbot. At his death, Cedd left the abbacy to Chad. According to Bede, Chad was "a holy man, modest in his ways, learned in the Scriptures, and zealous in carrying out their teaching."

Impressed by Chad's qualities, the king appointed him Bishop of York. Chad was ordained by "bishops of the British race who had not been canonically ordained," Bede tells us. Chad was, Bede also notes, "a man who kept the church in truth and purity, humility, and temperance." Following apostolic example, he traveled about his diocese on foot.

The new Archbishop of Canterbury, Theodore, arrived in England four years after Chad's ordination as bishop. Theodore made it clear that Chad's ordination had been irregular, that is, not according to Roman custom, and Chad humbly offered to resign from office. "Indeed, I never believed myself worthy of it," he said.

Theodore, impressed by such humility, re-ordained him, and appointed him Bishop of Mercia and Northumbria. Chad continued his custom of traveling on foot until Theodore ordered him to ride, at least on longer journeys. When Chad hesitated, the Archbishop is said to have lifted him bodily onto the horse, "determined to compel him to ride when the need arose."

Chad administered his new diocese with devout concern. He built a monastery, and established monasticism at Barrow. In his see city of Lichfield, where he had an official dwelling, he preferred to read and meditate in a small house he had built nearby.

Two and a half years after his re-ordination, plague broke out, killing many residents of the diocese including Chad himself, whose death Bede describes thus: "He joyfully beheld . . . the day of the Lord, whose coming he had always anxiously awaited. He was mindful to his end of all that the Lord did." He died on March 2, 672, and was buried at the Cathedral Church of St. Peter in Lichfield.

Chad of Lichfield

Bishop, 672

I Heavenly Father, whose son our Lord Jesus Christ didst take the form of a servant for the sake of his brothers and sisters: Strengthen us with the prayers and example of thy servant Chad, who became the least of all to minister to all; through the same Christ our Lord, who liveth and reigneth with thee and the Holy Ghost, one God, now and for ever. *Amen.*

II Heavenly Father, whose son our Lord Jesus Christ took the form of a servant for the sake of his brothers and sisters: Strengthen us with the prayers and example of your servant Chad, who became the least of all to minister to all; through the same Christ our Lord, who lives and reigns, with you and the Holy Spirit, one God, now and for ever. *Amen.*

Lessons and Psalm

Leviticus 10:1-3
Psalm 103:13-18
Philippians 4:10-13
Luke 14:1-14

Preface of a Saint (2)

John was the fifteenth, and Charles the eighteenth, child of Samuel Wesley, Rector of Epworth, Lincolnshire, and his wife, Susannah. John was born on June 17, 1703, and Charles on December 18, 1707. Of the nineteen Wesley siblings, only ten lived to maturity. Under their mother's tutelage, all of them were schooled each day in six-hour sessions, always begun and concluded with the singing of psalms.

Their theological writings and sermons are still widely appreciated, but it is through their hymns—especially those of Charles, who wrote over six thousand of them—that their religious experience, and their Christian faith and life, continue to touch the hearts of many.

Both Wesleys were educated at Christ Church, Oxford, John later being elected a fellow of Lincoln College, where they gathered a few friends to join a "Holy Club" in strict adherence to the worship and discipline of the Prayer Book, and were thus given the name "Methodists." John was ordained in 1728 and Charles in 1735. Both were profoundly attached to the doctrine and worship of the Church of England, although they were deeply moved by and critical of the church's neglect of the poor. Their affection for the Church of England remained despite abusive opposition to their cause and methods.

The two brothers went together to Georgia in 1735, John as a missionary of the Society for the Propagation of the Gospel, and Charles as secretary to James Oglethorpe, the Governor. The mission was a disaster, and both brothers returned to England, dejected and disappointed. Shortly after their return home, however, they each experienced an inner conversion. On May 21, 1738—Pentecost—Charles "felt the Spirit of God striving with his spirit 'till by degrees He chased away the darkness of unbelief." Three days later, at a meeting on May 24 in Aldersgate Street in London with a group of Moravians, during a reading of Luther's *Preface to the Epistle to the Romans,* John recorded, "I felt my heart strangely warmed. I felt I did trust in Christ, Christ alone, for salvation; and an assurance was given me that he had taken away my sins, even mine, and saved me from the law of sin and death."

So the revival was born. The two brothers placed a strong emphasis on preaching, and appointed lay people, both men and women, as preachers and evangelists to work together with the clergy in proclaiming the gospel.

The formal separation of the Methodists from the Church of England occurred only after the deaths of the two brothers in London—Charles on March 29, 1788, and John on March 2, 1791. In recent decades there has been increased cooperation and growth in agreement between Anglicans and Methodists, and growing appreciation for our common heritage.

John and Charles Wesley

Priests, 1791, 1788

I Lord God, who didst inspire thy servants John and Charles Wesley with burning zeal for the sanctification of souls and didst endow them with eloquence in speech and song: Kindle such fervor in thy church, we beseech thee, that those whose faith has cooled may be warmed, and those who have not known thy Christ may turn to him and be saved; who liveth and reigneth with thee and the Holy Ghost, one God, now and for ever. *Amen.*

II Lord God, you inspired your servants John and Charles Wesley with burning zeal for the sanctification of souls and endowed them with eloquence in speech and song: Kindle such fervor in your church, we entreat you, that those whose faith has cooled may be warmed, and those who have not known Christ may turn to him and be saved; who lives and reigns with you and the Holy Spirit, one God, now and for ever. *Amen.*

Lessons and Psalm

Isaiah 6:1-8
Psalm 129
Romans 12:11-17
Luke 9:1-6

Preface of Pentecost

Vibia Perpetua, born in 181, was a young widow, mother of an infant, and owner of several slaves, including Felicity and Revocatus. With two other young Carthaginians, Secundulus and Saturninus, they were all catechumens preparing together for baptism.

Early in the third century, Emperor Septimius Severus decreed that all persons should sacrifice to the emperor. Many Christians, confessing faith in the one Lord Jesus Christ, believed that they could not do this. Perpetua, Felicity, and the other catechumens were arrested and held in prison under miserable conditions. At the public hearing before the proconsul, Perpetua refused even the entreaties of her aged father. Pointing to a water pot, she asked him, "See that pot lying there? Can you call it by any other name than what it is?" Her father answered, "Of course not." Perpetua responded, "Neither can I call myself by any name other than what I am—a Christian."

Felicity was eight months pregnant at the time they were arrested. Because pregnant women could not be executed, she was anxious lest the others be executed apart from her, while she would be condemned to die at another time alone. Two days before the scheduled execution, however, she gave birth to a baby girl, who was adopted and raised by an anonymous Christian woman in Carthage.

A document that is attributed to Perpetua recounts the visions that she had while in prison. One was of a ladder to heaven, which she climbed to reach a large garden; another was of her brother who had died when young of a dreadful disease, but was now well and drinking the water of life; the last was of herself as a warrior battling the devil and defeating him to win entrance to the gate of life. "And I awoke, understanding that I should fight, not with beasts, but with the Devil."

On March 7, 203, Perpetua and Felicity, encouraging one another to bear bravely whatever pain they might suffer, were sent to the arena to be mangled by a leopard, a boar, a bear, and a savage cow. Perpetua and Felicity, tossed by the cow, were bruised and disheveled, but Perpetua, "lost in spirit and ecstasy," hardly knew that anything had happened. To her companions she cried, "Stand fast in the faith and love one another. And do not let what we suffer be a stumbling block to you."

Eventually, both Perpetua and Felicity were put to death by a stroke of a sword through the throat. The soldier who struck Perpetua was inept. His first blow merely pierced her throat between the bones. She shrieked with pain, then aided the man to guide the sword properly. The report of her death concludes, "Perhaps so great a woman, feared by the unclean spirit, could not have been killed unless she so willed it."

Perpetua and Felicity

Martyrs, 202

I O God, the King of Saints, who didst strengthen thy servants Perpetua, Felicity, and their companions to make a good confession and to encourage one another in the time of trial: Grant that we who cherish their blessed memory may share their pure and steadfast faith, and win with them the palm of victory; through Jesus Christ our Lord, who liveth and reigneth with thee and the Holy Ghost, one God, now and for ever. *Amen.*

II O God, the King of Saints, who strengthened your servants Perpetua, Felicity, and their companions to make a good confession and to encourage one another in the time of trial: Grant that we who cherish their blessed memory may share their pure and steadfast faith, and win with them the palm of victory; through Jesus Christ our Lord, who lives and reigns with you and the Holy Spirit, one God, now and for ever. *Amen.*

Lessons and Psalm

Daniel 6:10-16
Psalm 124
Hebrews 10:32-39
Matthew 24:9-14

Preface of a Saint (3)

Gregory was a man enchanted with Christ and dazzled by the meaning of his Passion. He was born in Caesarea in Cappadocia around 334, the younger brother of Basil the Great and, in his youth, a reluctant Christian.

When he was twenty, the transfer of the relics of the Forty Martyrs of Sebaste to the family chapel at Annesi quickened Gregory's faith, and he became a practicing Christian and a lector. He later abandoned this ministry, however, to become a rhetorician like his father.

His brother Basil, in his struggle against the Emperor Valens, compelled Gregory to become Bishop of Nyssa, a town ten miles from Caesarea. Knowing himself to be unfit for the charge, Gregory described his ordination as the most miserable day of his life. He lacked the important episcopal skills of tact and understanding, and had no sense of the value of money. Falsely accused of embezzling church funds, Gregory went into hiding for two years, not returning to his diocese until Valens died.

Although he resented his brother's dominance, Gregory was shocked by Basil's death in 379. Several months later, he received another shock: his beloved sister Macrina was dying. Gregory hastened to Annesi and conversed with her for two days about death, the soul, and the meaning of the resurrection. Macrina died in her brother's arms.

The two deaths, while stunning Gregory, also freed him to develop as a deeper and richer philosopher and theologian. He reveals his delight in the created order in his treatise, *On the Making of Man*. He exposes the depth of his contemplative and mystical nature in his *Life of Moses* and again in his *Commentary on the Song of Songs*. His *Great Catechism* is considered second only to Origen's treatise *On First Principles*, and his treatise *On Virginity* is a masterpiece of ascetical theology.

Gregory's theological writings have received a resurgence of interest among Christian theologians starting in the mid-twentieth century, and he is regarded as one of the "Cappadocian Fathers" together with his brother Basil and their friend Gregory of Nazianzus. Gregory died on March 9, probably in Nyssa, around the year 394.

Gregory of Nyssa

Bishop and Theologian, c. 394

I Almighty God, who hast revealed to thy Church thine eternal Being of glorious majesty and perfect love as one God in Trinity of Persons: Give us grace that, like thy bishop Gregory of Nyssa, we may continue steadfast in the confession of this faith, and constant in our worship of thee, Father, Son, and Holy Ghost; who livest and reignest now and for ever. *Amen.*

II Almighty God, who has revealed to your Church your eternal Being of glorious majesty and perfect love as one God in Trinity of Persons: Give us grace that, like your bishop Gregory of Nyssa, we may continue steadfast in the confession of this faith, and constant in our worship of you, Father, Son and Holy Spirit; who live and reign for ever and ever. *Amen.*

Lessons and Psalm

Wisdom 7:24-8:1
Psalm 119:97-104
Ephesians 2:17-22
John 14:23-26

Preface of Trinity Sunday

Slave births were recorded under property, not as persons with names, but we know that Harriet Ross was born sometime during 1820 on a Maryland Chesapeake Bay plantation, the sixth of eleven children born to Ben Ross and Harriet Green. Although her parents were loving and they enjoyed a cheerful family life inside their cabin, they lived in fear of the children being sold off at any time.

Harriet suffered beatings and a severe injury, but grew up strong and defiant, refusing to appear happy and smiling to her owners. To cope with brutality and oppression, she turned to religion. Her favorite Bible story was about Moses, who led the Israelites out of slavery. The slaves prayed for a Moses of their own.

When she was about 24, Harriet escaped to Canada but could not forget her parents and other slaves she left behind. Working with the Quakers, she made at least nineteen trips back to Maryland between 1851 and 1861, freeing over three hundred people by leading them into Canada. She was so successful that $40,000 was offered for her capture.

Guided by God through omens, dreams, and warnings, she claimed her struggle against slavery had been commanded by God. She foresaw the Civil War in a vision. When it began, she quickly joined the Union Army, serving as cook and nurse, caring for both Confederate and Union soldiers. She served as a spy and a scout. She led 300 Black troops on a raid that freed over 750 slaves, making her the first American woman to lead troops into military action.

In 1858–1859, she moved to upstate New York, where she opened her home to African American orphans and to helpless old people. Although she was illiterate, she founded schools for African American children. She joined the fight for women's rights, working with Elizabeth Cady Stanton and Susan B. Anthony, but supported African American women in their efforts to found their own organizations to address equality, work, and education. She died on March 10, 1913, in Auburn, New York.

Harriet Ross Tubman

Social Reformer, 1913

I O God, whose Spirit guideth us into all truth and maketh us free: Strengthen and sustain us as thou didst thy servant Harriet Ross Tubman. Give us vision and courage to stand against oppression and injustice and all that worketh against the glorious liberty to which thou dost call all thy children; through Jesus Christ our Savior, who liveth and reigneth with thee and the Holy Ghost, one God, for ever and ever. *Amen.*

II O God, whose Spirit guides us into all truth and makes us free: Strengthen and sustain us as you did your servant Harriet Ross Tubman. Give us vision and courage to stand against oppression and injustice and all that works against the glorious liberty to which you call all your children; through Jesus Christ our Savior, who lives and reigns with you and the Holy Spirit, one God, for ever and ever. *Amen.*

Lessons and Psalm

Judges 9:50-55
Psalm 146
James 2:14-17
Luke 11:5-10

Preface of Baptism

Gregory was born into a patrician family about 540 and became Prefect of Rome in 573. Shortly thereafter, however, he retired to a monastic life in a community which he founded in his ancestral home on the Coelian Hill. Pope Pelagius II made him Ambassador to Constantinople in 579, where he learned much about the larger affairs of the church. Not long after his return home, Pope Pelagius died of the plague, and in 590, Gregory was elected as his successor.

Gregory wrote eloquently about the demands of the pastoral office and the dangers of seeking it too rashly. He said: "Those who aspire to the priesthood usually delude themselves into thinking that they are seeking it out of a desire to perform good works, although this actually stems from pride and a desire to accomplish great things. Thus one thing takes place in their conscious mind, but another motive is hidden secretly within. For the mind frequently lies to itself about itself, pretending that it loves the good work when it does not, and that it does not care for worldly glory when in fact it does. The mind often has appropriate trepidation about seeking office, but once a leadership position has been secured, it assumes that it has achieved what it rightly deserved. When it begins to enjoy its newfound superiority, it quickly forgets all of the spiritual thoughts that it once had. Therefore, when thoughts begin to stray, it is good to direct them back to the past, and for a person to consider how he behaved while still under authority. In this way he will judge himself more accurately, for no one can learn humility in a position of leadership who did not learn it when he was in a position of subjection. No one will know how to flee from praise when it abounds if he secretly yearned for praise when it was absent. Therefore, let each person judge his own character on the basis of his past life so that the fantasy of his thoughts will not deceive him."

Gregory's pontificate was one of strenuous activity. He organized the defense of Rome against the attacks of the Lombards and fed its populace from papal granaries in Sicily. In this, as in other matters, he administered "the patrimony of St. Peter" with energy and efficiency. His ordering of the church's liturgy and chant has molded the spirituality of Western Christianity until the present day. His writings provided succeeding generations with a number of influential texts, especially his *Pastoral Care,* which remains to this day a classic text on the work of Christian ministry. Gregory understood well the intricacies of the human heart, and the ease with which growth in holiness may be compromised by self-deception. He wrote: "The pastor must understand that vices commonly masquerade as virtues. The person who is not generous claims to be frugal, while the one who is a prodigal describes himself as generous. Thus, it is necessary that the director of souls discern between vices and virtues with great care."

In the midst of all his cares and duties, Gregory prepared and fostered the evangelizing mission to the Anglo-Saxons under Augustine and other monks from his own monastery. For this reason, the English historian Bede justly called Gregory "The Apostle of the English." Gregory died on March 12, 604, and was buried in Saint Peter's Basilica. His life was a true witness to the title he assumed for his office: "Servant of the servants of God."

Gregory the Great

Bishop and Theologian, 604

I Almighty and merciful God, who didst raise up Gregory of Rome to be a servant of the servants of God, and didst inspire him to send missionaries to preach the Gospel to the English people: Preserve thy church in the catholic and apostolic faith, that thy people, being fruitful in every good work, may receive the crown of glory that never fades away; through Jesus Christ our Lord, who liveth and reigneth with thee and the Holy Ghost, one God, for ever and ever. *Amen.*

II Almighty and merciful God, you raised up Gregory of Rome to be a servant of the servants of God, and inspired him to send missionaries to preach the Gospel to the English people: Preserve your church in the catholic and apostolic faith, that your people, being fruitful in every good work, may receive the crown of glory that never fades away; through Jesus Christ our Lord, who lives and reigns with you and the Holy Spirit, one God, for ever and ever. *Amen.*

Lessons and Psalm

Genesis 18:1-15
Psalm 66:1-8
Colossians 1:28—2:3
Mark 10:42-45

Preface of Apostles and Ordinations

James Theodore Augustus Holly was born a free African American in Washington, D.C., on October 3, 1829. Baptized and confirmed in the Roman Catholic Church, he later became an Episcopalian. Holly was ordained as a deacon at St. Matthew's Church in Detroit on June 17, 1855, and ordained as a priest by the bishop of Connecticut on January 2, 1856. He was then appointed rector of St. Luke's in New Haven. In the same year he founded the Protestant Episcopal Society for Promoting the Extension of the Church among Colored People, an antecedent of the Union of Black Episcopalians. He became a friend of Frederick Douglass, and the two men worked together on many programs.

In 1861, Holly resigned as rector of St. Luke's to lead a group of African Americans settling in Haiti. Although his wife, his mother, and two of his children died during the first year, along with other settlers, Holly stayed on with two small sons, proclaiming that just "as the last surviving apostle of Jesus was in tribulation . . . on the forlorn isle of Patmos, so, by His Divine Providence, [Christ] had brought this tribulation upon me for a similar end on this isle in the Caribbean Sea." He welcomed the opportunity to speak of God's love to a people who needed to hear it.

Through an agreement between the House of Bishops of the Episcopal Church and the Orthodox Apostolic Church of Haiti, Holly was consecrated a missionary bishop to build the church in Haiti on November 8, 1874, making him the first African American to be raised to the office of bishop in the Episcopal Church. In 1878, Bishop Holly attended the Lambeth Conference, the first African American to do so, and he preached at Westminster Abbey on St. James' Day of that year.

In the course of his ministry, he doubled the size of his diocese, and established medical clinics where none had been before.

Bishop Holly served the Diocese of Haiti until his death in Haiti on March 13, 1911. He had charge of the Diocese of the Dominican Republic as well, from 1897 until he died. He is buried on the grounds of St. Vincent's School for Handicapped Children in Port-au-Prince.

James Theodore Holly

Bishop, 1911

I Most gracious God, whose servant James Theodore Holly labored to build a church in which all might be free: Grant that we might overcome our prejudice, and honor those whom thou dost call from every family, language, people, and nation; through Jesus Christ our Lord, who liveth and reigneth with thee and the Holy Ghost, one God, now and for ever. *Amen.*

II Most gracious God, whose servant James Theodore Holly labored to build a church in which all might be free: Grant that we might overcome our prejudice, and honor those whom you call from every family, language, people, and nation; through Jesus Christ our Lord, who lives and reigns with you and the Holy Spirit, one God, now and for ever. *Amen.*

Lessons and Psalm

Deuteronomy 6:20-25
Psalm 86:11-17
Acts 8:26-39
John 4:31-38

Preface of Apostles and Ordinations

Born into a family of peasant farmers in the village of Pouy in Gascony in 1581, Vincent de Paul showed an early aptitude for reading and writing. His father sold his oxen in order to send the boy to seminary, hoping that a clerical career would allow him to support the family. Later kidnapped by pirates and sold as a slave, he studied alchemy under his master. While traveling to Istanbul, the alchemist died; Vincent was sold again, this time to a former Franciscan who had likewise been enslaved, but became a Muslim in exchange for his freedom. Vincent shared the Gospel with his new master's wife; she was baptized and convinced her husband to return to the faith of Christ and escape to France. Later, while serving as a parish priest near Paris, Vincent began to devote his attention to serving the poor and destitute. With the support of the noble women of the parish, a ministry developed for visiting, feeding, and nursing the poor in and around Paris. As this ministry grew, he came to rely on a widow, Louise de Marillac, to oversee their efforts.

Louise de Marillac was born to a wealthy family near Le Jeux in Picardy; by the time she was fifteen years old both of her parents had died. She longed to become a nun, but was discouraged; instead, she wed Antoine Le Gras. Her husband died twelve years later; the union produced one child, a son with special needs. Francis de Sales, later Bishop of Geneva, who wrote the highly influential *Introduction to the Devout Life,* became her spiritual director. At age thirty-two it was revealed to her in a vision that God would bring her a new spiritual director, whose face she was shown. When she met Vincent de Paul, she recognized his face from her vision. He invited Louise to assist in his expanding charitable ministry. She accepted his offer, poured herself into this ministry, and soon became the leader of the sisterhood. She led the order until her death in 1660.

In 1633, Vincent de Paul and Louise de Marillac formally founded the Sisters of Charity of Saint Joseph (later the Company of the Daughters of Charity of Saint Vincent de Paul), or more commonly, the "Grey Sisters," the first non-cloistered religious order for women devoted to acts of charity. The ministry of the Grey Sisters grew to include founding hospitals, orphanages, and schools. The nineteenth-century revival of religious orders within Anglicanism was greatly influenced by the spirituality and the work of the Daughters of Charity.

Vincent de Paul

Priest, 1660

and Louise de Marillac

Vowed Religious, 1660

I Most Gracious God, who hast bidden us to act justly, love mercy, and walk humbly before thee; Teach us, like thy servants Vincent de Paul and Louise de Marillac, to see and to serve Christ by feeding the hungry, welcoming the stranger, clothing the naked, and caring for the sick; that we may know him to be the giver of all good things, through the same, Jesus Christ our Lord. *Amen.*

II Most Gracious God, who has bidden us to act justly, love mercy, and walk humbly before you; Teach us, like your servants Vincent de Paul and Louise de Marillac, to see and to serve Christ by feeding the hungry, welcoming the stranger, clothing the naked, and caring for the sick; that we may know him to be the giver of all good things, through the same Jesus Christ our Lord. *Amen.*

Lessons and Psalm

Micah 3:1-12
Psalm 37:1-17
Philippians 2:12-15
Matthew 18:18-20

Preface of Baptism

Patrick was born into a Christian family somewhere on the northwest coast of Britain around 390. His grandfather had been a Christian priest and his father, Calpornius, a deacon. Calpornius was an important official in the late Roman imperial government of Britain.

When Patrick was about sixteen, he was captured by a band of Irish slave-raiders. He was carried off to Ireland and forced to serve as a shepherd. When he was about twenty-one, he escaped and returned to Britain, where he was educated as a Christian. He tells us that he was ordained as both priest and bishop, although no particular see is known as his at this time. A vision then called him to return to Ireland, and he did so around the year 431.

Tradition holds that Patrick landed not far from the place of his earlier captivity, near what is now known as Downpatrick (a "down" or "dun" is a fortified hill, the stronghold of a local Irish king). He then began a remarkable process of missionary conversion throughout the country that continued until his death, probably in 461. He made his appeal to the local kings and through them to their tribes. Christianizing the old pagan religion as he went, Patrick erected Christian churches over sites already regarded as sacred, had crosses carved on old druidic pillars, and put sacred wells and springs under the protection of Christian saints.

Many legends of Patrick's Irish missionary travels possess substrata of truth, especially those telling of his conversion of the three major Irish High Kings. At Armagh, he is said to have established his principal church. To this day, Armagh is regarded as the primatial see of all Ireland.

Two works are attributed to Patrick: an autobiographical *Confession,* in which he tells us, among other things, that he was criticized by his contemporaries for lack of learning, and a *Letter to Coroticus,* a British chieftain. The *Lorica* or *St. Patrick's Breastplate* ("I bind unto myself today") was probably not written by him, dating most probably from the eighth century rather than from the fifth, but it does express his faith and zeal.

Patrick of Ireland

Bishop and Missionary, 461

I Almighty God, who in thy providence didst choose thy servant Patrick to be the apostle to the Irish people, to bring those who were wandering in darkness and error to the true light and knowledge of thee: Grant us so to walk in that way that we may come at last to the light of everlasting life; through Jesus Christ our Lord, who liveth and reigneth with thee and the Holy Ghost, one God, for ever and ever. *Amen.*

II Almighty God, in your providence you chose your servant Patrick to be the apostle to the Irish people, to bring those who were wandering in darkness and error to the true light and knowledge of you: Grant us so to walk in that way that we may come at last to the light of everlasting life; through Jesus Christ our Lord, who lives and reigns with you and the Holy Spirit, one God, for ever and ever. *Amen.*

Lessons and Psalm

Ezekiel 36:33-38
Psalm 97
1 Thessalonians 2:1-8
Matthew 28:16-20

Preface of Apostles and Ordinations

Born in Jerusalem about 315, Cyril became bishop of that city probably in 349. In the course of political and ecclesiastical disputes, he was banished and restored three times. Cyril is the one we have most to thank for the development of catechetical instruction and liturgical observances during Lent and Holy Week. His *Catechetical Lectures on the Christian Faith,* given before Easter to candidates for baptism, were probably written sometime between 348 and 350.

The work consists of an introductory lecture, or *Procatechesis,* and eighteen *Catecheses* based upon the articles of the creed of the church in Jerusalem. All these lectures (the earliest catechetical materials surviving today) may have been used many times over by Cyril and his successors, and considerably revised in the process. They were probably part of the pre-baptismal instruction that Egeria, a pilgrim nun from western Europe, witnessed at Jerusalem in the fourth century and described with great enthusiasm in the account of her pilgrimage. Many of the faithful would also attend these instructions.

Cyril's five *Mystagogical Catecheses on the Sacraments,* intended for the newly baptized after Easter, are now thought to have been composed, or at least revised, by John, Cyril's successor as Bishop of Jerusalem, from 386 to 417.

It is likely that it was Cyril who instituted the observances of Palm Sunday and Holy Week during the latter years of his episcopate in Jerusalem. In doing so, he was taking practical steps to organize devotions for countless pilgrims and local inhabitants around the sacred sites. In time, as pilgrims returned to their homes from Palestine, these services were to influence the development of Holy Week observances throughout the entire church. Cyril attended the Second Ecumenical Council at Constantinople, in 381, and died in Jerusalem on March 18, 386.

Cyril's writings have greatly enriched the observance of Holy Week in the 1979 Book of Common Prayer.

Cyril of Jerusalem

Bishop and Theologian, 386

I Strengthen, O God, thy church in the sacraments of thy grace, that we, in union with the teaching and prayers of thy servant Cyril of Jerusalem, may enter more fully into thy Paschal mystery; through Jesus Christ our Lord, who liveth and reigneth with thee and the Holy Ghost, one God, now and for ever. *Amen.*

II Strengthen, O God, your church in the sacraments of your grace, that we, in union with the teaching and prayers of your servant Cyril of Jerusalem, may enter more fully into your Paschal mystery; through Jesus Christ our Lord, who lives and reigns with you and the Holy Spirit, one God, now and for ever. *Amen.*

Lessons and Psalm

Ecclesiasticus 47:2-10
Psalm 29
Hebrews 13:14-21
Mark 9:38-41

Preface of Apostles and Ordinations

In the face of circumstances that distressed even a man of such tenderness and obedience to God as Joseph, he accepted the vocation of protecting Mary and being a father to Jesus. He is honored in Christian tradition for the nurturing care and protection he provided for the infant Jesus and his mother in taking them to Egypt to escape Herod's slaughter of the innocents, and in rearing him as a faithful Jew at Nazareth.

The Gospel according to Matthew pictures Joseph as a man of deep devotion, open to mystical experiences, and as a man of compassion, who accepted his God-given responsibility with gentleness and humility.

Joseph was a pious Jew, a descendant of David, and a carpenter by trade. As Joseph the Carpenter, he is considered the patron saint of the working man, one who not only worked with his hands, but taught his trade to Jesus. The little that is told of him is a testimony to the trust in God which values simple everyday duties, and gives an example of a loving husband and father.

Saint Joseph

I O God, who from the family of thy servant David didst raise up Joseph to be the guardian of thy incarnate Son and the spouse of his virgin mother: Give us grace to imitate his uprightness of life and his obedience to thy commands; through the same thy Son Jesus Christ our Lord, who liveth and reigneth with thee and the Holy Ghost, one God, for ever and ever. *Amen.*

II O God, who from the family of your servant David raised up Joseph to be the guardian of your incarnate Son and the spouse of his virgin mother: Give us grace to imitate his uprightness of life and his obedience to your commands; through Jesus Christ our Lord, who lives and reigns with you and the Holy Spirit, one God, for ever and ever. *Amen.*

Lessons and Psalm

2 Samuel 7:4, 8-16
Psalm 89:1-29 *or* 89:1-4, 26-29
Romans 4:13-18
Luke 2:41-52

Preface of the Epiphany

Cuthbert was the most popular saint of the pre-Conquest Anglo-Saxon Church. He was born about 625. Bede, who wrote a life of Cuthbert, tells us that in his youth, while tending sheep one night and praying, "as was his custom," he saw a stream of light break through the darkness, and in its midst, "a company of the heavenly host descended to the earth, and having received among them a spirit of surpassing brightness, returned without delay to their heavenly home." Learning the next day that Aidan of Lindisfarne had died at that very time, Cuthbert "determined immediately to enter a monastery."

Trained in the austere traditions of Celtic monasticism, Cuthbert was Prior of Melrose Abbey from 651 to 664, and then of Lindisfarne for twelve years. Bede says that he was accustomed to make visitations even to remote villages to preach to people who, "neglecting the sacrament of their creed, had recourse to idolatrous remedies; as if by charms or amulets, or any other mysteries of the magical art, they were able to avert a stroke inflicted upon them by the Lord . . ." Bede says that Cuthbert "often remained a week, sometimes two or three, even a whole month, without returning home; but dwelling among the mountains, taught the poor people, both by words of his preaching, and also by his own holy conduct."

Archbishop Theodore recognized Cuthbert's greatness of character and made him Bishop of Hexham in 684, but Cuthbert continued to make his see at Lindisfarne. He returned two years later to his hermitage on the neighboring island of Farne, where he died on March 20, 687.

Cuthbert accepted the decisions of the synod of Whitby in 663 that brought the usages of the English Church into line with Roman practice. He was thus a "healer of the breach" that threatened to divide the Church into Celtic and Roman factions.

At the time of the Viking invasions, the monks of Lindisfarne carefully protected his relics during their wanderings, until finally they brought them to Durham, where pilgrims come to visit his shrine to this day.

Cuthbert

Bishop, 687

I Merciful God, who didst call Cuthbert from following the flock to be a shepherd of thy people: Mercifully grant that we also may go without fear to dangerous and remote places, to seek the indifferent and the lost; through Jesus Christ our Lord, who liveth and reigneth with thee and the Holy Ghost, one God, for ever and ever. *Amen.*

II Merciful God, who called Cuthbert from following the flock to be a shepherd of your people: Mercifully grant that we also may go without fear to dangerous and remote places, to seek the indifferent and the lost; through Jesus Christ our Lord, who lives and reigns with you and the Holy Spirit, one God, for ever and ever. *Amen.*

Lessons and Psalm

Job 38:1, 12-21
Psalm 23
2 Corinthians 6:1-10
Luke 5:12-16

Preface of a Saint (2)

Thomas Ken was born at Berkhampsted, Hertfordshire, England, in 1637. Throughout his life he was both rewarded and punished for his integrity. His close relationship with the royal family began when he became chaplain to Princess Mary of Orange at The Hague. Ken was appalled at the Prince of Orange's treatment of his wife, and rebuked him publicly.

In 1683, Ken returned to England and became chaplain to Charles II. His integrity stirred him to rebuke Charles for lax behavior. When Ken was notified that the King's mistress, the actress Nell Gwyn, was to be lodged at his house, he refused, saying, "a woman of ill-repute ought not to be endured in the house of a clergyman, and especially the King's chaplain." The King took no offense, but in the next year made Ken the Bishop of Bath and Wells, declaring that none should have the position except "the little . . . fellow that refused his lodging to poor Nelly."

In 1688, when Charles' successor, James II, tried to undermine the authority of the Church of England and restore Roman Catholicism, Ken was one of seven bishops who refused to read the King's Declaration of Indulgence, which offered toleration to Protestant non-conformists and to Roman Catholics. The seven bishops were sent to the Tower, but were acquitted in the courts, and became popular heroes. After the Revolution of 1688, however, Ken's conscience did not permit him to swear allegiance to William of Orange, who became King William III. As a Non-Juror, Ken was deprived of his see.

Ken's conscience would not let him rest and his disagreement with others of the "Non-Juring" party over various matters troubled him for the rest of his life. He deplored the Non-Juror schism, and after the accession of Queen Anne in 1702, he made his peace with the Church of England, encouraging his fellow Non-Jurors to return to their parish churches in 1710. Ken announced his intention to do the same, but died on March 19, 1711, before doing so.

A man of deep piety, Ken was the author of several religious works, which were immensely popular in the eighteenth century. He is best known as a writer of hymns, particularly the well-known evening hymn "All praise to thee, my God, this night" (*The Hymnal 1982,* #43), which concludes with his doxology, "Praise God from whom all blessings flow." One of the most compelling products of his piety and his pen is the prayer, "Our God, amidst the deplorable division of your church, let us never widen its breaches, but give us universal charity to all who are called by your name. Deliver us from the sins and errors, the schisms and heresies of the age. Give us grace daily to pray for the peace of your church, and earnestly to seek it and to excite all we can to praise and love you; through Jesus Christ, our one Savior and Redeemer."

Thomas Ken

Bishop, 1711

I Almighty God, who didst give thy servant Thomas Ken grace and courage to bear witness to the truth before rulers and kings: Give us strength also that we may constantly defend what is right, boldly reprove what is evil, and patiently suffer for the truth's sake; through Jesus Christ our Lord, who liveth and reigneth with thee and the Holy Ghost, one God, for ever and ever. *Amen.*

II Almighty God, you gave your servant Thomas Ken grace and courage to bear witness to the truth before rulers and kings: Give us strength also that we may constantly defend what is right, boldly reprove what is evil, and patiently suffer for the truth's sake; through Jesus Christ our Lord, who lives and reigns with you and the Holy Spirit, one God, for ever and ever. *Amen.*

Lessons and Psalm

Deuteronomy 26:16-19
Psalm 22:27-31
Philippians 4:4-9
Luke 19:1-9

Preface of a Saint (2)

James De Koven was born in Middletown, Connecticut, on September 19, 1831, ordained by Bishop Kemper in 1855, and appointed professor of ecclesiastical history at Nashotah House. In addition, he administered a preparatory school and assisted at the Church of St. John Chrysostom in Delafield, Wisconsin.

Nashotah House was associated, from the time of its foundation, with many of the principles of the Oxford Movement, above all in its emphasis on the sacramental life of the church and the expression of devotion to the Eucharist—including such practices as bowing to the altar, at the name of Jesus, and before receiving Communion. In 1859, De Koven became Warden of Racine College at Racine, Wisconsin.

De Koven came to national attention at the General Conventions of 1871 and 1874, when the controversy over "ritualism" was at its height. In 1871, he asserted that the use of candles on the altar, incense, and genuflections were lawful, because they symbolized "the real, spiritual presence of Christ" which the Episcopal Church upheld, along with the Orthodox and the Lutherans. To the General Convention of 1874, De Koven expressed the religious conviction that underlay his churchmanship: "You may take away from us, if you will, every external ceremony; you may take away altars, and super-altars, lights and incense and vestments . . . and we will submit to you. But, gentlemen . . . to adore Christ's Person in his Sacrament—that is the inalienable privilege of every Christian and Catholic heart. How we do it, the way we do it, the ceremonies with which we do it, are utterly, utterly, indifferent. The thing itself is what we plead for."

Because of his advocacy of the "ritualist" cause, consents were not given to his consecration as Bishop of Wisconsin in 1874, and of Illinois in 1875.

Despite calls to serve at prominent parishes in New York City, Boston, Cincinnati, and Philadelphia, he remained in his post at Racine College, where his students admired him as "a model of great learning, gracious manners, personal holiness, and extraordinary compassion." He died there on March 19, 1879, and is buried on the grounds.

James De Koven

Priest, 1879

I Almighty and everlasting God, who led thy servant James De Koven to honor thy presence at the altar, and constantly to point to Christ: Grant that all ministers and stewards of thy mysteries may impart to thy faithful people the knowledge of thy presence and the truth of thy grace; through the same Jesus Christ our Lord, who liveth and reigneth with thee and the Holy Ghost, one God, for ever and ever. *Amen.*

II Almighty and everlasting God, who led your servant James De Koven to honor your presence at the altar, and constantly to point to Christ: Grant that all ministers and stewards of your mysteries may impart to your faithful people the knowledge of your presence and the truth of your grace; through the same Jesus Christ our Lord, who lives and reigns with you and the Holy Spirit, one God, for ever and ever. *Amen.*

Lessons and Psalm

Exodus 24:1-8
Psalm 84:7-12
2 Timothy 2:10-15
Luke 16:1-15

Preface of a Saint (1)

Armenia is traditionally regarded as the first kingdom to become officially Christian, and this set a precedent for the legalization of Christianity by the Emperor Constantine. As a buffer state between the more powerful empires of Rome and Persia, Armenia endured many shifts of policy, as first one and then the other empire took it "under protection." Armenia's conversion was actually preceded by those of two other small buffer kingdoms between Persia and Rome: Adiabene and Osroene. However, by the third century neither of these kingdoms existed as a self-governing entity.

The accounts of Gregory, known as the Illuminator (or Enlightener) and as "Apostle of the Armenians," are a mixture of legend and fact. He was born about 257. After his father assassinated the Persian King Chosroes I, the infant boy was rescued and taken to Caesarea in Cappadocia, where he was brought up as a Christian. He married a woman named Mary, who bore him two sons. About 280, he returned to Armenia and, after experiencing various fortunes of honor and imprisonment, succeeded in converting King Tiridates to his faith. With the help of the king, the country was Christianized and paganism was rooted out. About 300, Gregory was ordained a bishop at Caesarea. He established his cathedral at Valarshapat, with his center of work nearby at Echmiadzin, which is still the spiritual center of Armenian Christianity.

There is no record that Gregory attended the First Ecumenical Council at Nicaea in 325, but a tradition records that he sent in his stead his younger son Aristages, whom he ordained as his successor. His last years were spent in solitude, and he died about 332.

Gregory the Illuminator

Bishop and Missionary, c. 332

I Almighty God, who didst raise up thy servant Gregory to be a light in the world, and to preach the Gospel to the people of Armenia: Illuminate our hearts, that we also in our own generation may show forth thy praise, who hast called us out of darkness and into thy marvelous light; through Jesus Christ our Lord, who liveth and reigneth with thee and the Holy Ghost, one God, now and for ever. *Amen.*

II Almighty God, who raised up your servant Gregory to be a light in the world, and to preach the Gospel to the people of Armenia: Illuminate our hearts, that we also in our own generation may show forth your praise, who called us out of darkness and into your marvelous light; through Jesus Christ our Lord, who lives and reigns with you and the Holy Spirit, one God, now and for ever. *Amen.*

Lessons and Psalm

Ecclesiastes 2:1-11
Psalm 33:6-11
Acts 17:22-31
Mark 2:18-22

Preface of Apostles and Ordinations

Óscar Arnulfo Romero y Galdémez was born on August 15, 1917, in San Salvador. At the age of twelve, he was apprenticed to a carpenter. He was later able to attend seminary, but his family's economic circumstances forced him to withdraw to work in a gold mine. Ultimately he entered another seminary and was eventually sent to the Gregorian University in Rome to study theology. After his ordination to the priesthood, he returned to his native land, where he worked among the poor, served as an administrator for the church, and started an Alcoholics Anonymous group in San Miguel.

When he was appointed a bishop, radicals distrusted his conservative sympathies. However, after his appointment as Archbishop of San Salvador in 1977, a progressive Jesuit friend of his, Rutilio Grande, was assassinated, and Romero began protesting the government's injustice to the poor and its policies of torture. He met with Pope John Paul II in 1980 and complained that the leaders of El Salvador engaged in terror and assassinations. He also pleaded with the American government to stop military aid to his country, but this request was ignored.

Romero was shot to death while celebrating Mass at a small hospital chapel near his cathedral on March 24, 1980. The previous day, he had preached a sermon calling on soldiers to disobey orders that violated human rights. He had said, "A bishop will die, but the Church of God which is the people will never perish."

Romero was not the only Christian leader who was assassinated in El Salvador during this time. Almost nine months after Romero's assassination, four women—two Maryknoll Sisters, an Ursuline Sister, and a lay missioner—were also killed in the course of their ministry by the army. Six Jesuit priests, their housekeeper, and her daughter were similarly murdered in November of 1989.

The Roman Catholic Church canonized Romero on October 14, 2018, and he is honored as a martyr by many Christian churches worldwide. A statue of Romero stands at the door of Westminster Abbey in London as part of a commemoration of twentieth-century martyrs.

Óscar Romero

Archbishop and Martyr, 1980

and the Martyrs of El Salvador

I Almighty God, who didst call thy servant Óscar Romero to be a voice for the voiceless poor, and to give his life as a seed of freedom and a sign of hope: Grant that we, inspired by his sacrifice and the example of the martyrs of El Salvador, may without fear or favor witness to thy Word who abides, thy Word who is Life, even Jesus Christ our Lord, to whom, with thee and the Holy Ghost, be praise and glory now and for ever. *Amen.*

II Almighty God, you called your servant Óscar Romero to be a voice for the voiceless poor, and to give his life as a seed of freedom and a sign of hope: Grant that we, inspired by his sacrifice and the example of the martyrs of El Salvador, may without fear or favor witness to your Word who abides, your Word who is Life, even Jesus Christ our Lord, to whom, with you and the Holy Spirit, be praise and glory now and for ever. *Amen.*

Lessons and Psalm

1 Kings 21:1-19
Psalm 31:15-24
Revelation 7:13-17
John 12:20-26

Preface of a Saint (3)

Today's feast commemorates how God made known to a young Jewish woman that she was to be the mother of his Son. The Annunciation has been a major theme in Christian art, in both East and West, and innumerable sermons and poems have been composed about it. The term coined by Cyril of Alexandria for the Blessed Virgin, Theotokos ("the God-bearer"), was affirmed by the General Council of Ephesus in 431.

Many theologians stress that Mary accepted her vocation with perfect conformity of will. Mary's self-offering in response to God's call has been compared to that of Abraham, the father of believers. Just as Abraham was called to be the father of the chosen people, and accepted his call, so Mary was called to be the mother of the faithful, the new Israel. She is God's human agent in the mystery of the Incarnation. Her response to the angel, "Let it be to me according to your word," is identical with the faith expressed in the prayer that Jesus taught: "Your will be done on earth as in heaven."

But while many Christians emphasize the submissiveness of Mary, according to the sixth-century Syriac writer Jacob of Sarug, the most important words that Mary spoke were not those of quiet acquiescence but rather, "How can this be?" Indeed, in Jacob's account of the gospel encounter, Mary's response is much more than a single question. Instead, a teenage girl takes on an archangel in a theological debate and freely consents only when she has been convinced that the angel's word is true. In this interpretation, it is Mary's eagerness to understand God's plan and her own role in it that makes her exemplary rather than her meek consent. Jacob contrasts her behavior with Eve, who did not question the serpent that tempted her in the garden but uncritically accepted the claim that she and Adam would become like gods without testing it first. In Eve's case, "lack of doubt gave birth to death" because she simply believed whatever she was told and "was won over without any debate."

In both of these interpretations, however, our salvation is only possible because of Mary's free cooperation with God in that salvation. It has been said, "God made us without us, and redeemed us without us, but cannot save us without us." Mary's assent to God's call opened the way for God to accomplish the salvation of the world. It is for this reason that all generations have called her "blessed."

The Annunciation of Our Lord Jesus Christ to the Blessed Virgin Mary

I We beseech thee, O Lord, pour thy grace into our hearts, that we who have known the incarnation of thy Son Jesus Christ, announced by an angel to the Virgin Mary, may by his cross and passion be brought unto the glory of his resurrection; who liveth and reigneth with thee, in the unity of the Holy Ghost, one God, now and for ever. *Amen.*

II Pour your grace into our hearts, O Lord, that we who have known the incarnation of your Son Jesus Christ, announced by an angel to the Virgin Mary, may by his cross and passion be brought to the glory of his resurrection; who lives and reigns with you, in the unity of the Holy Spirit, one God, now and for ever. *Amen.*

Lessons and Psalm

Isaiah 7:10-14
Psalm 45 *or* 40:5-10 *or* Canticle 3 *or* 15
Hebrews 10:4-10
Luke 1:26-38

Preface of the Epiphany

The revival of monastic life in the Anglican tradition, both in England and in the United States, is a great story of vision and commitment shown in the lives of men and women responding to God's call despite opposition and misunderstanding. One of the earliest orders, the Community of Saint John Baptist, grew out of a mission in Clewer, one of the neighborhoods of Windsor, which offered safe shelter and rehabilitation to women caught by poverty in a life of destitution and human trafficking. This work caught the imagination of Harriet Monsell, whose husband, a priest of the Church of England, had recently died. Her brother-in-law, also a priest, had settled in the area, and so the connection was made that drew her into the work that would form the basis for a new sisterhood. On Ascension Day, 1851, Harriet made her first commitment to the religious life, and within a year, two others joined her. On St. Andrew's Day, 1852, she made her profession and was installed as superior by Samuel Wilberforce, Bishop of Oxford.

At this time, there were no permanent vows taken; the Bishop shared a common aversion to what was understood as a restrictive and debilitating structure. The Community had a twofold focus in both the contemplative and active life. Devotion and a full appropriation of the Daily Office was a key part of the community's worship. They also made one of the first efforts to produce an English-language version of the Breviary.

Deeply rooted in earnest prayer, Mother Harriet spoke clearly of the crucial call to active service: "I suppose the Sisters must always be ready to leave God for God . . . to leave God in devotion to seek God in those for whom [Christ] shed His Blood . . . to be ready to use broken prayer for themselves and for them."

Mother Harriet served as superior of the order until her health made retirement a necessity in 1875. She continued to take an active interest in the work of her sisters and in the affairs of the larger world, however, and all of this was the focus of her prayer and intercession. One of the prayers she wrote for her community begins: "Grant unto us, O great and glorious God, that we may be faithful souls, fervent in prayer, still in God, zealous for souls, ardent seekers after holiness, full of love and tenderness . . . ever being drawn into the Divine Unity, into the fellowship of the Blessed Trinity, that we may reveal the mind of Christ . . ."

Mother Harriet died on Easter Day, March 26, 1883. The community continues its ministry of prayer and service today in both the Episcopal Church and in the Church of England.

Harriet Monsell

Monastic, 1883

I Gracious God, who didst lead thy servant Harriet Monsell through grief to a new vocation; grant that we, inspired by her example, may grow in the life of prayer and the work of service, so that in all our sorrows and in all our joys, thy presence may evermore increase among us, and that our lives may be so ordered as to reveal the mind of Christ, to whom with thee and the Holy Ghost, be honor and glory, now and for ever. *Amen.*

II Gracious God, who led your servant Harriet Monsell through grief to a new vocation; grant that we, inspired by her example, may grow in the life of prayer and the work of service so that in sorrow or joy, your presence may increase among us and our lives reveal the mind of Jesus Christ, to whom, with you and the Holy Spirit be honor and glory, now and for ever. *Amen.*

Lessons and Psalm

Isaiah 66:1-4
Psalm 133
1 Timothy 6:6-10
John 3:25-30

Preface of a Saint (3)

Charles Henry Brent was born at New Castle, Ontario, Canada, on April 9, 1862, and was educated at Trinity College of the University of Toronto. Ordained as a priest in 1887 in Canada, he came to the United States for his first call as an assistant at St. Paul's Cathedral in Buffalo, New York. In 1888 he became associate rector at St. John the Evangelist in Boston, Massachusetts, with responsibility for St Augustine's, an African American congregation. He was serving at St. Stephen's, Boston, when, in 1901, he was elected by the House of Bishops as Missionary Bishop of the Philippines.

In the Philippines, he began a crusade against the opium traffic, a campaign he later expanded to the Asian continent. He became President of the Opium Conference in Shanghai in 1909, and represented the United States on the League of Nations Narcotics Committee. He also established cordial relations with the Philippine Independent Church, which led, ultimately, to a relationship of full communion with that church.

Bishop Brent served as Senior Chaplain of the American Expeditionary Forces in World War I. When General Pershing was given the command in 1917, he asked Brent to organize the chaplaincy for the force and then persuaded him to stay on to run the organization he had created, a first for the U.S. Army in terms of scale and centralization, and the precedent for the creation of the post of Chief of Chaplains in 1920. In 1918, he accepted election as Bishop of Western New York, having declined three previous elections in order to remain at his post in the Philippines.

Brent was the outstanding figure of the Episcopal Church on the world scene for two decades. The central focus of his life and ministry was the cause of Christian unity. After attending the World Missionary Conference in Edinburgh in 1910, he led the Episcopal Church in the movement that culminated in the first World Conference on Faith and Order, which was held in Lausanne, Switzerland, in 1927, and over which he presided. He died in 1929 and is buried in the main cemetery in Lausanne in the section reserved for "honored foreigners"; his tomb is still often visited and adorned with commemorative plaques brought by delegations from the Philippines.

The historian James Thayer Addison described Brent as "a saint of disciplined mental vigor, one whom soldiers were proud to salute and whom children were happy to play with, who could dominate a parliament and minister to an invalid, a priest and bishop who gloried in the heritage of his church, yet who stood among all Christian brothers as one who served . . . He was everywhere an ambassador of Christ."

Brent was also a man of prayer. One of his prayers for the mission of the church has been included in the Book of Common Prayer: "Lord Jesus Christ, you stretched out your arms of love on the hard wood of the cross that everyone might come within the reach of your saving embrace: So clothe us with your Spirit that we, reaching forth our hands in love, may bring those who do not know you to the knowledge and love of you; for the honor of your Name."

Charles Henry Brent

Bishop, 1929

I Heavenly Father, whose Son prayed that we all might be one: Deliver us from arrogance and prejudice, and give us wisdom and forbearance, that, following thy servant Charles Henry Brent, we may be united in one family with all who confess the Name of thy Son Jesus Christ; who liveth and reigneth with thee and the Holy Ghost, one God, now and for ever. *Amen.*

II Heavenly Father, whose Son prayed that we all might be one: Deliver us from arrogance and prejudice, and give us wisdom and forbearance, that, following your servant Charles Henry Brent, we may be united in one family with all who confess the Name of your Son Jesus Christ; who lives and reigns with you and the Holy Spirit, one God, now and for ever. *Amen.*

Lessons and Psalm

I Isaiah 56:6-8
Psalm 122
Ephesians 4:1-6
Matthew 9:35-38

Preface of Pentecost

James Solomon Russell was born into slavery on December 20, 1857, near Palmer Springs, Virginia. He became known as the father of St. Paul's College (one of the three historically Black Episcopal colleges) and was the founder of numerous congregations, a missionary, and a writer.

He was the first student of St. Stephen's Normal and Theological Institute (which later became the Bishop Payne Divinity School) in Petersburg, Virginia. In 1888, one year after his ordination as a priest in the Episcopal Church, Russell and his wife Virginia opened St. Paul's Normal School in Lawrenceville, Virginia. Russell's vision for the school was to provide both a literary and an industrial education. Religion was a mandatory subject, and students attended chapel twice daily. Russell served as the school's principal and chaplain until his retirement in 1929.

For 52 years of ordained ministry in the Diocese of Southern Virginia, he worked tirelessly to encourage Black candidates to offer themselves for ordination so that they could care for the growing numbers of Black Episcopalians. In 1893, Russell was named the first Archdeacon for Colored Work. Southern Virginia soon had the largest population of African American Episcopalians in the United States, thanks in large measure to Russell's evangelistic efforts. In 1927, Russell was the first African American elected bishop in the Episcopal Church. However, he declined election as Suffragan Bishop for Colored Work in the Dioceses of Arkansas and North Carolina, and he was glad that his action helped defeat the idea of subordinate racial bishops.

Russell's ministry continued until his death on March 28, 1935. His autobiography, *Adventure in Faith,* was published the following year.

James Solomon Russell

Priest, 1935

I O God, the font of resurrected life, draw us into the wilderness and speak tenderly to us, so that we might love and worship thee as did thy servant James Solomon Russell, in assurance of the saving grace of Jesus Christ, who liveth and reigneth with thee and the Holy Ghost, one God, for ever and ever. *Amen.*

II O God, the font of resurrected life, draw us into the wilderness and speak tenderly to us, so that we might love and worship you as your servant James Solomon Russell did, in assurance of the saving grace of Jesus Christ, who lives and reigns with you and the Holy Spirit, one God, for ever and ever. *Amen.*

Lessons and Psalm

1 Kings 5:1-12
Psalm 127
1 Timothy 6:11-16
Matthew 18:12-24

Preface of a Saint (1)

John Keble was born on April 23, 1792, and received his early education in his father's vicarage. At fourteen, he won a scholarship to Oxford and graduated in 1811 with highest honors. He served the university in several capacities, including ten years as Professor of Poetry. After ordination in 1816, he served in a series of rural curacies, and finally settled in 1836 into a thirty-year pastorate at the village of Hursley, near Winchester.

Among his cycle of poems entitled *The Christian Year* (1827), which he wrote to restore among Anglicans a deep feeling for the liturgical year, is a familiar hymn (*The Hymnal 1982,* #10):

> New ev'ry morning is the love
> Our wakening and uprising prove:
> Through sleep and darkness safely brought,
> Restored to life and power and thought.

The work went through ninety-five editions, but this was not a fame he sought: his consuming desire was to be a faithful pastor, and he found his fulfillment in daily services, confirmation classes, visits to village schools, and a voluminous correspondence with those seeking spiritual counsel.

England was going through a turbulent change from a rural to an industrial and urban society. England and Ireland were incorporated in 1801 and the (Protestant) Church of Ireland became part of the Church of England. Up until 1833, Ireland had twenty-two Anglican bishops and archbishops for a population of about 800,000 persons, a ratio considerably smaller than that of the English dioceses. The "Irish Church Measure" of 1833 would have reduced the number of Anglican bishops and archbishops by ten, amalgamating episcopal oversight to a proportion equal in both countries and saving money needed at the parish level. Keble vigorously attacked this Parliamentary action as a "National Apostasy" undermining the independence of the church in a sermon by that title, now referred to as his Assize Sermon of 1833.

This sermon was the spark that ignited the Oxford Movement. Those drawn to the Movement began to publish a series of "Tracts for the Times" (hence the popular name "Tractarians")—which sought to recall the church to its ancient sacramental heritage. John Henry Newman was the intellectual leader of the Movement, Edward Bouverie Pusey was the prophet of its devotional life, and John Keble was its pastoral inspiration. Though bitterly attacked, his loyalty to his church was unwavering. Within three years of his death at Bournemouth on March 29, 1866, at age 74, a college bearing his name was established at Oxford "to give an education in strict fidelity to the Church of England." For Keble, this would have meant dedication to learning in order "to live more nearly as we pray."

John Keble

Priest and Poet, 1866

I Grant, O God, that in all time of our testing we may know thy presence and obey thy will, that, following the example of thy servant John Keble, we may accomplish with integrity and courage that which thou givest us to do and endure that which thou givest us to bear; through Jesus Christ our Lord, who liveth and reigneth with thee and the Holy Ghost, one God, for ever and ever. *Amen.*

II Grant, O God, that in all time of our testing we may know your presence and obey your will, that, following the example of your servant John Keble, we may accomplish with integrity and courage what you give us to do and endure what you give us to bear; through Jesus Christ our Lord, who lives and reigns with you and the Holy Spirit, one God, for ever and ever. *Amen.*

Lessons and Psalm

Jeremiah 18:1-11
Psalm 150
Romans 12:9-21
Mark 1:9-13

Preface of a Saint (1)

Mary of Egypt was a fifth-century Christian hermit, but most of what is known about her is based on a seventh-century text by Sophronius of Jerusalem. According to this account, Mary was an Alexandrian prostitute who traveled to Jerusalem at the age of 29 with the aim of seducing pilgrims.

After attempting to visit the Holy Sepulchre, Mary found herself physically unable to cross the threshold of the church, even as others entered unobstructed. This invisible blockade proved to be strong medicine for Mary, who repented of her sins and became a solitary contemplative and ascetic in the desert beyond the Jordan River, where she remained for the next forty-seven years.

Two years before her death, she provided spiritual direction to a monk named Zosimus, who gave her his cloak and returned the following year to bring her communion. When Zosimus came back the next year, he found Mary lying dead with her face turned to the East. Several traditions hold that her grave was dug by a lion, an ancient symbol of Christ.

As early as the sixth century Mary's life was being commemorated in the Orthodox churches during Lent, an example of repentance categorized by continual self-emptying, as opposed to a realized state of sanctity.

This process is captured by Goethe, who casts Mary as one of the three penitent saints who pray to the Virgin Mary for the forgiveness of Faust:

By the consecrated place
Where the Lord's body lay:
By the warning arm, against my face,
That thrust me far from the doorway:
By my forty years' repentance,
Faithful, in that desert land:
By the blissful final sentence
That I wrote there on the sand -

Mary of Egypt

Monastic, c. 421

I Merciful Lord, who dost raise up sinners by thy boundless compassion and mercy: Cause the desert sun to burn away our coarseness and to melt our hardness of heart, that, like thy servant Mary of Egypt, we may not depart from this life until we understand the ways of repentance and the benefits of prayer; through Jesus Christ our Lord, who liveth and reigneth with thee and the Holy God, one God, for ever and ever. *Amen.*

II Merciful Lord, who raises up sinners by your boundless compassion and mercy: Cause the desert sun to burn away our coarseness and to melt our hardness of heart, that, like your servant Mary of Egypt, we may not depart from this life until we understand the ways of repentance and the benefits of prayer; through Jesus Christ our Lord, who lives and reigns with you and the Holy Spirit, one God, now and for ever. *Amen.*

Lessons and Psalm

Hosea 11:1-4, 8-9
Psalm 48:8-14
Hebrews 11:32-40
John 8:1-11

Preface of a Saint (2)

"Any man's death diminishes me, because I am involved in mankind. And therefore never send to know for whom the bell tolls: It tolls for thee."

These words are familiar to many; their author, John Donne, is one of the greatest of English poets. In his own time, he was the best-known preacher in the Church of England, but he came to that eminence by a tortuous path. Born into a wealthy and pious Roman Catholic family on January 21, 1572, in London, he was educated at both Oxford and Cambridge, and studied law at Lincoln's Inn. Some time later he conformed to the Established Church and embarked upon a promising political career of service to the State. The revelation of his secret marriage in 1601 to the niece of his employer, the Lord Keeper of the Great Seal, brought his public career to an end. In 1615, he was persuaded by King James I and others to receive ordination.

Following several brief parish pastorates, Donne rose rapidly in popularity as Dean of St. Paul's Cathedral, London, from 1621 until his death. He drew great throngs to the cathedral and to Paul's Cross, a nearby open-air pulpit. His sermons reflect the wide learning of the scholar, the passionate intensity of the poet, and the profound devotion of one struggling in his own life to relate the freedom and demands of the gospel to the concerns of a common humanity, on every level and in all its complexities.

The hymn "Wilt thou forgive that sin where I begun" (*The Hymnal 1982,* #140) is one of his poetic legacies. In another famous poem, he writes:

> Batter my heart, three-person'd God, for you
> As yet but knock, breathe, shine, and seek to mend;
> That I may rise and stand, o'erthrow me, and bend
> Your force to break, blow, burn, and make me new.
> I, like an usurp'd town to another due,
> Labor to admit you, but oh, to no end;
> Reason, your viceroy in me, me should defend,
> But is captiv'd, and proves weak or untrue.
> Yet dearly I love you, and would be lov'd fain,
> But am betroth'd unto your enemy;
> Divorce me, untie or break that knot again,
> Take me to you, imprison me, for I,
> Except you enthrall me, never shall be free,
> Nor ever chaste, except you ravish me.

John Donne died in London on March 31, 1631.

John Donne

Priest and Poet, 1631

I O God of eternal glory, whom no one living can see and yet whom to see is to live; grant that with thy servant John Donne, we may see thy glory in the face of thy Son, Jesus Christ, and then, with all our skill and wit, offer thee our crown of prayer and praise, until by his grace we stand in that last and everlasting day, when death itself will die, and all will live in thee, who with the Holy Ghost and the same Lord Jesus Christ art one God in everlasting light and glory. *Amen.*

II O God of eternal glory, whom no one living can see and yet whom to see is to live; grant that with your servant John Donne, we may see your glory in the face of your Son, Jesus Christ, and then, with all our skill and wit, offer you our crown of prayer and praise, until by his grace we stand in that last and everlasting day, when death itself will die, and all will live in you, who with the Holy Spirit and the same Lord Jesus Christ are one God in everlasting light and glory. *Amen.*

Lessons and Psalm

Ecclesiastes 9:1-12
Psalm 16
1 Corinthians 15:20-28
John 5:19-24

Preface of the Epiphany

In the same year that Karl Marx declared religion to be the "opiate of the people," Frederick Denison Maurice wrote, "We have been dosing our people with religion when what they want is not this but the living God." Like Marx, Maurice wanted to solve the questions of our complex society; unlike Marx, he called for a radical, but non-violent, reform, by the renewal of "faith in a God who has redeemed mankind, in whom I may vindicate my rights as a man." Maurice was a founder of the Christian Socialist Movement, which, he wrote, "will commit us at once to the conflict we must engage in sooner or later with the unsocial Christians and unchristian Socialists."

Maurice was born in 1805 into the family of a Unitarian minister whose life was marked by intense religious controversy. Maurice studied civil law at Cambridge, but refused the degree in 1827, because, as a Dissenter, he could not subscribe to the Thirty-Nine Articles of Religion. After several personal crises, however, he became an Anglican and was ordained in 1834. Soon afterwards he was appointed Professor of English Literature and History at King's College, London, and, in 1846, to the chair of Theology.

In his book *The Kingdom of Christ,* published in 1838, Maurice investigates the causes and cures of Christian divisions. The book has become a source of Anglican ecumenism. Maurice was dismissed from his professorships because of his leadership in the Christian Socialist Movement, and because of the alleged unorthodoxy of his *Theological Essays* (1853).

Maurice saw worship as the meeting point of time and eternity, and as the fountain of energies for the church's mission. He wrote, "I do not think we are to praise the liturgy but to use it. When we do not want it for our life, we may begin to talk of it as a beautiful composition."

After the death of the Christian Socialist Movement in 1854, Maurice founded the Working Men's College, and resumed teaching at Queen's College, London. Maurice awakened Anglicanism to the need for concern with the problems of society. In later years, he was honored even by former opponents. He served as rector of two parishes, and was professor of Moral Theology at Cambridge from 1866 until his death.

Frederick Denison Maurice

Priest, 1872

I Almighty God, who hast restored our human nature to heavenly glory through the perfect obedience of our Savior Jesus Christ: Enliven in thy Church, we beseech thee, the passion for justice and truth, that, like thy servant Frederick Denison Maurice, we may work and pray for the triumph of the kingdom of Christ; who liveth and reigneth with thee and the Holy Ghost, one God, now and for ever. *Amen.*

II Almighty God, who has restored our human nature to heavenly glory through the perfect obedience of our Savior Jesus Christ: Enliven in your Church, we pray, the passion for justice and truth, that, like your servant Frederick Denison Maurice, we may work and pray for the triumph of the kingdom of Christ; who lives and reigns with you and the Holy Spirit, one God, now and for ever. *Amen.*

Lessons and Psalm

Numbers 21:4-9
Psalm 145
Acts 2:42-47
John 18:33-37

Preface of Baptism

James Lloyd Breck was one of the most important missionaries of the Episcopal Church in the nineteenth century. He was called "The Apostle of the Wilderness."

Breck was born in Philadelphia in 1818, and like many important churchmen of his time, was greatly influenced by the pastoral devotion, liturgical concern, and sacramental emphasis of William Augustus Muhlenberg. Breck attended Muhlenberg's school in Flushing, New York, before entering the University of Pennsylvania. Muhlenberg inspired him, when he was sixteen years old, to dedicate himself to a missionary life. The dedication was crystallized when Breck, with three other classmates from the General Theological Seminary, founded a religious community at Nashotah, Wisconsin, which in 1844 was on the frontier.

Nashotah became a center of liturgical observance, of pastoral care, and of education. Isolated families were visited, mission stations established, and, probably for the first time since the Revolution, Episcopal missionaries were the first to reach the settlers.

Although Nashotah House flourished, and became one of the seminaries of the Episcopal Church, the "religious house" ideal did not. Breck moved on to St. Paul, Minnesota, where he began the work of the Episcopal Church there. At Gull Lake, he organized St. Columba's Mission for the Chippewa. Although the mission did not survive, it laid the foundation for work among the Native Americans by their own native priests.

In 1855, Breck married, and in 1858 settled in Faribault, Minnesota, where his mission was associated with one of the first cathedrals established in the Episcopal Church in the United States. He also founded Seabury Divinity School, which later merged with Western Theological Seminary, to become Seabury-Western. In 1867, Breck went on to California, inspired principally by the opportunity of founding a new theological school. His schools in Benicia, California, did not survive, but the five parishes he founded did, and the church in California was strengthened immensely through his work. He died of exhaustion, at the age of 57, in 1876.

James Lloyd Breck

Priest, 1876

I O God, who sent thy Son to preach peace to those who are far off and to those who are near: call us from comfortable complacency to preach, teach, and plant thy church on new frontiers, after the example of thy servant James Lloyd Breck; through Jesus Christ our Lord, who liveth and reigneth with thee and the Holy Ghost, one God, for ever and ever. *Amen.*

II O God, who sent your Son to preach peace to those who are far off and to those who are near: call us from comfortable complacency to preach, teach, and plant your church on new frontiers, after the example of your servant James Lloyd Breck; through Jesus Christ our Lord, who lives and reigns with you and the Holy Spirit, one God, for ever and ever. *Amen.*

Lessons and Psalm

Joshua 24:14-18
Psalm 119:145-152
1 Corinthians 3:1-7
Luke 7:1-10

Preface of Pentecost

Born in Burford, Worcestershire, around 1197, Richard and his older brother Robert were quite young when their parents died, leaving a rich estate with a guardian to manage it. The guardian allowed the estate to dwindle, and Richard worked long hours to restore it.

Pressure was put on Richard to marry, but he, who from earliest years had preferred books to almost anything else, turned the estate over to his brother and went to Oxford. Often hungry, cold, and not always sure of his next day's keep, Richard managed to succeed in his studies under such teachers as Robert Grosseteste.

He continued to study law at Paris and Bologna, earned a doctorate, and returned to Oxford to become the university chancellor. Shortly afterward, the Archbishop of Canterbury, Edmund Rich, appointed him to be his own chancellor. The friendship between the primate and his young assistant was close: Richard also became his biographer. Conflict with King Henry III eventually forced the archbishop into exile in France, where Richard nursed him in his final illness. After the archbishop's death, Richard moved to the Dominican house at Orleans for further study and teaching. He was ordained as a priest in 1243.

He then returned to England, and was elected Bishop of Chichester in 1244. King Henry opposed the election, confiscated all of the revenues of the diocese, and even locked Richard out of the episcopal dwelling. Richard was given lodging by a priest, Simon of Tarring. During these years he functioned as a missionary bishop, traveling about the diocese on foot, visiting fishermen and farmers, holding synods with great difficulty, and endeavoring to establish order. Threatened by the Pope, Henry finally acknowledged Richard as bishop in 1246.

For eight years, he served his diocese as preacher, confessor, teacher, and counselor. He died in 1253. Nine years after his death, he was canonized. His best remembered words are:

> Dear Lord, of thee three things I pray:
> To see thee more clearly,
> Love thee more dearly,
> Follow thee more nearly.

Richard of Chichester

Bishop, 1253

I Almighty and most merciful God, who callest thy people to thyself, we pray that, following the example of thy bishop Richard of Chichester, we may see thy Son Jesus Christ more clearly, love him more dearly, and follow him more nearly; who liveth and reigneth with thee and the Holy Ghost, one God, now and for ever. *Amen.*

II Almighty and most merciful God, who calls your people to yourself, we pray that, following the example of your bishop Richard of Chichester, we may see your Son Jesus Christ more clearly, love him more dearly, and follow him more nearly; who lives and reigns with you and the Holy Spirit, one God, now and for ever. *Amen.*

Lessons and Psalm

Proverbs 16:16-20
Psalm 101:1-4
Jude 17-25
Luke 3:7-14

Preface of a Saint (2)

Martin Luther King, Jr., was born on January 15, 1929, in Atlanta. As the son and grandson of Baptist preachers, he was steeped in the Black Church tradition. Following graduation from Morehouse College in 1948, King entered Crozer Theological Seminary, having been ordained the previous year into the ministry of the National Baptist Church. He graduated from Crozer in 1951 and received a doctorate in theology from Boston University in 1955.

In 1954, King became pastor of a church in Montgomery, Alabama. There, Black indignation at inhumane treatment on segregated buses culminated in December 1955, in the arrest of Rosa Parks for refusing to give up her seat to a white man. King was catapulted into national prominence as the leader of the Montgomery bus boycott. He became increasingly the articulate prophet, who could not only rally the Black masses, but could also move the consciences of Whites.

King founded the Southern Christian Leadership Conference to spearhead non-violent mass demonstrations against racism. Many confrontations followed, most notably in Birmingham and Selma, Alabama, and in Chicago. King's campaigns were instrumental to the passage of the Civil Rights Acts of 1964, 1965, and 1968. King then turned his attention to economic empowerment of the poor and to opposition to the Vietnam War, contending that racism, poverty, and militarism were interrelated. He was awarded the Nobel Peace Prize in 1964 for his commitment to non-violent social change.

King lived in constant danger: his home was dynamited, he was almost fatally stabbed, and he was harassed by death threats. He was even jailed thirty times; but through it all he was sustained by his deep faith. In 1957, he received, late at night, a vicious telephone threat. Alone in his kitchen he wept and prayed. He relates that he heard the Lord speaking to him and saying, "Martin Luther, stand up for righteousness, stand up for justice," and promising never to leave him alone—"No, never alone." King refers to his vision as his "Mountain-Top Experience."

After preaching at Washington Cathedral on March 31, 1968, King went to Memphis in support of sanitation workers in their struggle for better wages. There, he proclaimed that he had been "to the mountain-top" and had seen "the Promised Land," and that he knew that one day he and his people would be "free at last." On the following day, April 4, he was cut down by an assassin's bullet.

Martin Luther King, Jr.

Pastor and Martyr, 1968

I Almighty God, who by the hand of Moses thy servant didst lead thy people out of slavery, and didst make them free at last: Grant that thy church, following the example of thy prophet Martin Luther King, may resist oppression in the name of thy love, and may strive to secure for all thy children the blessed liberty of the Gospel of Jesus Christ; who liveth and reigneth with thee and the Holy Ghost, one God, now and for ever. *Amen.*

II Almighty God, by the hand of Moses your servant you led your people out of slavery, and made them free at last: Grant that your church, following the example of your prophet Martin Luther King, may resist oppression in the name of your love, and may strive to secure for all your children the blessed liberty of the Gospel of Jesus Christ; who lives and reigns with you and the Holy Spirit, one God, now and for ever. *Amen.*

Lessons and Psalm

Exodus 3:7-12
Psalm 77:11-20
Ephesians 6:10-20
Luke 6:27-36

Preface of Baptism

Harriet Starr Cannon was one of the founding sisters, and first superior, of the Community of St. Mary, the first religious order for women formally recognized in the Episcopal Church.

Mother Harriet was born in Charleston, South Carolina, in 1823, and was orphaned in 1824 when her parents died of yellow fever. She grew up with her sister, her only surviving sibling, in Bridgeport, Connecticut. Following the death of her sister, Harriet entered the Sisterhood of the Holy Communion, an order founded by William Augustus Muhlenberg, Rector of the Church of the Holy Communion in New York City. The sisters were heavily involved in the operation of clinics and care facilities that would become St. Luke's Hospital in the City of New York, and Harriet served as a nurse.

Over time, however, she and other sisters began to yearn for a more traditionally monastic form of the religious life. When agreement could not be reached with the Sisters of the Holy Communion, a small group of them discerned a call to begin a new order. On the Feast of the Presentation, February 2, 1865, Bishop Horatio Potter of the Diocese of New York received from Harriet Cannon and her sisters the traditional monastic vows of poverty, chastity, and obedience at St. Michael's Church in Manhattan. The sisters began life together as the Community of St. Mary, and Harriet became the community's first Superior.

The apostolate of the Community of St. Mary began with nursing and the care of women who had endured difficult circumstances. After a time, however, the sisters became increasingly committed to providing schools for the education of young women in addition to their medical work. The Community continued to grow and developed schools for girls, hospitals, and orphanages in New York, Tennessee, and Wisconsin. They continue their ministries to this day in Greenwich, New York, Sewanee, Tennessee, Milwaukee, Wisconsin, and Luwinga, Malawi.

Mother Harriet died on April 5, 1896, in Peekskill, New York.

Harriet Starr Cannon

Monastic, 1896

I Gracious God, who didst call Harriet Starr Cannon and her companions to revive the monastic vocation in the Episcopal Church and to dedicate their lives to thee: Grant that we, after their example, may ever surrender ourselves to the revelation of thy holy will; through our Lord and Savior Jesus Christ, who liveth and reigneth with thee and the Holy Ghost, one God for ever and ever. *Amen.*

II Gracious God, who called Harriet Starr Cannon and her companions to revive the monastic vocation in the Episcopal Church and to dedicate their lives to you: Grant that we, after their example, may ever surrender ourselves to the revelation of your holy will; through our Lord and Savior Jesus Christ, who lives and reigns with you and the Holy Spirit, one God, for ever and ever. *Amen.*

Lessons and Psalm

Wisdom 16:20-26
Psalm 131
Hebrews 13:7-16
Mark 9:33-37

Preface of a Saint (2)

Vasily Ivanovich Belavin (Tikhon's given name) was born January 19, 1865. He grew up in a rural area among peasants in a village where his father was a priest of the Russian Orthodox Church. Even as a child, he loved religion, and by age thirteen he began his seminary training, where his classmates nicknamed him "Patriarch." At 23, he graduated as a layman and began to teach moral theology. Three years later, he became a monk and was given the name Tikhon.

By 1897, he was consecrated Bishop of Lublin, and in 1898 became Archbishop of the Aleutians and Alaska, the leader of Russian Orthodoxy in North America. Tikhon was held in such esteem that the United States made him an honorary citizen. While living there, he established many new cathedrals and churches, and participated in ecumenical events with other denominations, in particular the Episcopal Church. In 1900, at the consecration of Bishop Reginald Weller as coadjutor of the Diocese of Fond du Lac, the diocesan bishop, Charles Grafton, invited Tikhon to sit on his own throne. The Archbishop would have participated in the laying-on-of-hands if the Episcopal Church's House of Bishops had not forbidden it. Tikhon later established warm relations with the Diocese of California.

In 1907, Tikhon returned to Russia and a decade later was elected Patriarch of Moscow. The outbreak of the Russian Revolution threw the Church into disarray. When a severe famine caused many peasants to starve in 1921, the Patriarch ordered the sale of many church treasures to purchase food for the hungry. Soon the government began seizing church property for itself, and many believers were killed in defense of their faith. The Communists tried to wrest control of the church from Tikhon, while he, in turn, attempted to shelter his people. To this end, he discouraged the clergy from making political statements that might antagonize the government. He prayed, "May God teach every one of us to strive for His truth, and for the good of the Holy Church, rather than something for our sake."

Imprisoned by the Soviet government for more than a year, he was criticized both by the Communist Party and by those Orthodox bishops who believed he had compromised too much with the government. On April 7, 1925, he died, worn out by his struggles. In 1989, the Council of Bishops of the Russian Orthodox Church glorified Patriarch Tikhon, numbering him among the saints of the church.

Tikhon

Bishop and Ecumenist, 1925

I Holy God, holy and mighty, who hast called us together into one communion and fellowship: Open our eyes, we pray thee, as thou didst open the eyes of thy servant Tikhon, that we may see the faithfulness of others as we strive to be steadfast in the faith delivered unto us, that the world may see and know thee; through Jesus Christ our Lord, to whom, with thee and the Holy Ghost, be glory and praise unto ages of ages. *Amen.*

II Holy God, holy and mighty, you call us together into one communion and fellowship: Open our eyes, we pray, as you opened the eyes of your servant Tikhon, that we may see the faithfulness of others as we strive to be steadfast in the faith delivered unto us, that the world may see and know you; through Jesus Christ our Lord, to whom, with you and the Holy Spirit, be glory and praise unto ages of ages. *Amen.*

Lessons and Psalm

Jeremiah 31:10-14
Psalm 72
2 Peter 1:3-11
Matthew 21:28-32

Preface of Trinity Sunday

William Augustus Muhlenberg was born in Philadelphia in 1796, into a prominent German Lutheran family, and was drawn to the Episcopal Church by its use of English. He deliberately chose to remain unmarried in order to free himself for a variety of ministries. As a young priest, he was deeply involved in the Sunday School movement, and was concerned that the church should minister to all social groups. Aware of the limitations of the hymnody of his time, he wrote hymns and compiled hymnals, thus widening the range of music in Episcopal churches.

For twenty years he was head of a boys' school in Flushing, New York. The use of music, flowers, and color, and the emphasis on the Church Year in the worship there became a potent influence. In 1846, he founded the Church of the Holy Communion in New York City. Again, he was bold and innovative, establishing free pews for everyone, a parish school, a parish unemployment fund, and trips to the country for poor city children. His conception of beauty in worship, vivid and symbolic, had at its heart the Holy Communion itself, celebrated every Sunday. It was there that Anne Ayres founded the Sisterhood of the Holy Communion. In 1857, the two of them founded St. Luke's Hospital, where Muhlenberg was the pastor-superintendent and she the matron.

Muhlenberg's concern for sacramental worship and evangelism led him and several associates to memorialize the General Convention of 1853, calling for flexibility in worship and polity to enable the church better to fulfill its mission. The insistence of the "Memorial" on traditional Catholic elements—the Creeds, the Eucharist, and Episcopal ordination—together with the Reformation doctrine of grace, appealed to people of varying views. Although the church was not ready to adopt the specific suggestions of the Memorial, its influence was great, notably in preparing the ground for liturgical reform and ecumenical action.

Muhlenberg's last great project was an experiment in Christian social living, St. Johnland on Long Island. Although his dream of a Christian city was not realized, several of its philanthropic institutions survive.

William Augustus Muhlenberg

Priest, 1877

I Open the eyes of thy church, O Lord, to the plight of the poor and neglected, the homeless and destitute, the old and the sick, the lonely and those who have none to care for them. Give unto us the vision and compassion with which thou didst so richly endow thy servant William Augustus Muhlenberg, that we may labor tirelessly to heal those who are broken in body or spirit, and to turn their sorrow into joy; through Jesus Christ our Lord, who liveth and reigneth with thee and the Holy Ghost, one God, for ever and ever. *Amen.*

II Open the eyes of your church, O Lord, to the plight of the poor and neglected, the homeless and destitute, the old and the sick, the lonely and those who have none to care for them. Give to us the vision and compassion with which you so richly endowed your servant William Augustus Muhlenberg, that we may labor tirelessly to heal those who are broken in body or spirit, and to turn their sorrow into joy; through Jesus Christ our Lord, who lives and reigns with you and the Holy Spirit, one God, for ever and ever. *Amen.*

Lessons and Psalm

Isaiah 63:7-9
Psalm 100
James 1:12-18
Matthew 21:12-16

Preface of a Saint (1)

Dietrich Bonhoeffer was born in Breslau, Germany (now Wroclaw, Poland), on February 4, 1906. He studied theology at the universities of Berlin and Tübingen, and his doctoral thesis was published in 1930 as *Communio Sanctorum*. Still canonically too young to be ordained at the age of 24, he undertook postdoctoral study and teaching at Union Theological Seminary in New York City.

From the first days of the Nazi accession to power in 1933, Bonhoeffer was involved in protests against the regime. From 1933 to 1935 he was the pastor of two small congregations in London, but nonetheless was a leading spokesman for the Confessing Church, the center of Protestant resistance to the Nazis. In 1935, Bonhoeffer was appointed to organize and head a new seminary for the Confessing Church at Finkenwald. He described the community in his classic work *Life Together*. He later wrote *The Cost of Discipleship*, which quickly became a modern classic.

Bonhoeffer was acutely aware of the difficulties of life in community, and the easy disillusionment that could come when the experience did not live up to the imagined idea. Yet he also wrote eloquently of the gift and privilege of Christian community. “It is not simply to be taken for granted that the Christian has the privilege of living among other Christians. Jesus Christ lived in the midst of his enemies. At the end all of his disciples deserted him. On the Cross he was utterly alone, surrounded by evildoers and mockers. For this cause he had come, to bring peace to the enemies of God. So the Christian, too, belongs not in the seclusion of a cloistered life but in the thick of foes. There is his commission, his work . . . So between the death of Christ and the Last Day it is only by a gracious anticipation of the last things that Christians are privileged to live in visible fellowship with other Christians.”

Bonhoeffer became increasingly involved in the political struggle after 1939, when he was introduced to a group seeking Hitler’s overthrow. Bonhoeffer considered refuge in the United States, but he returned to Germany where he was able to continue his resistance. Bonhoeffer was arrested April 5, 1943, and imprisoned in Berlin. After an attempt on Hitler’s life failed on July 20, 1944, documents were discovered linking Bonhoeffer to the conspiracy. He was taken to Buchenwald concentration camp, then to Schoenberg Prison. On Sunday, April 8, 1945, just as he concluded a service in a school building in Schoenberg, two men came in with the chilling summons, “Prisoner Bonhoeffer . . . come with us.” He said to another prisoner, “This is the end. For me, the beginning of life.” Bonhoeffer was hanged the next day, April 9, at Flossenburg Prison.

There is in Bonhoeffer’s life a remarkable unity of faith, prayer, writing, and action. The pacifist theologian came to accept the guilt of plotting the death of Hitler, because he was convinced that not to do so would be a greater evil. Discipleship was to be had only at great cost.

Dietrich Bonhoeffer

Pastor and Theologian, 1945

I Embolden our lives, O Lord, and inspire our faiths, that we, following the example of thy servant Dietrich Bonhoeffer, might embrace thy call with undivided hearts; through Jesus Christ our Savior, who liveth and reigneth with thee and the Holy Ghost, one God, for ever and ever. *Amen.*

II Embolden our lives, O Lord, and inspire our faiths, that we, following the example of your servant Dietrich Bonhoeffer, might embrace your call with undivided hearts; through Jesus Christ our Savior, who lives and reigns with you and the Holy Spirit, one God, for ever and ever. *Amen.*

Lessons and Psalm

Judges 7:1-8a
Psalm 119:81-88
Romans 6:3-11
Matthew 13:47-52

Preface of a Saint (2)

"If we are to follow Christ, it must be in our common way of spending every day. If we are to live unto God at any time or in any place, we are to live unto him in all times and in all places. If we are to use anything as the gift of God, we are to use everything as his gift." So wrote William Law in 1728 in *A Serious Call to a Devout and Holy Life*.

This quiet schoolmaster of Putney, England, could hardly be considered a revolutionary, and yet his book had near-revolutionary repercussions. His challenge to take Christian living very seriously received a more enthusiastic response than he could ever have imagined, especially in the lives of Henry Venn, George Whitefield, and John Wesley, all of whom he strongly influenced. More than any other man, William Law laid the foundation for the religious revival of the eighteenth century, the Evangelical Movement in England, and the Great Awakening in America.

Law came to typify the devout priest in the eyes of many. His life was characterized by simplicity, devotion, and works of charity. Because he was a Non-Juror, who refused to swear allegiance to the House of Hanover, he was deprived of the usual means of making a living as a clergyman in the Church of England. He therefore worked as a tutor to the father of the historian Edward Gibbon from 1727 to 1737.

Law also organized schools and homes for the poor. He stoutly defended the sacraments and scriptures against attacks by the Deists, and he spoke out eloquently against the warfare of his day. His richly inspired sermons and writings have gained him a permanent place in Christian literature.

Law died at Kings Cliffe on April 9, 1761.

William Law

Priest, 1761

I Almighty God, whose servant William Law taught us to hear and follow your call to a devout and holy life: Grant that we, loving thee above all things and in all things, may seek thy purpose and shape our actions to thy will, that we may grow in all virtue and be diligent in prayer all the days of our lives, through Jesus Christ our Lord, to whom with thee and the Holy Ghost be all honor and glory now and for ever. *Amen.*

II Almighty God, whose servant William Law taught us to hear and follow your call to a devout and holy life: Grant that we, loving you above all things and in all things, may seek your purpose and shape our actions to your will, that we may grow in all virtue and be diligent in prayer all the days of our lives, through Jesus Christ our Lord, to whom with you and the Holy Spirit be all honor and glory now and for ever. *Amen.*

Lessons and Psalm

Ecclesiasticus 1:11-20
Psalm 128
2 Peter 1:3-11
Matthew 6:1-8

Preface of a Saint (2)

George Augustus Selwyn was born on April 5, 1809, at Hampstead, London. He was educated at Eton, and in 1831 graduated from St. John's College, Cambridge, of which he became a Fellow.

Ordained in 1833, Selwyn served as a curate at Windsor until his selection as the first Bishop of New Zealand in 1841. On the voyage to his new field, he mastered the Maori language and was able to preach in it upon his arrival. In the tragic ten-year war between the English and the Maoris, Selwyn was able to minister to both sides and to keep the affection and admiration of both the Maori and colonists. He began missionary work in the Pacific islands in 1847.

In addition to learning the Maori language and customs, Selwyn became an accomplished navigator, cartographer, and sailor in order to spread the gospel through the Pacific Islands. Reportedly, a sailor once noted, "To see the bishop handle a boat was almost enough to make a man a Christian."

Selwyn's first general synod in 1859 laid down a constitution, influenced by that of the Episcopal Church, which became important for all English colonial churches.

After the first Lambeth Conference in 1867, Selwyn was reluctantly persuaded to accept the See of Lichfield in England. He died on April 11, 1878, and his grave in the cathedral close has become a place of pilgrimage for the Maoris to whom he first brought the light of the gospel.

Bishop Selwyn twice visited the Episcopal Church in the United States, and was the preacher at the 1874 General Convention.

George Augustus Selwyn

Bishop, 1878

I Almighty and everlasting God, whose servant George Augustus Selwyn didst lay a firm foundation for the growth of thy church in many nations: Raise up in this and every land evangelists and heralds of thy kingdom, that thy church may proclaim the unsearchable riches of our Lord Jesus Christ; who liveth and reigneth with thee and the Holy Ghost, one God, now and for ever. *Amen.*

II Almighty and everlasting God, whose servant George Augustus Selwyn laid a firm foundation for the growth of your church in many nations: Raise up in this and every land evangelists and heralds of your kingdom, that your church may proclaim the unsearchable riches of our Lord Jesus Christ; who lives and reigns with you and the Holy Spirit, one God, now and for ever. *Amen.*

Lessons and Psalm

Ecclesiasticus 1:1-10
Psalm 21:1-4
Ephesians 2:8-10
Matthew 10:7-16

Preface of a Saint (2)

Zenaida, Philonella, and Hermione were three early Christian women who are commemorated in the Orthodox Church as the first "unmercenary physicians"—Christian medical doctors who offered their skill to everyone and refused to accept payment.

According to Orthodox tradition, Zenaida and Philonella were sisters, born into a well-educated and wealthy Jewish family in the city of Tarsus. They were baptized by their brother Jason after his conversion and ordination as a priest.

Both sisters were said to have been well educated at home in both philosophy and medicine, but they were unable to find employment in either field in an era when both professions were controlled by men. Therefore, they built a chapel, two cells, and a medical clinic on the outskirts of the city of Thessaly, where they devoted themselves to treating all who came to them regardless of their ability to pay, and refused to accept any money in exchange for their services.

Philonella was said to be skilled in experimental treatments for diseases that were regarded as incurable, and Zenaida specialized in pediatric medicine and the treatment of psychological disorders, particularly depression. Zenaida became particularly renowned as a spiritual director as well as a physician. Three of her male disciples founded a monastery a short distance away from the sisters. Varying accounts are given of their death, with one tradition relating that they were killed by robbers, and others relating that they continued in their ministry until dying peacefully of old age.

Hermione is the third early Christian woman to be given the title of "unmercenary physician." She is reported to be one of the daughters of Philip the Deacon (Acts 6). After studying medicine in Caesarea, she went to Ephesus in the hopes of meeting the Apostle John, but found that he had already died. She therefore used her income to open up a medical clinic, with the help of her younger sister Eukhidia. Eventually, she expanded the clinic into a residential facility to allow for more extended treatment. Orthodox Christians believe that this was the first example of a Christian hospital, and it became the inspiration for later developments in Christian medical care, particularly in the Christian East.

Zenaida, Philonella, and Hermione

Unmercenary Physicians, c. 100, c. 117

I Merciful God, whose most dear Son came to heal the sick, raise the dead, cast out demons, and preach good news to the poor: Lead us by the example of thy servants, Zenaida, Philonella, and Hermione, to freely give even as we have freely received; through Jesus Christ our Lord. *Amen.*

II Merciful God, whose most dear Son came to heal the sick, raise the dead, cast out demons, and preach good news to the poor: Lead us by the example of your servants, Zenaida, Philonella, and Hermione, to freely give even as we have freely received; through Jesus Christ our Lord. *Amen.*

Lessons and Psalm

Ecclesiasticus 38:1-15
Psalm 147
Acts 2:42-47
Mark 1:29-34

Preface of a Saint (3)

Fr. Damien was born Joseph de Veuster in 1840 in Belgium, the son of a farmer. At the age of 18, he joined the Congregation of the Sacred Hearts of Jesus and Mary. He made his first vows in 1859 and took the name Damien, after the ancient physician and martyr. When his older brother became ill and was unable to join the mission endeavor in Hawai'i, Damien volunteered to take his place.

As Father Damien began his ministry in Hawai'i, leprosy was spreading rapidly throughout the Islands. In 1863, King Kamehameha V ordered those with leprosy to be sent to Kalaupapa, an isolated peninsula on the northern coast of Molokai. There, on the side of the peninsula known as Kalawao, those afflicted by the disease were left with no aid.

Damien was among the first priests to arrive in Kalawao, and he remained there for the rest of his life, building houses, an orphanage, a church, and a hospital. He ate with those he served, worshipped with them, and invited them into his home. He eventually contracted leprosy, later known as Hansen's disease, and died in 1889.

Like Father Damien, Marianne Cope aspired to a religious vocation at an early age. She entered the Sisters of St. Francis in Syracuse, New York, in 1862, and in 1870, she began work as a nurse and administrator at St. Joseph's Hospital in Syracuse, where she was criticized for accepting alcoholics and other undesirable patients.

In 1883, she received a letter from a priest in Hawai'i asking for help managing the hospitals and ministry to leprosy patients. She arrived in Honolulu in 1883 and immediately took over supervision of the Kaka'ako Branch Hospital, which served as a receiving center for leprosy patients from all over the islands. She also opened a care center for the healthy children of leprosy victims.

In 1884, she met Father Damien, and in 1886, she alone ministered to him when his illness made him unwelcome among church and government leaders. She continued her work with hospitals and sufferers of Hansen's disease until her death in 1918.

Damien
Priest, 1889
and Marianne Cope
Monastic, 1918
# of Hawai‘i

I Bind up the wounds of thy children, O God, and help us to be bold and loving in service to all who are shunned for the diseases they suffer, following the example of thy servants Damien and Marianne, that thy grace may be poured forth upon all; through Jesus Christ our Lord, who with thee and the Holy Ghost liveth and reigneth, one God, for ever and ever. *Amen.*

II Bind up the wounds of your children, O God, and help us to be bold and loving in service to all who are shunned for the diseases they suffer, following the example of your servants Damien and Marianne, that your grace may be poured forth upon all; through Jesus Christ our Lord, who with you and the Holy Spirit lives and reigns, one God, for ever and ever. *Amen.*

Lessons and Psalm

Isaiah 57:14-19
Psalm 32:7-12
1 Corinthians 4:9-13
Matthew 11:1-6

Preface of a Saint (1)

Peter Williams Cassey was ordained as a deacon in 1866, the first person of color ordained in the Episcopal Church west of the Mississippi River. He was a fourth-generation freed African American. His great-grandfather bought his freedom and founded the first Black church in New York, the African Methodist Episcopal Zion Church. His grandfather was the first African American Episcopal priest in New York and founder of St. Philip's, Manhattan. His parents, Joseph and Amy Cassey, were prominent abolitionists in Philadelphia.

Peter received the best classical education available at the time, learning to read Greek, Hebrew, and Latin fluently. Arriving in San Francisco in 1853, he worked as a barber and formed an abolitionist group to help free slaves. He helped organize a community association to protect African Americans and other persons of color. In the late 1850s he moved to San José, California.

Peter married Anna Besant, who came from another prominent African American family. They were among the founding members of Trinity Parish, San José, California, in 1861. At the same time, they rented the former Bascom School for Girls and established St. Philip's Mission for Colored People and opened St. Philip's Academy. The school was not only for African Americans, but also for Native American, Mexican, and Chinese students because no children of color could attend public schools.

Bishop William Ingraham Kip, first Bishop of California, recognized St. Philip's as a mission congregation out of Trinity Church and in 1866 ordained Peter as a deacon. In 1872, Bishop Kip directed him to establish Christ Church for Colored People in San Francisco while Anna kept St. Philip's going. Later this church would split into the African American Church of St. Cyprian and Christ Nippon Sei Ko Kai (Japanese American Episcopal Church). In 1881 Peter was called to St. Cyprian's Episcopal Church in New Bern, North Carolina, as the first African American rector in that state. In 1884 he accepted a call to Florida where he served three parishes in succession until he died at the age of 86 on April 16, 1917. He was never ordained a priest because of the racism of the clergy and Standing Committees of the three dioceses in which he served, even though the bishops favored his ordination.

The Bishop of Florida, Edwin Gardner Weed, said at Peter's funeral that "no other clergyman in the diocese came close to the theological maturity and scholarship that Peter Williams Cassey exhibited in his ministry and teachings. We should be proud of these great souls that helped lay the foundations of this diocese."

Peter Williams Cassey

Deacon, 1917

and Anna Besant Cassey

1875

I O God of justice and mercy, we remember before thee thy servants Peter Williams Cassey and Anna Besant Cassey, who, in the face of slavery and discrimination, gave the blessings of education and spiritual haven to the marginalized; Grant us to be fearless in the face of injustice and to work for blessings that will touch those whom the world does not count of value; through Jesus Christ our Lord, who with thee and the Holy Ghost liveth and reigneth for ever and ever. *Amen.*

II O God of justice and mercy, we remember before you your servants Peter Williams Cassey and Anna Besant Cassey, who, in the face of slavery and discrimination, gave the blessings of education and spiritual haven to the marginalized; Grant us to be fearless in the face of injustice and to work for blessings that will touch those whom the world does not count of value; through Jesus Christ our Lord, who with you and the Holy Spirit lives and reigns for ever and ever. *Amen.*

Lessons and Psalm

Proverbs 22:1-9
Psalm 13
Romans 8:31-39
Matthew 5:13-16

Preface of a Saint (3)

Tekakwitha, "She who bumps into things," was born in the Mohawk village of Ossernon in upstate New York around 1656. Her childhood and adolescence were marked by hardship. A smallpox epidemic, which claimed the lives of her parents and younger brother, also scarred her face and severely impaired her vision. Her aunt and uncle, as adoptive parents, attempted to pressure her to marry beginning at age 11, but she resisted every attempt.

Moved by the preaching of Jesuit missionaries, Tekakwitha followed in the path of her late mother and converted to Christianity. She was baptized on Easter Sunday, 1676, at 19 years of age. As part of her conversion, she took the name Kateri, in honor of Catherine of Siena. Kateri Tekakwitha devoted her life to chastity, pledging to marry only Jesus Christ, and asking the Virgin Mary to accept her as a daughter.

Her piety was mocked and derided by her fellow villagers, some of whom threatened her life. She fled to a village south of Montreal, where with her friend Marie-Therese, she attempted to begin a monastic community of indigenous women. They were dissuaded by the local priests, who believed they did not have enough experience to begin such a community. Kateri therefore accepted an "ordinary" life of vowed singleness and good works among the people, especially the elderly and sick.

At age 24, she succumbed to a serious illness. Tradition accords her final words as being "Jesus, I love you," as she entered eternal life on the Wednesday of Holy Week, 1680. Following her death, it was reported that her body softened and her face took on the appearance of a child, even including a smile. The pockmarks of her childhood smallpox faded, and her skin became smooth. Pilgrimages were made to her grave as early as 1684.

Kateri Tekakwitha is known as the Lily of the Mohawks, and was the first Native American to be canonized in the Roman Catholic Church, where she is considered the patron of ecology and the environment, as well as of persons in exile.

Kateri Tekakwitha

Lay Contemplative, 1680

I Almighty and everliving God, who didst open the heart of Kateri Tekakwitha to receive the Good News of Jesus Christ and to devote her life to thy service: Grant us the same zeal of devotion to persevere in faith through the trials and tribulations of our lives, through Jesus Christ our Lord. *Amen.*

II Almighty and everliving God, who opened the heart of Kateri Tekakwitha to receive the Good News of Jesus Christ and to devote her life to your service: Grant us the same zeal of devotion to persevere in faith through the trials and tribulations of our lives, through Jesus Christ our Lord. *Amen.*

Lessons and Psalm

1 Kings 19:19-21
Psalm 6
1 Thessalonians 5:16-24
Matthew 8:18-22

Preface of a Saint (3)

Juana Inés de Asbaje y Ramirez de Santillana was born the illegitimate daughter of a Spanish captain and a creole woman on November 12, 1648, in the town of San Miguel Nepantla near Mexico City, Mexico.

Raised by her grandparents in Amecameca, Juana Inés established herself from a young age as a talented thinker and writer. She is reported to have learned to read and write by the age of three, to do accounting by the age of five, to compose religious poetry by the age of eight, to teach Latin to children by age thirteen, and to master Greek logic by adolescence.

Prevented from university studies in Mexico City because she was a woman, Juana Inés continued to study privately while serving as a lady-in-waiting to the Vicereine Leonor Carreto, who also served as Juana Inés' tutor, confidant, and friend. By the time she was seventeen, Juana Inés was able to sit before a tribunal of theologians, philosophers, justices, and poets to defend her knowledge and skill, thus expanding her renown as a scholar and a poet.

Juana Inés spent a short time in 1667 living in a cloistered monastery of Carmelite nuns, but found the community's discipline too severe to allow her academic and creative genius room to grow. In 1669 Juana Inés entered the monastery of the Order of Saint Jerome, a more relaxed community, and took the religious name Sor Juana Inés de la Cruz (Sister Joan Agnes of the Cross in English).

Sor Juana Inés' literary career blossomed in the monastery, which drew both the affirmation and ire of ecclesiastical and secular society. Her detractors insisted that a nun had no business writing about secular studies such as philosophy or natural science, while her admirers praised her concise theories and elegant prose. In the midst of a very public intellectual career, Sor Juana Inés managed to balance religious devotion and life in community. She is claimed to have said: "One can perfectly well philosophize while cooking supper."

Giving in to threats of official ecclesiastical censure, Sor Juana Inés stopped publishing her writing by 1693. Following her retirement from public intellectual life, Sor Juana Inés is reported to have sold her collection of musical and scientific instruments, as well as her library of more than 4,000 books. Of her extensive correspondence and publications, only a few of her writings have survived but she is hailed by contemporary critics as a major figure in indigenous Mexican literature.

Sor Juana Inés de la Cruz died on April 17, 1695, while serving her religious community during an outbreak of the plague.

Juana Inés de la Cruz

Monastic and Theologian, 1695

I Almighty God, Source of all knowledge, we give thee thanks for the witness of thy servant Juana Inés de la Cruz in her fierce passion for learning and creativity. Teach us, we beseech thee, so to be faithful stewards of our minds and hearts, that, following her example, we might forever proclaim the riches of thine unending love in Christ Jesus our Lord. Through the same Jesus Christ who, with thee and the Holy Ghost, livest and reignest for ever and ever. *Amen.*

II Almighty God, Source of all knowledge, we give you thanks for the witness of your servant Juana Inés de la Cruz in her fierce passion for learning and creativity. Teach us to be faithful stewards of our minds and hearts, so that, following her example, we might forever proclaim the riches of your unending love in Jesus Christ our Lord. Through Jesus Christ who, with you and the Holy Spirit, lives and reigns, one God, for ever and ever. *Amen.*

Lessons and Psalm

Judith 16:1-10
Psalm 56:8-12
Ephesians 4:20-27
Matthew 5:17-20

Preface of a Saint (2)

Born in 954, Alphege (or Aelfheah) gave his witness in the troubled time of the second wave of Scandinavian invasion and settlement in England. After serving as a monk at Deerhurst, and then as Abbot of Bath, he became, in 984, through Archbishop Dunstan's influence, Bishop of Winchester. He was instrumental in bringing the Norse King Olaf Tryggvason, only recently baptized, to King Aethelred in 994 to make his peace and to be confirmed at Andover.

Transferred to Canterbury in 1005, Alphege was captured by the Danes in 1011. He refused to allow a personal ransom to be collected from his already over-burdened people. Seven months later he was brutally murdered, despite the Viking commander Thorkell's effort to save him by offering all his possessions except his ship for the Archbishop's life.

The Anglo-Saxon Chronicle relates that the Danes were "much stirred against the bishop, because he would not promise them any fee, and forbade that any man should give anything for him. They were also much drunken . . . and took the bishop, and led him to their hustings, on the eve of the Saturday after Easter . . . and then they shamefully killed him. They overwhelmed him with bones and horns of oxen; and one of them smote him with an axe-iron on the head; so that he sunk downwards with the blow. And his holy blood fell on the earth, whilst his sacred soul was sent to the realm of God."

Alphege

Archbishop of Canterbury and Martyr, 1012

I Lord Jesus Christ, who didst willingly walk the way of the cross: Strengthen thy church through the example and prayers of thy servant Alphege to hold fast to the path of discipleship; for with the Father and the Holy Ghost thou livest and reignest, one God, for ever and ever. *Amen.*

II Lord Jesus Christ, who willingly walked the way of the cross: Strengthen your church through the example and prayers of your servant Alphege to hold fast to the path of discipleship; for with the Father and Holy Spirit you live and reign, one God, for ever and ever. *Amen.*

Lessons and Psalm

Micah 2:1-11
Psalm 30:1-5
Colossians 1:24-29
Luke 12:35-40

Preface of a Saint (3)

Anselm was born in Italy about 1033 and took monastic vows in 1060 at the Abbey of Bec in Normandy. He succeeded his teacher Lanfranc as Prior of Bec in 1063, and as Archbishop of Canterbury in 1093. His episcopate was stormy, in continual conflict with the crown over the rights and freedom of the church. His greatest talent lay in theology and spiritual direction.

As a pioneer in the scholastic method, Anselm remains the great exponent of the so-called "ontological argument" for the existence of God: God is "that than which nothing greater can be thought." Even the fool, who (in Psalm 14) says in his heart "There is no God," must have an idea of God in his mind, the concept of an unconditional being (*ontos*) than which nothing greater can be conceived; otherwise he would not be able to speak of "God" at all. And so this something, "God," must exist outside the mind as well; because, if he did not, he would not in fact be that than which nothing greater can be thought. Since the greatest thing that can be thought must have existence as one of its properties, Anselm asserts, "God" can be said to exist in reality as well as in the intellect, but is not dependent upon the material world for verification. To some, this "ontological argument" has seemed mere deductive rationalism; to others it has the merit of showing that faith in God need not be contrary to human reason.

Anselm is also the most famous exponent of the "satisfaction theory" of the atonement. Anselm explains the work of Christ in terms of the feudal society of his day. If a vassal breaks his bond, he has to atone for this to his lord; likewise, sin violates a person's bond with God, the supreme Lord, and atonement or satisfaction must be made. Of ourselves, we are unable to make such atonement, because God is perfect and we are not. Therefore, God himself has saved us, becoming perfect man in Christ, so that a perfect life could be offered in satisfaction for sin.

Undergirding Anselm's theology is a profound piety. His spirituality is best summarized in the phrase, "faith seeking understanding." He writes, "I do not seek to understand that I may believe, but I believe in order that I may understand. For this, too, I believe, that unless I first believe, I shall not understand."

Anselm of Canterbury

Archbishop of Canterbury and Theologian, 1109

I Almighty God, whose servant Anselm helped thy church to understand its faith in thine eternal Being, perfect justice, and saving mercy: Provide thy church in all ages with devout and learned scholars and teachers, that we may be able to give a reason for the hope that is in us; through Jesus Christ our Lord, who liveth and reigneth with thee and the Holy Ghost, one God, for ever and ever. *Amen.*

II Almighty God, whose servant Anselm helped your church to understand its faith in your eternal Being, perfect justice, and saving mercy: Provide your church in all ages with devout and learned scholars and teachers, that we may be able to give a reason for the hope that is in us; through Jesus Christ our Lord, who lives and reigns with you and the Holy Spirit, one God, for ever and ever. *Amen.*

Lessons and Psalm

Wisdom 6:12-16
Psalm 108:1-6
Romans 5:1-11
Matthew 11:25-30

Preface of the Epiphany

Little is known about the life of Hadewijch apart from her influential corpus of spiritual writings. She was almost certainly a Beguine, a member of a group of women who lived in a quasi-monastic community but did not take formal vows. Instead, they pledged to be bound by the traditional vows of poverty, chastity, and obedience only as long as they lived in the community.

The Beguine movement was particularly attractive to women who could not afford the (often substantial) dowry that was required by many monasteries, but the level of Hadewijch's education suggests that she was probably from a wealthy background. Her writings show that, in addition to her native language of Dutch, she was conversant with theological writings in both Latin and French, and also with French courtly poetry.

Hadewijch is considered one of the creators of Dutch lyrical poetry, which includes compositions in which she co-opts the French trouvêre form to extoll the love between the speaker and God rather than worldly love. She also wrote poems in couplets on religious themes, as well as prose letters and a *Book of Visions* in which she engages Christ in dialogue.

In a number of her works, she explicitly genders Love as female:

"Of great Love in high thought
I long to think, day and night.
She with her terrible might
so opens my heart.
I must surrender all to her."

And also,

"Sweet as Love's nature is,
Where can she come by the strange hatred
With which she continually pursues me,
And that pierces the depths of my heart with storm?
I wander in darkness without clarity,
Without liberating consolation, and in strange fear."

While her works were widely known in the fourteenth and fifteenth centuries, by the time of the sixteenth century she had been largely forgotten. However, recent scholarly research has uncovered the profound impact that her writings had on better-known male mystics such as Meister Eckhart and John of Ruusbroec, which has resulted in increased attention and appreciation for the originality and import of her works.

Hadewijch of Brabant

Poet and Mystic, thirteenth century

I Triune God of Love, overwhelming and all-encompassing: Visit us in our solitude and in our companionship, and draw us ever more deeply into union with thee, who art ever present and ever mysterious; that we, like thy servant Hadewijch, might know thee ever more fully, even as we have been fully known. *Amen.*

II Triune God of Love, overwhelming and all-encompassing: Visit us in our solitude and in our companionship, and draw us ever more deeply into union with you, who are ever present and ever mysterious; that we, like your servant Hadewijch, might know you ever more fully, even as we have been fully known. *Amen.*

Lessons and Psalm

Isaiah 52:13—53:12
Psalm 57:6-11
Galatians 5:22-26
John 19:31-37

Preface of the Epiphany

George is the patron saint of England by declaration of King Edward II in 1347. He is remembered as a martyr, having given his life in witness to the gospel during the persecution of the church in the early fourth century. Very few details of his life have survived, and his story is replete with legend. By the middle of the fifth century, he was commemorated in local calendars and historical records of the period.

George was a soldier by vocation, serving as an officer in the Roman army. It is said that he "gave his goods to the poor, and openly confessed Christianity before the court."

George's initial notoriety may well have resulted from his faithfulness and witness to Christ during the Diocletian persecutions, 303–304, a particularly destructive period through which the church suffered.

Much of the legend of George dates back only to the eighth century, and more of it developed in the centuries that followed. The infamous story of George slaying the dragon, probably developed from Greek mythology, is not associated with him until the twelfth century. The inclusion of George's story in the thirteenth century manuscript, *The Golden Legend,* accounts for his growing popularity in the Middle Ages.

In the twelfth century George was recognized as the patron saint of soldiers and he was called upon in support of those who would fight in the Crusades. The shield under which his soldier's fought became a symbol of national pride for the English and in time was adapted into the national flag. Interestingly, the "St. George's Shield"—white shield emblazoned with a red cross—is the basis of the Episcopal Church flag and seal.

[George of Lydda]

Soldier and Martyr, c. 304

I Almighty God, who didst commission thy holy martyr George to bear before the rulers of this world the banner of the cross: Strengthen us in our battles against the great serpent of sin and evil, that we too may attain the crown of eternal life; through Jesus Christ our Redeemer, who liveth and reigneth with thee and the Holy Spirit, one God, for ever and ever. *Amen.*

II Almighty God, you commissioned your holy martyr George to bear before the rulers of this world the banner of the cross: Strengthen us in our battles against the great serpent of sin and evil, that we too may attain the crown of eternal life; through Jesus Christ our Redeemer, who lives and reigns with you and the Holy Spirit, one God, for ever and ever. *Amen.*

Lessons and Psalm

Joshua 1:7-9
Psalm 3
Revelation 12:7-12
John 15:18-21

Preface of Lent (I)

Toyohiko Kagawa, born on July 10, 1888, in Kobe, Japan, was a Japanese evangelist, advocate of social change, and pacifist.

Kagawa was the son of a wealthy Kobe Buddhist business entrepreneur-politician and his concubine, both of whom died when Kagawa was four years old. The youth was raised by Presbyterian missionaries and had a conversion experience at the age of fifteen. "O God, make me like Christ," he prayed repeatedly.

Kagawa studied at theological seminaries in Japan and at Princeton University and Princeton Theological Seminary, but was increasingly drawn to an evangelism of social reform, seeking to apply Christ's teachings directly to Japan's poor in a theologically uncomplicated way. From 1910 to 1924, he lived for the most part in a six-foot-square windowless shed in Kobe's slums. A skilled organizer, he helped found trade unions and credit unions among dock workers, factory laborers, and subsistence farmers. Trade unions were forbidden at the time, and Kagawa was twice imprisoned. He was also a pacifist and organized the National Anti-War League in 1928. Kagawa was arrested in 1940 for publicly apologizing to the people of China for Japan's invasion of that country. An advocate for universal male suffrage (granted in 1925), he later became a voice for women's right to vote as well.

A prolific author, his autobiographical novel, *Crossing the Death Line* (1920), became a best seller, and many of his other novels and writings in a Christian Socialist vein were translated into English. He used the revenues from his substantial book sales to fund his extensive slum work. Although Kagawa was under police surveillance much of his life, the Japanese government called on him to organize the rebuilding of Tokyo after a 1923 earthquake and again at the end of World War II to serve as head of the country's social welfare programs.

Although some knew him best as a social reformer and pacifist, Kagawa saw himself first of all an evangelist. "Christ alone can make all things new," he said. "The spirit of Christ must be the soul of all real social reconstruction."

Kagawa died on April 23, 1960, in Tokyo.

Toyohiko Kagawa

Social Reformer, 1960

I Strengthen and protect, O God, all those who suffer for their fidelity to Jesus Christ; that, like thy servant Toyohiko Kagawa, they might persevere in seeking and serving Christ in all persons, and work tirelessly for the advancement of thy kingdom; through the same Jesus Christ our Lord, to whom with thee and the Holy Ghost be all honor and glory now and for ever. *Amen.*

II Strengthen and protect, O God, all those who suffer for their fidelity to Jesus Christ; that, like your servant Toyohiko Kagawa, they might persevere in seeking and serving Christ in all persons, and work tirelessly for the advancement of your kingdom; through the same Jesus Christ our Lord, to whom with you and the Holy Spirit be all honor and glory now and for ever. *Amen.*

Lessons and Psalm

Job 13:13-22
Psalm 140
Philippians 1:10-20
Luke 22:47-53

Preface of a Saint (1)

A disciple of Jesus, named Mark, appears in several places in the New Testament. If all references to Mark can be accepted as referring to the same person, we learn that he was the son of a woman who owned a house in Jerusalem. Church tradition suggests that Mark may have been the young man who fled naked when Jesus was arrested in the Garden of Gethsemane. In his letter to the Colossians, Paul refers to "Mark the cousin of Barnabas," who was with him in his imprisonment. Mark set out with Paul and Barnabas on their first missionary journey, but he turned back for reasons which failed to satisfy Paul (Acts 15:36-40). When another journey was planned, Paul refused to have Mark with him. Instead, Mark went with Barnabas to Cyprus. The breach between Paul and Mark was later healed, and Mark became one of Paul's companions in Rome, as well as a close friend of Peter's.

An early tradition recorded by Papias, Bishop of Hieropolis in Asia Minor at the beginning of the second century, names Mark as the author of the Gospel bearing his name, drawing his information from the teachings of Peter. In his First Letter, Peter refers to "my son Mark," which shows a close relationship between the two men (1 Peter 5:13).

The Church of Alexandria in Egypt claimed Mark as its first bishop and most illustrious martyr, and the great Church of St. Mark in Venice commemorates the disciple who progressed from turning back while on a missionary journey with Paul and Barnabas to proclaiming in his Gospel Jesus of Nazareth as Son of God, and bearing witness to that faith in his later life as friend and companion to the apostles Peter and Paul.

Saint Mark the Evangelist

I Almighty God, who by the hand of Mark the evangelist hast given to thy church the Gospel of Jesus Christ the Son of God: We thank thee for this witness, and pray that we may be firmly grounded in its truth; through the same Jesus Christ our Lord, who liveth and reigneth with thee and the Holy Ghost, one God, for ever and ever. *Amen.*

II Almighty God, by the hand of Mark the evangelist you have given to your church the Gospel of Jesus Christ the Son of God: We thank you for this witness, and pray that we may be firmly grounded in its truth; through Jesus Christ our Lord, who lives and reigns with you and the Holy Spirit, one God, for ever and ever. *Amen.*

Lessons and Psalm

Isaiah 52:7-10
Psalm 2 *or* 2:7-10
Ephesians 4:7-8, 11-16
Mark 1:1-15 *or* 16:15-20

Preface of All Saints

Zita was born in the early thirteenth century in the village of Montsegradi in Tuscany; she died on April 12, 1271. Zita was born into a poor family, but one in which the Christian faith was emphasized. One of her uncles was a hermit, a sister became a nun, and the entire family was faithful in worship together, both at church and in their home.

At the age of twelve she entered the service of the Fatinelli family in Lucca. Although little more than a child, she maintained the serious faith that she had been taught by her family. Scrupulous in the exercise of her domestic duties, she embodied Paul's advice in Colossians 3:23, "Whatever your task, put yourselves into it, as done for the Lord and not for your masters." Her earnest diligence, however, was first met with scorn from both her employers and her fellow servants. Nevertheless, she continued faithfully in her work and exhibited a peace that surpassed comprehension. Through her perseverance in doing good, she eventually earned the respect and affection of the whole household.

In due course, the once despised servant became the housekeeper. As head of the household staff, Zita demonstrated such Christlike benevolence that she came to be venerated throughout Lucca even before her death. Mindful of the poverty in which she had been raised, she gave away most of her income to those in need.

After her death, the popularity of her cult spread as far as England, where she is called Sitha; images of her may be found in churches throughout southern England. In popular piety, she is often entreated in order to find lost keys.

Zita of Tuscany

Worker of Charity, 1271

I Merciful God, who hast given unto us all things that pertain unto life and godliness; Grant that we, like thy servant Zita, may be faithful in the exercise of our duties and that, whatsoever thou givest us to do, we may do it heartily unto thee for the honor and glory of thy Name; through him who hast called us to virtue, Jesus Christ, thy Son, our Lord. *Amen.*

II Merciful God, who has given to us all things necessary for life and godliness; Grant that we, like your servant Zita, may be faithful in the exercise of our duties and that, whatever you give us to do, we may do it heartily to you for the honor and glory of your Name; through him who has called us to virtue, Jesus Christ, your Son, our Lord. *Amen.*

Lessons and Psalm

Exodus 1:15-21
Psalm 16
James 2:1-7
Mark 12:41-44

Preface of a Saint (1)

Catherine Benincasa was the youngest of twenty-five children of a dyer of Siena. At six years of age, she had a remarkable vision that decided her life's vocation. Walking home from a visit, she stopped on the road and gazed upward, oblivious to everything around her. "I beheld our Lord seated in glory with St. Peter, St. Paul, and St. John." She went on to say later that the Savior smiled on her and blessed her.

From then on, Catherine spent most of her time in prayer and meditation, despite her mother's attempts to force her to be like other girls. To settle matters, Catherine cut off her hair, her chief beauty. Her family harassed her continually; but in the end, convinced that she was deaf to all opposition, her father let her do as she wished: close herself away in a darkened room, fast, and sleep on boards. Eventually, she was accepted as a third order Dominican postulant.

Catherine had numerous visions, and was also tried most severely by temptations. Frequently, she felt totally abandoned by God. At last, in 1366, the Savior appeared with Mary and the Heavenly Host, and espoused her to himself, thus ending her years of lonely prayer and struggle. She became a nurse, as Dominican tertiaries regularly did, caring for patients with leprosy and cancer, whom other nurses disliked to treat.

Opinion in Siena was sharply divided about whether she was a saint or a fanatic, but when the Bishop of Capua was appointed as her confessor, he helped her to win full support from the Dominican Mother House. Catherine was a courageous worker in a time of severe plague. She visited prisoners condemned to death, and she was constantly called upon to arbitrate feuds and to prepare troubled sinners for confession.

During the great schism of the papacy, with rival popes in Rome and Avignon, Catherine wrote tirelessly to princes, kings, and popes, urging them to restore the unity of the church. She even went to Rome to press further for the cause.

Besides her many letters to all manner of people, Catherine wrote a *Dialogue,* a mystical work dictated in ecstasy. Exhausted and paralyzed, she died at the age of thirty-three.

Catherine of Siena

Mystic and Prophetic Witness, 1380

I Almighty and everlasting God, who didst kindle the flame of thy love in the heart of thy servant Catherine of Siena: Grant unto us the same strength of conviction and power of love that, as we rejoice in her triumph, we may profit by her example; through Jesus Christ our Lord. *Amen.*

II Almighty and everlasting God, who kindled the flame of your love in the heart of your servant Catherine of Siena: Grant unto us the same strength of conviction and power of love that, as we rejoice in her triumph, we may profit by her example; through Jesus Christ our Lord. *Amen.*

Lessons and Psalm

Lamentations 3:31-36
Psalm 36
1 John 1:5—2:2
Luke 12:22-31

Preface of a Saint (2)

The two apostles commemorated on this day are among those about whom little is known, except for their mention in the Gospels. James the Less is so called to distinguish him from James the son of Zebedee and from James "the brother of the Lord," or perhaps to indicate youth or lack of stature. He is known to us from the list of the Twelve, where he is called James the son of Alpheus. He may also be the person referred to in Mark's Gospel as James the younger, who, with his mother Mary and the other women, watched the crucifixion from a distance.

Philip figures in several important incidents in Jesus' ministry as reported in John's Gospel. There we read that Jesus called Philip soon after calling Andrew and Peter. Philip, in turn, found his friend Nathanael, and convinced him to come and see Jesus, the Messiah. Later, when Jesus saw the hungry crowd, he asked Philip, "How are we to buy bread, so that these people may eat?" (John 6:5). Philip's practical response, "Two hundred denarii would not buy enough bread for each of them to get a little" (John 6:7), was the prelude to the feeding of the multitude with the loaves and fishes. In a later incident in John's Gospel, some Greeks came to Philip asking to see Jesus. At the Last Supper, Philip's request, "Lord, show us the Father, and we shall be satisfied," evokes the response, "Have I been with you so long, and yet you do not know me, Philip? He who has seen me has seen the Father" (John 14:8, 9).

The Apostles Saint Philip and Saint James

I Almighty God, who didst give to thine apostles Philip and James grace and strength to bear witness to the truth: Grant that we, being mindful of their victory of faith, may glorify in life and death the Name of our Lord Jesus Christ; who liveth and reigneth with thee and the Holy Ghost, one God, now and for ever. *Amen.*

II Almighty God, who gave to your apostles Philip and James grace and strength to bear witness to the truth: Grant that we, being mindful of their victory of faith, may glorify in life and death the Name of our Lord Jesus Christ; who lives and reigns with you and the Holy Spirit, one God, now and for ever. *Amen.*

Lessons and Psalm

Isaiah 30:18-21
Psalm 119:33-40
2 Corinthians 4:1-6
John 14:6-14

Preface of Apostles and Ordinations

Athanasius was born around 295 in Alexandria and was ordained as a deacon in 319. He quickly attracted attention by his opposition to the presbyter Arius, whose teaching that the Second Person of the Trinity was a creature was gaining widespread acceptance. Alexander, the Bishop of Alexandria, took Athanasius as his secretary and adviser to the first Ecumenical Council, at Nicaea in 325, which dealt with the Arian conflict. Athanasius was successful in winning approval for the phrase in the Nicene Creed which has ever since been recognized as expressing unequivocally the full divinity of the Son: "of one Being with the Father" *(homoousios)*.

When Alexander died in 328, Athanasius became bishop. He fearlessly defended Nicene Christology against emperors, magistrates, bishops, and theologians. Five times he was sent into exile. He often seemed to stand alone for the orthodox faith. "*Athanasius contra mundum*" (Athanasius against the world) became a by-word. Yet, by the time of his last exile, his popularity among the citizens of Alexandria was so great that the emperor had to recall him to avoid insurrection in the city.

Athanasius wrote extensively, including biblical interpretation, theological exposition, sermons, and letters. His treatise, *On the Incarnation of the Word of God,* is a still widely read theological classic, and his work *The Life of Antony* became profoundly influential in the spread of the early monastic movement.

In *On the Incarnation,* he writes, "The Savior of us all, the Word of God, in his great love took to himself a body and moved as Man among men, meeting their senses, so to speak, halfway. He became himself an object for the senses, so that those who were seeking God in sensible things might apprehend the Father through the works which he, the Word of God, did in the body. Human and human-minded as people were, therefore, to whichever side they looked in the sensible world, they found themselves taught the truth."

Athanasius died in Alexandria in the year 373, after devoting his final years to preaching, writing, and giving spiritual direction.

Athanasius of Alexandria

Bishop and Theologian, 373

I O Lord, who didst establish thy servant Athanasius, through wisdom, in thy truth: Grant that we, perceiving the humanity and divinity of thy Son Jesus Christ, may follow in his footsteps and ascend the way to eternal life; who liveth and reigneth with thee and the Holy Ghost, one God, now and for ever. *Amen.*

II O Lord, who established your servant Athanasius, through wisdom, in your truth: Grant that we, perceiving the humanity and divinity of your Son Jesus Christ, may follow in his footsteps and ascend the way to eternal life, who lives and reigns with you and the Holy Spirit, one God, now and for ever. *Amen.*

Lessons and Psalm

Ezekiel 3:1-14
Psalm 71:1-8
1 John 5:1-5
Matthew 10:22-32

Preface of the Epiphany

Elisabeth Cruciger was a friend and coworker of Martin Luther, and the first female hymn writer of the Protestant Reformation. Elisabeth entered monastic life as a young woman, but through books that were smuggled into the monastery she became convinced of the teachings of the Protestant Reformation and left the convent for Wittenberg. She would eventually marry Caspar Cruciger, who was a professor of theology.

Elisabeth embarked on an active ministry as a hymn writer, producing a number of compositions that helped to teach the Christian faith to laypeople. According to one account, she once dreamed she was standing in the pulpit of the Wittenberg church preaching. When she told Caspar this, he replied that whenever the church sang one of her hymns, she was indeed preaching, just as much as if she had spoken the words from the pulpit. She died when she was in her mid-thirties.

Elisabeth's hymn "Lord Christ, God's Only Dear Son" was translated into English by Miles Coverdale, and was one of the most popular hymns used by Anglicans in the sixteenth century. It is still included in most Lutheran hymnals, and is #309 in *Evangelical Lutheran Worship,* the current hymnal of the Evangelical Lutheran Church in America.

The following is the English translation of her hymn translated by Anglican priest Arthur Tozer Russell in 1850:

> 1. The only Son from heaven, foretold by ancient seers, by God the Father given, in human form appears. No sphere his light confining, no star so brightly shining, As he, our Morningstar.
> 2. Oh, times of God appointed, Oh bright and holy morn! He comes, the king anointed, the Christ, the virgin-born, Grim death to vanquish for us, to open heav'n before us And bring us life again.
> 3. Awaken, Lord, our spirit to know and love you more, In faith to stand unshaken, in spirit to adore, That we, through this world moving, each glimpse of heaven proving, May reap his fullness there.
> 4. O Father, here before you with God the Holy Ghost, And Jesus we adore you, O pride of angel host: Before you mortals lowly cry: "Holy, holy, holy, O blessed Trinity!"

Elisabeth Cruciger

Poet and Hymnographer, 1535

I Pour out thy Spirit upon all of thy sons and daughters, Almighty God, that like thy servant Elisabeth Cruciger our lips may praise thee, our lives may bless thee, and our worship may give thee glory; through Jesus Christ our Lord. *Amen.*

II Pour out your Spirit upon all of your sons and daughters, Almighty God, that like your servant Elisabeth Cruciger our lips may praise you, our lives may bless you, and our worship may give you glory; through Jesus Christ our Lord. *Amen.*

Lessons and Psalm

Joel 2:23-29
Psalm 26
Colossians 3:11-17
Mark 4:26-29

Preface of a Saint (3)

Monica's life story is enshrined in the spiritual autobiography of her eldest son, *The Confessions of Saint Augustine*. Born in North Africa about 331, of Berber parents, Monica was married to a pagan Latinized provincial of Tagaste named Patricius. Early in their marriage Patricius could be violent and abusive, although over the course of their life together he seems to have worked to improve his temper. In Monica's earlier years she was not without worldly ambitions and tastes, and in particular she struggled with a tendency to drink too much wine—a temptation that she gradually overcame. Over time, she grew in Christian maturity and spiritual insight through an ever-deepening life of prayer.

Her ambition for her gifted son was transformed into a passionate desire for his conversion to Christ. She had longed for all three of her children to be baptized, but her husband insisted that nothing be done until they were adults and could decide for themselves. Augustine took a particularly slow and circuitous path to Christianity, but Monica never gave up hope for his conversion. After his baptism in Milan in 387 by Bishop Ambrose, Augustine and his mother, together with a younger brother, planned to return home to Africa. While awaiting ship at Ostia, the port of Rome, however, Monica fell ill.

Augustine writes, "One day during her illness she had a fainting spell and lost consciousness for a short time. We hurried to her bedside, but she soon regained consciousness and looked up at my brother and me as we stood beside her. With a puzzled look, she asked, 'Where was I?' Then, watching us closely as we stood there speechless with grief, she said, 'You will bury your mother here.'"

Augustine's brother expressed sorrow, for her sake, that she would die so far from her own country. She said to the two brothers, "It does not matter where you bury my body. Do not let that worry you. All I ask of you is that, wherever you may be, you should remember me at the altar of the Lord." To the question of whether she was afraid at the thought of leaving her body in an alien land, she replied, "Nothing is far from God, and I need have no fear that he will not know where to find me, when he comes to raise me to life at the end of the world."

Recent excavations at Ostia have uncovered her original tomb. Her mortal remains, however, were transferred in 1430 to the Church of St. Augustine in Rome.

Monica

Mother of Augustine of Hippo, 387

I Deepen our devotion, O Lord, and use us in accordance with thy will; that inspired by the example of your servant Monica, we may bring others to acknowledge Jesus Christ as Savior and Lord; who with thee and the Holy Ghost lives and reigns, one God, for ever and ever. *Amen.*

II Deepen our devotion, O Lord, and use us in accordance with your will; that inspired by the example of your servant Monica, we may bring others to acknowledge Jesus Christ as Savior and Lord; who with you and the Holy Spirit lives and reigns, one God, for ever and ever. *Amen.*

Lessons and Psalm

1 Samuel 1:10-20
Psalm 115:12-18
Galatians 4:1-12a
Luke 7:11-17

Preface of Baptism

The Roman Catholic Church commemorates the Forty Martyrs of England and Wales on May 4: men and women who were executed for treason between 1535 and 1679 for their allegiance to the Catholic Church. In recent years, the Church of England has shared this commemoration, broadening it to all of the English saints and martyrs of the Reformation era. This commemoration remembers not only Anglican martyrs like Thomas Cranmer, Hugh Latimer, and Nicholas Ridley, who died for their adherence to the Church of England, but those Catholics who were killed by Anglicans—along with all other Christians who were persecuted by their fellow Christians for their beliefs, most notably the Anabaptists and the Quakers.

Ecumenical dialogues around the five hundredth anniversary of the Reformation have led many Christians to soul-searching questions about the role that our churches played in the persecution of other Christians for their beliefs. Without minimizing the seriousness of the theological disagreements or the inextricable links between religion and politics in that time, this commemoration asks us to recognize that within the heritage of our own tradition there were both victims and persecutors, and that there was a deeply Christian courage and holiness present in the martyrs from various confessions who were willing to die for their faith. It is a sobering reminder of just how swiftly Christians have often turned from being persecuted and oppressed to being the persecutors and the oppressors of others.

By our baptisms we are incorporated into God's one church, and thus we are the heirs of both the martyrs and their executioners. It is this double heritage that must spur our efforts to heal our divisions and to work and pray for a future when Christ's prayer that his followers might be truly one as he and the Father are one (John 17:21) will be fulfilled.

Martyrs of the Reformation Era

I Almighty and Most Merciful God, give to thy church that peace which the world cannot give, and grant that those who have been divided on earth may be reconciled in heaven, and share together in the vision of thy glory; through Jesus Christ thy Son our Lord, who liveth and reigneth with thee, in the unity of the Holy Ghost, one God, now and for ever. *Amen.*

II Almighty and Most Merciful God, give to your church that peace which the world cannot give, and grant that those who have been divided on earth may be reconciled in heaven, and share together in the vision of your glory; through Jesus Christ your Son our Lord, who lives and reigns with you, in the unity of the Holy Spirit, one God, now and for ever. *Amen.*

Lessons and Psalm

Ezekiel 34:1-10
Psalm 51:10-17
2 Corinthians 4:7-12
Matthew 7:1-6

Preface of God the Holy Spirit

Of Julian's early life we know little, only the probable date of her birth (1342). Her own writings in her *Revelations of Divine Love* are concerned only with her visions, or "showings," that she experienced when she was thirty years old rather than with the details of her biography.

Julian had been gravely ill and was given last rites. Suddenly, on the seventh day, all pain left her, and she had fifteen visions of Christ's Passion. These brought her great peace and joy. "From that time I desired oftentimes to learn what was our Lord's meaning," she wrote, "and fifteen years after I was answered in spiritual understanding: 'Would you learn the Lord's meaning in this thing? Learn it well. Love was his meaning. Who showed it you? Love. What did he show you? Love. Why did he show it? For Love.'"

Julian had long desired three gifts from God: "the mind of his passion, bodily sickness in youth, and three wounds—of contrition, of compassion, of will-full longing toward God." Her illness brought her the first two wounds, which then passed from her mind. The third, "will-full longing" (divinely inspired longing), never left her.

She became a recluse, an anchoress, at Norwich soon after her recovery from illness, living in a small dwelling attached to the parish church. Even in her lifetime, she was famed as a mystic and spiritual counselor and was frequently visited by clergy and lay persons, including the mystic Margery Kempe. Kempe says of Julian: "This anchoress was expert in knowledge of our Lord and could give good counsel. I spent much time with her talking of the love of our Lord Jesus Christ."

Julian understood that God was both Father and Mother to us, and understood Christ as exemplifying this maternal face of God. "Thus Jesus Christ, who does good against evil, is our very Mother. We have our being in him, where the ground of motherhood begins . . . As truly as God is our Father, so truly is God our Mother."

Julian's book is a tender and beautiful exposition of God's eternal and all-embracing love, showing how his charity toward human beings is exhibited in the Passion. Again and again Julian referred to Christ as "our courteous Lord." Many have found strength in the words that the Lord had given her: "I can make all things well; I will make all things well; I shall make all things well; and you can see for yourself that all manner of things shall be well."

Julian of Norwich

Mystic and Theologian, c. 1417

I Triune God, Father and Mother to us all, who in thy compassion didst grant to your servant Julian many revelations of thy nurturing and sustaining love: Move our hearts, like hers, to seek thee above all things, for in giving us thyself thou givest us all. *Amen.*

II Triune God, Father and Mother to us all, who showed your servant Julian revelations of your nurturing and sustaining love: Move our hearts, like hers, to seek you above all things, for in giving us yourself you give us all. *Amen.*

Lessons and Psalm

Isaiah 49:13-18
Psalm 27:7-11
Hebrews 10:19-24
John 4:21-26

Preface of the Epiphany

Gregory of Nazianzus, one of the Cappadocian Fathers, loved God, the art of letters, and the human race—in that order. He was born about 330 in Nazianzus in Cappadocia (now Turkey), the son of a local bishop. He studied rhetoric in Athens with his friend Basil of Caesarea, and Julian, later to be the apostate emperor.

In 361, against his will, Gregory was ordained as a priest, which he described as an "act of tyranny." At first he fled with Basil to Pontus where he lived a monastic life of seclusion, but eventually he returned home to assume the work of a priest. His Oration 2, "In Defense of his Flight to Pontus," remains one of the classic treatments of the weight and responsibilities of the pastoral office. He writes: "I was ashamed of all of those men who intrude into these most sacred offices when they are no better than ordinary people. Indeed, it is really very lucky if they are not a good deal worse, with unwashed hands and uninstructed souls, laying claim to the sanctuary before being worthy even to approach the temple, and pushing and shoving their way up to the holy altar as if they thought that the priesthood was simply a way of earning a living rather than a pattern of virtue, or as though it were an absolute authority instead of a ministry for which we will have to render an account. Indeed, such priests are almost more numerous than those whom they are supposed to govern, pathetic with respect to piety and completely lacking in dignity, so that it seems to me that as time and evil progress, they will eventually have no one left to rule because everyone will be a teacher."

In time, however, Gregory reconciled himself to his calling and felt prepared to undertake it, and settled down to live an austere, priestly life. He was not to have peace for long. Basil, in his fight against the Arian Emperor Valens, compelled Gregory to become Bishop of Sasima. According to Gregory, it was "a detestable little place without water or grass or any mark of civilization." He felt, he said, like "a bone flung to the dogs." His friendship with Basil suffered a severe break. Deaths in his family, and then that of his estranged friend Basil, brought Gregory himself to the point of death, and he withdrew into seclusion again for healing.

In 379, Gregory moved to Constantinople, a new man and no longer in despair. He appeared as one afire with the love of God. His fame as a theologian rests on five sermons he delivered during this period on the doctrine of the Trinity. They are marked by clarity, strength, and cheerfulness, and remain to this day one of the most influential expositions of Trinitarian theology. The next year, the new Emperor Theodosius entered Constantinople and expelled its Arian bishop and clergy. Then, on a rainy day, the crowds in the Great Church of Hagia Sophia acclaimed Gregory bishop, after a ray of sunlight suddenly shone on him.

Gregory was asked to preside over the ecumenical council in Constantinople in 381. However, exhausted by the politicking and infighting that beset the task, he shocked the assembled bishops by abruptly tendering his resignation. He retired to his home town of Nazianzus, where he continued to write and minister to the people until his death in 389.

Gregory of Nazianzus

Bishop and Theologian, 389

I Almighty God, who hast revealed to thy Church thine eternal Being of glorious majesty and perfect love as one God in Trinity of Persons: Give us grace that, like thy bishop Gregory of Nazianzus, we may continue steadfast in the confession of this faith, and constant in our worship of thee, Father, Son, and Holy Ghost; who livest and reignest for ever and ever. *Amen.*

II Almighty God, who has revealed to your Church your eternal Being of glorious majesty and perfect love as one God in Trinity of Persons: Give us grace that, like your bishop Gregory of Nazianzus, we may continue steadfast in the confession of this faith, and constant in our worship of you, Father, Son, and Holy Spirit; who live and reign for ever and ever. *Amen.*

Lessons and Psalm

Jonah 1:1-16
Psalm 19:7-14
Ephesians 3:14-21
John 8:25-32

Preface of Trinity Sunday

Johann Arndt and Jacob Boehme were two of the most prominent Lutheran mystical writers.

Born in Edderitz near Ballenstedt, in Anhalt-Köthen, Johann Arndt (1555–1621) was orphaned at age ten. He began his studies with a divided focus on medicine and divinity. After recovering from a grave illness, he came to look on his life as a gift and felt duty-bound to devote it to God's service. He turned his attention exclusively to divinity, which he studied in several different German and Swiss universities.

An irenic spirit, Arndt hoped, like Philipp Melanchthon, to help heal the divisions between the Reformed (Calvinist) and Evangelical (Lutheran) branches of Protestantism. Although a diligent pastor, this high aspiration met with continual frustration in his ministry; the posthumous influence of his writing, however, has contributed to this hope by drawing many across theological divides to closer personal union with Christ.

In Arndt's major work, *True Christianity,* he seeks to correct an over-emphasis on the legal aspect of salvation (justification by faith) by emphasizing the need for the believer to abide in Christ through personal prayer, scripture-reading, and godliness. This work became a standard manual among German Pietists as well as the Mennonites. Philipp Jakob Spener (1635-1705) looked to Arndt as a forerunner of his work. Similarly, Arndt influenced John Wesley and the birth of Methodism within the Church of England. In the twentieth century, Albert Schweitzer called Johann Arndt the prophet of interior Protestantism. *True Christianity* has provided a model for countless other devotional texts by both Protestant and Roman Catholic writers.

Jacob Boehme (1575-1624) was born in Alt Seidenburg to a family of cattle-herders. Deemed too weak for cattle-herding, he was sent to school where he learned to read and write and eventually became apprentice to a shoe-maker.

He was given to mystical visions, even in his youth. A particularly compelling vision in 1600 led Boehme to write *Die Morgenroete im Aufgang* (The Rising of Dawn). Although he never intended the work for publication, it was circulated among friends and eventually came to the attention of the pastor of Görlitz, who harshly condemned it. It was many years before Boehme took up the pen again. However, in 1618 he began to write and produced a remarkable number of works on mystical theology and cosmology in the six years before his death. While Boehme remained a Lutheran, his theological speculations caused considerable controversy for departing from the Lutheran Orthodoxy of his day.

Boehme writings influenced the radical pietists, including the Society of Friends (Quakers). William Law (1686–1761) became a great admirer of the German mystic later in his life, and produced an English edition of Boehme's work. However, this admiration was not uncontroversial; Law's student John Wesley called his writings "sublime nonsense." Boehme also had a great influence on both German and English Romanticism, most notably William Blake.

Johann Arndt and Jacob Boehme

Mystics, 1621 and 1624

I Holy God, who dwellest with them that are of a contrite and humble spirit: Revive our spirits; purify us from deceitful lusts; and clothe us in righteousness and true holiness; though Jesus Christ our Lord, who liveth and reigneth with thee and the Holy Ghost, one God now and for ever. *Amen.*

II Holy God, who dwells with those who have a contrite and humble spirit: Revive our spirits; purify us from deceitful lusts; and clothe us in righteousness and true holiness; though Jesus Christ our Lord, who lives and reigns with you and the Holy Spirit, one God now and for ever. *Amen.*

Lessons and Psalm

Exodus 17:1-7
Psalm 119:25-32
Romans 7:21-25
Mark 6:45-52

Preface of a Saint (3)

Frances Perkins was an active member of the Episcopal Church and the first woman to serve a President of the United States as a member of the cabinet. Born in Boston on April 10, 1880, and educated at Mount Holyoke College and Columbia University, Perkins was passionate about the social problems occasioned by the continuing effects of industrialization and urbanization.

As a young adult, she discovered the Episcopal Church and was confirmed at the Church of the Holy Spirit in Lake Forest, Illinois, on June 11, 1905. She remained a faithful and active Episcopalian for the remainder of her life.

After moving to New York, she became an advocate for industrial safety and persistent voice for the reform of what she believed were unjust labor laws. This work got the attention of two of New York's governors, Al Smith and Franklin D. Roosevelt, in whose state administrations she took part. President Roosevelt later appointed her to a cabinet post as Secretary of Labor, a position she would hold for twelve years. As Secretary of Labor, Perkins would have a major role in shaping the New Deal legislation signed into law by President Roosevelt, most notably the establishment of the Social Security program.

During her years of public service, Frances Perkins depended upon her faith, her life of prayer, and the guidance of her church for the support she needed to assist the United States and its leadership to face the enormous problems of the time. During her time as Secretary of Labor, she would take time away from her duties on a monthly basis and make a retreat at the Episcopal convent of the All Saints Sisters of the Poor in nearby Catonsville, Maryland. She spoke publicly of how the Christ's incarnation informed her conviction that people ought to work with God to create a just Christian social order.

Following her public service, she became a professor of industrial and labor relations at Cornell University. She remained active in teaching, social justice advocacy, and in the mission and ministry of the Episcopal Church. She was an eloquent example of lay ministry, writing that "the special vocation of the laity is to conduct and carry on the worldly and secular affairs of modern society . . . in order that all men may be maintained in health and decency." She died in New York City on May 14, 1965.

Frances Perkins

Social Reformer, 1965

I Loving God, we bless thy Name for Frances Perkins, who in faithfulness to her baptism envisioned a society in which all might live in health and decency: Help us, following her example and in union with her prayers, to contend tirelessly for justice and for the protection of all, that we may be faithful followers of Jesus Christ; who with thee and the Holy Ghost liveth and reigneth, one God, for ever and ever. *Amen.*

II Loving God, we bless your Name for Frances Perkins, who in faithfulness to her baptism envisioned a society in which all might live in health and decency: Help us, following her example and in union with her prayers, to contend tirelessly for justice and for the protection of all, that we may be faithful followers of Jesus Christ; who with you and the Holy Spirit lives and reigns, one God, for ever and ever. *Amen.*

Lessons and Psalm

Deuteronomy 15:7-11
Psalm 37:27-31
Ephesians 4:25—5:2
Luke 9:10-17

Preface of Baptism

Pachomius is commonly regarded as the founder of coenobitic monasticism, the form of Christian monasticism in which members live together in community rather than individually as hermits, and he was the author of the first formal monastic rule of life.

Born to a pagan family in 292, Pachomius first encountered Christianity when he was imprisoned as part of a forced military conscription. The Christians of the city visited everyone in the prison, bringing them food, supplies, and comfort, and Pachomius was astonished. He asked the other prisoners, "Why are these people so good to us when they do not even know us?" They answered, "They are Christians, and therefore they treat us with love for the sake of the God of heaven." When he was released from prison, he was baptized, and began to lead an ascetic life of manual labor, prayer, and care for the poor.

In time, a community of people was drawn to Pachomius, and they began to organize themselves into a formal monastic community. This way of life was particularly attractive to those who were drawn to monasticism but could not withstand the hardship of a solitary life, particularly those who might be elderly or ill or very young. Before long, a federation of monastic communities was created, with houses for both men and women, which were organized into a common structure. Pachomius and his disciples wrote the first monastic rules to organize the life of these communities.

The new monastic movement was controversial in its day, and was initially opposed by many bishops and priests. When the monks were building their first monastery, the local bishop came with a mob to try to tear it down. Others came to respect the monks and their way of life, but wanted to unite them more closely to official church institutions. The bishops Serapion and Athanasius visited the community with the hope of ordaining Pachomius to the priesthood, but he hid from them until they finally went away. Indeed, the life of Pachomius states that originally "he did not want any clergy in his monasteries at all for fear of jealousy and vainglory." In time, however, the new monastic movement and the church hierarchy developed a mutual respect for the differing gifts and responsibilities that each of them bore within the church.

By the time that Pachomius died, his monastic federation included several thousand monks and nuns, and within a generation the monastic movement would spread from Egypt to Palestine, Turkey, and Western Europe.

Pachomius of Tabenissi

Monastic, 348

I Set us free, O God, from all false desires, vain ambitions, and everything that would separate us from thy love; that, like thy servant Pachomius, we might give ourselves fully to a life of discipleship, seeking thee alone and serving those whom thou hast given us to serve; through Jesus Christ, our only mediator and advocate. *Amen.*

II Set us free, O God, from all false desires, vain ambitions, and everything that would separate us from your love; that, like your servant Pachomius, we might give ourselves fully to a life of discipleship, seeking you alone and serving those whom you have given us to serve; through Jesus Christ, our only mediator and advocate. *Amen.*

Lessons and Psalm

1 Samuel 10:20-27
Psalm 16
2 Timothy 2:1-6
Matthew 6:24-33

Preface of a Saint (3)

Thurgood Marshall was a distinguished American jurist and the first African American to become an Associate Justice of the United States Supreme Court.

Marshall was born on July 2, 1908, in Baltimore, Maryland. He attended Frederick Douglass High School in Baltimore and Lincoln University in Pennsylvania. Although he was pushed toward other professions, Marshall was determined to be an attorney. He was denied admission to the University of Maryland Law School due to its segregationist admissions policy. He enrolled and graduated magna cum laude from the Law School of Howard University in Washington.

Marshall began the practice of law in Baltimore in 1933 and began representing the local chapter of the NAACP in 1934, eventually becoming the legal counsel for the national organization, working in New York City. He won his first major civil rights decision in 1936, *Murray v. Pearson,* which forced the University of Maryland to open its doors to Black people.

At the age of 32, Marshall successfully argued his first case before the United States Supreme Court and went on to win 29 of the 32 cases he argued before the court. As a lawyer, his crowning achievement was arguing successfully for the plaintiffs in *Brown v. Board of Education of Topeka,* in 1954. The Supreme Court ruled that the "separate but equal" doctrine was unconstitutional and ordered the desegregation of public schools across the nation.

President Lyndon Johnson appointed Marshall as the ninety-sixth Associate Justice of the United States Supreme Court in 1967, a position he held for 24 years. Marshall compiled a long and impressive record of decisions on civil rights, not only for African Americans, but also for women, Native Americans, and the incarcerated; he was a strong advocate for individual freedoms and human rights. He adamantly believed that capital punishment was unconstitutional and should be abolished.

As a child, Marshall attended St. Katherine's Church, one of Baltimore's historic African American parishes. While living in New York, he was the senior warden of St. Phillip's Church in Harlem and served as a deputy to General Convention in 1964. During his years in Washington, Marshall and his family were members of St. Augustine's Episcopal Church, where he was affectionately known as "the Judge." He is remembered as "a wise and godly man who knew his place and role in history and obeyed God's call to follow justice wherever it led." Thurgood Marshall died on January 24, 1993.

Thurgood Marshall

Public Servant, 1993

I Eternal and ever-gracious God, who didst bless thy servant Thurgood Marshall with grace and courage to discern and speak the truth: Grant that, following his example, we may know thee and recognize that we are all thy children, brothers and sisters of Jesus Christ, who liveth and reigneth with thee and the Holy Ghost, one God, for ever and ever. *Amen.*

II Eternal and ever-gracious God, who blessed your servant Thurgood Marshall with grace and courage to discern and speak the truth: Grant that, following his example, we may know you and recognize that we are all your children, brothers and sisters of Jesus Christ, who lives and reigns with you and the Holy Spirit, one God, for ever and ever. *Amen.*

Lessons and Psalm

Amos 5:10-15
Psalm 34:15-22
1 Corinthians 13:1-13
Matthew 23:1-12

Preface of Baptism

In the ninth century, under King Alfred the Great, England had achieved considerable military, political, cultural, and even some ecclesiastical recovery from the Viking invasions. It was not until the following century, however, that there was a revival of monasticism and spirituality. In that, the leading figure was Dunstan.

Dunstan was born about 909 into a family with royal connections. He became a monk and, in 943, was made Abbot of Glastonbury. During a year-long political exile in Flanders, he encountered the vigorous currents of the Benedictine monastic revival. King Edgar recalled Dunstan to England in 957, appointed him Bishop of Worcester, then of London; and, in 960, named him Archbishop of Canterbury. Together with his former pupils, Bishops Aethelwold of Winchester and Oswald of Worcester (later of York), Dunstan was a leader of the English church. All three have been described as "contemplatives in action"—bringing the fruits of their monastic prayer life to the immediate concerns of church and state. They sought better education and discipline among the clergy, the end of landed family interest in the church, the restoration of former monasteries and the establishment of new ones, a revival of monastic life for women, and a more elaborate and carefully ordered liturgical worship.

This reform movement was set forth in the "Monastic Agreement," a common code for English monasteries drawn up by Aethelwold about 970, primarily under the inspiration of Dunstan. It called for continual intercession for the royal house, and emphasized the close tie between the monasteries and the crown.

The long-term effects of this tenth-century reform resulted in the retention of two peculiarly English institutions: the "monastic cathedral," and the Celtic pattern of "monk-bishops."

Dunstan is also reputed to have been an expert craftsman. His name is especially associated with the working of metals and the casting of bells, and he was regarded as the patron saint of those crafts. He died at Canterbury in 988.

Dunstan

Archbishop of Canterbury, 988

I Direct thy Church, O Lord, into the beauty of holiness, that, following the good example of thy servant Dunstan, we may honor thy Son Jesus Christ with our lips and in our lives; to the glory of his Name, who liveth and reigneth with thee and the Holy Ghost, one God, now and for ever. *Amen.*

II Direct your Church, O Lord, into the beauty of holiness, that, following the good example of your servant Dunstan, we may honor your Son Jesus Christ with our lips and in our lives; to the glory of his Name, who lives and reigns with you and the Holy Spirit, one God, now and for ever. *Amen.*

Lessons and Psalm

Exodus 25:31-40
Psalm 67:1-11
Ephesians 5:15-20
Matthew 24:42-47

Preface of the Dedication of the Church

Alcuin was born about 730 near York, into a noble family related to Willibrord, the first missionary to the Netherlands. He was educated at the cathedral school in York under Archbishop Egbert, a pupil of Bede. He thus inherited the best traditions of learning and zeal of the early English church.

After ordination as a deacon in 770, he became head of the York school. It was not uncommon for theologians and intellectuals in the early and medieval church to be ordained as deacons, teaching and scholarship being understood by the church as a diaconal ministry as well as care for the poor and the needy.

Following a meeting in 781 with the Emperor Charlemagne in Pavia (Italy), Alcuin was persuaded to become the Emperor's "prime minister," with special responsibility for the revival of education and learning in the Frankish dominions. He was named Abbot of Tours in 796, where he died on May 19, 804, and was buried in the church of St. Martin.

Alcuin was a man of vast learning, personal charm, and integrity of character. In his direction of Charlemagne's Palace School at Aachen, he was chiefly responsible for the preservation of the classical heritage of Western civilization. Schools were revived in cathedrals and monasteries, and manuscripts of both pagan and Christian writings of antiquity were collated and copied.

Under the authority of Charlemagne, the liturgy was reformed, and service books gathered from Rome were edited and adapted. To this work we owe the preservation of many of the collects that have come down to us, including the Collect for Purity at the beginning of the Holy Eucharist.

Alcuin of York

Deacon, 804

I Almighty God, who didst raise up thy servant Alcuin as a beacon of learning: Shine in our hearts, we pray, that we may also show forth thy praise in our own generation, for thou hast called us out of darkness and into thy marvelous light; through Jesus Christ our Lord, who liveth and reigneth with thee and the Holy Ghost, one God, now and for ever. *Amen.*

II Almighty God, who raised up your servant Alcuin as a beacon of learning: Shine in our hearts, we pray, that we may also show forth your praise in our own generation, for you have called us out of darkness and into your marvelous light; through Jesus Christ our Lord, who lives and reigns with you and the Holy Spirit, one God, now and for ever. *Amen.*

Lessons and Psalm

Ecclesiastes 3:1-8
Psalm 107:1-8
Titus 2:1-3
Matthew 13:24-30

Preface of a Saint (1)

Lydia of Thyatira was Paul's first European convert. She was a Gentile woman living in Philippi who, like many others, was interested in the Jewish faith, but had not converted. As what the Jewish community called a "God-fearer," she was undoubtedly accorded some level of respect by the Jewish community, but would not have been treated as a full member of the Jewish community in Philippi.

Paul encountered her on a riverbank where she and a group of women had gathered for Sabbath prayers. Paul and his companions began to talk with the women, and God "opened her heart" to hear what Paul had to say about Christ and the Gospel. Lydia believed what she heard and, as was the custom when the head of a household converted, her whole household was baptized along with her.

Lydia was a prosperous cloth merchant and had the means to offer hospitality to the apostles during their time in Philippi. Her home, having served as a base of operations for Paul and his companions, became the location of a house church in Philippi. Although she is not mentioned by name outside of Acts 16, her significant role in enabling the spread of the Gospel in Philippi has led to her recognition as a saint in a wide range of Christian traditions, including the Roman Catholic Church, the Orthodox Church, and many Protestant traditions. In the Orthodox Church she is given the title "Equal to the Apostles" for her role in spreading the Christian faith.

Lydia of Thyatira

Coworker of the Apostle Paul

I Eternal God, who givest good gifts to all people and dost grant the spirit of generosity: Give unto us, we pray thee, hearts always open to hear thy word, that, following the example of thy servant Lydia, we may show hospitality to those who are in any need or trouble; through Jesus Christ our Lord who lives and reigns with thee and the Holy Ghost, one God, now and for ever. *Amen.*

II Eternal God, who gives good gifts to all people, and who grants the spirit of generosity: Give us, we pray you, hearts always open to hear your word, that, following the example of your servant Lydia, we may show hospitality to those who are in any need or trouble; through Jesus Christ our Lord who lives and reigns with you and the Holy Spirit, one God, now and for ever. *Amen.*

Lessons and Psalm

Malachi 3:16-18
Psalm 100
Acts 16:11-15
Luke 15:8-10

Preface of Pentecost

Helena was the mother of the Emperor Constantine of Rome and a devout Christian, but she is perhaps most renowned for her discoveries of holy sites related to the life of Jesus.

Helena was born into a lower-class family in the middle of the third century, though we are unsure about where. Many believe she was born in Drepana (now Helenopolis) in northern Asia Minor but this is uncertain. There are also later legends that place her birth in England, and for that she is honored with numerous holy wells across the country. Regardless of birthplace she would eventually become the wife, or at least consort, of Constantius I, who was co-emperor and ruled over Gaul (France) and Britannia (Britain). During this time Helena would give birth to a son, Constantine, in the year 272, but she would soon be divorced and live in the East in the palace of Diocletian.

Once her son gained the Western Empire in the year 312, she returned to Rome and was granted the title Augusta, or Empress, in 325. It was during this time that she made her famous journey to the Holy Land to find the places mentioned in the Gospels, with the most important finds being the Cross of the Crucifixion and the site of the Resurrection.

Long after the destruction of Jerusalem in the year 70, the Emperor Hadrian had the area rebuilt. As part of this restoration a pagan temple was built on the very site of the Resurrection. Helena ordered this temple destroyed, had the area excavated, and discovered three crosses along with the epitaph that said, "Jesus, King of the Jews." To ensure it was truly the cross of Christ, a woman near death was carried to the site and touched each cross in turn. On the third one she was cured and Helena declared this to be the one. She ordered that a church be built which would be called the Church of the Holy Sepulchre.

Regardless of the truth of the legend itself, it is certain that she claimed to have found this and many other holy sites and relics on her journey, and that many of these remain prominent sites of Christian pilgrimage to this day. Unfortunately, she would not live to see the completion of the Church of the Holy Sepulchre, as she died in 330, five years before its completion.

Helena also had a reputation as a faithful Christian who cared for the poor. After her death several towns would be named in her honor and she would also eventually be given the title of "Equal to the Apostles" in the Orthodox Church. Helena's faith in her Lord was not a detached spirituality, but an embodied and historical one, such that she eagerly sought to find the very places where the Son of God had walked, taught, died, and rose again.

Helena of Constantinople

Protector of the Holy Places, 330

I Most Merciful God, who didst vouchsafe to bless thy servant Helena with such grace and devotion to thee that she didst venerate the very footsteps of our Savior; Grant unto us the same grace that, aided by her prayers and example, we too may evermore behold thy glory in the cross of thy Son. Through the same Jesus Christ our Lord; who liveth and reigneth with thee, in the unity of the Holy Ghost, one God, for ever and ever. *Amen.*

II Most Merciful God, who blessed your servant Helena with such grace and devotion to you that she venerated the very footsteps of our Savior; Grant unto us the same grace that, aided by her prayers and example, we also may always behold your glory in the cross of your Son. Through the same Jesus Christ our Lord; who lives and reigns with you, in the unity of the Holy Spirit, one God, for ever and ever. *Amen.*

Lessons and Psalm

Micah 4:1-4
Psalm 2
1 Corinthians 3:8-15
Luke 23:26-32

Preface of Holy Week

When the General Convention of 1835 declared all the members of the Episcopal Church to be members also of the Domestic and Foreign Missionary Society, it provided at the same time for missionary bishops to serve in the wilderness and in foreign countries. Jackson Kemper was the first such bishop. Although he was assigned to Missouri and Indiana, he also laid foundations in Iowa, Wisconsin, Minnesota, Nebraska, and Kansas, and made extensive missionary tours in the South and Southwest.

Kemper was born in Pleasant Valley, New York, on December 24, 1789. He graduated from Columbia College in 1809 and was ordained as a deacon in 1811 and as a priest in 1814. He served Bishop White as his assistant at Christ Church, Philadelphia. At his urging, Bishop White made his first and only visitation in western Pennsylvania. In 1835, Kemper was ordained as a bishop, and immediately set out on his travels.

Because Episcopal clergy, mostly from well-to-do Eastern homes, found it hard to adjust to the harsh life of the frontier—scorching heat, drenching rains, and winter blizzards—Kemper established Kemper College in St. Louis, Missouri, the first of many similar attempts to train clergy and laity for specialized tasks in the church. The College failed in 1845 from the usual malady of such projects in the church—inadequate funding. Nashotah House, in Wisconsin, which he founded in 1842 with the help of James Lloyd Breck and his companions, was more successful. So was Racine College, founded in 1852. Both these institutions reflected Kemper's devotion to beauty in ritual and worship.

Kemper pleaded for more attention to the Native Americans and encouraged the translation of services into native languages. He described a service among the Oneida which was marked by "courtesy, reverence, worship—and obedience to that Great Spirit in whose hands are the issues of life."

From 1859 until his death, Kemper was diocesan Bishop of Wisconsin, but he is more justly honored by his unofficial title, "The Bishop of the Whole Northwest."

Jackson Kemper

Bishop and Missionary, 1870

I O God, who didst send thy son Jesus Christ to preach peace to those who are far off and to those who are near: Grant that we, like thy servant Jackson Kemper, may proclaim the Gospel in our own day, with courage, vision, and perseverance; through the same Jesus Christ our Lord, who with thee and the Holy Ghost liveth and reigneth, now and for ever. *Amen.*

II O God, who sent your son Jesus Christ to preach peace to those who are far off and to those who are near: Grant that we, like your servant Jackson Kemper, may proclaim the Gospel in our own day, with courage, vision, and perseverance; through the same Jesus Christ our Lord,who with you and the Holy Spirit lives and reigns, now and for ever. *Amen.*

Lessons and Psalm

Exodus 15:22-25
Psalm 67
1 Corinthians 3:8-15
Luke 13:1-9

Preface of Pentecost

At the age of seven, Bede's parents brought him to the nearby monastery at Jarrow (near Durham in northeast England) for his education. There, as he later wrote, "spending all the remaining time of my life . . . I wholly applied myself to the study of Scripture, and amidst the observance of regular discipline, and the daily care of singing in the church, I always took delight in learning, teaching, and writing." Bede was ordained as a deacon at nineteen, and as a priest at thirty.

Bede was the greatest scholar of his day in the Western church. He wrote commentaries on the Scriptures based on patristic interpretations. His treatise on chronology remained standard for centuries. He also wrote on orthography, poetic meter, and especially on history. His most famous work, *The Ecclesiastical History of the English People,* remains the primary source for the period from 597 to 731, when Anglo-Saxon culture developed and Christianity triumphed.

Bede took his vocation as a historian seriously. He consulted many documents, carefully evaluated their reliability, and cited his sources. His interpretations were largely balanced and judicious. He also wrote *The History of the Abbots* (of Wearmouth and Jarrow), and a notable biography of Cuthbert, both in prose and in verse.

He died on the eve of the Ascension in 735 while dictating a vernacular translation of the Gospel of John. Around 1020, his body was removed to Durham and placed in the Lady Chapel at the west end of the cathedral nave. Together with Cuthbert, who is also buried in the cathedral, he remains beloved by the Christian community in Durham and by pilgrims from around the world.

Bede

Priest and Historian, 735

I Almighty God, who hast enriched thy church with the learning and holiness of thy servant Bede: Grant us to find in Scripture and disciplined prayer the image of thy Son our Savior Jesus Christ, and to fashion our lives according to his likeness, to the glory of thy great Name and to the benefit of thy holy church; through the same Jesus Christ our Lord. *Amen.*

II Almighty God, who has enriched your church with the learning and holiness of your servant Bede: Grant us to find in Scripture and disciplined prayer the image of your Son our Savior Jesus Christ, and to fashion our lives according to his likeness, to the glory of your great Name and to the benefit of your holy church; through the same Jesus Christ our Lord. *Amen.*

Lessons and Psalm

Ecclesiastes 12:9-14
Psalm 139:10-17
1 Corinthians 15:1-8
Matthew 13:31-33

Preface of a Saint (1)

Although Christianity had existed in Britain before the invasions of Angles and Saxons in the fifth century, Pope Gregory the Great decided in 596 to send a mission to the pagan Anglo-Saxons. He selected, from his own monastery on the Coelian hill in Rome, a group of monks, led by their prior, Augustine. They arrived in Kent in 597, carrying a silver cross and an image of Jesus Christ painted on a board, which thus became, so far as we know, "Canterbury's first icon."

King Ethelbert tolerated their presence and allowed them the use of an old church built on the east side of Canterbury, dating from the Roman occupation of Britain. Here, says Bede, they assembled "to sing the psalms, to pray, to say Mass, to preach, and to baptize." This church of St. Martin is the earliest place of Christian worship in England still in use.

Probably in 601, Ethelbert was converted, thus becoming the first Christian king in England. Around the same time, Augustine was ordained as a bishop somewhere in France and named "Archbishop of the English Nation." Thus, the see of Canterbury and its Cathedral Church of Christ owe their establishment to Augustine's mission, as does the nearby Abbey of Saints Peter and Paul, later re-named for Augustine. The "chair of St. Augustine" in Canterbury Cathedral, however, dates from the thirteenth century.

Some correspondence between Augustine and Gregory survives. One of the Pope's most famous counsels to the first Archbishop of Canterbury has to do with diversity in the young English church. Gregory writes, "If you have found customs, whether in the Roman, Gallican, or any other churches that may be more acceptable to God, I wish you to make a careful selection of them, and teach the church of the English, which is still young in the faith, whatever you can profitably learn from the various churches. For things should not be loved for the sake of places, but places for the sake of good things." This counsel bears on the search for Christian "unity in diversity" of the ecumenical movement of today.

Augustine died on May 26, probably in 605.

Augustine

First Archbishop of Canterbury, 605

I O Lord our God, who by thy Son Jesus Christ didst call thy servant Augustine to preach the Gospel to the English people: We pray that all whom thou dost call and send may do thy will, bide thy time, and see thy glory; through the same Jesus Christ our Lord, who liveth and reigneth with thee and the Holy Ghost, one God, for ever and ever. *Amen.*

II O Lord our God, who by your Son Jesus Christ called your servant Augustine to preach the Gospel to the English people: We pray that all whom you call and send may do your will, bide your time, and see your glory; through the same Jesus Christ our Lord, who lives and reigns with you and the Holy Spirit, one God, for ever and ever. *Amen.*

Lessons and Psalm

Tobit 13:1, 10-11
Psalm 66:1-8
2 Corinthians 5:17-21
Luke 5:1-11

Preface of Apostles and Ordinations

Mechthild of Magdeburg was one of the most original medieval mystics, and the first to write in the German language. She was a Beguine, a member of a group of women who lived in a quasi-monastic community but did not take formal vows. Instead, they pledged to be bound by the traditional vows of poverty, chastity, and obedience only for as long as they lived in the community. Typically, Beguines lived in a communal house and supported themselves through their own work, such as nursing, weaving, embroidery, burial of the dead, and housework.

Mechthild is known to us primarily through her work *The Flowing Light of the Godhead,* which consists of seven books written over a period of thirty years. It is clear from the work that she was familiar with courtly poetry and vernacular literature, but she does not seem to have had any formal training in theology or in Latin.

Her work alternates between passionate descriptions of her love for God and scathing denunciations of many clergy and of the laxity that she perceived in the official church of her time. Because of these criticisms, her work was at times controversial. Shortly after her death, a Latin translation of her work was produced by Dominican priests, who faithfully conveyed the majority of the text, but significantly toned down both her erotic imagery and her critiques of the vices of the clergy.

Mechthild spent the last years of her life at a Cistercian convent in Helfta, whose nuns were famous for their education and scholarship. It is clear that she felt somewhat uncomfortable in this very different environment, but the sisters seem to have warmly welcomed her and protected her from anyone who criticized her work. During the last years of her life, she became blind, and so the last chapters of her book were dictated to one of the sisters of the convent.

In one famous passage of her book, she writes:

"A fish cannot drown in water,
A bird does not fall in air.
In the fire of creation,
God doesn't vanish:
The fire brightens.
Each creature God made
must live in its own true nature;
How could I resist my nature,
That lives for oneness with God?"

Mechthild of Magdeburg

Mystic, c. 1282

I Draw the souls of thy people into thy love, O God, that, like thy servant Mechthild, we may yearn to be fully thine, for thou dost know us better than we can know ourselves; through Jesus Christ our Lord, who liveth and reigneth with thee and the Holy Ghost, one God now and for ever. *Amen.*

II Draw the souls of your people into your love, O God, that like your servant Mechthild, we may yearn to be fully yours, for you know us better than we can know ourselves; through Jesus Christ our Lord, who lives and reigns with you and the Holy Spirit, one God now and for ever. *Amen.*

Lessons and Psalm

Song of Songs 3:1-5
Psalm 71:17-23
1 Thessalonians 3:6-13
Mark 8:22-26

Preface of a Saint (1)

This feast commemorates the visit of the Blessed Virgin to her cousin Elizabeth, recorded in the Gospel according to Luke (1:39-56).

Elizabeth, who was then pregnant with John the Baptist, greeted Mary with the words, "Blessed are you among women, and blessed is the fruit of your womb." Mary broke into the song of praise and thanksgiving which we call the Magnificat, "My soul proclaims the greatness of the Lord."

In this scene, the unborn John the Baptist, the prophet who was to prepare the way of the Lord, rejoices in the presence of him whose coming he is later to herald publicly to all Israel, for the Gospel records that when Mary's greeting came to her kinswoman's ears, the babe in Elizabeth's womb leaped for joy.

The Visitation of the Blessed Virgin Mary

I Father in heaven, by whose grace the virgin mother of thy incarnate Son was blessed in bearing him, but still more blessed in keeping thy word: Grant us who honor the exaltation of her lowliness to follow the example of her devotion to thy will; through the same Jesus Christ our Lord, who liveth and reigneth with thee and the Holy Ghost, one God, for ever and ever. *Amen.*

II Father in heaven, by your grace the virgin mother of your incarnate Son was blessed in bearing him, but still more blessed in keeping your word: Grant us who honor the exaltation of her lowliness to follow the example of her devotion to your will; through Jesus Christ our Lord, who lives and reigns with you and the Holy Spirit, one God, for ever and ever. *Amen.*

Lessons and Psalm

1 Samuel 2:1-10
Psalm 113
Romans 12:9-16b
Luke 1:39-57

Preface of the Epiphany

In the middle of the second century, there came into the young Christian community a seeker for the truth, whose wide interests, noble spirit, and able mind greatly enriched it.

Justin was born into a Greek-speaking pagan family about the year 110 in Samaria, near Shechem. He was educated in Greek philosophy. Like Augustine after him, he was left restless by all this knowledge. During a walk along the beach at Ephesus, he began speaking with a stranger, who told him about Christ. "Straightway a flame was kindled in my soul," he writes, "and a love of the prophets and those who are friends of Christ possessed me." He became a Christian as a result of this encounter, and thereafter regarded Christianity as the only "safe and profitable philosophy."

Around 150, Justin moved to Rome. As philosophers did in those days, he started a school—in this case, a school of Christian philosophy—and accepted students. He also wrote. Three of his works survive: a dialogue in Platonic style with a Jew named Trypho, and two apologies in defense of the Christian faith. Justin's *First* and *Second Apologies* defend Christianity against the Greek charge of irrationality and against the Roman charge of disloyalty to the empire. These two works provide us with important insights into the developing theological ideas and liturgical practices of early Christianity.

While teaching in Rome, he engaged in a public debate with a philosopher of the Cynic school named Crescens, accusing him of ignorance and immorality. Angered, Crescens brought legal charges against him. Justin and six of his students were arrested and brought before the prefect Rusticus. As the custom was, Rusticus gave them an opportunity to renounce their faith. All steadfastly refused to do so. Justin and his students were all put to death around the year 167.

Justin

Martyr, 167

I O God, who hast given thy church wisdom and revealed to it deep and secret things: Grant that we, like thy servant Justin and in union with his prayers, may find thy Word an abiding refuge all the days of our lives; through Jesus Christ our Lord, who with thee and the Holy Ghost liveth and reigneth, one God, in glory everlasting. *Amen.*

II O God, who has given your church wisdom and revealed to it deep and secret things: Grant that we, like your servant Justin and in union with his prayers, may find your Word an abiding refuge all the days of our lives; through Jesus Christ our Lord, who with you and the Holy Spirit lives and reigns, one God, in glory everlasting. *Amen.*

Lessons and Psalm

Deuteronomy 7:7-9
Psalm 116:1-9
1 Corinthians 1:18-25
John 12:44-50

Preface of a Saint (3)

In the second century, after a brief respite, Christians in many parts of the Roman empire were once again subjected to persecution. At Lyons and Vienne, in Gaul, there were missionary centers which had drawn many Christians from Asia and Greece. They were living a devout life under the guidance of Pothinus, the elderly Bishop of Lyons, when persecution began in 177.

At first, the Christians were socially excluded from Roman homes, the public baths, and the market place; insults, stones, and blows were rained on them by pagan mobs, and Christian homes were vandalized. Soon after, the imperial officials forced Christians to come to the marketplace for harsh questioning, followed by imprisonment.

Some slaves from Christian households were tortured to extract public accusations that Christians practiced cannibalism, incest, and other perversions. These false accusations roused the mob to such a pitch of wrath that any leniency toward the imprisoned Christians was impossible. Even friendly pagans now turned against them.

The fury of the mob fell most heavily on Sanctus, a deacon; Attalus; Maturus, a recent convert; and Blandina, a slave. According to Eusebius, Blandina was so filled with power to withstand torments that her torturers gave up. "I am a Christian," she said, "and nothing vile is done among us." Sanctus was tormented with red-hot irons. The aged Pothinus, badly beaten, died soon after. Finally, the governor decided to set aside several days for a public spectacle in the amphitheater.

Eusebius depicts Blandina in particular as standing in the person of Christ: "Blandina was suspended on a stake, and exposed to be devoured by the wild beasts who should attack her. And because she appeared as if hanging on a cross, and because of her earnest prayers, she inspired the combatants with great zeal. For they looked on her in her conflict, and beheld with their outward eyes, in the form of their sister, him who was crucified for them, that he might persuade those who believe in him that every one who suffers for the glory of Christ has fellowship always with the living God."

On the final day of the spectacle, writes Eusebius, "Blandina, last of all, like a noble mother who had encouraged her children and sent them ahead victorious to the King, hastened to join them." Beaten, torn, burned with irons, she was wrapped in a net and tossed about by a wild bull. The spectators were amazed at her endurance.

Eusebius concludes: "They offered up to the Father a single wreath, but it was woven of diverse colors and flowers of all kinds. It was fitting that the noble athletes should endure a varied conflict, and win a great victory, that they might be entitled in the end to receive the crown supreme of life everlasting."

Blandina and Her Companions, the Martyrs of Lyons

177

I Almighty God, who didst give such courage and endurance to Blandina and her companions, that by their deaths many hearts were turned to thee; Grant that we, in accordance with their example, may also gladly endure all that is required of us as we witness to thee in our own day; through Jesus Christ our Lord, who liveth and reigneth with thee and the Holy Ghost, one God, now and for ever. *Amen.*

II Almighty God, who gave such courage and endurance to Blandina and her companions that by their deaths many hearts were turned to you; Grant that we, in accordance with their example, may also gladly endure all that is required of us as we witness to you in our own day; through Jesus Christ our Lord, who lives and reigns with you and the Holy Spirit, one God, now and for ever. *Amen.*

Lessons and Psalm

Jeremiah 12:1-4
Psalm 3
1 Peter 1:3-9
Mark 14:32-42

Preface of a Saint (3)

On June 3, 1886, thirty-two young men, pages of the court of King Mwanga of Buganda, were burned to death at Namugongo for their refusal to renounce Christianity. In the following months many other Christians throughout the country died by fire or spear for their faith.

These martyrdoms greatly changed the dynamic of Christian growth in Uganda. Introduced by a handful of Anglican and Roman Catholic missionaries after 1877, the Christian faith had been preached only to the immediate members of the court, by order of King Mutesa. His successor, Mwanga, became increasingly angry as he realized that the first converts put loyalty to Christ above the traditional loyalty to the king.

The martyrdoms began in 1885. Mwanga first forbade anyone to go near a Christian mission on pain of death, but when he found himself unable to cool the ardor of the converts, he resolved to wipe out Christianity.

The Namugongo martyrdoms produced a result entirely opposite to Mwanga's intentions. The example of these martyrs, who walked to their death singing hymns and praying for their enemies, so inspired many of the bystanders that they began to seek instruction from the remaining Christians. Within a few years the original handful of converts had multiplied many times and had spread far beyond the court. The martyrs had left the indelible impression that Christianity was truly African, not simply a white man's religion. Most of the missionary work was carried out by Africans rather than by white missionaries, and Christianity spread steadily.

Renewed persecution of Christians by a Muslim military dictatorship in the 1970s proved the vitality of the example of the Namugongo martyrs. Among the thousands of new martyrs, both Anglican and Roman Catholic, was Janani Luwum, Archbishop of the Anglican Church of Uganda, whose courageous ministry and death inspired not only members of his own country, but also Christians throughout the world.

The Martyrs of Uganda

1886

I O God, by whose providence the blood of the martyrs is the seed of the church: Grant that we who remember before thee the blessed martyrs of Uganda, may, like them, be steadfast in our faith in Jesus Christ, to whom they gave obedience unto death, and by their sacrifice brought forth a plentiful harvest; through Jesus Christ our Lord, who liveth and reigneth with thee and the Holy Ghost, one God, for ever and ever. *Amen.*

II O God, by whose providence the blood of the martyrs is the seed of the church: Grant that we who remember before you the blessed martyrs of Uganda, may, like them, be steadfast in our faith in Jesus Christ, to whom they gave obedience even to death, and by their sacrifice brought forth a plentiful harvest; through Jesus Christ our Lord, who lives and reigns with you and the Holy Spirit, one God, for ever and ever. *Amen.*

Lessons and Psalm

Habakkuk 2:9-14
Psalm 138
Hebrews 10:32-39
Matthew 24:9-14

Preface of Holy Week

Born in Northern Italy in 1881, Angelo Giuseppe Roncalli was trained in Roman Catholic schools from an early age. After service in the military, Roncalli was ordained as a priest in 1904. His passion for social justice for working people and for the poor was formed early and remained an important commitment of his ministry.

Roncalli often received complicated assignments. He was made an archbishop in 1925 and sent as the papal envoy to Bulgaria, where he was responsible for reducing the tensions between Eastern Rite and Latin Rite Catholics during a difficult period. Some years later, he was the papal representative to Greece and Turkey when anti-religious sentiments were running high. His leadership in Turkey anticipated on a local scale some of the developments of later decades on a universal scale: putting the liturgy and the official documents of the church in the language of the people, and opening conversations with Orthodox Christians and those of other faiths.

While serving as the papal nuncio in Turkey, Roncalli actively aided Jews fleeing Nazi persecution and encouraged priests under him to do the same. Near the end of the Second World War, he was made the papal nuncio to Paris with the task of trying to heal the divisions caused by the war. In 1953, at the age of 72, he was made a cardinal and appointed patriarch of Venice, the first time he had ever been the bishop ordinary of a diocese.

In 1958, Cardinal Roncalli was elected Pope and took the name John XXIII. After the long pontificate of Pius XII, it was widely assumed that John XXIII would be a brief "placeholder" pope of minor consequence. During the first year of his pontificate, however, he called the Second Vatican Council for the purpose of renewing and revitalizing the church. The work of the Council transformed the church of the twentieth century, not only for Roman Catholics, but for all Christians. With its emphasis on liturgical renewal, ecumenism, world peace, and social justice, the legacy of the Council continues to inspire the mission of the church among Christians of all traditions.

John XXIII died on June 3, 1963.

John XXIII (Angelo Giuseppe Roncalli)

Bishop, 1963

I God of all truth and peace, who didst raise up thy bishop John to be servant of the servants of God and bestowed on him wisdom to call for the work of renewing thy church: Grant that, following his example, we may reach out to other Christians in the love of thy Son, and labor throughout the nations of the world to kindle a desire for justice and peace; through Jesus Christ our Lord, who livest and reignest with thee and the Holy Ghost, one God, now and for ever. *Amen.*

II God of all truth and peace, who raised up your bishop John to be servant of the servants of God and bestowed on him wisdom to call for the work of renewing your church: Grant that, following his example, we may reach out to other Christians in the love of your Son, and labor throughout the nations of the world to kindle a desire for justice and peace; through Jesus Christ our Lord, who lives and reigns with you and the Holy Spirit, one God, now and for ever. *Amen.*

Lessons and Psalm

Numbers 11:10-17
Psalm 50:1-6
1 Peter 5:1-4
Luke 5:36-39

Preface of a Saint (1)

Boniface is justly called one of the "Makers of Europe." He was born at Crediton in Devonshire, England, about 675, and received the English name of Winfred. He was educated at Exeter, and later at Nursling, near Winchester, where he was professed as a monk and ordained to the priesthood.

Inspired by the examples of Willibrord and others, Winfred decided to become a missionary, and made his first Journey to Frisia (the Netherlands) in 716—a venture with little success. In 719 he started out again, but this time he first went to Rome to seek papal approval. Pope Gregory II commissioned him to work in Germany, and gave him the name of Boniface.

For the rest of his days, Boniface devoted himself to reforming, planting, and organizing churches, monasteries, and dioceses in Hesse, Thuringia, and Bavaria. Many helpers and supplies came to him from friends in England. In 722 the Pope ordained him as a bishop, ten years later made him an archbishop, and in 743 gave him a fixed see at Mainz.

The Frankish rulers also supported his work. At their invitation, he presided over reforming councils of the Frankish Church, and in 752, with the consent of Pope Zacharias, he anointed Pepin (Pippin) as King of the Franks. Thus, the way was prepared for Charlemagne, son of Pepin, and the revival of a unified Christian dominion in western Europe.

In 753 Boniface resigned his see in order to spend his last years again as a missionary in Frisia. On June 5, 754, while awaiting a group of converts for confirmation, he and his companions were murdered by a band of pagans, near Dokkum. His body was buried at Fulda, a monastery he had founded in 744, near Mainz.

Boniface

Bishop and Missionary, 754

I Pour out thy Holy Ghost, O God, upon thy church in every land, that like thy servant Boniface we might proclaim the Gospel unto all nations, that thy kingdom might be enlarged and that thy holy Name might be glorified in all the world; through Jesus Christ our Lord, who liveth and reigneth with thee and the same Holy Ghost, one God, for ever and ever. *Amen.*

II Pour out your Holy Spirit, O God, upon your church in every land, that like your servant Boniface we might proclaim the Gospel to all nations, that your kingdom might be enlarged and that your holy Name might be glorified in all the world; through Jesus Christ our Lord, who lives and reigns with you and the same Spirit, one God, for ever and ever. *Amen.*

Lessons and Psalm

Ecclesiastes 3:16-22
Psalm 115:1-8
Acts 20:17-28
Mark 8:27-30

Preface of Apostles and Ordinations

Melania was a part of the first generation of Roman aristocrats who were encouraged to embrace Christianity,and lived to see it become the official religion of the Roman Empire. She was born in 341 in Spain and moved to Rome following her marriage, where she was widowed at the age of 22. Only one of her children, a son, survived, and she gave him into the care of a guardian so that she might pursue a monastic vocation.

Leaving Rome, she went to Alexandria where she used her fortune to support monastics, teachers, and pilgrims. While in Egypt, Melania studied asceticism and theology with the desert fathers and mothers. During a purge of the monasteries by the Arian bishop of Alexandria, Melania traveled to Palestine where she would spend the majority of her life.

Arriving in Jerusalem sometime after 372, she founded two monasteries on the Mount of Olives. These communities practiced hospitality for the many pilgrims who came to the sites of Christ's passion and resurrection—all paid for by Melania. Her work of hospitality was especially significant for the many women making pilgrimage: the roads were not a safe place for travelers, and women were particularly vulnerable.

In an era when aristocratic Roman widows were expected to embrace the virtues of modesty and reserve, Melania was theologically outspoken and never shied away from expressing her passion for asceticism and for learning. She promoted theological tolerance and the unity of Christianity. A committed scholar, she studied the works of Origen, Basil the Great, and Gregory of Nazianzus. She was a teacher and spiritual director to many of the most prominent theologians and spiritual writers of her day, most notably Evagrius, whom she counseled through a spiritual crisis and then clothed as a monk. His *Letter to Melania* is one of his most profound works of ascetical and mystical theology.

Late in her life, on a visit to Rome to see her son, she inspired his daughter, also named Melania, to embrace the monastic life. Known as Melania the Younger, she followed her grandmother back to Jerusalem. Melania the Elder entered into eternal life in 410.

Melania the Elder

Monastic, 410

I Most High and Merciful God, who didst call thy servant Melania to forsake earthly comforts that she might devote herself to studying the scriptures and to welcoming the poor: Instruct us in the ways of poverty and the grace of hospitality, that we might comfort those who have no place to rest and teach the way of thy love; through Jesus Christ our Lord. *Amen.*

II Most High and Merciful God, who called your servant Melania to forsake earthly comforts in order to devote herself to studying the scriptures and to welcoming the poor: Instruct us in the ways of poverty and the grace of hospitality, that we might comfort those who have no place to rest and teach the way of your love; through Jesus Christ our Lord. *Amen.*

Lessons and Psalm

Exodus 4:24-26
Psalm 119:113-120
Romans 8:18-25
Mark 8:14-21

Preface of a Saint (3)

Columba was born in Ireland in 521, and early in life showed scholarly and pastoral ability. He entered the monastic life, and almost immediately set forth on missionary travels. Even before ordination as a priest in 551, he had founded monasteries at Derry and Durrow.

Twelve years after his ordination, Columba and a dozen companions set out for northern Britain, where the Picts were still generally unaware of Christianity. Columba was kindly received, and allowed to preach, convert, and baptize. He was also given possession of the island of Iona, where, according to legend, his tiny boat had washed ashore. Here he founded the celebrated monastery which became the center for the conversion of the Picts. From Iona, also, his disciples went out to found other monasteries, which, in turn, became centers of missionary activity.

Columba made long journeys through the Highlands, as far as Aberdeen. He often returned to Ireland to attend synods, and thus established Iona as a link between Irish and Pictish Christians. For thirty years, he evangelized, studied, wrote, and governed his monastery at Iona. He supervised his monks in their work in the fields and workrooms, in their daily worship and Sunday Eucharist, and in their study and teaching.

He died peacefully in 597 while working on a copy of the Psalter. He had put down his pen, rested a few hours, and at Matins was found dead before the altar, a smile on his face. He is quoted by his biographer Adamnan as having said, "This day is called in the sacred Scriptures a day of rest, and truly to me it will be such, for it is the last of my life and I shall enter into rest after the fatigues of my labors."

Today the abbey at Iona is home to the Iona Community, an ecumenical retreat center that has shaped the spirituality of many Christians since it was founded in 1938, and which continues as an important place of pilgrimage and spiritual renewal to this day.

Columba of Iona

Monastic, 597

I O God, who by the preaching of thy servant Columba didst cause the light of the Gospel to shine in Scotland: Grant, we beseech thee that, having his life and labors in remembrance, we may follow the example of his zeal and patience; through Jesus Christ our Lord, who liveth and reigneth with thee and the Holy Ghost, one God, for ever and ever. *Amen.*

II O God, who by the preaching of your servant Columba caused the light of the Gospel to shine in Scotland: Grant, we pray, that, remembering his life and labors, we may follow the example of his zeal and patience; through Jesus Christ our Lord, who lives and reigns with you and the Holy Spirit, one God, for ever and ever. *Amen.*

Lessons and Psalm

Wisdom 19:18-22
Psalm 111
1 Corinthians 3:16-23
Luke 10:17-20

Preface of Apostles and Ordinations

Ephrem of Nisibis was a teacher, poet, orator, and defender of the faith, and the foremost Christian theologian who wrote in the Syriac language. The Syrians called him "The Harp of the Holy Spirit," and his hymns still enrich the liturgies of the Syriac churches. Ephrem was one whose writings were influential in the development of Christian doctrine. Jerome writes: "I have read in Greek a volume of his on the Holy Spirit, and though it was only a translation, I recognized therein the sublime genius of the man."

Ephrem was born at Nisibis in Mesopotamia. At eighteen, he was baptized by James, Bishop of Nisibis. It is believed that Ephrem accompanied James to the famous Council of Nicaea in 325 and served as his secretary, deacon, and theological assistant. He lived at Nisibis until 363, when the Persians captured the city and drove out the Christians.

Ephrem retired to a cave in the hills above the city of Edessa. There he wrote most of his spiritual works. Discovering that hymns could be of great value in support of the Christian faith, he opposed Gnostic hymns with his own, sung by choirs of women. An example is "From God Christ's deity came forth" (*The Hymnal 1982,* #443). This establishment of female choirs gave an important liturgical role to women within the early Syriac church, and the strong theological content of the hymns meant that women were also being educated in theology. Catechizing women was considered to be the most effective way of teaching the faith because of the influence that they would likely have on their children. Therefore, women's education was a high priority.

Ephrem's homilies and poems often employ vivid and memorable imagery. In describing the death and resurrection of Christ in his *Homily on Our Lord,* he wrote: "When Death came confidently as usual, to feed on mortal fruit, Life, the killer of Death, was lying in wait . . . Because of one thing which it could not eat, Death had to give back everything inside that it had eaten, for when a person's stomach is upset, he vomits out what had agreed with him as well as what disagrees with him. Thus Death's stomach became upset, and when it vomited out the Medicine of Life which had soured it, it vomited out with Him all those whom it had been pleased to swallow."

During a famine in 372–373, Ephrem distributed food and money to the poor and organized a sort of ambulance service for the sick. He died of exhaustion, brought on by his long hours of relief work.

Of his writings, there remain dozens of poems and hymns, commentaries on the Old and New Testaments, and numerous homilies. In his commentary on the Passion, he wrote: "No one has seen or shall see the things which you have seen. The Lord himself has become the altar, priest, and bread, and the chalice of salvation. He alone suffices for all, yet none suffices for him. He is Altar and Lamb, victim and sacrifice, priest as well as food."

Ephrem of Nisibis

Deacon and Poet, 373

I Pour out upon us, O Lord, that same Spirit by which thy deacon Ephrem declared the mysteries of faith in sacred song; that, with gladdened hearts, we too might proclaim the riches of thy glory; through Jesus Christ our Lord, who liveth and reigneth with thee and the Holy Ghost, one God, now and for ever. *Amen.*

II Pour out upon us, O Lord, that same Spirit by which your deacon Ephrem declared the mysteries of faith in sacred song; that, with gladdened hearts, we too might proclaim the riches of your glory; through Jesus Christ our Lord, who lives and reigns with you and the Holy Spirit, one God, now and for ever. *Amen.*

Lessons and Psalm

Job 38:1-11
Psalm 68:11-18
Ephesians 3:8-12
Mark 9:38-41

Preface of a Saint (1)

"Joseph, a Levite born in Cyprus, whom the apostles called Barnabas (which means son of encouragement), sold a field he owned, brought the money, and turned it over to the apostles" (Acts 4:36-37). This first reference in the New Testament to Barnabas introduces one whose missionary efforts would cause him to be called, like the Twelve, an apostle.

As a Jew of the diaspora, Barnabas had much in common with Paul. When Paul came to Jerusalem after his conversion, the disciples were afraid to receive him. It was Barnabas who brought Paul to the apostles, and declared to them how, on the road to Damascus, Paul had seen the Lord, and had preached boldly in the name of Jesus (Acts 9:27). Later, Barnabas, having settled in Antioch, sent for Paul to join him in leading the Christian church in that city.

Barnabas and Paul were sent by the disciples in Antioch to carry famine relief to the church in Jerusalem. Upon their return, the church in Antioch sent them on their first missionary journey beginning at Cyprus. At Lystra in Asia Minor, the people took them to be gods, supposing the eloquent Paul to be Mercury, the messenger of the gods, and Barnabas to be Jupiter, the chief of the gods, a testimony to the commanding presence of Barnabas.

The association of Barnabas and Paul was broken, after their journey, by a disagreement about Mark, who had left the mission to return to Jerusalem. After attending the Council of Jerusalem with Barnabas, Paul made a return visit to the churches that he and Barnabas had founded in Asia Minor. Barnabas and Mark went to Cyprus, where Barnabas is traditionally honored as the founder of the church. Tradition has it that he was martyred at Salamis in Cyprus.

Saint Barnabas the Apostle

I Grant, O God, that we may follow the example of thy faithful servant Barnabas, who, seeking not his own renown but the well-being of thy church, gave generously of his life and substance for the relief of the poor and the spread of the Gospel; through Jesus Christ our Lord, who liveth and reigneth with thee and the Holy Ghost, one God, for ever and ever. *Amen.*

II Grant, O God, that we may follow the example of your faithful servant Barnabas, who, seeking not his own renown but the well-being of your church, gave generously of his life and substance for the relief of the poor and the spread of the Gospel; through Jesus Christ our Lord, who lives and reigns with you and the Holy Spirit, one God, for ever and ever. *Amen.*

Lessons and Psalm

Isaiah 42:5-12
Psalm 112
Acts 11:19-30; 13:1-3
Matthew 10:7-16

Preface of Apostles and Ordinations

John Johnson Enmegahbowh, an Odawa (Ottawa) Indian from Canada, born in 1807, was raised both in the Midewiwin traditional healing way of his grandfather and the Christian religion of his mother. He came into the United States as a Methodist missionary in 1832. At one point Enmegahbowh attempted to abandon missionary work and return to Canada, but the boat was turned back by storms on Lake Superior, providing him a vision: "Here Mr. Jonah came before me and said, 'Ah, my friend Enmegahbowh, I know you. You are a fugitive. You have sinned and disobeyed God. Instead of going to the city of Nineveh, where God sent you to spread his word to the people, you started to go, and then turned aside. You are now on your way to the city of Tarsish . . .'"

Enmegahbowh invited James Lloyd Breck to Gull Lake, where together they founded St. Columba's Mission in 1852. The mission was later moved to White Earth, where Enmegahbowh served until his death in 1902. Unwelcome for a time among some Ojibway groups because he warned the community at Fort Ripley about the 1862 uprising, Enmegahbowh was consistent as a man of peace, inspiring the Waubanaquot (Chief White Cloud) mission, which obtained a lasting peace between the Ojibway and the Dakota peoples.

Enmegahbowh ("The one who stands before his people") is the first recognized Native American priest in the Episcopal Church. He was ordained as a deacon in 1859 and as a priest in the cathedral at Faribault in 1867.

Enmegahbowh helped train many others to serve as deacons throughout northern Minnesota. The powerful tradition of Ojibway hymn singing is a living testimony to their ministry. His understanding of Native tradition enabled him to enculturate Christianity in the language and traditions of the Ojibway. He tirelessly traveled throughout Minnesota and beyond, actively participating in the development of mission strategy and policy for the Episcopal Church.

Enmegahbowh died at the White Earth Indian Reservation in northern Minnesota on June 12, 1902.

Enmegahbowh

Priest and Missionary, 1902

I Almighty God, who didst lead thy pilgrim people of old by fire and cloud: Grant that the ministers of thy church, following the example of thy servant Enmegahbowh, may lead thy people with fiery zeal and gentle humility; through Jesus Christ, who liveth and reigneth with thee in the unity of the Holy Ghost, one God, now and for ever. *Amen.*

II Almighty God, who led your pilgrim people of old by fire and cloud: Grant that the ministers of your church, following the example of your servant Enmegahbowh, may lead your people with fiery zeal and gentle humility; through Jesus Christ, who lives and reigns with you in the unity of the Holy Spirit, one God, now and for ever. *Amen.*

Lessons and Psalm

Isaiah 52:1-6
Psalm 129
1 Peter 5:1-4
Luke 6:17-23

Preface of a Saint (1)

The first Book of Common Prayer came into use on the Day of Pentecost, June 9, 1549, in the second year of the reign of King Edward VI. From it have descended all subsequent editions and revisions of the Book in the Churches of the Anglican Communion.

Though prepared by a commission of learned bishops and priests, the format, substance, and style of the Prayer Book were primarily the work of Thomas Cranmer, Archbishop of Canterbury, 1533–1556. The principal sources employed in its compilation were the medieval Latin service books of the Use of Sarum (Salisbury), with enrichments from the Greek liturgies, certain ancient Gallican rites, the vernacular German forms prepared by Luther, and a revised Latin liturgy of the reforming Archbishop Hermann of Cologne. The Psalter and other biblical passages were drawn from the English "Great Bible" authorized by King Henry VIII in 1539, and the Litany was taken from the English form issued as early as 1544.

The originality of the Prayer Book, apart from the felicitous translations and paraphrases of the old Latin forms, lay in its simplification of the complicated liturgical usages of the medieval church, so that it was suitable for use by the laity as well as by the clergy. The Book thus became both a manual of common worship for Anglicans and a primary resource for their personal spirituality.

The First Book of Common Prayer

1549

I Almighty and everliving God, who through the Book of Common Prayer didst restore the language of the people in the prayers of thy church: Make us always thankful for this heritage; and help us so to pray in the Spirit and with understanding, that we may worthily magnify thy holy Name; through Jesus Christ our Lord, who liveth and reigneth with thee and the Holy Ghost, one God, for ever and ever. *Amen.*

II Almighty and everliving God, who through the Book of Common Prayer restored the language of the people in the prayers of your church: Make us always thankful for this heritage; and help us so to pray in the Spirit and with understanding, that we may worthily magnify your holy Name; through Jesus Christ our Lord, who lives and reigns with you and the Holy Spirit, one God, for ever and ever. *Amen.*

Lessons and Psalm

1 Kings 8:54-61
Psalm 103:8-12
Acts 2:38-42
Luke 18:16-18

Preface of Pentecost

Basil was born about 329, in Caesarea of Cappadocia, into a Christian family of wealth and distinction. Educated in classical Hellenism, Basil might have continued in academic life, had it not been for the death of a beloved younger brother and the faith of his sister, Macrina. He was baptized at the age of twenty-eight, and ordained as a deacon soon after.

Macrina had founded a monastic community at the family home in Annesi. Inspired by her example, Basil made a journey to study the life of anchorites in Egypt and elsewhere. In 358 he returned to Cappadocia and founded the first monastery for men at Ibora. Assisted by Gregory of Nazianzus, he compiled *The Longer* and *Shorter Rules,* which transformed the solitary anchorites into a disciplined community of prayer and work. These *Rules* became the foundation for all Orthodox Christian monastic discipline.

Basil was ordained as a priest in 364. During the conflict between the Arians (supported by an Arian Emperor) and Nicene Christians, Basil was elected Bishop of Caesarea, Metropolitan of Cappadocia, and Exarch of Pontus. He was relentless in his efforts to restore the faith and discipline of the clergy, and in defense of the Nicene faith. When the Emperor Valens sought to undercut Basil's power by dividing the See of Cappadocia, Basil forced his younger brother Gregory to become Bishop of Nyssa.

Basil also argued forcefully for the full divinity of the Holy Spirit. In his treatise, *On the Holy Spirit,* Basil maintained that both the language of Scripture and the faith of the church require that the same honor, glory, and worship is to be paid to the Spirit as to the Father and the Son. It was entirely proper, he asserted, to adore God in liturgical prayer, not only with the traditional words, "Glory be to the Father through the Son in the unity of the Holy Spirit"; but also with the formula, "Glory be to the Father with the Son together with the Holy Spirit."

Basil was also concerned about the poor and, when he died, he willed to Caesarea a complete new town, built on his estate, with housing, a hospital and staff, a church for the poor, and a hospice for travelers. He died at the age of fifty, in 379, just two years before the Second Ecumenical Council, which affirmed the Nicene faith.

Basil of Caesarea

Bishop and Theologian, 379

I Almighty God, who hast revealed to thy church thine eternal Being of glorious majesty and perfect love as one God in Trinity of Persons: Give us grace that, like thy bishop Basil of Caesarea, we may continue steadfastly in the confession of this faith and remain constant in our worship of thee, Father, Son, and Holy Ghost; ever one God, for ever and ever. *Amen.*

II Almighty God, who has revealed to your church your eternal Being of glorious majesty and perfect love as one God in Trinity of Persons: Give us grace that, like your bishop Basil of Caesarea, we may continue steadfastly in the confession of this faith and remain constant in our worship of you, Father, Son, and Holy Spirit; ever one God, for ever and ever. *Amen.*

Lessons and Psalm

Ezekiel 22:23-30
Psalm 139:1-9
1 Corinthians 2:6-13
Luke 10:21-24

Preface of Trinity Sunday

The only child of a prominent barrister and his wife, Evelyn Underhill was born in Wolverhampton, England, on December 6, 1875, and grew up in London. She was educated there and in a girls' school in Folkestone, where she was confirmed in the Church of England. She had little other formal religious training, but her spiritual curiosity was naturally lively, and she read widely, developing quite early a deep appreciation for mysticism. At sixteen, she began a lifelong devotion to writing.

Evelyn had few childhood companions, but one of them, Hubert Stuart Moore, she eventually married. Other friends, made later, included Laurence Housman, Maurice Hewlett, and Sarah Bernhardt. Closest of all were Ethel Ross Barker, a devout Roman Catholic, and Baron Friedrich von Hügel, who became her spiritual director.

In the 1890s, Evelyn began annual visits to the European continent, and especially to Italy. There she became influenced by the paintings of the Italian masters and by the Roman Catholic Church. She spent nearly fifteen years wrestling painfully with the idea of converting to Roman Catholicism, but in the end she discerned that she was called to remain as an Anglican.

In 1921, Evelyn Underhill became reconciled to her Anglican roots, while remaining what she called a "Catholic Christian." She continued with her life of reading, writing, meditation, and prayer. She had already published her first great spiritual work, *Mysticism*. This was followed by many other books, culminating in her most widely read and studied book, *Worship* (1937).

Evelyn Underhill's most valuable contribution to spiritual literature must surely be her conviction that the mystical life is not only open to a saintly few, but to anyone who cares to nurture it and weave it into everyday experience, and also (at the time, a startling idea) that modern psychological theories and discoveries, far from hindering or negating spirituality, can actually enhance and transform it. In *Mysticism,* she writes: "We are, then, one and all the kindred of the mystics; and it is by dwelling upon this kinship, by interpreting—so far as we may—their great declarations in the light of our little experience, that we shall learn to understand them best. Strange and far away though they seem, they are not cut off from us by some impassable abyss. They belong to us. They are our brethren; the giants, the heroes of our race. As the achievement of genius belongs not to itself only, but also to the society that brought it forth; as theology declares that the merits of the saints avail for all; so, because of the solidarity of the human family, the supernal accomplishment of the mystics is ours also."

Evelyn Underhill's writings proved appealing to many, resulting in a large international circle of friends and disciples, making her much in demand as a lecturer and retreat director. She died, at age 65, on June 15, 1941.

Evelyn Underhill

Mystic and Writer, 1941

I O God, Origin, Sustainer, and End of all creatures: Grant that thy church, taught by thy servant Evelyn Underhill, may continually offer to thee all glory and thanksgiving, and attain with thy saints to the blessed hope of everlasting life, which thou hast promised us by our Savior Jesus Christ; who with thee and the Holy Ghost liveth and reigneth, one God, now and for ever. *Amen.*

II O God, Origin, Sustainer, and End of all creatures: Grant that your church, taught by your servant Evelyn Underhill, may continually offer to you all glory and thanksgiving, and attain with your saints to the blessed hope of everlasting life, which you have promised us by our Savior Jesus Christ; who with you and the Holy Spirit lives and reigns, one God, now and for ever. *Amen.*

Lessons and Psalm

2 Kings 22:14-20
Psalm 96:7-13
1 Corinthians 4:1-5
John 4:19-24

Preface of a Saint (1)

Joseph Butler was born in Berkshire in 1692, into a Presbyterian family. His early education was in dissenting academies, but in his early twenties he became an Anglican. He entered Oxford in 1715 and was ordained in 1718.

Butler distinguished himself as a preacher while serving Rolls Chapel, Chancery Lane, London, and then went on to serve several parishes before being appointed Bishop of Bristol in 1738. He declined the primacy of Canterbury, but accepted translation to Durham in 1750. He died on June 16, 1752, in Bath, and his body was entombed in Bristol Cathedral.

Butler's importance rests chiefly on his acute apology for orthodox Christianity against the Deistic thought prevalent in England in his time in his work *The Analogy of Religion, Natural and Revealed, to the Constitution and Course of Nature,* 1736. He maintained the "reasonable probability" of Christianity, with action upon that probability as a basis for faith.

Butler's was a rational exposition of the faith grounded in deep personal piety, a worthy counterpoint to the enthusiasm of the Wesleyan revival of the same period.

Joseph Butler

Bishop and Theologian, 1752

I O God, who dost raise up scholars for thy church in every generation; we praise thee for the wisdom and insight granted to thy bishop and theologian Joseph Butler, and pray that thy church may never be destitute of such gifts; through Jesus Christ our Lord, who with thee and the Holy Ghost liveth and reigneth, one God, for ever and ever. *Amen.*

II O God, who raises up scholars for your church in every generation; we praise you for the wisdom and insight granted to your bishop and theologian Joseph Butler, and pray that your church may never be destitute of such gifts; through Jesus Christ our Lord, who with you and the Holy Spirit lives and reigns, one God, for ever and ever. *Amen.*

Lessons and Psalm

Ecclesiastes 1:12-18
Psalm 134
Acts 13:38-44
Luke 10:25-28

Preface of a Saint (1)

Marina was born in present-day Lebanon, in the fifth century. She was the only child of her parents, and her mother died when she was still a young girl. Her father refused to remarry, and instead raised her himself until she was a teenager. At that point, he hoped to find her a husband and then retire to live the life of a monk.

Marina, however, rejected this plan, saying: "Why would you save your own soul at the cost of destroying mine?" Instead, she shaved off her hair and exchanged her clothing for men's clothes. When her father saw her determination, he relented. Selling all of their possessions, they went together to the monastic settlement in the Qadisha Valley, where he introduced her as his son "Marinos."

After ten years of living the monastic life together, the father died. Marinos continued to live at the monastery without revealing his identity to anyone. In time, however, a local girl who had become pregnant accused Marinos of fathering her child. Rather than respond to this accusation with the obvious denial, Marinos accepted responsibility rather than reveal his secret or subject the girl to further reproach. When the child was born, the infant was given to Marinos to raise at the monastery, and he accepted the boy as though he were truly his own son, and bore patiently all of the scorn and abuse that the other monks heaped upon him for his alleged violation of his monastic vows.

After many years Marinos also died, and it was only when the monks went to prepare the body for burial that they discovered it was actually the body of a woman, who had obviously been innocent of the accusation of having fathered a child. The monks and villagers lamented their false accusation and judgment, and after their repentance many miracles were performed at Marina's tomb.

While some aspects of this story may be legendary, there are numerous accounts in early Christianity of women disguising themselves as men and entering male monasteries, and this is one of the examples that is considered to be the most historically reliable.

Marina/Marinos is particularly venerated today in Lebanon, Cyprus, and Italy, usually under the name of "Marina the Monk."

Marina the Monk

Monastic, fifth century

I Give us grace, Lord God, to refrain from judgments about the sins of others; that, like thy servant Marina the Monk, we may hold fast to the path of discipleship in the midst of unjust judgments; through Jesus Christ our Lord, who liveth and reigneth with thee and the Holy Ghost, one God, for ever and ever. *Amen.*

II Give us grace, Lord God, to refrain from judgments about the sins of others; that, like your servant Marina the Monk, we may hold fast to the path of discipleship in the midst of unjust judgments; through Jesus Christ our Lord who lives and reigns with you and the Holy Spirit, one God, for ever and ever. *Amen.*

Lessons and Psalm

Susanna 34-46
Psalm 148
James 1:19-27
Luke 18:18-30

Preface of a Saint (2)

Bernard Mizeki was born around the year 1861 in Portuguese East Africa (Mozambique). In his early teens, he left his native land and came to Cape Town, South Africa, where he was befriended by Anglican missionaries. He was baptized on March 9, 1886, and trained as a catechist, becoming a much-beloved teacher.

In 1891, Bernard Mizeki volunteered to serve as catechist for the pioneer mission in Mashonaland (a region in what is now northern Zimbabwe) and was stationed at Nhowe. On June 18, 1896, during an uprising of the native people against the Europeans and their African friends, Bernard was marked out especially. Though warned to flee, he would not desert his converts at the mission station. He was stabbed to death, but his body was never found, and the exact site of his burial is unknown.

A shrine near Bernard's place of martyrdom attracts many pilgrims today, and the Anglican Churches of Central and Southern Africa honor him as their primary native martyr and witness.

Bernard Mizeki

Martyr, 1896

I Almighty and everlasting God, who kindled the flame of thy love in the heart of thy holy martyr Bernard Mizeki: Grant unto us thy servants a like faith and power of love, that we, who rejoice in his triumph, may profit by his example; through Jesus Christ our Lord, who liveth and reigneth with thee and the Holy Ghost, one God, for ever and ever. *Amen.*

II Almighty and everlasting God, who kindled the flame of your love in the heart of your holy martyr Bernard Mizeki: Grant unto us your servants a like faith and power of love, that we, who rejoice in his triumph, may profit by his example; through Jesus Christ our Lord, who lives and reigns with you and the Holy Spirit, one God, for ever and ever. *Amen.*

Lessons and Psalm

Nehemiah 6:6-11
Psalm 70
Revelation 7:13-17
Luke 12:1-12

Preface of Holy Week

Adelaide Teague Case was born in St. Louis, Missouri, on January 10, 1887, but her family soon moved to New York City. She received her undergraduate education at Bryn Mawr College and her graduate degrees from Columbia University. By the time she had completed her doctorate, a position had been created for her on the faculty of the Teachers' College at Columbia, where she rose to the status of full professor and head of the department of religious education. She is remembered for advocating a child-centered rather than teacher-centered approach to education.

In 1941, when her professional accomplishments were at their height, the Episcopal Theological School in Cambridge, Massachusetts, was able to convince her to leave her distinguished and comfortable position at Columbia, and she was appointed Professor of Christian Education. Although other women had taught occasional courses in the seminaries of the church, Case was the first to take her place as a full-time faculty member at the rank of Professor.

Case identified with the liberal Catholic tradition in Anglicanism. This is reflected in her first book, *Liberal Christianity and Religious Education,* in which she emphasized teaching children to engage in reasonable inquiry into their faith. Case was also active in the Religious Education Association, the Episcopal Pacifist Fellowship, and the Women's Auxiliary of the Episcopal Church. From 1946 to 1948, she served on the National Council of the Episcopal Church. Case was a proponent of women's ordination and a frequent preacher in the chapel at ETS. She continued to teach at ETS until her death on June 19, 1948, in Boston.

Students and faculty colleagues remember her contagious faith in Christ, her deep sense of humanity, and her seemingly boundless compassion. Although she carried herself with style and grace, Case had struggled with health problems her entire life, but those who knew her testify to the fact that in spite of those challenges she was spirited, energetic, and fully devoted to her work. It was often said of her that she was a true believer in Christ, and that one saw Christ living in and through her.

Case believed that the point of practicing the Christian faith was to make a difference in the world. As an advocate for peace, she believed that Christianity had a special vocation to call people into transformed, reconciled relationships for the sake of the wholeness of the human family. She is said to have discovered these things not in theology or educational theory, but in a life of common prayer and faithful eucharistic practice.

Adelaide Teague Case

Educator, 1948

I Almighty and everlasting God, who dost raise up educators and teachers of the faith in every generation of thy church: Grant that following the example of thy servant Adelaide Teague Case, we might be bold to proclaim the reconciling power of Christ's love in our own generation. Through the same Jesus Christ our Lord, who liveth and reigneth with thee and the Holy Ghost, one God, in glory everlasting. *Amen.*

II Almighty and everlasting God, who raises up educators and teachers of the faith in every generation of your church: Grant that following the example of your servant Adelaide Teague Case, we might be bold to proclaim the reconciling power of Christ's love in our own generation. Through the same Jesus Christ our Lord, who lives and reigns with you and the Holy Spirit, one God, in glory everlasting. *Amen.*

Lessons and Psalm

Proverbs 4:1-9
Psalm 134
Hebrews 5:11—6:1
Mark 4:21-25

Preface of a Saint (1)

Alban is the earliest Christian in Britain who is known by name and, according to tradition, the first British martyr. He was a soldier in the Roman army, stationed at Verulamium, a city about twenty miles northeast of London, which is now called St. Albans.

Alban gave shelter to a Christian priest who was fleeing from persecution and was converted by him. When officers came to Alban's house, he dressed himself in the garments of the priest and gave himself up. Alban was tortured and martyred in place of the priest, on the hilltop where the Cathedral of St. Albans now stands. The traditional date of his martyrdom is 303 or 304, although the dates 209 and 251 have also been suggested by some scholars.

The site of Alban's martyrdom soon became a shrine. King Offa of Mercia established a monastery there about the year 793, and, in the high Middle Ages, St. Albans ranked as the premier abbey in England.

Bede gives this account of Alban's trial: "When Alban was brought in, the judge happened to be standing before an altar, offering sacrifice to demons . . . 'What is your family and race?' demanded the judge. 'How does my family concern you?' replied Alban; 'If you wish to know the truth about my religion, know that I am a Christian and am ready to do a Christian's duty.' 'I demand to know your name,' insisted the judge. 'Tell me at once.' 'My parents named me Alban,' he answered, 'and I worship and adore the living and true God, who created all things.'"

Alban

Martyr, c. 304

I Almighty God, by whose grace and power thy holy martyr Alban triumphed over suffering and was faithful even unto death: Grant us, who now remember him in thanksgiving, to be so faithful in our witness to thee in this world that we may receive with him the crown of life; through Jesus Christ our Lord, who liveth and reigneth with thee and the Holy Ghost, one God, for ever and ever. *Amen.*

II Almighty God, by whose grace and power your holy martyr Alban triumphed over suffering and was faithful even unto death: Grant us, who now remember him in thanksgiving, to be so faithful in our witness to you in this world that we may receive with him the crown of life; through Jesus Christ our Lord, who lives and reigns with you and the Holy Spirit, one God, for ever and ever. *Amen.*

Lessons and Psalm

Wisdom 3:1-9
Psalm 125
1 John 3:13-16
Matthew 10:34-42

Preface of a Saint (3)

John the Baptist, the prophet, and forerunner of Jesus, was the son of elderly parents, Elizabeth and Zechariah, and according to the Gospel of Luke, he was related to Jesus on his mother's side. His birth is celebrated six months before Christmas Day, since, according to Luke, Elizabeth became pregnant six months before the angel Gabriel appeared to Mary.

John figures prominently in all four Gospels, but the account of his birth is given only in the Gospel according to Luke. His father, Zechariah, a priest of the Temple at Jerusalem, was struck speechless because he doubted a vision foretelling John's birth. When his speech was restored, Zechariah uttered a canticle of praise, the Benedictus, which is one of the canticles used in the Daily Office, traditionally at Morning Prayer.

John lived ascetically in the desert. He was clothed with camel's hair, with a leather belt, and ate locusts and wild honey. He preached repentance, and called upon people to prepare for the coming of the Kingdom and of the Messiah, baptizing his followers to signify their repentance and new life. Jesus himself was baptized by John in the Jordan River.

John is remembered during Advent as a prophet, and at Epiphany as the baptizer of Jesus. The Gospel according to John quotes the Baptist as saying to his followers that Jesus is the Lamb of God, and prophesying, "He must increase, but I must decrease" (John 3:30).

The Nativity of Saint John the Baptist

I Almighty God, by whose providence thy servant John the Baptist was wonderfully born, and sent to prepare the way of thy Son our Savior by preaching repentance: Make us so to follow his doctrine and holy life, that we may truly repent according to his preaching; and after his example constantly speak the truth, boldly rebuke vice, and patiently suffer for the truth's sake; through the same thy Son Jesus Christ our Lord, who liveth and reigneth with thee and the Holy Ghost, one God, for ever and ever. *Amen.*

II Almighty God, by whose providence your servant John the Baptist was wonderfully born, and sent to prepare the way of your Son our Savior by preaching repentance: Make us so to follow his teaching and holy life, that we may truly repent according to his preaching; and, following his example, constantly speak the truth, boldly rebuke vice, and patiently suffer for the truth's sake; through Jesus Christ your Son our Lord, who lives and reigns with you and the Holy Spirit, one God, for ever and ever. *Amen.*

Lessons and Psalm

Isaiah 40:1-11
Psalm 85 *or* 85:7-13
Acts 13:14b-26
Luke 1:57-80

Preface of Advent

Isabel Hapgood, a lifelong and faithful Episcopalian, was a force behind ecumenical relations between the Episcopal Church and Russian Orthodoxy in the United States around the turn of the twentieth century. Born in Massachusetts on November 21, 1851, Hapgood was a superior student with a particular talent for the study of languages. In addition to the standard fare of the time—Latin and French—she also mastered most of the Romance and Germanic languages of Europe, as well as Russian, Polish, and Church Slavonic. She possessed the particular gift of being able to translate the subtleties of Russian into equally nuanced English. Her translations made the works of Dostoyevsky, Tolstoy, Gorky, and Chekhov, among others, available to English readers.

From 1887 until 1889, Hapgood traveled extensively in Russia, cementing her lifelong love of Russia, its language and culture, and particularly the Russian Orthodox Church. She would make return visits to Russia almost every year for the rest of her life.

Her love of Russian Orthodoxy and its Divine Liturgy led her to seek the permission of the hierarchy to translate the rites into English. Hapgood's already established reputation as a sensitive translator certainly contributed, but in the meantime she had developed close relationships with Russian clergy and musicians at all levels. The work, *Service Book of the Holy Orthodox-Catholic Church,* took eleven years to complete. It received support of the Russian Orthodox bishops in North America, particularly Archbishop Tikhon, who was later to give Hapgood's work a second blessing when he became Patriarch of Moscow.

Isabel Florence Hapgood is faithfully remembered among Russian Orthodox Christians in North America for her contribution to their common life, her desire for closer relations between Orthodox and Anglican Christians, and for her making the liturgical treasures of their tradition available to the English-speaking world.

She died on June 26, 1928.

Isabel Florence Hapgood

Ecumenist, 1928

I Teach thy divided church, O God, so to follow the example of thy servant Isabel Florence Hapgood that we might look upon one another with a holy envy, to honor whatever is good and right in our separate traditions, and to continually seek the unity that thou desirest for all thy people. We ask this in the name of Jesus Christ our Lord, who didst pray that his church might be one. *Amen.*

II Teach your divided church, O God, so to follow the example of your servant Isabel Florence Hapgood that we might look upon one another with a holy envy, to honor whatever is good and right in our separate traditions, and to continually seek the unity that you desire for all your people. We ask this in the name of Jesus Christ our Lord, who prayed that his church might be one. *Amen.*

Lessons and Psalm

Numbers 27:1-11
Psalm 24
Revelation 5:8-14
John 15:5-8

Preface of All Saints

There is considerable doubt about the year of Irenaeus' birth; estimates vary from 97 to 160. According to tradition, he learned the Christian faith in Ephesus at the feet of Polycarp, who in turn had known John the Evangelist. Some years before 177, probably while Irenaeus was still a teenager, he carried the tradition of Christianity to Lyons in southern France.

The year 177 brought hardship to the mission in Gaul. Persecution broke out, and theological divisions within the fledgling Christian community threatened to engulf the church. Irenaeus, by now a priest, was sent to Rome to mediate the dispute regarding Montanism, which the Bishop of Rome, Eleutherus, seemed to embrace. While Irenaeus was on this mission, the aged Bishop of Lyons, Pothinus, died in prison during a local persecution. When Irenaeus returned to Lyons, he was elected bishop to succeed Pothinus.

Irenaeus' enduring fame rests mainly on a large treatise, entitled *The Refutation and Overthrow of Gnosis, Falsely So-Called,* usually shortened to *Against Heresies*. In it, Irenaeus describes the major Gnostic systems, thoroughly, clearly, and often with biting humor. It is one of our chief sources of knowledge about Gnosticism. He also makes a case for orthodox Christianity which has become a classic, resting heavily on Scripture and on the continuity between the teaching of the Apostles and the teaching of bishops, generation after generation. Against the Gnostics, who despised the flesh and exalted the spirit, he stressed two doctrines: that of creation being good, and that of the resurrection of the body. He famously wrote that "the glory of God is a human being fully alive, and full human life consists in the vision of God."

A late and uncertain tradition claims that he suffered martyrdom around the year 202.

Irenaeus of Lyon

Bishop and Theologian, c. 202

I Almighty God, who didst strengthen thy servant Irenaeus to defend thy truth against every blast of vain doctrine: Keep us, we pray, steadfast in thy true religion, that in constancy and peace we may walk in the way that leads to eternal life; through Jesus Christ our Lord, who liveth and reigneth with thee and the Holy Ghost, one God, now and for ever. *Amen.*

II Almighty God, who strengthened your servant Irenaeus to defend thy truth against every blast of vain doctrine: Keep us, we pray, steadfast in your true religion, that in constancy and peace we may walk in the way that leads to eternal life; through Jesus Christ our Lord, who lives and reigns with you and the Holy Spirit, one God, now and for ever. *Amen.*

Lessons and Psalm

Proverbs 8:6-11
Psalm 8
2 Timothy 2:22-26
Luke 11:33-36

Preface of the Epiphany

Peter and Paul, the two greatest leaders of the early church, are also commemorated separately, Peter on January 18, for his confession of Jesus as the Messiah, and Paul on January 25, for his conversion, but they are commemorated together on June 29 in observance of the tradition of the church that they both died as martyrs in Rome during the persecution under Nero in 64.

Paul, the well-educated and cosmopolitan Jew of the diaspora, and Peter, the uneducated fisherman from Galilee, had differences of opinion in the early years of the church concerning the mission to the Gentiles. More than once, Paul speaks of rebuking Peter for his continued insistence on Jewish exclusiveness; yet their common commitment to Christ and the proclamation of the Gospel proved stronger than their differences; and both eventually carried that mission to Rome, where they were martyred. According to tradition, Paul was granted the right of a Roman citizen to be beheaded by a sword, but Peter suffered the fate of his Lord, crucifixion, although with his head downward.

A generation after their martyrdom, Clement of Rome, writing to the church in Corinth, probably in the year 96, wrote: "Let us come to those who have most recently proved champions; let us take up the noble examples of our own generation. Because of jealousy and envy the greatest and most upright pillars of the church were persecuted and competed unto death. Let us bring before our eyes the good apostles—Peter, who because of unrighteous jealousy endured not one or two, but numerous trials, and so bore a martyr's witness and went to the glorious place that he deserved. Because of jealousy and strife Paul pointed the way to the reward of endurance; seven times he was imprisoned, he was exiled, he was stoned, he was a preacher in both East and West, and won renown for his faith, teaching uprightness to the whole world, and reaching the farthest limit of the West, and bearing a martyr's witness before the rulers, he passed out of the world and was taken up into the holy place, having proved a very great example of endurance."

The Apostles Saint Peter and Saint Paul

I Almighty God, whose blessed apostles Peter and Paul glorified thee by their martyrdom: Grant that thy church, instructed by their teaching and example, and knit together in unity by thy Spirit, may ever stand firm upon the one foundation, which is Jesus Christ our Lord; who liveth and reigneth with thee, in the unity of the same Spirit, one God, for ever and ever. *Amen.*

II Almighty God, whose blessed apostles Peter and Paul glorified you by their martyrdom: Grant that your Church, instructed by their teaching and example, and knit together in unity by your Spirit, may ever stand firm upon the one foundation, which is Jesus Christ our Lord; who lives and reigns with you, in the unity of the same Spirit, one God, now and for ever. *Amen.*

Lessons and Psalm

Ezekiel 34:11-16
Psalm 87
2 Timothy 4:1-8
John 21:15-19

Preface of Apostles and Ordinations

Pauli Murray was an early and committed civil rights activist and the first African American woman ordained as a priest in the Episcopal Church.

Born in Baltimore in 1910, Murray was raised in Durham, North Carolina, and graduated from Hunter College in 1933. After seeking admission to graduate school at the University of North Carolina in 1938, she was denied entry due to her race. She went on to graduate from Howard University Law School in 1944. While a student at Howard, she participated in sit-in demonstrations that challenged racial segregation in drugstores and cafeterias in Washington, D.C. Denied admission to Harvard University for an advanced law degree because of her gender, Murray received her Master's of Law from the University of California, Berkeley, in 1945.

In 1948 the Women's Division of Christian Service of the Methodist Church hired Murray to compile information about segregation laws in the South. Her research led to a 1951 book, *States' Laws on Race and Color,* which became a foundational document for Thurgood Marshall in his work on the decisive Supreme Court decision *Brown v. Board of Education* in 1954.

Committed to dismantling barriers of race, Murray saw the civil rights and women's movements as intertwined and believed that Black women had a vested interest in the women's movement. In recent years, scholars have brought to light Murray's complex sexual and gender identity, including her attempts to access testosterone therapy as early as the 1930s.

In later life, she discerned a call to ordained ministry and began studies at General Theological Seminary in 1973. She was ordained as a deacon in June 1976, and, on January 8, 1977, she was ordained as a priest at Washington National Cathedral. Murray served at Church of the Atonement in Washington, D.C., from 1979 to 1981 and at Holy Nativity Church in Baltimore until her death in 1985.

Murray's books include the family memoir *Proud Shoes: Story of an American Family* (1956) and the personal memoir *Song in a Weary Throat: An American Pilgrimage* (1987).

Pauli Murray

Priest, 1985

I Liberating God, we give thee thanks for the steadfast courage of thy servant Pauli Murray, who didst fight long and well: Unshackle us from the chains of prejudice and fear, that we may show forth the reconciling love and true freedom which thou didst reveal in thy Son our Savior Jesus Christ; who liveth and reigneth with thee and the Holy Ghost, one God, now and for ever. *Amen.*

II Liberating God, we thank you for the steadfast courage of your servant Pauli Murray, who fought long and well: Unshackle us from the chains of prejudice and fear, that we may show forth the reconciling love and true freedom which you revealed in your Son our Savior Jesus Christ; who lives and reigns with you and the Holy Spirit, one God, now and for ever. *Amen.*

Lessons and Psalm

Isaiah 55:10-13
Psalm 119:17-24
Galatians 3:23-29
Mark 12:1-12

Preface of a Saint (1)

Moses of Ethiopia, commonly called Moses the Black in early Christian literature, was a fourth-century monk who lived in one of several isolated desert monasteries near Scete in Lower Egypt. He was described as being tall, strong, "black of body," and in his early life, the hot-blooded leader of a marauding robber band. While fleeing from the authorities, he took shelter with a group of monks. He was so impressed with their faithfulness and kindness that he chose to be baptized and to remain with them.

He led an ascetic life, lived in a simple cell, and ate only ten ounces of dry bread each day. Once, when the monks gathered to judge a member who had sinned, Moses arrived carrying a leaky basket filled with sand on his back. He explained that what he was holding behind him represented his own many sins, now hidden from his own view. "And now I have come to judge my brother for a small fault," he remarked. The other monks then each personally forgave their erring brother and returned to their cells.

It is to Moses that one of the most famous pieces of advice from desert monasticism is attributed: "Go, sit in your cell, and your cell will teach you everything."

When Moses was an old man, he was warned that an armed band of raiders was approaching and that the monks needed to flee. "Those who live by the sword shall die by the sword" (Matthew 26:52), the former robber-murderer calmly replied. "I have been waiting for this day to come for a long time." He and six other brothers waited patiently, and were all slain.

Moses the Black

Monastic and Martyr, c. 400

I Almighty God, whose blessed Son dost guide our footsteps into the way of peace: Deliver us from the paths of hatred and violence, that we, following the example of thy servant Moses, may serve thee with singleness of heart and attain to the tranquility of the world to come; through Jesus Christ our Lord, who liveth and reigneth with thee in the unity of the Holy Ghost, one God, now and for ever. *Amen.*

II Almighty God, whose blessed Son guides our footsteps in the way of peace: Deliver us from the paths of hatred and violence, that we, following the example of your servant Moses, may serve you with singleness of heart and attain to the tranquility of the world to come; through Jesus Christ our Lord, who lives and reigns with you in the unity of the Holy Spirit, one God, now and for ever. *Amen.*

Lessons and Psalm

2 Chronicles 28:8-15
Psalm 62
Acts 22:6-21
Luke 23:39-43

Preface of a Saint (1)

Proper Psalms, Lessons, and Prayers were first appointed for this national observance in the Proposed Prayer Book of 1786. They were deleted, however, by the General Convention of 1789, primarily as a result of the intervention of Bishop William White. Though himself a supporter of the American Revolution, he felt that the required observance was inappropriate, since the majority of the Church's clergy had, in fact, been loyal to the British crown.

Writing about the Convention which had called for the observance of the day throughout "this Church, on the fourth of July, for ever," White said, "The members of the convention seem to have thought themselves so established in their station of ecclesiastical legislators, that they might expect of the many clergy who had been averse to the American revolution the adoption of this service; although, by the use of it, they must make an implied acknowledgment of their error, in an address to Almighty God . . . The greater stress is laid on this matter because of the notorious fact, that the majority of the clergy could not have used the service, without subjecting themselves to ridicule and censure. For the author's part, having no hindrance of this sort, he contented himself with having opposed the measure, and kept the day from respect to the requisition of the convention; but could never hear of its being kept, in above two or three places beside Philadelphia."

In the 1928 revision of the Book of Common Prayer, provision was again made for the liturgical observance of Independence Day.

Independence Day (United States)

I Lord God Almighty, in whose Name the founders of this country won liberty for themselves and for us, and lit the torch of freedom for nations then unborn: Grant, we beseech thee, that we and all the people of this land may have grace to maintain these liberties in righteousness and peace; through Jesus Christ our Lord, who liveth and reigneth with thee and the Holy Ghost, one God, for ever and ever. *Amen.*

II Lord God Almighty, in whose Name the founders of this country won liberty for themselves and for us, and lit the torch of freedom for nations then unborn: Grant that we and all the people of this land may have grace to maintain our liberties in righteousness and peace; through Jesus Christ our Lord, who lives and reigns with you and the Holy Spirit, one God, for ever and ever. *Amen.*

Lessons and Psalm

Deuteronomy 10:17-21
Psalm 145 *or* 145:1-9
Hebrews 11:8-16
Matthew 5:43-48

Preface of Trinity Sunday

Eva Lee Matthews was born on February 9, 1862, in Glendale, Ohio. She grew up as an active member of the Episcopal Church, and felt a call to service in the church from a young age. While working at Bethany Mission House, an Episcopal charitable organization designed to help the less fortunate residents of Cincinnati, she and her coworker Beatrice Henderson discerned a call to create a new Episcopal religious order. The purpose of this order was to assist Cincinnati's poor, especially children. Eva became the community's first superior, taking the name Mother Eva Mary.

On August 6, 1898, Episcopal Church officials formally recognized Matthews and Henderson's order, naming the group the Community of the Transfiguration. The Community of the Transfiguration remained in Cincinnati for only a short time. The order soon relocated a short distance away to Glendale, Matthews' childhood home. The order grew slowly, but by the 1920s the Community of the Transfiguration had members engaged in ministries in Painesville, Ohio; Cleveland, Ohio; Woodlawn, Ohio; Hawai'i; and China.

Matthews served as the leader of the Community of the Transfiguration until her death in July 1928. The community she founded continues to serve the church through a variety of ministries in Ohio, California, and the Dominican Republic.

Eva Lee Matthews

Monastic, 1928

I O God, whose blessed Son became poor that we through his poverty might be rich: Deliver us, we pray thee, from an inordinate love of this world, that, inspired by the devotion of thy servant Eva Lee Matthews, we may serve thee with singleness of heart, and attain to the riches of the age to come; through the same Jesus Christ our Lord, who liveth and reigneth with thee, in the unity of the Holy Spirit, one God, now and for ever. *Amen.*

II O God, whose blessed Son became poor that we through his poverty might be rich: Deliver us from an inordinate love of this world, that, inspired by the devotion of your servant Eva Lee Matthews, we may serve you with singleness of heart, and attain to the riches of the age to come; through the same Jesus Christ our Lord, who lives and reigns with you, in the unity of the Holy Spirit, one God, now and for ever. *Amen.*

Lessons and Psalm

Micah 6:6-8
Psalm 90:1-12
Acts 4:32-35
Matthew 26:6-13

Common of a Saint (2)

When Paul came to Corinth (probably in the year 50), he met Priscilla and her husband Aquila. Like Paul, they were tentmakers by trade, and had just arrived from Rome, from which the Emperor Claudius had recently expelled the Jewish community. It is not clear whether Aquila and Priscilla were already Christians before meeting Paul, or were converted by his preaching. After eighteen months, the three of them went together to Ephesus, where Priscilla and Aquila remained while Paul continued to Antioch.

Soon after, a man named Apollos came to Ephesus, who had heard and believed a portion of the Christian message, and was promoting that belief with eloquent preaching, based on a thorough knowledge of the Hebrew Scriptures. Aquila and Priscilla befriended him and explained the Gospel to him more fully, after which he continued to preach with even greater effectiveness.

Priscilla and Aquila were apparently in Rome when Paul wrote to that congregation, and in Ephesus with Timothy when Paul wrote his last letter to Timothy. When Paul wrote to the Corinthians from Ephesus, he joined their greetings with his own. Clearly they were dear to Paul, and were earnest and effective in spreading the Good News of Christ and His saving work.

Altogether, Aquila and Priscilla are mentioned six times in the New Testament (Acts 18:2; Acts 18:18-19; Acts 18:26; Romans 16:3; 1 Corinthians 16:19; 2 Timothy 4:19), and the observant reader may note that in half of these Aquila's name comes first, while in the other half, Priscilla's comes first, as if to emphasize that they are being mentioned on equal terms.

Priscilla and Aquila

Coworkers of the Apostle Paul

I God of grace and might, who didst plenteously endow thy servants Priscilla and Aquila with gifts of zeal and eloquence to make known the truth of the Gospel: Raise up, we pray thee, in every country, heralds and evangelists of thy kingdom, that the world may know the immeasurable riches of our Savior Jesus Christ; who liveth and reigneth with thee and the Holy Ghost, one God, now and for ever. *Amen.*

II God of grace and might, who gave to your servants Aquila and Priscilla gifts of zeal and eloquence to make known the truth of the Gospel: Raise up, we pray, in every country, heralds and evangelists of your kingdom, so that the world may know the immeasurable riches of our Savior Jesus Christ; who lives and reigns with you and the Holy Spirit, one God, now and for ever. *Amen.*

Lessons and Psalm

Jeremiah 23:23-32
Psalm 18:30-36
Acts 18:1-4, 18-21, 24-28
Luke 24:28-35

Preface of a Saint (3)

Benedict is generally considered the father of Western monasticism. He was born around 480, at Nursia in central Italy, and was educated at Rome. Rome at this time was in the midst of considerable political and social instability. Benedict's disapproval of the manners and morals of his society led him to a vocation of ascetic renunciation. He withdrew to a hillside cave above Lake Subiaco, about forty miles east of Rome, where there was already at least one other hermit.

Gradually, after many setbacks and considerable opposition, a community grew up around Benedict. Sometime between 525 and 530, he moved south with some of his disciples to Monte Cassino, midway between Rome and Naples, where he established another community, and, around 540, composed his famous monastic *Rule*. He died sometime between 540 and 550 and was buried in the same grave as his sister, Scholastica.

It has been said that no personality or text in the history of monasticism has occasioned more studies than Benedict and his rule. The major problem for historians is the question of how much of the rule is original. This is closely related to the question of the date of another, very similar but anonymous, rule for monks, known as *The Rule of the Master,* which may antedate Benedict's *Rule* by ten years. This does not detract from the fact that Benedict's firm but reasonable rule has been the basic source document from which most subsequent Western monastic rules were derived. Its average day provides for a little over four hours to be spent in liturgical prayer, a little over five hours in spiritual reading, about six hours of work, one hour for eating, and about eight hours of sleep. The entire Psalter is to be recited in the Divine Office once every week. At profession, the new monk or nun takes vows of "stability, conversion of life, and obedience."

The prologue to the *Rule* says: "And so we are going to establish a school for the service of the Lord. In founding it we hope to introduce nothing harsh or burdensome. But if a certain strictness results from the dictates of equity for the amendment of vices or the preservation of charity, do not be at once dismayed and fly from the way of salvation, whose entrance cannot but be narrow (Matthew 7:14). For as we advance in the religious life and in faith, our hearts expand and we run the way of God's commandments with unspeakable sweetness of love. Thus, never departing from his school, but persevering in the monastery according to his teaching until death, we may by patience share in the sufferings of Christ (1 Peter 4:13) and deserve to have a share also in his kingdom."

Gregory the Great wrote Benedict's *Life* in the second book of his *Dialogues*. He also adopted Benedictine monasticism as an instrument of evangelization when, in 596, he sent Augustine and his companions to convert the Anglo-Saxon people. In the Anglican Communion today, not only are there several Benedictine communities, but the rules of many other religious orders also have been strongly influenced by the Benedictine rule.

Benedict of Nursia

Monastic, c. 543

I Gracious God, whose service is perfect freedom and in whose commandments there is nothing harsh nor burdensome: Grant that we, with thy servant Benedict, may listen with attentive minds, pray with fervent hearts, and serve thee with willing hands, so that we might live at peace with one another and in obedience to thy Word, Jesus Christ our Lord, who with thee and the Holy Ghost liveth and reigneth, one God, now and for ever. *Amen.*

II Gracious God, whose service is perfect freedom and in whose commandments there is nothing harsh nor burdensome: Grant that we, with your servant Benedict, may listen with attentive minds, pray with fervent hearts, and serve you with willing hands, so that we might live at peace with one another and in obedience to your Word, Jesus Christ our Lord, who with you and the Holy Spirit lives and reigns, one God, now and for ever. *Amen.*

Lessons and Psalm

1 Kings 17:2-6
Psalm 4:1-5
Philippians 2:12-18
Luke 14:27-33

Preface of a Saint (2)

Argula von Grumbach would have been a remarkable woman in any age, but her brilliance shines especially brightly in her setting—Germany in the sixteenth century. She became the first published Protestant woman writer, and participated publicly in the theological and political debates of her time.

Argula was born in 1492 into a noble family in the Bavarian countryside. When she was ten, her father presented her with an illustrated copy of the German Bible—a lavish gift which seems to have made an impression on the young Argula. Her education continued when she was a lady-in-waiting at the court, in a time when renaissance and reform were stirring the air in Munich and Germany.

Her parents died when she was 17; she married at 18 and moved to another country town, where she managed the household, finances, and land; bore, raised, and oversaw the education of four children; and pursued her interests in theology.

Argula took on a more public role when, in September of 1523, she learned that the theologians at the nearby University of Ingolstadt had forced a young Lutheran tutor to recant his beliefs in public. He was saved from burning at the stake, but was to be exiled and imprisoned. Argula wrote a letter to these clerics, accusing them of "foolish violence against the word of God," and noting that "nowhere in the Bible do I find that Christ, or his apostles, or his prophets put people in prison, burnt or murdered them, or sent them into exile." She defends the writings of "Martin and Melancthon," which she has read, and decries the University's failed attempts to hide the truth of these reformers and of Scripture.

Despite her being a lay person and a woman, she says she is compelled to speak by her divine duty as a Christian to confess God's name (she quotes Matthew 10) and to be unashamed of Christ (Luke 9). Her knowledge of Scripture and artful use of it was striking to her readers of the time, and is striking now. Her letter is a variegated composition with textures from across the Bible, picking up Gospels, Psalms, and prophets to form the skeleton and teeth of her impassioned arguments.

She closes by saying, "What I have written to you is no woman's chit-chat, but the word of God; and (I write) as a member of the Christian Church, against which the gates of Hell cannot prevail." Her letter was immediately printed as a pamphlet, which was then reprinted in fourteen editions over two months. More pamphlets, letters, and poems followed, and consequences followed too. However, she did not seem ever to regret that she—like her beloved forebears Judith, Esther, and Jael—had been called by God into decisive action.

Argula von Grumbach

Scholar and Church Reformer, c. 1554

I Almighty God, who didst give to thy servant Argula von Grumbach a spirit of wisdom and power to love thy Word and to boldly draw others unto its truth: Pour out that same spirit upon us, that we, knowing and loving thy Holy Word, may be unashamed of Christ and may not sin against the Holy Spirit that is within us. *Amen.*

II Almighty God, who gave your servant Argula von Grumbach a spirit of wisdom and power to love your Word and to boldly draw others to its truth: Pour out that same spirit upon us, that we, knowing and loving your Holy Word, may be unashamed of Christ and may not sin against the Holy Spirit that is within us. *Amen.*

Lessons and Psalm

Judges 4:4-9
Psalm 118:19-29
James 2:8-13
Matthew 7:24-29

Preface of a Saint (1)

William White was born in Philadelphia on March 24, 1747, and was educated at the college of that city, graduating in 1765. In 1770 he went to England, where he was ordained as a deacon on December 23, and as a priest on April 25, 1772.

Upon his return home, he became assistant minister of Christ and St. Peter's from 1772 to 1779, and rector from that year until his death on July 17, 1836. He also served as chaplain of the Continental Congress from 1777 to 1789, and then of the United States Senate until 1800. Chosen unanimously as first Bishop of Pennsylvania in 1786, he went to England again, with Samuel Provoost, Bishop-elect of New York; and the two men were consecrated in Lambeth Chapel on Septuagesima Sunday, February 4, 1787, by the Archbishops of Canterbury and York and the Bishops of Bath and Wells and of Peterborough.

Bishop White was the chief architect of the Constitution of the American Episcopal Church and the overseer of its life during the first generation of its history. He was the Presiding Bishop at its organizing General Convention in 1789, and again from 1795 until his death in Philadelphia on July 17, 1836.

He was a theologian of significant ability, and among his protégés, in whose formation he had a large hand, were many leaders of a new generation such as John Henry Hobart, Jackson Kemper, and William Augustus Muhlenberg. White's gifts of statesmanship and reconciling moderation steered the American Church through the first decades of its independent life.

William White

Bishop, 1836

I O Lord, who in a time of turmoil and confusion didst raise up thy servant William White to lead thy church into ways of stability and peace; Hear our prayer, and give us wise and faithful leaders, that, through their ministry, thy people may be blessed and thy will be done; through Jesus Christ our Lord, who liveth and reigneth with thee and the Holy Ghost, one God, for ever and ever. *Amen.*

II O Lord, who in a time of turmoil and confusion raised up your servant William White to lead your church into ways of stability and peace; Hear our prayer, and give us wise and faithful leaders, that, through their ministry, your people may be blessed and your will be done; through Jesus Christ our Lord, who lives and reigns with you and the Holy Spirit, one God, for ever and ever. *Amen.*

Lessons and Psalm

Jeremiah 1:4-10
Psalm 40:4-10
1 Timothy 3:1-10
Mark 4:30-34

Preface of a Saint (1)

Macrina the younger (340–379) was a monastic, theologian, and teacher. She is described as having lived a "philosophical life" and she founded one of the earliest Christian monastic communities in the Cappadocian countryside, on the crossroad of Annisa. Macrina left no writings; we know of her through the works of her brother, Gregory of Nyssa. Gregory used the *Life of Macrina* not only to preserve the memory of his renowned sister, but also as a template in which to flesh out a practical theology of Christian holiness and union with God that supplements his more theoretical works.

Gregory relates that when Macrina's prospective fiancé died, she refused to marry anyone else because of her conviction that there is but one marriage and because of her "hope in the resurrection." This hope was the basis of her monastic, that is, her philosophical, life. Although he says that she, like other philosophers, chose to live "on her own," Gregory immediately describes how Macrina lived as a student and servant to her mother, Emilia. He goes on to show Macrina taking a leadership role when she persuades her mother to join her by living on the same level as their servants. In setting out Macrina's relationship with her brother, Peter, Gregory also shows the mutuality of Christian community. He not only describes Macrina as being everything to Peter—father, mother, and teacher of all good things—but Peter as being the person from whom Macrina learned the most.

Gregory credits Macrina with being the spiritual and theological intelligence behind her brothers' notable leadership in the church. She is shown challenging them, telling Gregory that his fame was not due to his own merit, but to the prayers of his parents, and taking Basil in hand when he returned from Athens "monstrously conceited about his skill in rhetoric." Notably, although Gregory and Basil, as well as Peter, became bishops, in the *Life* it is Macrina who is portrayed saying a priestly, and thoroughly liturgical, prayer.

Gregory visited Macrina as she lay dying. It is only at this point in the story that he unveils how the hope of the resurrection with which Macrina began her philosophical life after the death of her fiancé was the inspiration for her decisions to free slaves and the reason why she could cross over otherwise firmly established gender divisions. He shows, too, that her belief in one marriage and her hope of union with her fiancé was, in fact, ultimately a striving toward the true bridegroom, Jesus Christ. In both his *Life of Macrina* and in his later treatise *On the Soul and Resurrection,* Gregory presents Macrina admiringly as a Christian Socrates, delivering eloquent deathbed prayers and teachings about the resurrection. This presentation of Macrina by Gregory serves as one sort of "Rule." Basil also wrote a formal monastic rule for community life, ensuring that Macrina's ideas for Christian community would have lasting authority through the centuries.

Macrina of Caesarea

Monastic and Teacher, 379

I Merciful God, who didst call thy servant Macrina to reveal in her life and teaching the riches of thy grace and truth: Grant that we, following her example, may seek after thy wisdom and live according to the way of thy Son our Savior Jesus Christ, who liveth and reigneth with thee and the Holy Ghost, one God, for ever and ever. *Amen.*

II Merciful God, who called your servant Macrina to reveal in her life and teaching the riches of your grace and truth: Grant that we, following her example, may seek after your wisdom and live according to the way of your Son our Savior Jesus Christ; who lives and reigns with you and the Holy Spirit, one God, for ever and ever. *Amen.*

Lessons and Psalm

Ecclesiasticus 51:13-22
Psalm 119:121-128
Philippians 3:7-11
Mark 3:20-34

Preface of a Saint (2)

Elizabeth Cady Stanton, 1815–1902

Born on November 12, 1815, into an affluent, strict Calvinist family in Johnstown, New York, Elizabeth, as a young woman, took seriously the Presbyterian doctrines of predestination and human depravity. She became very depressed, but resolved her mental crises through action. She dedicated her life to righting the wrongs perpetrated upon women by the church and society.

She and four other women organized the first Women's Rights Convention at Seneca Falls, New York, July 19-20, 1848. The event set her political and religious agenda for the next 50 years. She held the Church accountable for oppressing women by using Scripture to enforce the subordination of women in marriage and to prohibit them from ordained ministry. She held society accountable for denying women equal access to professional jobs, property ownership, the vote, and for granting less pay for the same work.

In 1881, the Revised Version of the Bible was published by a committee which included no women scholars. Elizabeth founded her own committee of women to write a commentary on Scripture, and applying the Greek she had learned as a child from her minister, focused on passages used to oppress and discriminate against women.

Although Elizabeth blamed male clergy for women's oppression, she attended Trinity Episcopal Church in Seneca Falls with her friend Amelia Bloomer. As a dissenting prophet, Elizabeth preached hundreds of homilies and political speeches in pulpits throughout the nation. Wherever she visited, she was experienced as a holy presence and a liberator. She never lost her sense of humor, despite years of contending with opposition, even from friends. In a note to Susan B. Anthony, she said: "Do not feel depressed, my dear friend; what is good in us is immortal, and if the sore trials we have endured are sifting out pride and selfishness, we shall not have suffered in vain." Shortly before she died in New York City, on October 26, 1902, she said: "My only regret is that I have not been braver and bolder and truer in the honest conviction of my soul."

Amelia Jenks Bloomer, 1818–1894

Amelia Jenks, the youngest of six children, was born in New York on May 27, 1818, to a pious Presbyterian family. Early on she demonstrated a kindness of heart and a strict regard for truth and right. As a young woman, she joined in the temperance, anti-slavery, and women's rights movements.

Amelia Jenks Bloomer never intended to make dress reform a major platform in women's struggle for justice. But women's fashion of the day prescribed waist-cinching corsets, even for pregnant women, resulting in severe health problems. Faith and fashion collided explosively when she published in her newspaper, *The Lily,* a picture of herself in loose-fitting Turkish trousers, and began wearing them publicly. Clergy, from their pulpits, attacked women who wore them, citing Moses: "Women should not dress like men." Amelia fired back: "It matters not what Moses had to say to the men and women of his time about what they should wear. If clergy really cared about what Moses said about clothes, they would all put fringes and blue ribbons on their garments." Her popularity soared as she engaged clergy in public debate.

She insisted that "certain passages in the Scriptures relating to women had been given a strained and unnatural meaning." And, of St. Paul, she said: "Could he have looked into the future and foreseen all the sorrow and strife, the cruel exactions and oppression on the one hand and the blind submission and cringing fear on the other, that his words have sanctioned and caused, he would never have uttered them." And of women's right to freedom, she wrote: "the same Power that brought the slave out of bondage will, in His own good time and way, bring about the emancipation of woman, and make her the equal in power and dominion that she was in the beginning."

Later in life, in Council Bluffs, Iowa, a frontier town, she worked to establish churches, libraries, and school houses. She provided hospitality for traveling clergy of all denominations, and for temperance lecturers and reformers. Trinity Episcopal Church, Seneca Falls, New York, where she was baptized, records her as a "faithful Christian missionary all her life." Amelia Jenks Bloomer died in Council Bluffs on December 30, 1894.

Sojourner Truth, "Miriam of the Later Exodus"
1797–8 to 1883

Sojourner Truth, born Isabella Baumfree to James and Elizabeth Baumfree near the turn of the nineteenth century, spent the first twenty-eight years of her life as a slave in the state of New York. During that time, she was separated first from her siblings and then from her children as they were sold to various slaveholders. In 1826, when her owner refused to honor his promise to emancipate her ahead of New York's abolition of slavery, Sojourner took her infant daughter and, in her words, "walked off, believing that to be all right." She later learned that her young son Peter had been illegally sold by her former master, and was enslaved in Alabama. She filed suit, and in 1828, two years after her escape, she won her case, becoming one of the first Black women to ever prevail in an American court over a white man.

With slavery abolished in the state, Sojourner moved to New York City as a free woman. Having undergone a religious conversion after her escape, she became involved in the African Methodist Episcopal Church, founded when white members of St. George's Episcopal Church in Philadelphia would not permit African Americans to worship alongside them as equals. Heartened by the knowledge that a Black woman, Jarena Lee, had been ordained as a minister in the AME tradition, Truth was known to preach and pray and sing with remarkable passion and eloquence. She also worked at a shelter for homeless women, convinced that showing Christ's love required meeting the material needs of the poor and vulnerable. The next decades of her life would prove tumultuous for Sojourner. She was abused by men in positions of religious authority, and in 1835 was falsely accused of crimes she did not commit. She was acquitted of all charges, and later successfully sued her accusers for slander.

At approximately forty-six years old, Sojourner heard a call from God, telling her to go east and preach the gospel, telling the truth of her experiences as a slave and proclaiming the Christian imperative to support the abolition of slavery. It was at this time that she abandoned the names given to her by her master at birth, taking up for herself the name Sojourner Truth. After over a year of itinerant preaching, she joined an abolitionist co-operative in Northampton, Massachusetts, which had been founded on principles of women's rights and pacifism in addition to its abolitionist mission.

Sojourner became a traveling preacher, approaching white religious meetings and campgrounds and asking to speak. Captivated by her charismatic presence, her wit, and her wisdom, they found her hard to refuse. She never learned to read or write, but quoted extensive Bible passages from memory in her sermons. Her reputation grew and she became part of the abolitionist and women's rights speakers' network.

During a women's rights convention in Ohio, Sojourner gave the speech for which she is best remembered, now known as "Ain't I a Woman." She had listened for hours to clergy attack women's rights and abolition, using the Bible to support their oppressive logic: God had created women to be weak and Black people to be a subservient race. Speaking extemporaneously, she exposed the hypocrisy of the white male ministers, pointing out the ways in which slavery had forced her to become as strong as any man, and noting that Jesus himself never turned women away or refused to teach them on account of their gender. Until her death, she continued to speak and preach, advocating for the right to vote to be expanded to all women, not only white women. Sojourner passed away at her home in Michigan on November 26, 1883.

Elizabeth Cady Stanton, Amelia Bloomer, and Sojourner Truth

Social Reformers, 1902, 1894, and 1883

I O God, whose Spirit guideth us into all truth and maketh us free: Strengthen and sustain us as thou didst thy servants Elizabeth, Amelia, and Sojourner. Give us vision and courage to stand against oppression and injustice and all that worketh against the glorious liberty to which thou dost call all thy children; through Jesus Christ our Savior, who liveth and reigneth with thee and the Holy Ghost, one God, for ever and ever. *Amen.*

II O God, whose Spirit guides us into all truth and makes us free: Strengthen and sustain us as you did your servants Elizabeth, Amelia, and Sojourner. Give us vision and courage to stand against oppression and injustice and all that works against the glorious liberty to which you call all your children; through Jesus Christ our Savior, who lives and reigns with you and the Holy Spirit, one God, for ever and ever. *Amen.*

Lessons and Psalm

Esther 1:1-21
Psalm 146
1 Peter 4:10-11
Luke 11:5-10

Preface of Baptism

Maria Skobtsova was born to a well-to-do family in 1891. She was given the name Elizaveta, known as Liza to her family. In 1906, after the death of her father, her mother took the family to St. Petersburg, where she became involved in radical intellectual circles. After her divorce from her first husband, she was drawn to Christianity. She married her second husband, Daniel Skobtsov, and they emigrated to Paris in 1923. Three years later, her youngest child died, and she separated from her second husband. After this, Liza began to work more directly with those who were in need.

In 1932, Liza's bishop encouraged her to take vows as a nun, which she did, taking the name Maria. She realized that Christian asceticism was not primarily about self-mortification and the cloistered life, but responding with love to the needs of others while trying to create better social structures. She could often be found sitting along the Boulevard Montparnasse, in front of a café, with a glass of beer, smoking cigarettes, and talking with simple workers in full monastic robes. Maria made a rented house in Paris her "convent." It was a place with an open door for refugees, the needy and the lonely. It also soon became a center for intellectual and theological discussion. For Maria, these two elements—service to the poor and theology—went hand-in-hand.

When the Nazis took Paris in 1940, Maria began to provide a safe haven for Jewish Parisians. Many came to her hoping to receive baptismal certificates, which they believed would prevent their deportation. Her chaplain, Father Dimitri, gladly provided them. As the occupation became more dangerous, the community hid more Jewish people, providing shelter and helping many to escape. Eventually, this work of the community was discovered by the Gestapo. Maria, her son Yuri, her mother Sophia, and Dmitri Klepinin were all taken into custody.

Maria was sent to the concentration camp in Ravensbrück, Germany. While imprisoned, she encouraged the other inmates. Her faith was strengthened by her claim that "each person is the very icon of God incarnate in the world." With this recognition came the need "to accept this awesome revelation of God unconditionally, to venerate the image of God" in her brothers and sisters.

On Holy Saturday, March 31, 1945, Mother Maria was taken to the gas chamber and entered eternal life. It is suggested that she took the place of a Jewish woman who had been selected for death. A week later, the camp was liberated by the Red Army. In the Orthodox Church she is commemorated on July 20.

Maria Skobtsova

Monastic and Martyr, 1945

I O Creator and Giver of Life, who didst crown thy martyr Maria Skobtsova with glory and didst give her as an example of service to the suffering and poor even unto death: Teach us to love Christ in our neighbors, and thereby battle injustice and evil with the light of the Resurrection; through Jesus Christ our Lord, who livest and reignest with thee and the Holy Ghost, one God in glory everlasting. *Amen.*

II O Creator and Giver of Life, who crowned your martyr Maria Skobtsova with glory and gave her as an example of service to the suffering and poor even unto death: Teach us to love Christ in our neighbors, and thereby battle injustice and evil with the light of the Resurrection; through Jesus Christ our Lord, who lives and reigns with you and the Holy Spirit, one God in glory everlasting. *Amen.*

Lessons and Psalm

Judges 5:1-9
Psalm 9:7-10
Romans 8:28-30
John 2:1-10

Preface of a Saint (3)

Mary of Magdala, a town near Capernaum, was one of several women who followed Jesus and ministered to him in Galilee. The Gospel according to Luke records that Jesus "went on through cities and villages, preaching and bringing the good news of the kingdom of God. And the Twelve were with him, and also some women who had been healed of evil spirits and infirmities: Mary, called Magdalene, from whom seven demons had gone out . . ." (Luke 8:1-2). The Gospels tell us that Mary was healed by Jesus, followed him, and was one of those who stood near his cross at Calvary.

It is clear that Mary Magdalene's life was radically changed by Jesus' healing. Her ministry of service and steadfast companionship, even as a witness to the crucifixion, has, through the centuries, been an example of the faithful ministry of women to Christ. All four Gospels name Mary as one of the women who went to the tomb to mourn and to care for Jesus' body. Her weeping for the loss of her Lord strikes a common chord with the grief of all others over the death of loved ones. Jesus' tender response to her grief—meeting her in the garden, revealing himself to her by calling her name—makes her the first witness to the risen Lord. She is given the command, "Go to my brethren and say to them, I am ascending to my Father and your Father, to my God and your God" (John 20:17). As the first messenger of the resurrection, she tells the disciples, "I have seen the Lord" (John 20:18).

In the tradition of the Eastern Church, Mary is considered "equal to the apostles" and "apostle to the apostles"; and she is held in veneration as the patron saint of the great cluster of monasteries on Mount Athos.

Saint Mary Magdalene

I Almighty God, whose blessed Son restored Mary Magdalene to health of body and mind, and called her to be a witness of his resurrection: Mercifully grant that by thy grace we may be healed of all our infirmities and know thee in the power of his endless life; Through the same Jesus Christ our Lord, who with thee and the Holy Ghost liveth and reigneth, one God, now and for ever. *Amen.*

II Almighty God, whose blessed Son restored Mary Magdalene to health of body and of mind, and called her to be a witness of his resurrection: Mercifully grant that by your grace we may be healed from all our infirmities and know you in the power of his unending life; Through the same Jesus Christ our Lord, who with you and the Holy Spirit lives and reigns, one God, now and for ever. *Amen.*

Lessons and Psalm

Judith 9:1, 11-14
Psalm 42:1-7
2 Corinthians 5:14-18
John 20:11-18

Preface of All Saints

Born in Romania around 365, John Cassian struggled with the problems of living the Christian life in a time when the world seemed to be falling apart. As a young man he traveled to a monastery in Bethlehem and later moved to Egypt, where he sought the tutelage of the great founders of the ascetic movement of the desert, such as Evagrius and Macarius.

At the heart of desert monasticism was the idea that the image of God in each person, tarnished by sin but not destroyed, yearns to and has the capacity to love God with the purity of heart with which God loves us. Their aim in desert solitude was to rid themselves of the anxieties and distractions that called their attention away from loving God.

Cassian was initiated into this tradition before political pressures arising from theological controversies forced him to leave Egypt in about 399. After a period in Constantinople, where he was ordained as a deacon, he moved to southern Gaul. In about 415, he founded a house in Marseilles for monks, and later a house for nuns. Though Cassian's goal, like that of his desert mentors, was the perfection of the individual soul, he insisted that no one should embark on a monastic vocation alone. One should enter a house where others are pursuing the same goal, live according to a time-tested rule, and thereby gain the guidance and companionship of the community.

Though Cassian remained committed to the desert ideal of individual perfection, his insistence on the necessity of Christian community and loving moderation was the basis for Benedictine monasticism. It was perhaps a paradox that only in community could the Christian soul "lose sight of earthly things in proportion to the inspiration of its purity so that . . . with the inner gaze of the soul it sees the glorified Jesus coming in the splendor of his majesty."

Cassian died in Marseilles around the year 435.

John Cassian

Monastic and Theologian, 435

I Holy God, whose beloved Son Jesus Christ didst bless the pure in heart: Grant that we, together with thy servant John Cassian and in union with his prayers, may ever seek the purity with which to behold thee as thou art; one God in Trinity of persons now and for ever. *Amen.*

II Holy God, whose beloved Son Jesus Christ blessed the pure in heart: Grant that we, together with your servant John Cassian and in union with his prayers, may ever seek the purity with which to behold you as you are; one God in Trinity of persons now and for ever. *Amen.*

Lessons and Psalm

2 Kings 2:9-15
Psalm 145:1-7
1 John 3:1-3
John 1:1-14

Preface of Lent (1)

Thomas à Kempis is one of the best known and most beloved medieval Christian spiritual writers. Millions of Christians have found his work *The Imitation of Christ* to be a treasured and constant source of edification, and it has been translated into an astonishingly wide range of languages.

Thomas Hammerken was born at Kempen in the Duchy of Cleves about 1380. He was educated at Deventer by the Brethren of the Common Life, and joined their order in 1399 at their house of Mount St. Agnes in Zwolle (in the Low Countries).

The Order of the Brethren of the Common Life was founded by Gerard Groote (1340–1384) at Deventer. It included both clergy and lay members who cultivated a biblical piety of a practical rather than speculative nature, with stress upon the inner life and the practice of virtues. They supported themselves by copying manuscripts and teaching. Many have seen in them harbingers of the Reformation; but the Brethren had little interest in the problems of the institutional church. Their spirituality, known as the "New Devotion" (*Devotio moderna*), has influenced both Catholic and Protestant traditions of prayer and meditation.

In *The Imitation of Christ,* Thomas wrote: "A humble knowledge of oneself is a surer road to God than a deep searching of the sciences. Yet learning itself is not to be blamed, nor is the simple knowledge of anything whatsoever to be despised, for true learning is good in itself and ordained by God; but a good conscience and a holy life are always to be preferred. But because many are more eager to acquire much learning than to live well, they often go astray, and bear little or no fruit. If only such people were as diligent in the uprooting of vices and the planting of virtues as they are in the debating of problems, there would not be so many evils and scandals among the people, nor such laxity in communities. At the Day of Judgement, we shall not be asked what we have read, but what we have done; not how eloquently we have spoken, but how holily we have lived. Tell me, where are now all those Masters and Doctors whom you knew so well in their lifetime in the full flower of their learning? Other men now sit in their seats, and they are hardly ever called to mind. In their lifetime they seemed of great account, but now no one speaks of them."

Thomas died on July 25, 1471.

Thomas à Kempis

Priest and Mystic, 1471

I Holy Father, who hast nourished and strengthened thy church by the writings of thy servant Thomas à Kempis: Grant that we may learn from him to know what is necessary to be known, to love what is to be loved, to praise what highly pleases thee, and always to seek to know and to follow thy will; through Jesus Christ our Lord, who liveth and reigneth with thee and the Holy Ghost, one God, for ever and ever. *Amen.*

II Holy Father, you have nourished and strengthened your church by the writings of your servant Thomas à Kempis: Grant that we may learn from him to know what is necessary to be known, to love what is to be loved, to praise what highly pleases you, and always to seek to know and to follow your will; through Jesus Christ our Lord, who lives and reigns with you and the Holy Spirit, one God, for ever and ever. *Amen.*

Lessons and Psalm

Ecclesiastes 1:1-11
Psalm 113
Ephesians 4:32—5:2
Matthew 18:18-20

Preface of a Saint (2)

James, the brother of John, is often known as James the Greater, to distinguish him from the other Apostle of the same name who is commemorated on May 1 with Philip, and also from James "the brother of our Lord."

He was the son of a Galilean fisherman, Zebedee, and with his brother John left his home and his trade in obedience to the call of Christ. With Peter and John, he seems to have belonged to an especially privileged group, whom Jesus chose to be witnesses to the Transfiguration, to the raising of Jairus' daughter, and to his agony in the Garden of Gethsemane.

Apparently, James shared John's hot-headed disposition, and Jesus nicknamed the brothers "Boanerges" (Sons of Thunder). James' expressed willingness to share the cup of Christ was realized in his being the first of the Apostles to die for him. As the Acts of the Apostles records, "About that time Herod the King laid violent hands upon some who belonged to the Church. He killed James the brother of John with the sword" (Acts 12:1-2).

According to an old tradition, the body of James was taken to Compostela, Spain, which has been a shrine for pilgrims for centuries.

Saint James the Apostle

I O Gracious God, we remember before thee this day thy servant and apostle James, first among the Twelve to suffer martyrdom for the Name of Jesus Christ; and we pray that thou wilt pour out upon the leaders of thy church that spirit of self-denying service by which alone they may have true authority among thy people; through the same Jesus Christ our Lord, who liveth and reigneth with thee and the Holy Ghost, one God, now and for ever. *Amen.*

II O Gracious God, we remember before you today your servant and apostle James, first among the Twelve to suffer martyrdom for the Name of Jesus Christ; and we pray that you will pour out upon the leaders of your church that spirit of self-denying service by which alone they may have true authority among your people; through Jesus Christ our Lord, who lives and reigns with you and the Holy Spirit, one God, now and for ever. *Amen.*

Lessons and Psalm

Jeremiah 45:1-5
Psalm 7:1-10
Acts 11:27—12:3
Matthew 20:20-28

Preface of Apostles and Ordinations

The gospels tell us little about the home of our Lord's mother. She is thought to have been of Davidic descent and to have been brought up in a devout Jewish family that cherished the hope of Israel for the coming kingdom of God, in remembrance of the promise to Abraham and his descendants.

In the second century, devout Christians sought to supply a more complete account of Mary's birth and family, to satisfy the interest and curiosity of believers. An apocryphal gospel, known as the *Protevangelium of James* or *The Nativity of Mary,* appeared. It included legendary stories about Mary's parents, Joachim and Anne. These stories were built out of Old Testament narratives of the births of Isaac and of Samuel (whose mother's name, Hannah, is the original form of Anne), and from traditions of the birth of John the Baptist. In these stories, Joachim and Anne—the childless, elderly couple who grieved that they would have no posterity—were rewarded with the birth of a girl, whom they dedicated in infancy to the service of God under the tutelage of the temple priests.

In 550, the Emperor Justinian I erected in Constantinople the first church to Saint Anne. The Eastern churches observe her festival on July 25. Not until the twelfth century did her feast become known in the West. Pope Urban VI fixed her day, in 1378, to follow the feast of Saint James. Joachim has had several dates assigned to his memory; but the new Roman Calendar of 1969 joined his festival to that of Anne on this day.

The Parents of the Blessed Virgin Mary

I Almighty God, heavenly Father, we remember in thanksgiving this day the parents of the Blessed Virgin Mary; and we pray that we all may be made one in the heavenly family of thy Son Jesus Christ our Lord; who with thee and the Holy Ghost liveth and reigneth, one God, for ever and ever. *Amen.*

II Almighty God, heavenly Father, we remember in thanksgiving this day the parents of the Blessed Virgin Mary; and we pray that we all may be made one in the heavenly family of your Son Jesus Christ our Lord; who with you and the Holy Spirit lives and reigns, one God, for ever and ever. *Amen.*

Lessons and Psalm

Genesis 17:1-8
Psalm 132:11-19
1 Thessalonians 1:1-5
Luke 1:26-33

Preface of the Incarnation

"First presbyter of the Church" was the well-deserved, if unofficial, title of the sixth rector of Grace Church, New York City. William Reed Huntington provided a leadership characterized by breadth, generosity, scholarship, and boldness. He was the acknowledged leader in the House of Deputies of the Episcopal Church's General Convention during a period of intense stress and conflict within the Church. His reconciling spirit helped preserve the unity of the Episcopal Church in the painful days after the beginning of the schism that resulted in the formation of the Reformed Episcopal Church.

In the House of Deputies, of which he was a member from 1871 until 1907, Huntington showed active and pioneering vision in making daring proposals. As early as 1871, his motion to revive the primitive order of "deaconesses" began a long struggle, which culminated in 1889 in canonical authorization for that order. Huntington's parish immediately provided facilities for this new ministry, and Huntington House became a training center for deaconesses and other women workers in the Church.

Christian unity was Huntington's great passion throughout his ministry. In his book, *The Church Idea* (1870), he attempted to articulate the essentials of Christian unity. The grounds he proposed as a basis for unity were presented to, and accepted by, the House of Bishops in Chicago in 1886, and, with some slight modification, were adopted by the Lambeth Conference in 1888. The "Chicago-Lambeth Quadrilateral" has become a historic landmark for the Anglican Communion. It is included on pages 876-878 of the Book of Common Prayer, among the Historical Documents of the Church.

In addition to his roles as ecumenist and statesman, Huntington is significant as a liturgical scholar. It was his bold proposal to revise the Prayer Book that led to the revision of 1892, providing a hitherto unknown flexibility and significant enrichment. His Collect for Monday in Holy Week, now used also for Fridays at Morning Prayer, is itself an example of skillful revision. In it he takes two striking clauses from the exhortation to the sick in the 1662 Prayer Book and uses them as part of a prayer for grace to follow the Lord in his sufferings.

William Reed Huntington

Priest, 1909

I O Lord our God, we thank thee for instilling in the heart of thy servant William Reed Huntington a fervent love for thy church and its mission in the world; and we pray that, with unflagging faith in thy promises, we may make known to all people thy blessed gift of eternal life; through Jesus Christ our Lord, who liveth and reigneth with thee and the Holy Ghost, one God, for ever and ever. *Amen.*

II O Lord our God, we thank you for instilling in the heart of your servant William Reed Huntington a fervent love for your church and its mission in the world; and we pray that, with unflagging faith in your promises, we may make known to all people your blessed gift of eternal life; through Jesus Christ our Lord, who lives and reigns with you and the Holy Spirit, one God, for ever and ever. *Amen.*

Lessons and Psalm

Joel 2:12-17
Psalm 133
Galatians 6:14-18
John 17:20-26

Preface of Baptism

Johann Sebastian Bach was born in Eisenach, Germany, in 1685, into a family of musicians. As a child, he studied violin and organ and served as a choirboy at the parish church. By early adulthood, Bach had already achieved an enviable reputation as a composer and performer.

His assignments as a church musician began in 1707 and, a year later, he became the organist and chamber musician for the court of the Duke of Weimar. In 1723, Bach was appointed cantor of the St. Thomas School in Leipzig and parish musician at both St. Thomas and St. Nicholas churches, where he remained until his death in 1750.

A man of deep Lutheran faith, Bach's music was an expression of his religious convictions. Among his many works are included musical interpretations of the Bible, which are his "Passions." The most famous of these is the *Passion According to St. Matthew*. This composition, written in 1727 or 1729, tells the story of chapters 26 and 27 of the Gospel of Matthew and was performed as part of a Good Friday service. He also wrote music for eucharistic services, the most renowned of which may be his Mass in B Minor.

Bach's music compositions continue to be widely used and to profoundly influence the musical traditions of many Christian churches. Even beyond their technical merits, they may be understood as deeply theological interpretations of the Christian faith which have been translated into the language of music.

Johann Sebastian Bach

Composer, 1750

I Sound out thy majesty, O God, and call us to thy work; that, like thy servant Johann Sebastian Bach, we might present our lives and our works to thy glory alone; through Jesus Christ our Lord, who liveth and reigneth with thee and the Holy Ghost, one God, for ever and ever. *Amen.*

II Sound out your majesty, O God, and call us to your work; that, like thy servant Johann Sebastian Bach, we might present our lives and our works to your glory alone; through Jesus Christ our Lord, who lives and reigns with you and the Holy Spirit, one God, for ever and ever. *Amen.*

Lessons and Psalm

2 Chronicles 5:11-14
Psalm 150
Colossians 2:2-6
Luke 2:8-14

Preface of a Saint (3)

This commemoration celebrates The Philadelphia Eleven -- the first eleven women ordained to the priesthood in The Episcopal Church on July 29, 1974 at the Church Advocate in Philadelphia.

Through most of the history of the Christian Church, women were relegated to positions secondary to those held by men and excluded from leadership roles. During the first half of the twentieth century that began to shift as the Episcopal Church experienced an expansion of the participation of women in the church as "Deaconesses"—a separate order from male Deacons. Deaconesses were set apart to care for "the sick, the afflicted, and the poor," but precluded from functioning liturgically.

In 1970, laywomen were seated for the first time in General Convention as Deputies with voice and vote. Calling for a vote to eliminate the canonical distinctions between male deacons and female deaconesses, their intent was to make clear that women seeking ordination should be recognized as full and equal deacons. Once that motion was adopted, The Episcopal Church was presented with the issue of whether to ordain women as priests and bishops, too.

A resolution was put forward by the women deputies at the 1970 General Convention to approve women's ordination to the priesthood and episcopate. It failed to pass the House of Deputies, but nonetheless had much positive support. A similar resolution narrowly failed to pass at the next General Convention in 1973.

By July 1974, supporters of women's ordination to the priesthood grew restless with the stalled legislative process and an ordination service was scheduled to ordain women to the priesthood by three retired bishops: Daniel Corrigan, retired bishop suffragan of Colorado; Robert L. DeWitt, recently resigned Bishop of Pennsylvania; and Edward R. Welles, retired Bishop of West Missouri.

Eleven women who were deacons presented themselves as ready for ordination to the priesthood, and plans for the service proceeded. These women, who came to be called the "The Philadelphia Eleven", were Merrill Bittner, Alla Bozarth-Campbell, Alison Cheek, Emily Hewitt, Carter Heyward, Suzanne Hiatt, Marie Moorefield, Jeannette Piccard, Betty Schiess, Katrina Swanson, and Nancy Wittig. They were ordained on July 29, 1974 at the Church of the Advocate in Philadelphia, Pennsylvania.

The ordinations inspired both celebration and controversy in the Episcopal Church. The House of Bishops declared them "irregular" and the Philadelphia Eleven were prohibited from officially exercising priestly functions. Nevertheless, the movement for the ordination of women continued to move forward. At the 65th General Convention in September 1976, the ordination of women to the priesthood was approved to begin on January 1, 1977, the previous "irregular" ordinations were regularized, and the way was opened for women to respond to the call to ordination in the Episcopal Church.

[The Ordination of the Philadelphia Eleven]

I O God of Persistent Grace, who didst call the Philadelphia Eleven to the priesthood and didst grant them courage and boldness to respond, thereby opening the eyes of thy church to the giftedness and equality of all: grant us so to hear, trust, and follow thy Holy Spirit wheresoever she may lead, that the gifts of all thy people may flourish throughout the earth, through Christ our Savior. *Amen.*

II O God of Persistent Grace, you called the Philadelphia Eleven to the priesthood and granted them courage and boldness to respond, thereby opening the eyes of your church to the giftedness and equality of all: grant us so to hear, trust, and follow your Holy Spirit wherever she may lead, that the gifts of all your people may flourish throughout the earth, through Christ our Savior. *Amen.*

Lessons and Psalm

Exodus 1:15-21
Sirach 1:4-15 (in place of the Psalm)
Galatians 3:23-29
Luke 24:1-11

Preface of Baptism

Mary and Martha of Bethany are described in the Gospels according to Luke and John as close and well-loved friends of Jesus. Luke records the well-known story of their hospitality, which has made Martha a symbol of the active life and Mary of the contemplative.

John's Gospel sheds additional light on the characters of Mary and Martha. When their brother Lazarus is dying, Jesus delays his visit to the family and arrives after Lazarus' death. Martha comes to meet him, still trusting in his power to heal and restore. The exchange between them evokes Martha's deep faith and acknowledgment of Jesus as the Messiah (John 11:21-27).

John also records the supper at Bethany at which Mary anointed Jesus' feet with fragrant ointment and wiped them with her hair. This tender gesture of love evoked criticism from the disciples. Jesus interpreted the gift as a preparation for his death and burial.

The devotion and friendship of Mary and Martha have been an example of fidelity and service to the Lord. Their hospitality and kindness, and Jesus' enjoyment of their company, show us the beauty of human friendship and love at its best.

Many Christian writers have interpreted Martha and Mary as symbolizing the active and contemplative lives. In most cases, however, they stressed that this division of action and contemplation was not a simple dichotomy. Although most ancient and medieval theologians tended to prioritize the contemplative life, all of them stressed the necessity for the different vocations of both sisters in the church.

In his sermon 104, Augustine of Hippo writes that "Martha has to set sail in order that Mary can remain quietly in port." Although in some ways he thinks that the adoring worship of Christ is indeed superior, it does no good to adore Christ without serving and feeding him as Martha did, and as all Christians can do by serving those in need.

The Cistercian theologian Aelred of Rievaulx wrote that just as Mary and Martha dwelt as sisters within one house, so also the active and contemplative life should ideally dwell within the same soul.

Although most premodern writers did tend to view Mary as superior to Martha, the medieval mystic Meister Eckhart argued in his sermon 86 that Martha was the more spiritually advanced of the two sisters, suggesting that she is mature enough that she is no longer enamored by religious feelings and experiences, but able to move on from them to the practical work of service. In this case, Jesus' words that Mary "has chosen the better part" are meant to reassure Martha that her sister is on the right track, and that when she is ready, she too will eventually move on from only seeking spiritual consolation to serving where she is needed.

Mary and Martha of Bethany

I O God, heavenly Father, whose Son Jesus Christ enjoyed rest and refreshment in the home of Mary and Martha of Bethany: Give us the will to love thee, open our hearts to hear thee, and strengthen our hands to serve thee in others for his sake; who liveth and reigneth with thee and the Holy Ghost, one God, now and for ever. *Amen.*

II O God, heavenly Father, your Son Jesus Christ enjoyed rest and refreshment in the home of Mary and Martha of Bethany: Give us the will to love you, open our hearts to hear you, and strengthen our hands to serve you in others for his sake; who lives and reigns with you and the Holy Spirit, one God, now and for ever. *Amen.*

Lessons and Psalm

1 Samuel 25:18-38
Psalm 36:1-5
Romans 12:9-13
Luke 10:38-42

Preface of the Epiphany

The life of William Wilberforce refutes the popular notion that a politician cannot be a saintly Christian, dedicated to the service of humanity.

Wilberforce was born into an affluent family in Hull, Yorkshire, on August 24, 1759, and was educated at St. John's College, Cambridge. In 1780, he was elected to the House of Commons, and he served in it until 1825. He died in London, July 29, 1833, and was buried in Westminster Abbey.

His conversion to an evangelical Christian life occurred in 1784, several years after he entered Parliament. Fortunately, he was induced by his friends not to abandon his political activities after this inward change in his life, but thereafter he steadfastly refused to accept high office or a peerage.

He gave himself unstintingly to the promotion of overseas missions, popular education, and the reformation of public manners and morals. He also supported parliamentary reform and Catholic emancipation. Above all, his fame rests upon his persistent, uncompromising, and single-minded crusade for the abolition of slavery and the slave-trade. That sordid traffic was abolished in 1807. He died just one month before Parliament put an end to slavery in the British dominions. One of the last letters written by John Wesley was addressed to Wilberforce. In it Wesley gave him his blessing for his noble enterprise.

Wilberforce's eloquence as a speaker, his charm in personal address, and his profound religious spirit, made him a formidable power for good; and his countrymen came to recognize in him a man of heroic greatness.

William Wilberforce

Social Reformer, 1833

I Let thy continual mercy, O Lord, enkindle in thy Church the never-failing gift of love; that, following the example of thy servant William Wilberforce, we may have grace to defend the poor, and maintain the cause of those who have no helper; for the sake of him who gave his life for us, thy Son our Savior Jesus Christ, who liveth and reigneth with thee and the Holy Ghost, one God, now and for ever. *Amen.*

II Let your continual mercy, O Lord, kindle in your Church the never-failing gift of love; that, following the example of your servant William Wilberforce, we may have grace to defend the poor, and maintain the cause of those who have no helper; for the sake of him who gave his life for us, your Son our Savior Jesus Christ, who lives and reigns with you and the Holy Spirit, one God, now and for ever. *Amen.*

Lessons and Psalm

2 Samuel 12:1-10
Psalm 35:23-28
Romans 12:9-13
Matthew 20:1-16

Preface of a Saint (2)

Ignatius was born into a noble Basque family in 1491. In his autobiography he tells us that until the age of 26 he was "a man given over to the vanities of the world and took special delight in the exercise of arms with a great and vain desire of winning glory." An act of reckless heroism at the Battle of Pamplona in 1521 led to his being seriously wounded. During his convalescence at Loyola, Ignatius experienced a profound spiritual awakening. Following his recovery and an arduous period of retreat, a call to be Christ's knight in the service of God's kingdom was deepened and confirmed.

Ignatius began to share the fruits of his experience with others, making use of a notebook which eventually became the text of the *Spiritual Exercises*. Since his time, many have found the *Exercises* to be a way of encountering Christ as intimate companion and responding to Christ's call: "Whoever wishes to come with me must labor with me."

The fact that Ignatius was an unschooled layman made him suspect in the eyes of church authorities and led him, at the age of 37, to study theology at the University of Paris in preparation for the priesthood. While there, Ignatius gave the *Exercises* to several of his fellow students; and in 1534, he and six companions took vows to live lives of strict poverty and to serve the needs of the poor. Thus, what later came to be known as the Society of Jesus was born.

In 1540 the Society was formally recognized, and Ignatius became its first Superior General. According to his journals and many of his letters, a profound sense of sharing God's work in union with Christ made the season of intense activity which followed a time of great blessing and consolation.

Ignatius died on July 31, 1556, in the simple room which served both as his bedroom and chapel, having sought God in all things and having tried to do all things for God's greater glory.

Ignatius of Loyola

Priest and Spiritual Writer, 1556

I Almighty God, who didst call Ignatius of Loyola to the service of thy Divine Majesty and to seek thee in all things; Give us also the grace to labor without counting the cost and to seek no reward other than knowing that we do thy will; through Jesus Christ our Lord, who liveth and reigneth with thee and the Holy Ghost, one God, now and for ever. *Amen.*

II Almighty God, who called Ignatius of Loyola to the service of your Divine Majesty and to seek you in all things; Give us also the grace to labor without counting the cost and to seek no reward other than knowing that we do your will; through Jesus Christ our Lord, who lives and reigns with you and the Holy Spirit, now and for ever. *Amen.*

Lessons and Psalm

Genesis 32:22-31
Psalm 22:27-31
1 Corinthians 10:31—11:1
Luke 9:57-62

Preface of a Saint (3)

Joseph of Arimathea was a secret disciple of our Lord whose intervention with Pilate ensured a burial for Jesus' crucified body. After the Crucifixion, when many of Jesus' disciples went into hiding for fear of the authorities, Joseph courageously came forward to ask Pilate's permission to remove Jesus' body from the cross in accordance with pious Jewish practice, namely, to provide the deceased with a timely and proper burial. Moreover, Joseph freely offered his own newly dug tomb for Jesus, preventing further desecration by humans or animals.

Although we know nothing of his further role in the early Christian movement, legends developed in later centuries about Joseph's possible subsequent leadership, including medieval traditions connecting him to Glastonbury in Britain. However, Joseph's remembrance depends primarily upon the gospel narratives of Jesus' burial, attesting to his devotion, his generous compassion, and his brave willingness to take action on behalf of another when such action mattered.

Joseph of Arimathea

I Merciful God, whose servant Joseph of Arimathea with reverence and godly fear prepared the body of our Lord and Savior for burial and laid it in his own tomb: Grant to us, thy faithful people, grace and courage to love and serve Jesus with sincere devotion all the days of our life; through the same Jesus Christ our Lord, who liveth and reigneth with thee and the Holy Ghost, one God, for ever and ever. *Amen.*

II Merciful God, whose servant Joseph of Arimathea with reverence and godly fear prepared the body of our Lord and Savior for burial and laid it in his own tomb: Grant to us, your faithful people, grace and courage to love and serve Jesus with sincere devotion all the days of our life; through the same Jesus Christ our Lord, who lives and reigns with you and the Holy Spirit, one God, for ever and ever. *Amen.*

Lessons and Psalm

Proverbs 4:10-18
Psalm 128
James 1:17-18
Luke 23:50-56

Preface of a Saint (1)

Joanna, Mary, and Salome are traditionally counted as the three women who came to Jesus' tomb early in the morning on the day of the resurrection in order to anoint his body with myrrh and other spices. They were followers of Jesus during his earthly ministry and remained with him throughout his arrest, crucifixion, and burial, and they discovered his empty tomb after his resurrection.

Little is known about the lives of Joanna, Mary, and Salome beyond their faithful and unwavering devotion and service to Christ. Joanna is identified in the Gospel of Luke as the wife of Chuza, a steward of Herod, and in Luke 8:2-3 is counted among the women who followed and provided for Jesus after having been healed by him.

The Gospel of Mark includes Salome in a list of women present at the crucifixion without any further information; according to early Christian tradition Salome was a relative of Mary the Mother of Jesus.

In addition to Joanna, Salome, and Mary Magdalene, Matthew 28:1 lists a woman it refers to as "the other Mary." Mark 16:1 refers to her as Mary the mother of James. John 19:25 recounts that Mary the wife of Cleopas was present at the crucifixion, and historically the Christian tradition has tended to assume that all three of these Marys are actually the same person.

The little information that we do have about these women shows them to be faithful disciples and worthy of our commemoration and, more importantly, emulation. There is a particular devotion to these "Holy Myrrhbearers" in the Orthodox Church, and the second Sunday after Easter is celebrated as "Myrrhbearers Sunday."

Joanna, Mary, and Salome

Myrrh-Bearing Women

I Almighty God, who didst reveal the resurrection of thy Son to Joanna, Mary, and Salome as they faithfully came bearing myrrh to his tomb: Grant that we too may perceive the presence of the risen Lord in the midst of pain and fear, and go forth proclaiming his resurrection; who liveth and reigneth with thee and the Holy Ghost, one God, now and for ever. *Amen.*

II Almighty God, who revealed the resurrection of your Son to Joanna, Mary, and Salome as they faithfully came bearing myrrh to his tomb: Grant that we too may perceive the presence of the risen Lord in the midst of pain and fear, and go forth proclaiming his resurrection; who lives and reigns with you and the Holy Spirit, one God, now and for ever. *Amen.*

Lessons and Psalm

Job 2:11-13
Psalm 50
Acts 2:29-36
Mark 16:1-8

Preface of a Saint (3)

The Transfiguration is not to be understood only as a spiritual experience of Jesus while at prayer, which three chosen disciples, Peter, James, and John, were permitted to witness. It is one of a series of spiritual manifestations by which God authenticated Jesus as his Son. It is at one with the appearance of the angels at the birth and at his resurrection, and with the descent of the Spirit at Jesus' baptism. Matthew records the voice from heaven saying, "This is my Son, the Beloved, with whom I am well pleased; listen to him" (Matthew 17:5). Briefly the veil is drawn aside, and a chosen few are permitted to see Jesus, not only as the human son of Mary, but also as the eternal Son of God. Moses and Elijah witness to Jesus as the fulfillment of the Law and the Prophets. In Luke's account of the event, they speak of the "exodus" which Jesus is to accomplish at Jerusalem. A cloud, a sign of divine presence, envelops the disciples, and a heavenly voice proclaims Jesus to be the Son of God.

Immediately thereafter, Jesus announces to Peter, James, and John the imminence of his death. As Paul was later to say of Jesus, "Though he was in the form of God, he did not count equality with God a thing to be grasped, but emptied himself, taking the form of a servant, and was born in human likeness. And, being found in human form, he humbled himself, and became obedient unto death, even death on a cross" (Philippians 2:6-8).

The Feast of the Transfiguration is held in the highest esteem by the Eastern Churches. The figure of the transfigured Christ is regarded as a foreshadowing of the Risen and Ascended Lord. The festival, however, was only accepted into the Roman calendar on the eve of the Reformation, and for that reason was not originally included in the reformed calendar of the Church of England. Since its inclusion in the American liturgical revision of 1892, it has been taken into most modern Anglican calendars.

The Transfiguration of Our Lord Jesus Christ

I O God, who on the holy mount didst reveal to chosen witnesses thy well-beloved Son, wonderfully transfigured, in raiment white and glistening: Mercifully grant that we, being delivered from the disquietude of this world, may by faith behold the King in his beauty; who with thee, O Father, and thee, O Holy Ghost, liveth and reigneth, one God, for ever and ever. *Amen.*

II O God, who on the holy mount revealed to chosen witnesses your well-beloved Son, wonderfully transfigured, in raiment white and glistening: Mercifully grant that we, being delivered from the disquietude of this world, may by faith behold the King in his beauty; who with you, O Father, and you, O Holy Spirit, lives and reigns, one God, for ever and ever. *Amen.*

Lessons and Psalm

Exodus 34:29-35
Psalm 99 *or* 99:5-9
2 Peter 1:13-21
Luke 9:28-36

Preface of the Epiphany

John Mason Neale was born in London in 1818, studied at Cambridge, where he also served as tutor and chaplain, and was ordained to the priesthood in 1842. Chronic ill health made parish ministry impractical, but in 1846, he was made warden of Sackville College, a charitable residence for the poor, which position he held for the rest of his life. Both a scholar and a creative poet, his skills in composing original verse and translating Latin and Greek hymns into effective English lyrics were devoted to the church and were but one expression of his active support for the Oxford Movement in its revival of medieval liturgical forms. With such familiar words as "Good Christian men, rejoice" (*The Hymnal 1982*, #107), "Come, ye faithful, raise the strain" (#199; #200), "All glory, laud, and honor" (#154; #155), "Sing, my tongue, the glorious battle" (#165; #166), and "Creator of the stars of night" (#60), he greatly enriched our hymnody.

Gentleness combined with firmness, good humor, modesty, patience, devotion, and an unbounded charity describe Neale's character. A prolific writer and compiler, his works include *Medieval Hymns and Sequences, Hymns of the Eastern Church, Essays on Liturgiology and Church History,* and a four-volume commentary on the Psalms. He established the Camden Society, later called the Ecclesiological Society, and, consistent with Anglo-Catholic principles that united liturgical piety with compassionate social action, he founded the Sisterhood of St. Margaret for the relief of suffering women and girls.

Neale faced active persecution for his liturgical and theological principles. He was forced to resign his first parish due to disagreements with his bishop. He was physically attacked several times, including at a funeral of one of the sisters. Mobs threatened both him and his family, believing him to be a secret agent of the Vatican attempting to destroy the Church of England from within.

Though his work was little appreciated in England, his contributions were recognized both in the United States and in Russia, where the Metropolitan presented him with a rare copy of the Old Believers' Liturgy. He died on the Feast of the Transfiguration in 1866, at the age of 46, leaving a lasting mark on Anglican worship.

John Mason Neale

Priest and Hymnographer, 1866

I Grant unto us, O God, that in all time of our testing we may know thy presence and obey thy will; that, following the example of thy servant John Mason Neale, we may with integrity and courage accomplish what thou givest us to do, and endure what thou givest us to bear; through Jesus Christ our Lord, who liveth and reigneth with thee and the Holy Ghost, one God, for ever and ever. *Amen.*

II Grant, O God, that in all time of our testing we may know your presence and obey your will; that, following the example of your servant John Mason Neale, we may with integrity and courage accomplish what you give us to do, and endure what you give us to bear; through Jesus Christ our Lord, who lives and reigns with you and the Holy Spirit, one God, for ever and ever. *Amen.*

Lessons and Psalm

2 Chronicles 20:20-21
Psalm 102:18-28
1 Corinthians 1:1-9
Matthew 13:44-46

Preface of the Dedication of a Church

Dominic was the founder of the Order of Preachers, commonly known as Dominicans. He was born around 1170 in Spain. Influenced by the contemporary search for a life of apostolic poverty, Dominic is reputed to have sold all his possessions to help the poor during a famine in 1191. Ordained in 1196, he soon became a canon and then sub-prior of the Cathedral of Osma, where a rule of strict discipline was established among the canons.

In 1203 he began a number of preaching tours in Languedoc, a region in Southern France, against the Cathars, who believed in a dualist version of Christianity that denigrated the physical world and the human body. In 1214, his plan to found a special preaching order for the conversion of the Cathars began to take shape, and in the following year, he took his followers to Toulouse. At the Fourth Lateran Council in October of 1215, Dominic sought confirmation of his order from Pope Innocent III. This was granted by Innocent's successor, Honorius III, in 1216 and 1217.

Over the next few years, Dominic traveled extensively, establishing friaries, organizing the order, and preaching, until his death on August 6, 1221. He is remembered as a man of austere poverty and heroic sanctity, always zealous to win souls by the preaching of pure doctrine.

The Dominican Constitutions, first formulated in 1216 and revised and codified by the Master-General of the Order, Raymond of Peñafort, in 1241, place a strong emphasis on learning, preaching, and teaching, and, partly through the influence of Francis of Assisi, on absolute poverty. The continuing Dominican apostolate embraces intellectual work and the arts of preaching, their major houses usually situated in university centers. Their Constitutions express the priority in this way: "In the cells, moreover, they can write, read, pray, sleep, and even stay awake at night, if they desire, on account of study."

Dominic

Priest and Friar, 1221

I Almighty God, grant unto thy people a hunger for thy Word and an urgent longing to share thy Gospel; that, like thy servant Dominic, we might labor to bring the whole world to the knowledge and love of thee as thou art revealed in thy Son Jesus Christ; who liveth and reigneth with thee and the Holy Ghost, one God, for ever and ever. *Amen.*

II Almighty God, grant unto your people a hunger for your Word and an urgent longing to share your Gospel; that, like your servant Dominic, we might labor to bring the whole world to the knowledge and love of you as you are revealed in your Son Jesus Christ; who lives and reigns with you and the Holy Spirit, one God, for ever and ever. *Amen.*

Lessons and Psalm

Ecclesiastes 12:1-7
Psalm 103:1-7
Romans 10:13-17
John 7:16-18

Preface of a Saint (2)

Edith Stein was born into a Jewish family in Breslau, Germany, in 1891. Although her family was religious observant, Edith became an atheist at the age of 14. A brilliant philosopher, she studied with Edmund Husserl and received her doctorate at the age of 25, even after having interrupted her studies to serve as a nurse during the First World War. She subsequently taught at the University of Freiburg.

Edith became a Christian in 1921 after encountering the autobiography of Teresa of Avila, and she was baptized the following year. Although she felt immediately drawn to the monastic life, particularly Teresa of Avila's own Carmelite tradition, she was dissuaded by her spiritual advisers from pursuing a monastic vocation so soon after her baptism. Instead, she spent several years teaching at a Catholic school and doing intensive study of Catholic philosophy and theology, particularly that of Thomas Aquinas. In 1933 she was forced to leave her teaching position as a result of the anti-Semitic policies of the German Nazi government, and thus she entered a Carmelite community in Cologne where she took the name Teresa Benedicta of the Cross. Even during her life as a nun, however, she continued to produce philosophical works.

In an effort to protect both Edith and her sister Rosa (who had also converted to Christianity and entered the convent) from the Nazis, the nuns transferred both of them to a convent in the Netherlands. Even here, however, they were not safe after the Nazi invasion of the Netherlands. In July of 1942, the Dutch Bishops Conference issued a statement condemning Nazi racism as incompatible with Christianity, which was read in every parish church. In retaliation, the Nazis ordered the arrest of 243 Dutch Christians of Jewish origin, including both Edith and Rosa. Both sisters were killed in the gas chambers of Auschwitz within days of their arrest.

Back in 1933, Edith had written forcefully to the pope, beseeching him to condemn the actions of the Nazi government. "Everything that happened and continues to happen on a daily basis originates with a government that calls itself 'Christian.' For weeks not only Jews but also thousands of faithful Catholics in Germany, and, I believe, all over the world, have been waiting and hoping for the Church of Christ to raise its voice to put a stop to this abuse of Christ's name. Is not this idolization of race and governmental power which is being pounded into the public consciousness by the radio open heresy? Isn't the effort to destroy Jewish blood an abuse of the holiest humanity of our Savior, of the most blessed Virgin and the apostles? Is not all this diametrically opposed to the conduct of our Lord and Savior, who, even on the cross, still prayed for his persecutors? And isn't this a black mark on the record of this Holy Year which was intended to be a year of peace and reconciliation? We all, who are faithful children of the Church and who see the conditions in Germany with open eyes, fear the worst for the prestige of the Church, if the silence continues any longer."

Her letter received no response. Edith Stein was canonized by the Roman Catholic Church in 1998.

Edith Stein (Teresa Benedicta of the Cross)

Philosopher, Monastic, and Martyr, 1942

I Pour out thy grace upon thy church, O God; that, like thy servant Edith Stein, we may always seek what is true, defend what is right, reprove what is evil, and forgive those who sin against us, even as thy Son hath commanded; through the same Jesus Christ our Lord, to whom with thee and the Holy Ghost be all honor and glory, now and for ever. *Amen.*

II Pour out your grace upon thy church, O God; that, like your servant Edith Stein, we may always seek what is true, defend what is right, reprove what is evil, and forgive those who sin against us, even as your Son commanded; through the same Jesus Christ our Lord, to whom with you and the Holy Spirit be all honor and glory, now and for ever. *Amen.*

Lessons and Psalm

Jeremiah 31:31-34
Psalm 119:49-56
2 Corinthians 21:1-10
John 3:1-15

Preface of a Saint (3)

Laurence the Deacon was martyred at Rome during a persecution initiated in 257 by the Emperor Valerian, aimed primarily at clergy and laity of the upper classes. Both of his parents, Orencio and Patientia, had been martyred earlier, but he had been spared in the first wave of persecution, and was subsequently ordained to the diaconate.

On August 4, 258, Pope Sixtus II and his seven deacons were apprehended in the Roman catacombs and summarily executed, except for the archdeacon, Laurence, who was martyred on August 10.

Ambrose relates a tradition that the prefect demanded information from Laurence about the church's treasures, since as archdeacon he had the primary responsibility for distributing alms to the poor and needy. Laurence asked for several days to gather all of the wealth together, during which time he worked quickly to give everything away to those in need. When the prefect again demanded the church's treasures, Laurence pointed to the sick and the poor and said, "These are the treasures of the church."

Laurence is believed to have been roasted alive on a gridiron. According to legend, while being roasted he cheerfully exclaimed, "I am done on this side; turn me over!"

Laurence of Rome

Deacon and Martyr, 258

I Almighty God, by whose grace and power thy servant Laurence didst triumph over suffering and didst despise death: Grant that we may be steadfast in service to the poor and outcast, and may share with him in the joys of thine everlasting kingdom; through Jesus Christ our Lord, who liveth and reigneth with thee and the Holy Ghost, one God, for ever and ever. *Amen.*

II Almighty God, by whose grace and power your servant Laurence triumphed over suffering and despised death: Grant that we may be steadfast in service to the poor and outcast, and may share with him in the joys of your everlasting kingdom; through Jesus Christ our Lord, who lives and reigns with you and the Holy Spirit, one God, for ever and ever. *Amen.*

Lessons and Psalm

Daniel 3:19-27
Psalm 126
2 Corinthians 9:6-10
Luke 14:12-14

Preface of a Saint (3)

In the latter part of the twelfth century, many Christians felt that the church had fallen on evil days and was weak and spiritually impoverished. It was then that Francis of Assisi renounced his wealth and established the mendicant order of Franciscans. At the first gathering of the order in 1212, Francis preached a sermon that was to make a radical change in the life of an eighteen-year-old young woman named Clare Offreduccio.

The daughter of a wealthy family, Clare was inspired by Francis' words with the desire to serve God and to give her life to the following of Christ's teaching. She sought out Francis and begged that she might become a member of his order, placing her jewelry and rich outer garments on the altar as an offering. Francis could not refuse her pleas. He placed her temporarily in a nearby Benedictine convent. When this action became known, friends and relatives tried to take Clare home again, but she remained adamant. She prevailed, and soon after was taken by Francis to a poor dwelling beside the Church of St. Damian at Assisi. Several other women soon joined her. She became the Superior of the order, which was called the "Poor Ladies of St. Damian," and, after her death, the "Poor Clares" in tribute to her.

The order's practices were austere. They embraced the Franciscan rule of absolute poverty. Their days were given over to begging and to works of mercy for the poor and the neglected. Clare herself was servant, not only to the poor, but to her nuns. Her biographer says that she "radiated a spirit of fervor so strong that it kindled those who but heard her voice."

Clare governed her community for 40 years, and outlived Francis by 27 years. After the death of Francis, the order that he had founded quickly began to relax its discipline of strict poverty, and it was Clare and the other sisters who continually urged the brothers to persevere in the commitment that they had made. She resisted several attempts by successive popes to impose a more traditional Benedictine rule on the sisters, since the discipline followed by her community was considered to be too austere for women. When Pope Gregory IX tried to absolve her from the obligation to follow the strict poverty of her rule, Clare replied: "I need to be absolved from my sins, not from the obligation of following Christ." Ultimately, her community and its rule were recognized by the church as a legitimate expression of religious life for women.

In 1253, her last illness began. Daily she weakened, and daily she was visited by devoted people, by priests, and even by the pope. On her last day, as she saw many weeping by her bedside, she exhorted them to love "holy poverty" and to share their possessions. She was heard to say: "Go forth in peace, for you have followed the good road. Go forth without fear, for he that created you has sanctified you, has always protected you, and loves you as a mother. Blessed be God, for having created me."

Clare of Assisi

Monastic, 1253

I O God, whose blessed Son became poor that we, through his poverty, might become rich: Deliver us, we pray thee, from an inordinate love of this world, that we, inspired by the devotion of thy servant Clare, might serve thee with singleness of heart and attain to the riches of the age to come; through Jesus Christ our Lord, who liveth and reigneth with thee, in the unity of the Holy Ghost, one God, now and for ever. *Amen.*

II O God, whose blessed Son became poor that we, through his poverty, might become rich: Deliver us from an inordinate love of this world, that we, inspired by the devotion of your servant Clare, might serve you with singleness of heart and attain to the riches of the age to come; through Jesus Christ our Lord, who lives and reigns with you and the Holy Spirit, one God, for ever and ever. *Amen.*

Lessons and Psalm

Ecclesiastes 5:8-15
Psalm 49:16-20
1 Peter 4:1-2
Luke 12:32-34

Preface of a Saint (2)

Florence Nightingale was born to a wealthy English family in Florence, Italy, on May 12, 1820. She trained as a nurse in a hospital run by a Lutheran order of Deaconesses at Kaiserwerth, and in 1853 became superintendent of a hospital for invalid women in London. In response to God's call and animated by a spirit of service, in 1854 she volunteered for duty during the Crimean War and recruited 38 nurses to join her. With them she organized the first modern nursing service in the British field hospitals of Scutari and Balaclava.

Making late-night rounds to check on the welfare of her charges, a hand-held lantern to aid her, the wounded identified her as "The Lady with the Lamp." By imposing strict discipline and high standards of sanitation, she radically reduced the drastic death toll and rampant infection then typical in field hospitals. She returned to England in 1856, and a fund of £50,000 was subscribed to enable her to form an institution for the training of nurses at St. Thomas's Hospital and at King's College Hospital. Her school at St. Thomas's Hospital became significant in helping to elevate nursing into a profession. She devoted many years to the question of army sanitary reform, to the improvement of nursing, and to public health in India. Her main work, *Notes on Nursing,* went through many editions.

An Anglican, she remained committed to a personal mystical religion, which sustained her through many years of poor health until her death in 1910. Until the end of her life, although her illness prevented her from leaving her home, she continued in frequent spiritual conversation with many prominent church leaders of the day, including the local parish priest, who regularly brought the Eucharist to her. By the time of her death on August 13, 1910, her accomplishments and legacy were widely recognized, and she is honored throughout the world as the founder of the modern profession of nursing.

Florence Nightingale

Nurse, 1910

I O God, who didst give grace to thy servant Florence Nightingale to bear thy healing love into the shadow of death: Grant unto all who heal the same virtues of patience, mercy, and steadfast love, that thy saving health may be revealed to all; through Jesus Christ, who liveth and reigneth with thee and the Holy Ghost, one God, now and for ever. *Amen.*

II O God, who gave grace to your servant Florence Nightingale to bear your healing love into the shadow of death: Grant to all who heal the same virtues of patience, mercy, and steadfast love, that your saving health may be revealed to all; through Jesus Christ, who lives and reigns with you and the Holy Spirit, one God, now and for ever. *Amen.*

Lessons and Psalm

Jeremiah 30:12-17
Psalm 41
1 Corinthians 12:4-11
Luke 10:29-37

Preface of a Saint (1)

Jeremy Taylor, one of the most influential of the "Caroline Divines," was educated at Cambridge and, through the influence of William Laud, became a Fellow of All Souls at Oxford. He was still quite young when he became chaplain to Charles I and later, during the Civil War, a chaplain in the Royalist army.

The successes of Cromwell's forces brought about Taylor's imprisonment and, after Cromwell's victory, Taylor spent several years in forced retirement as chaplain to the family of Lord Carberry in Wales. It was during this time that his most influential works were written, especially *Holy Living* and *Holy Dying* (1651). The opening of *Holy Living* reveals the impact that the Civil War, fought in part over religious concerns, had on him:

"I have lived to see religion painted upon banners, and thrust out of churches; and the temple turned into a tabernacle, and that tabernacle made ambulatory, and covered with skins of beasts and torn curtains; and God to be worshipped, not as he is 'the Father of our Lord Jesus,' (an afflicted Prince, the King of sufferings,) nor as the 'God of Peace,' (which two appellatives God newly took upon him in the New Testament, and glories in forever,) but he is owned now rather as 'the Lord of Hosts,' which title he was preached by the Prince of Peace. But when religion puts on armor, and God is not acknowledged by his New Testament titles, religion may have in it the power of the sword, but not the power of godliness; and we may complain of this to God, and amongst them that are afflicted, but we have no remedy but what we must expect from the fellowship of Christ's sufferings and the returns of the God of peace. In the meantime, and now that religion pretends to stranger actions upon the new principles; and men are apt to prefer a prosperous error before an afflicted truth; and some will think they are religious enough, if their worshippings have in them the great earnestness and passion, with much zeal and desire; that we refuse no labor; that we bestow upon it much time; that we use the best guides, and arrive at the end of glory by all the ways of grace, of prudence, and religion."

Among Taylor's other works, *Liberty of Prophesying* proved to be a seminal work in encouraging the development of religious toleration in the seventeenth century. The principles set forth in that book rank with those of Milton's *Areopagitica* in its plea for freedom of thought.

In later life, Taylor and his family moved to the northeastern part of Ireland where, after the restoration of the monarchy, he became Bishop of Down and Connor. To this was later added the small adjacent diocese of Dromore. As bishop, he labored tirelessly to rebuild churches, restore the use of the Prayer Book, and overcome continuing Puritan opposition. As Vice-Chancellor of Trinity College, Dublin, he took a leading part in reviving the intellectual life of the Church of Ireland. He died in 1667, having remained to the end a man of prayer and a pastor.

Jeremy Taylor

Bishop and Theologian, 1667

I O God, whose days are without end, and whose mercies cannot be numbered: Make us, we beseech thee, like thy servant Jeremy Taylor, deeply sensible of the shortness and uncertainty of human life; and let thy Holy Ghost lead us in holiness and righteousness all our days; through Jesus Christ our Lord, who liveth and reigneth with thee and the Holy Ghost, one God, now and for ever. *Amen.*

II O God, whose days are without end, and whose mercies cannot be numbered: Make us, like your servant Jeremy Taylor, deeply aware of the shortness and uncertainty of human life; and let your Holy Spirit lead us in holiness and righteousness all our days; through Jesus Christ our Lord, who lives and reigns with you and the Holy Spirit, one God, now and for ever. *Amen.*

Lessons and Psalm

Ecclesiastes 3:1-15
Psalm 114
Romans 14:7-12
Mark 13:32-37

Preface of a Saint (1)

Jonathan Myrick Daniels was born in Keene, New Hampshire, in 1939. Like many young adults, from high school in Keene to graduate school at Harvard, Jonathan wrestled with vocation. Attracted to medicine, ordained ministry, law, and writing, he found himself close to a loss of faith until his discernment was clarified by a profound conversion on Easter Day 1962 at the Church of the Advent in Boston. Jonathan then entered the Episcopal Theological School in Cambridge, Massachusetts.

In March 1965, the televised appeal of Martin Luther King, Jr., to come to Selma to secure for all citizens the right to vote touched Jonathan's passions for the well-being of others, the Christian witness of the church, and political justice. His conviction was deepened at Evening Prayer during the singing of the Magnificat: "He hath put down the mighty from their seat and hath exalted the humble and meek. He hath filled the hungry with good things." He wrote: "I knew that I must go to Selma. The Virgin's song was to grow more and more dear to me in the weeks ahead."

In Selma he found himself in the midst of a time and place where the nation's racism and the Episcopal Church's share in that inheritance were exposed. Greatly moved by what he saw and experienced, he returned to seminary, asked leave to work in Selma while continuing his studies, and returned there under the sponsorship of the Episcopal Society for Cultural and Racial Unity.

After a brief return to Cambridge in May to complete his exams, he returned to Alabama to resume his efforts assisting those engaged in the integration struggle. Jailed on August 14 for joining a picket line, Jonathan and his companions resolved to remain together until bail could be posted for all of them, as it was six days later. Released and aware that they were in danger, four of them walked to a small store. As sixteen-year-old Ruby Sales reached the top step of the entrance, a man with a shotgun appeared, cursing her. Jonathan pulled her to one side to shield her from the unexpected threats and was killed instantly by the 12-gauge blast.

Jonathan's letters and papers bear eloquent witness to the profound effect that Selma had upon him. He writes, "The doctrine of the creeds, the enacted faith of the sacraments, were the essential preconditions of the experience itself. The faith with which I went to Selma has not changed: it has grown . . . I began to know in my bones and sinews that I had been truly baptized into the Lord's death and resurrection . . . with them, the black men and white men, with all life, in him whose Name is above all the names that the races and nations shout . . . We are indelibly and unspeakably one."

Jonathan Myrick Daniels

Martyr, 1965

I O God of justice and compassion, who didst put down the proud and the mighty from their place, and dost lift up the poor and the afflicted: We give thee thanks for thy faithful witness Jonathan Myrick Daniels, who, in the midst of injustice and violence, risked and gave his life for another; and we pray that we, following his example, may make no peace with oppression; through Jesus Christ our Savior, who with thee and the Holy Ghost liveth and reigneth, one God, for ever and ever. *Amen.*

II O God of justice and compassion, who puts down the proud and mighty from their place, and lifts up the poor and the afflicted: We give you thanks for your faithful witness Jonathan Myrick Daniels, who, in the midst of injustice and violence, risked and gave his life for another; and we pray that we, following his example, may make no peace with oppression; through Jesus Christ our Savior, who lives and reigns with you and the Holy Spirit, one God, for ever and ever. *Amen.*

Lessons and Psalm

Amos 5:18-24
Psalm 89:7-13
Galatians 3:22-28
Luke 1:46-55

Preface of a Saint (2)

The honor paid to Mary, the Mother of Jesus Christ, goes back to the earliest days of the church. Two Gospels tell of the manner of Christ's birth, and the familiar Christmas story testifies to the church's conviction that he was born of a virgin. In Luke's Gospel, we catch a brief glimpse of Jesus' upbringing at Nazareth, when the child was in the care of his mother and her husband Joseph.

During Jesus' ministry in Galilee, we learn that Mary was often with the other women who followed Jesus and ministered to his needs. At Calvary, she was among the little band of disciples who kept watch at the cross. After the resurrection, she was to be found with the Twelve in the upper room, watching and praying until the coming of the Spirit at Pentecost.

Mary was the person closest to Jesus in his most impressionable years, and the words of the Magnificat, as well as her courageous acceptance of God's will, bear more than an accidental resemblance to the Lord's Prayer and the Beatitudes of the Sermon on the Mount.

Later devotion has claimed many things for Mary beyond the brief description that is given in Holy Scripture. What we can believe is that one who stood in so intimate a relationship with the incarnate Son of God on earth must, of all human beings, have the place of highest honor in the eternal life of God. A paraphrase of an ancient Greek hymn expresses this belief in very familiar words: "O higher than the cherubim, more glorious than the seraphim, lead their praises, alleluia."

Saint Mary the Virgin, Mother of Our Lord Jesus Christ

I O God, who hast taken to thyself the blessed Virgin Mary, mother of thy incarnate Son: Grant that we, who have been redeemed by his blood, may share with her the glory of thine eternal kingdom; through the same thy Son Jesus Christ our Lord, who liveth and reigneth with thee, in the unity of the Holy Ghost, one God, now and for ever. *Amen.*

II O God, you have taken to yourself the blessed Virgin Mary, mother of your incarnate Son: Grant that we, who have been redeemed by his blood, may share with her the glory of your eternal kingdom; through Jesus Christ our Lord, who lives and reigns with you, in the unity of the Holy Spirit, one God, now and for ever. *Amen.*

Lessons and Psalm

Isaiah 61:10-11
Psalm 34 *or* 34:1-9
Galatians 4:4-7
Luke 1:46-55

Preface of the Incarnation

Bernard was the son of a knight and landowner who lived near Dijon, France. He was born in 1090 and given a secular education, but in 1113 he entered the Benedictine Abbey of Citeaux. His family was not pleased with his choice of a monastic life, but he nevertheless persuaded four of his brothers and about twenty-six of his friends to join him. After only three years, the abbot of Citeaux deployed Bernard and a small company of monks to establish a monastery at Clairvaux in 1115.

The work at Clairvaux, and the extreme rigors of the Benedictine rule practiced by the Cistercian community, were taxing. Tasked with much, Bernard denied himself sleep to the detriment of his health that he might have time to write letters and sermons. He preached so persuasively that sixty new abbeys were founded, all affiliated with Clairvaux. Famed for the ardor with which he preached love for God without measure, he fulfilled his own definition of a holy man: “seen to be good and charitable, holding back nothing for himself, but using his every gift for the common good.”

By 1140, his writings had made him one of the most influential figures in Christendom. His guidance was sought by prelates and princes, drawing him into active participation in all manner of controversy involving the church, from settling disputes among secular rulers to sorting contentious theological debates. An ardent opponent of a growing movement of his time to reconcile inconsistencies of doctrine by reason, he felt that such an approach was a downgrading of the mysteries. This conflict took particular expression in his fierce opposition to the formidable theologian Abelard.

Among Bernard’s writings are treatises on humility and pride, on love, on the veneration of Mary, and a commentary on the Song of Songs. Among well-known hymns, he is credited with having written “O sacred head sore wounded” (*The Hymnal 1982*, #168; #169), “Jesus, the very thought of thee” (#642), and “O Jesus, joy of loving hearts” (#649; #650). He died on August 20, 1153.

Bernard of Clairvaux

Monastic and Theologian, 1153

I O God, by whose grace thy servant Bernard of Clairvaux, kindled with the flame of thy love, became a burning and a shining light in thy church: Grant that we also may be aflame with the spirit of love and discipline and walk before thee as children of light; through Jesus Christ our Lord, who liveth and reigneth with thee and the Holy Ghost, one God, now and for ever. *Amen.*

II O God, by whose grace your servant Bernard of Clairvaux, kindled with the flame of your love, became a burning and a shining light in your church: Grant that we also may be aflame with the spirit of love and discipline and walk before you as children of light; through Jesus Christ our Lord, who lives and reigns with you and the Holy Spirit, one God, now and for ever. *Amen.*

Lessons and Psalm

Song of Songs 1:1-8
Psalm 139:1-9
Jude 1-3
Mark 10:23-31

Preface of a Saint (1)

Bartholomew is one of the twelve Apostles known in the Gospels according to Matthew, Mark, and Luke only by name. His name means "Son of Tolmai," and he is sometimes identified with Nathanael, the friend of Philip, the "Israelite without guile" in John's Gospel, to whom Jesus promised the vision of angels ascending and descending on the Son of Man.

There is a tradition that Bartholomew traveled to India, and Eusebius reports that when Pantaenus of Alexandria visited India, between 150 and 200, he found there "the Gospel according to Matthew" in Hebrew, which had been left behind by "Bartholomew, one of the Apostles."

An ancient tradition maintains that Bartholomew was flayed alive at Albanopolis in Armenia.

Saint Bartholomew the Apostle

I Almighty and everlasting God, who didst give to thine apostle Bartholomew grace truly to believe and to preach thy Word: Grant, we beseech thee, that thy church may love what he believed and preach what he taught; through Jesus Christ our Lord, who liveth and reigneth with thee and the Holy Ghost, one God, for ever and ever. *Amen.*

II Almighty and everlasting God, who gave to your apostle Bartholomew grace truly to believe and to preach your Word: Grant that your church may love what he believed and preach what he taught; through Jesus Christ our Lord, who lives and reigns with you and the Holy Spirit, one God, for ever and ever. *Amen.*

Lessons and Psalm

Deuteronomy 18:15-18
Psalm 91 *or* 91:1-4
1 Corinthians 4:9-15
Luke 22:24-30

Preface of Apostles and Ordinations

Louis IX was born at Poissy on April 25, 1214. His father, Louis VIII, died when Louis IX was 11 years old; he was crowned King at Rheims on November 29, 1226. His mother and regent, Blanche of Castile, inspired his early religious exercises of devotion and asceticism. At age 20, Louis married Margaret of Provence, who bore him 11 children, 9 of whom lived past infancy. Blanche remained a major influence on her son Louis IX until her death in 1252.

A man of unusual purity of life and manners, he was sincerely committed to his faith and to its moral demands. Living simply, dressing plainly, visiting hospitals, helping the poor, and acting with integrity and honesty, Louis IX believed that the crown was given him by God and that God would hold him accountable for his reign.

A deplorable aspect of medieval Christianity was its anti-Semitism, and despite his attempts to cultivate holiness, Louis IX was complicit in official action against Jewish believers. Louis ordered the expulsion of all Jews engaged in usury and the confiscation of their property to finance his crusade. At the urging of Pope Gregory IX, Louis also ordered the burning in Paris in 1243 of some 12,000 manuscript copies of the Talmud and other Jewish books and increased the power and authority of the Inquisition in France.

In the winter of 1244, Louis fell gravely ill. In an act customary of the piety and politics of his time and culture, he vowed that if he recovered he would lead a Crusade against the Muslims. Leaving his mother Blanche in charge of the kingdom, Louis led the Seventh Crusade fortified with 36 ships and 15,000 soldiers, including two of his brothers. They began with an attack upon Damietta in Egypt, where Louis won an easy victory in June 1249 that quickly led to disaster as the troops progressed to Cairo. The Egyptian army was numerically superior, the French troops ravaged with famine and disease that forced the Crusaders back to Damietta. But on the way, the Egyptians defeated Louis at Fariskur on April 6, 1250, and he was taken captive. Released only after paying a very large ransom, Louis then went to Acre, where he engaged in a series of fruitless negotiations. When the money ran out, and learning of the death of his mother, Louis IX went home to France.

Back in France, Louis' piety inspired his patronage of the arts and encouraged the spread of Gothic architecture. One of his most notable commissions is Sainte-Chapelle ("Holy Chapel"), located within the royal palace complex in the center of Paris, erected as a shrine for the Crown of Thorns and a fragment of the True Cross, precious relics of the Passion of Jesus that Louis had purchased in 1239–1241 for a sum twice the total cost of the chapel itself.

The Eighth Crusade, launched by Louis IX in 1270 in response to Mamluk attacks against the Christian outposts in Syria, landed him in Tunis in July of 1270. Most of the soldiers dispatched ahead of him had developed diarrheal diseases from poor drinking water. Louis developed "flux of the stomach" and died August 25, 1270. Louis' brother, Charles of Anjou, continued the crusade to a negotiated settlement, and Louis' son, Philip III, succeeded his father as king.

Louis

King, 1270

I O God, who didst call thy servant Louis of France to an earthly throne that he might advance thy heavenly kingdom, and gave him zeal for thy church and love for thy people: Mercifully grant that we who commemorate him this day may be fruitful in good works and attain to the glorious crown of thy saints; through Jesus Christ our Lord, who liveth and reigneth with thee and the Holy Ghost, one God, for ever and ever. *Amen.*

II O God, you called your servant Louis of France to an earthly throne that he might advance your heavenly kingdom, and gave him zeal for your church and love for your people: Mercifully grant that we who commemorate him this day may be fruitful in good works and attain to the glorious crown of your saints; through Jesus Christ our Lord, who lives and reigns with you and the Holy Spirit, one God, for ever and ever. *Amen.*

Lessons and Psalm

Wisdom 7:1-6
Psalm 21:1-7
Colossians 2:6-10
Mark 2:13-17

Preface of Baptism

In the eighth chapter of the Acts of the Apostles, we find the story of Philip and the baptism of an unnamed Ethiopian eunuch. In the second century, the bishop and theologian Irenaeus of Lyons referred to him as Simeon Bachos; this is the name by which this unidentified figure is known in many parts of the Eastern church, including in the Ethiopian Orthodox Tewahedo Church.

According to Acts, he was familiar with the Hebrew scriptures, and his encounter with Philip took place as he traveled from Jerusalem, where he had worshipped at the temple. Some suggest that he was a Jewish convert, while others contend that he was a "Godfearer." Regardless of his previous religious affiliation, scripture records him as the first African person to be baptized.

Simeon Bachos was a person of great prestige, serving the Candace, or Queen, as both chamberlain and treasurer. His status as a eunuch indicates that he was a member of a sexual minority, either a castrated male, a deliberately celibate male, or a gender nonconformist.

Irenaeus describes Simeon Bachos' life after baptism, saying, "This man was also sent into the regions of Ethiopia, to preach what he had himself believed." In the fourth century, the historian Eusebius wrote that "the Eunuch became an apostle for his people." The tenth-century Synaxarion of Constantinople designates August 27 as the commemoration of Simeon Bachos.

As a person of a different race, ethnicity, and gender identification, Simeon Bachos stands at the intersection of multiple marginalized groups. His identity shows that the early church was able to transcend social categories in its evangelizing work and that the gospel's message would spread to the ends of the earth and to every person. Simeon Bachos calls Christians to be fully inclusive and welcoming of all people, empowering them for ministry and leadership.

Simeon Bachos, the Ethiopian Eunuch

I Holy One of love, thou didst call thy servant Simeon Bachos to study thy Word and led him to the waters of baptism, making him thy evangelist to Ethiopia: give to us the grace to follow where thou leadest, overcoming the barriers that divide and diminish thy people, that we may behold thee in all thy glory; through our Savior and Lord Jesus Christ, who with thee and the Holy Spirit liveth and reigneth for ever and ever. *Amen.*

II Holy One of love, you called your servant Simeon Bachos to study your word and led him to the waters of baptism, making him your evangelist to Ethiopia: give us the grace to follow where you lead, overcoming the barriers that divide and diminish your people, that we may behold you in all your glory; through our Savior and Lord Jesus Christ, who with you and the Holy Spirit lives and reign for ever and ever. *Amen.*

Lessons and Psalm

Isaiah 53:1-9
Psalm 68:28-29, 31-35
Acts 8:26-40
Matthew 19:3-12

Preface of a Saint (1)

Ministry to the deaf in the Episcopal Church begins with Thomas Gallaudet and his protégé, Henry Winter Syle. Without Gallaudet's genius and zeal for the spiritual well-being of deaf persons, it is improbable that a history of ministry to the deaf in the Episcopal Church could be written. He has been called "The Apostle to the Deaf."

Gallaudet was born June 3, 1822, in Hartford. He was the eldest son of Thomas Hopkins Gallaudet, founder of the West Hartford School for the Deaf, and his wife, Sophia, who was deaf.

After graduating from Trinity College in Hartford, Connecticut, Thomas announced his desire to become a priest in the Episcopal Church. His father, who was a Congregationalist minister, prevailed upon him to postpone a final decision, and to accept a teaching position in the New York Institution for Deaf-Mutes. There he met and married a deaf woman named Elizabeth Budd.

Gallaudet was ordained as a deacon in 1850 and served his diaconate at St. Stephen's Church, where he established a Bible class for deaf persons. Ordained as a priest in 1851, Gallaudet became Assistant Rector at St. Ann's Church, where he conceived a plan for establishing a church that would be a spiritual home for deaf people. This became a reality the following year, with the founding of St. Ann's Church for Deaf-Mutes. The congregation was able to purchase a church building in 1859, and it became a center for missionary work to the deaf continuing into its merger with the parish of Calvary-St. George in 1976. As a result of this ministry, mission congregations were established in many cities. Gallaudet died on August 27, 1902.

One fruit of Gallaudet's ministry was Henry Winter Syle. Born in China, he had lost his hearing as a young child as the result of scarlet fever. Educated at Trinity College, Hartford; St. John's College, Cambridge, England; and Yale University, Syle was a brilliant student, who persisted in his determination to obtain an education in spite of his deafness and fragile health. He was encouraged by Gallaudet to offer himself for ordination as a priest, and was supported in that call by Bishop William Bacon Stevens of Pennsylvania, against the opposition of many who believed that the impairment of one of the senses was an impediment to ordination. Syle was ordained as a deacon in 1876, the first deaf person to be ordained in this church, and later ordained as a priest in 1883. In 1888, he built All Souls Church for the Deaf in Philadelphia, the first Episcopal church constructed especially for deaf persons. He died on January 6, 1890.

Thomas Gallaudet and Henry Winter Syle

Priests, 1902 and 1890

I O Loving God, whose will it is that everyone shouldst come to thee and be saved: We bless thy holy Name for thy servants Thomas Gallaudet and Henry Winter Syle, and we pray that thou wilt continually move thy church to respond in love to the needs of all people; through Jesus Christ, who liveth and reigneth with thee and the Holy Ghost, one God, now and for ever. *Amen.*

II O Loving God, whose will it is that everyone should come to you and be saved: We bless your holy Name for your servants Thomas Gallaudet and Henry Winter Syle, and we pray that you will continually move your church to respond in love to the needs of all people; through Jesus Christ, who lives and reigns with you and the Holy Spirit, one God, now and for ever. *Amen.*

Lessons and Psalm

Isaiah 35:1-7
Psalm 119:1-8
2 Thessalonians 1:3-4
Mark 7:31-37

Preface of Pentecost

Augustine, perhaps the most influential theologian in the history of Western Christianity, was born in 354 at Tagaste in North Africa. In his restless search for truth, he was attracted by Manichaeism and Neoplatonism, and was constantly engaged in an inner struggle against sin. Finally, under the influence of his mother, Monica, Augustine surrendered to the Christian faith in the late summer of 386. He was baptized by Ambrose, Bishop of Milan, on Easter Eve in 387. After returning to North Africa in 391, Augustine found himself chosen by the people of Hippo to be a priest. Four years later he was chosen bishop of that city. His spiritual autobiography, *The Confessions,* written shortly before 400 in the form of an extended prayer, is a classic of Western spirituality. He famously wrote, "You have made us for yourself, O Lord, and our hearts are restless until they rest in you."

Augustine wrote countless treatises, letters, and sermons. They have provided a rich source of new and fresh insights into Christian truth, and became foundational of later Christian theology as it developed in the Western church.

Much of Augustine's theology developed in dialogue with those he disagreed with, and his training in rhetoric is on full display. The Manichaeans had attempted to solve the problem of evil by positing the existence of an independent agent eternally opposed to God. In refutation, Augustine affirmed that all creation is essentially good, having been created by God, and that evil is, properly speaking, the privation of good. A rigorist sect, the Donatists, had split from the rest of the church after the persecution of Diocletian in the early fourth century. Against them, Augustine asserted that the church was "holy," not because its members could be proved holy, but because holiness was a property of the church, to which all its members are called.

Stirred by Alaric the Visigoth's sack of Rome in 410, Augustine wrote his great work, *The City of God.* In it he writes: "Two cities have been formed by two loves: the earthly by love of self, even to the contempt of God, the heavenly by the love of God, even to the contempt of self. The earthly city glories in itself, the heavenly city glories in the Lord . . . In the one, the princes, and the nations it subdues, are ruled by the love of ruling; in the other, the princes and the subjects serve one another in love."

Augustine died on August 28, 430, as the Vandals were besieging his own earthly city of Hippo.

Augustine of Hippo

Bishop and Theologian, 430

I Lord God, the light of the minds that know thee, the life of the souls that love thee, and the strength of the hearts that serve thee: Help us, following the example of thy servant, Augustine of Hippo, so to know thee that we may truly love thee, and so to love thee that we may fully serve thee, whose service is perfect freedom; through Jesus Christ our Lord, who liveth and reigneth with thee and the Holy Ghost, one God, now and for ever. *Amen.*

II Lord God, the light of the minds that know you, the life of the souls that love you, and the strength of the hearts that serve you: Help us, following the example of your servant, Augustine of Hippo, so to know you that we may truly love you, and so to love you that we may fully serve you, whose service is perfect freedom; through Jesus Christ our Lord, who lives and reigns with you and the Holy Spirit, one God, now and for ever. *Amen.*

Lessons and Psalm

Wisdom 16:20-26
Psalm 87
Hebrews 12:22-29
John 14:5-15

Preface of Baptism

All four Gospels give an account of John the Baptist as a prophet and preacher whose ministry created expectation and awakened a wave of repentance leading to baptism among many different groups of people. Two Sundays in Advent focus on that preaching and the First Sunday after the Epiphany celebrates Jesus' baptism by John as a central moment where the fullness of Christ's humanity and divinity are revealed. In Mark's Gospel, John's arrest is the moment when Jesus begins his public ministry. John's death likewise has a profound impact on the narrative in the Gospels.

Herod, who regarded John with the apprehension of a tyrant for a leader among the people and with the superstitious dread of the wicked for true spiritual power, let himself be cornered into condemning John to death. The Gospel recounts the sordid tale of a young woman's manipulation and the foolish promise that Herod makes. Caught by his own rash promise and pride, Herod has the man he fears put to death and his head delivered on a platter to the girl, who takes it to her mother, Herodias. The gruesome narrative ends, as John's disciples take his body and bury it and then go to Jesus to tell him what has happened.

After the death of John the Baptist, Jesus, with his disciples, withdraws from the crowds, but they follow. No doubt the unjust execution of a fierce and admired prophet left many in fear, anger, and confusion. That day's teaching led to the Feeding of the Five Thousand and soon thereafter to the Transfiguration, Peter's Confession, and the First Prediction of the Passion. As John's ministry had been integral to the beginning of Jesus' ministry, John's death was part of the turning point as the narratives turn toward Jerusalem and the cross.

John's role as the one who points toward Jesus and who baptized him, the family connections that Luke's birth narrative relates, and the role that John plays in the spiritual life of the people give weight to his death which, like his preaching, foreshadowed Jesus' ministry and his death.

This feast, along with the Feast of the Nativity of St. John the Baptist, found its place in the church's calendar very early.

The Beheading of Saint John the Baptist

I Almighty God, who didst call thy servant John to be the forerunner of thy Son our Lord both in life and death; Grant, we beseech thee, that as we remember his faithfulness unto death, we may with boldness speak thy truth and with humility be ready to hear it; through Jesus Christ, the firstborn from the dead, who with Thee and the Holy Ghost, livest and reignest one God, for ever and ever. *Amen.*

II Almighty God, who called your servant John the Baptist to go before your Son our Lord both in life and death; Grant that we who remember his witness may with boldness speak your truth and in humility hear it when it is spoken to us, through Jesus Christ, the firstborn from the dead, who with you and the Holy Spirit lives and reigns one God for ever and ever. *Amen.*

Lessons and Psalm

Wisdom 2:23—3:9
Psalm 5:1-5
2 Corinthians 4:5-11
Matthew 14:1-12

Preface of a Saint (2)

To their credit, our sixteenth-century ancestors perceived a vital connection between politics, religion, and morality; to their shame, both Catholics and Protestants pursued the righteousness of Christ with the sword. Despite her pacific disposition and refusal to "make windows into men's souls," many Roman Catholics were persecuted as traitors by Anglican magistrates during the reign of Elizabeth I. Margaret Ward, Margaret Clitherow, and Anne Line, along with the Forty Martyrs of England and Wales canonized by Paul VI in 1970, fell victims to this Anti-Catholic violence. Though we rightly celebrate the flourishing of Anglicanism in the reign of Elizabeth, we must repent of zeal without knowledge and unjust violence.

Nothing is known of the early life of Margaret Ward, the Pearl of Tyburn. She helped a Roman Catholic priest, William (or Richard) Watson, to escape from Bridewell Prison. Discovered and arrested, Ward was questioned, kept in irons for eight days, hanged by the wrists and scourged; nevertheless, she refused to disclose the whereabouts of Watson. Liberty was offered if she would worship at an Anglican service and beseech pardon of the Queen. Refusing, Ward was executed by hanging on August 30, 1588.

Margaret Clitherow, called the Pearl of York, converted to the Roman Catholic faith. Her husband, whose brother was a Roman Catholic priest, remained in the Church of England. He paid the fines levied for his wife's lack of attendance at church and allowed her to harbor priests in their home, an offense punishable by death. Discovered and arrested, Clitherow refused to plea, sparing her children from testifying against their mother. To induce a plea, weights were placed on a board until she was crushed. Clitherow died on Good Friday 1586, which coincided with the Annunciation that year. Hearing of her cruel death, Elizabeth wrote to the people of York to protest the execution of a woman.

Anne Line and her brother were converts to the Roman faith disinherited by their Puritan father. Born Alice Higham, she took the name Anne after her conversion, and was married to Roger Line, who was also a disinherited convert. After her husband's death, Anne was entrusted to keep a house of refuge for fugitive priests by the Jesuit missionary-priest John Gerard. On Candlemas 1601, during the blessing of the candles, her house was raided. At her trial, Line told the court she only regretted not being able to harbor a thousand more priests. She was executed by hanging on February 27.

Margaret Ward, Margaret Clitherow, and Anne Line

Martyrs, 1588, 1586, and 1601

I Most Merciful God, who despisest not a broken and contrite heart and hath promised to fill those who hunger and thirst after righteousness; We humbly beseech thee, remember not the sins and offenses of our forefathers, but grant that, like thy servants Margaret Ward, Margaret Clitherow, and Anne Line, we may sanctify thee in our hearts and be always ready to answer for our faith with meekness and fear; through our only Mediator and Advocate, Jesus Christ our Lord. *Amen.*

II Most Merciful God, who despises not a broken and contrite heart and has promised to fill those who hunger and thirst after righteousness; We humbly beseech you, remember not the sins and offenses of our ancestors, but grant that, like your servants Margaret Ward, Margaret Clitherow, and Anne Line, we may sanctify you in our hearts and be always ready to answer for our faith with meekness and fear; through our only Mediator and Advocate, Jesus Christ our Lord. *Amen.*

Lessons and Psalm

Ezekiel 37:1-14
Psalm 43
Romans 1:16-17
Mark 13:3-13

Preface of Lent (1)

The Gospel first came to the northern English in 627, when King Edwin of Northumbria was converted by a mission from Canterbury led by Bishop Paulinus, who established his see at York. Edwin's death in battle in 632 was followed by a severe pagan reaction. A year later, Edwin's exiled nephew Oswald gained the kingdom, and proceeded at once to restore the Christian mission.

During his exile, Oswald had lived at Columba's monastery of Iona, where he had been converted and baptized. Hence he sent to Iona, rather than to Canterbury, for missionaries. The head of the new mission was a gentle monk named Aidan, who centered his work, not at York, but in imitation of his home monastery, on Lindisfarne, an island off the northeast coast of England.

With his fellow monks and the English youths whom he trained, Aidan restored Christianity in Northumbria, King Oswald often serving as his interpreter, and extended the mission through the midlands as far south as London.

Aidan died at the royal town of Bamborough, on August 31, 651. The historian Bede said of him: "He neither sought nor loved anything of this world, but delighted in distributing immediately to the poor whatever was given him by kings or rich men of the world. He traversed both town and country on foot, never on horseback, unless compelled by some urgent necessity. Wherever in his way he saw any, either rich or poor, he invited them, if pagans, to embrace the mystery of the faith; or if they were believers, to strengthen them in their faith and stir them up by words and actions to alms and good works."

Aidan of Lindisfarne

Bishop, 651

I O loving God, who didst call thy servant Aidan from the cloister to re-establish the Christian mission in northern England: Grant, we beseech thee, that we, following his example, may use what thou hast given us for the relief of human need, and may persevere in commending the saving Gospel of our Redeemer Jesus Christ; who liveth and reigneth with thee and the Holy Ghost, one God, for ever and ever. *Amen.*

II O loving God, you called your servant Aidan from the cloister to re-establish the Christian mission in northern England: Grant that we, following his example, may use what you have given us for the relief of human need, and may persevere in commending the saving Gospel of our Redeemer Jesus Christ; who lives and reigns with you and the Holy Spirit, one God, for ever and ever. *Amen.*

Lessons and Psalm

Proverbs 3:21-32
Psalm 103:13-18
1 Corinthians 9:16-23
Matthew 19:27-30

Preface of Apostles and Ordinations

"God's warrior" is an epithet by which David Pendleton Oakerhater is known among the Cheyenne Indians of Oklahoma. The title is an apt one, for this apostle of Christ to the Cheyenne was originally a soldier who fought against the United States government with warriors of other tribes in the disputes over Indian land rights. Born around the year 1851, by the late 1860s Oakerhater had distinguished himself for bravery and leadership as an officer in an elite corps of Cheyenne fighters.

In 1875, after a year of minor uprisings and threats of major violence, he and twenty-seven other warrior leaders were taken prisoner by the U.S. Army, charged with inciting rebellion, and sent to a disused military prison in Florida. Under the influence of a concerned Army captain, who sought to educate the prisoners, Oakerhater and his companions learned English, gave art and archery lessons to the area's many visitors, and had their first encounter with the Christian faith. The captain's example, and that of other concerned Christians from as far away as New York, had a profound effect on the young warrior. He was moved to answer the call to transform his leadership in war into a lifelong ministry of peace.

With sponsorship from the Diocese of Central New York and financial help from a Mrs. Pendleton of Cincinnati, he and three other prisoners went north to study for the ministry. At his baptism in Syracuse in 1878, he took the name David Pendleton Oakerhater, in honor of his benefactress. Soon after his ordination to the diaconate in 1881, Oakerhater returned to Oklahoma. There, he was instrumental in founding and operating schools and missions, through great personal sacrifice and often in the face of apathy from the church hierarchy and resistance from the government. He continued his ministry of service, education, and pastoral care among his people until his death on August 31, 1931.

Half a century before, the young deacon had told his people: "You all know me. You remember when I led you out to war I went first, and what I told you was true. Now I have been away to the East and I have learned about another captain, the Lord Jesus Christ, and he is my leader. He goes first, and all he tells me is true. I come back to my people to tell you to go with me now in this new road, a war that makes all for peace."

David Pendleton Oakerhater

Deacon, 1931

I O God of unsearchable wisdom and mercy; Liberate us from bondage to self, and empower us to serve thee and our neighbors that like thy servant David Oakerhater, we might bring those who do not know thee to the knowledge and love of thee; through Jesus Christ, the captain of our salvation, who liveth and reigneth with thee and the Holy Ghost, one God for ever and ever. *Amen.*

II O God of unsearchable wisdom and mercy; Liberate us from bondage to self, and empower us to serve you and our neighbors, that like your servant David Oakerhater, we might bring those who do not know you to the knowledge and love of you; through Jesus Christ, the captain of our salvation, who lives and reigns with you and the Holy Spirit, one God for ever and ever. *Amen.*

Lessons and Psalm

Daniel 1:1-17
Psalm 11
Romans 8:1-6
Luke 10:1-9

Preface of Apostles and Ordinations

New Guinea, the second-largest island in the world, is still one of the main frontiers of Christian mission, because of its difficult terrain and the cultural diversity of its peoples, who speak some 500 distinct languages. Christian missionaries first began work there in the 1860s and 1870s, with only limited success. The Anglican mission began in 1891, and the first bishop was consecrated in 1898.

During World War II, the suffering of both the native people and the missionaries was severe. One historian reckons that the total number of martyrs from all Christian denominations during this period was around 330. This feast day, observed in the Diocese of New Guinea and in the Church of Australia, marks the witness of nine Australian missionaries and two Papuan martyrs who died while serving those who needed them.

The missionaries were determined to remain with their people during the Japanese invasion and to continue their work of healing, teaching, and evangelism. Once the invasion occurred, however, they realized that their presence was a danger to the local people with whom they stayed; any people of European descent were considered enemy combatants, and villages harboring them were severely punished. Two of the missionaries, one Australian and one Papuan, were evacuating with the villagers when their boat was strafed and sunk by seaplanes. The remaining missionaries were captured in the bush. Some were executed by soldiers, and others by locals who feared retribution for their presence.

One of the Papuan martyrs, Lucian Tapiedi, is among the ten twentieth-century martyrs honored with a statue above the west door of Westminster Abbey in London. While accompanying his Australian companions as a guide, he was separated from the group and killed by a local Orokaiva named Hivijapa. After the war, Hivijapa converted to Christianity, was baptized as Hivijapa Lucian, and built a church at Embi in memory of the evangelist whom he had slain.

In 1950, the Primate of the Anglican Church in Japan gave several bamboo crosses to be erected at the parish churches of the martyrs as a mark of contrition. In addition to remembering those who gave up their lives, the day also includes remembrance of the faith and devotion of Papuan Christians of all churches, who risked their own lives to care for the wounded, and to save the lives of many who otherwise would have perished.

The Martyrs of New Guinea

1942

I Almighty God, we remember before thee this day the blessed martyrs of New Guinea, who, following the example of their Savior, laid down their lives for their friends, and we pray that we who honor their memory may imitate their loyalty and faith; through Jesus Christ our Lord, who liveth and reigneth with thee and the Holy Ghost, one God, for ever and ever. *Amen.*

II Almighty God, we remember before you this day the blessed martyrs of New Guinea, who, following the example of their Savior, laid down their lives for their friends, and we pray that we who honor their memory may imitate their loyalty and faith; through Jesus Christ our Lord, who lives and reigns with you and the Holy Spirit, one God, for ever and ever. *Amen.*

Lessons and Psalm

1 Chronicles 22:11-13
Psalm 130
Revelation 7:9-12
Luke 12:4-12

Preface of Holy Week

Phoebe appears once in Paul's letter to the Romans (16:1), where she is referred to as both a deacon in the church at Cenchreae, near Corinth, and a benefactor of Paul and others.

The fact that Paul commends her to the Roman church at the end of the letter suggests the possibility that she was the messenger, which would speak highly of Paul's trust in her. There may even have been more to her mission, as Paul commands the Christians in Rome to help her in whatever she needs.

It is unknown what other impact she had in the early church, but she is an example of the many early workers who supported Paul in the spreading of the Gospel, often personally carrying that message across the Empire. We may often think that Paul did it all himself, or at least with the help of only a few of the more prominent individuals such as Luke. But the brief mention of Phoebe gives us an example of the many women and men whose calling was to work faithfully in the background to ensure that the Gospel would spread throughout the world.

Phoebe

Deacon

I Eternal God, who didst raise up Phoebe as a deacon in thy church and minister of thy Gospel; Grant unto us the same grace, that aided by her prayers and example, we too may take the Gospel unto the ends of the earth; through Jesus Christ thy Son our Lord who liveth and reigneth with thee, in the unity of the Holy Ghost, one God, for ever and ever. *Amen.*

II Eternal God, who raised up Phoebe as a deacon in your church and minister of your Gospel; Grant us that same grace that, assisted by her prayers and example, we too may take the Gospel to the ends of the earth; through Jesus Christ your Son our Lord who lives and reigns with you, in the unity of the Holy Spirit, one God, for ever and ever. *Amen.*

Lessons and Psalm

Ezekiel 2:1-7
Psalm 40:4-10
Romans 16:1-7
Luke 22:24-27

Preface of Apostles and Ordinations

Paul Jones was born in 1880 in the rectory of St. Stephen's Church, Wilkes-Barre, Pennsylvania. After graduating from Yale University and the Episcopal Theological School in Cambridge, Massachusetts, he accepted a call to serve a mission in Logan, Utah. In 1914, he was appointed archdeacon of the Missionary District of Utah and, later that year, was elected its bishop. Meanwhile, World War I had begun.

As Bishop of Utah, Paul Jones did much to expand the church's mission stations and to strengthen diocesan institutions. At the same time, he spoke openly about his opposition to war. With the entry of the United States into the war, the Bishop of Utah's views became increasingly controversial. At a meeting of the Fellowship of Reconciliation in Los Angeles in 1917, Bishop Jones expressed his belief that "war is unchristian," for which he was attacked with banner headlines in the Utah press.

As a result of the speech and the reaction it caused in Utah, a commission of the House of Bishops was appointed to investigate the situation. In their report, the commission concluded that "The underlying contention of the Bishop of Utah seems to be that war is unchristian. With this general statement the Commission cannot agree . . ." The report went on to recommend that "The Bishop of Utah ought to resign his office," thus rejecting Paul Jones' right to object to war on grounds of faith and conscience.

In the spring of 1918, Bishop Jones, yielding to pressure, resigned as Bishop of Utah. In his farewell to the Missionary District of Utah in 1918, Bishop Jones said: "Where I serve the Church is of small importance, so long as I can make my life count in the cause of Christ . . . Expediency may make necessary the resignation of a bishop at this time, but no expedience can ever justify the degradation of the ideals of the episcopate which these conclusions seem to involve."

For the rest of his life, he continued a ministry within the church dedicated to peace and conscience, speaking always with a conviction and gentleness rooted in the gospel. Bishop Jones died on September 4, 1941.

Paul Jones

Bishop, 1941

I Merciful God, who didst send thy beloved Son to preach peace to those who are far off and to those who are near: Raise up in this and every land witnesses, who, after the example of thy servant Paul Jones, will stand firm in proclaiming the Gospel of the Prince of Peace, our Savior Jesus Christ, who liveth and reigneth with thee and the Holy Ghost, one God, now and for ever. *Amen.*

II Merciful God, you sent your beloved Son to preach peace to those who are far off and to those who are near: Raise up in this and every land witnesses who, after the example of your servant Paul Jones, will stand firm in proclaiming the Gospel of the Prince of Peace, our Savior Jesus Christ, who lives and reigns with you and the Holy Spirit, one God, now and for ever. *Amen.*

Lessons and Psalm

Malachi 2:17—3:5
Psalm 120
1 Peter 3:8-17
John 8:31-36

Preface of a Saint (3)

Katharina Schutz Zell was born in 1497 in Strasbourg. Reform and protest against abuses in the church reached her part of the world early on, and the twelve-person Schutz family—artisans, not nobility—were convinced. Katharina was especially interested in the new thinking and teaching about the church. She was intent on seeking a holy life; for a long time, this meant a dedicated celibacy, but as a Protestant, she was convinced of the holiness of marriage as a vocation, and late in 1523 she married Matthew Zell, the most popular priest and preacher in Strasbourg.

For clergy to marry was truly a startling thing for Christians in this time; even some of the new Protestant Christians found it difficult, distasteful, or immoral. In response to the city's reaction, Zell wrote a letter to the bishop building a Biblical defense of the marriage of priests, and describing the traits of a good pastor. Though she wanted to publish it, she accepted the city council's demand to keep quiet. In September of 1524, however, she published a pamphlet addressed to her fellow (lay) Christians explaining the Biblical basis for clerical marriage and for her ability (as a woman) to speak on such things. She argues that when a Christian speaks out in this way, it is significant as an act of love to her neighbor.

That same year, 150 men and their families were driven out of Kentzingen because of their beliefs; Katharina and her husband purportedly welcomed 80 of these people in their home. She wrote a "Letter to the suffering women of the Community of Kentzingen, who believe in Christ, sisters with me in Jesus Christ," in which she interpreted these women's painful experiences in light of Scripture and the promises of Christ, in order to encourage them on their path.

Throughout her life she continued to welcome refugees and to visit those sick with plague, syphilis, and other feared diseases. Some of her guests were more well known than others; she welcomed Martin Bucer (who had performed her marriage) when he fled Weissenburg, and John Calvin when he fled France. She also continued to write throughout her life—a funeral oration for her husband, pamphlets, letters (including a correspondence with Luther), and Scriptural commentary. Her last published work was a commentary on Psalm 50, Psalm 130, and the Lord's Prayer.

When, later in life, she was accused by her husband's successor of disturbing the peace of the city, she wrote, "Do you call this disturbing the peace that instead of spending my time in frivolous amusements I have visited the plague infested and carried out the dead? I have visited those in prison and under sentence of death. Often for three days and nights I have neither eaten or slept. I have never mounted the pulpit, but I have done more than any minister in visiting those in misery. Is this disturbing the peace of the church?"

Katharina Zell

Church Reformer and Writer, 1562

I Almighty God, whose servant Katharina Zell toiled for the reform of thy church both in word and in deed: Fill us with the wisdom to speak out in defense of thy truth, with love for thee and for our neighbor, that we may serve thee and welcome all thy people with a mother's heart; through Christ our Lord. *Amen.*

II Almighty God, whose servant Katharina Zell toiled for the reform of your church both in word and in deed: Fill us with the wisdom to speak out in defense of your truth, with love for you and for our neighbor, that we may serve you and welcome all your people with a mother's heart; through Christ our Lord. *Amen.*

Lessons and Psalm

Genesis 38:6-26
Psalm 71:17-23
Galatians 5:13-18
Luke 4:23-30

Preface of a Saint (2)

Hannah More brought a wide array of gifts and talents to her work in the church. She was a religious writer, poet and playwright, philanthropist, social reformer, and abolitionist.

More was born in Bristol in 1745 and was raised in the Church of England. She and her four sisters were instructed at home by their father, who was a local schoolteacher. When the oldest two sisters had reached adulthood, their father established a school for girls and placed them in charge of it. Hannah completed her education there and then taught at the school herself.

Hannah devoted considerable energy to writing even as a child. Her first works were poems and plays that were intended to be performed in girls' schools, with the characters being primarily women. In the 1780s, Hannah became friends with James Oglethorpe, an early abolitionist who was working to abolish the slave trade. Around this time, she began to address issues of religious concerns and social reform, particularly the evils of slavery. She also wrote on a number of other religious topics, with important works such as *Practical Piety* (1811), *Christian Morals* (1813), and *The Character of St. Paul* (1815). Her works were extremely popular in some circles but reviled in others. In his 1906 work *Hannah More Once More,* the lawyer and politician Augustine Birrell admits to burying all 19 volumes of her work in his garden in disgust.

More was heavily active in philanthropic work, establishing twelve schools for the education of poor children. She also donated money to Bishop Philander Chase for the establishment of Kenyon College, and established a number of Sunday Schools which offered instruction in both literacy and Christianity. Many of More's poems drew forceful attention to the evils of slavery and forced the issue into the public gaze. While their literary quality is often not to modern tastes, in their own day they were very influential, and raised awareness of the issue among literary circles who were not otherwise inclined to discussions of public policy and social reform. This is an excerpt from her poem *Slavery:*

> I see, by more than Fancy's mirrow shewn,
> The burning village, and the blazing town:
> See the dire victim torn from social life,
> The shrieking babe, the agonizing wife!
> She, wretch forlorn! is dragg'd by hostile hands,
> To distant tyrants sold, in distant lands!
> Transmitted miseries, and successive chains,
> The sole sad heritage her child obtains!
> Ev'n this last wretched boon their foes deny,
> To weep together, or together die.
> By felon hands, by one relentless stroke,
> See the fond links of feeling nature broke!
> The fibres twisting round a parent's heart,
> Torn from their grasp, and bleeding as they part.
> Hold, murderers, hold! not aggravate distress;
> Respect the passions you yourselves possess.

Hannah More

Religious Writer and Philanthropist, 1833

I Almighty God, whose only-begotten Son led captivity captive: Multiply among us faithful witnesses like thy servant Hannah More, who will fight for all who are oppressed or held in bondage, and bring us all, we pray, into the glorious liberty that thou hast promised to all thy children; through Jesus Christ our Lord, who liveth and reigneth with thee and the Holy Ghost, one God, for ever and ever. *Amen.*

II Almighty God, whose only-begotten Son led captivity captive: Multiply among us faithful witnesses like your servant Hannah More, who will fight for all who are oppressed or held in bondage, and bring us all, we pray, into the glorious liberty that you have promised to all your children; through Jesus Christ our Lord, who lives and reigns with you and the Holy Spirit, one God, for ever and ever. *Amen.*

Lessons and Psalm

Genesis 21:14-21
Psalm 146:4-9
Romans 13:8-10
John 9:1-12

Preface of Baptism

Élie Naud (also known as Elias Nead) was a French Huguenot (French Reformed) born in 1661. It was an era when French Roman Catholicism was increasingly dominant and the persecution of Protestants was becoming more violent. Naud fled France and landed in England, where he sojourned briefly before settling permanently in New York City. During his early years in New York, he traveled frequently to Europe to raise money for Huguenot causes, having to take passage in steerage because he was not a Roman Catholic. His unwillingness to renounce his French Reformed faith resulted in his imprisonment for nearly two years in the infamous Chateau d'If.

In New York City, Naud became a member of L'Eglise du Saint-Esprit, a French-speaking parish which eventually joined The Episcopal Church, and later of Trinity Church, Wall Street, where he served for fifteen years as a catechist among slaves and Native Americans, preparing them for baptism.

Naud founded a school for the children of the poor and for the children of slaves. Upon the recommendation of the Rector of Trinity Church, the Bishop of London, acting for the Society for the Propagation of the Gospel (SPG), licensed Naud as a missioner "to slaves and ragged people in the New World." Naud also worked to influence Parliament for the passage of British laws that would demand Christian instruction for the children of slaves and Native Americans and schools for their education. Only through these means, he believed, could an equal and free society be created. During the New York City slave riot of 1712, Naud remained faithful to his vision despite threats of death from those who believed education of slaves fueled such uprisings.

Naud continued to write hymns and poetry in his native French throughout his life. He died on September 7, 1722, and was buried in the churchyard at Trinity Church, Wall Street.

[Élie Naud]

Huguenot Witness to the Faith, 1722

I Blessed God, whose Son Jesus calmed the waves and knelt to serve his disciples: We give thee honor for the witness of the Huguenot Élie Naud, remembered as Mystic of the Galleys and Servant of Slaves; praying that, with him, we may proclaim Christ in suffering and joy alike, and call others to join us in ministry to those littlest and least, following Jesus who came not to be ministered to but to minister; who liveth and reigneth with thee and the Holy Spirit, one God, to whom be honor and glory for ever and ever. *Amen.*

II Blessed God, whose Son Jesus calmed the waves and knelt to serve his disciples: We honor you for the witness of the Huguenot Élie Naud, remembered as Mystic of the Galleys and Servant of Slaves; and we pray that we, with him, may proclaim Christ in suffering and joy alike, and call others to join us in ministry to those littlest and least, following Jesus who came not to be ministered to but to minister; who lives and reigns with you and the Holy Spirit, one God, to whom be honor and glory for ever and ever. *Amen.*

Lessons and Psalm

Daniel 6:10b-16, 19-23
Psalm 30
James 1:2-4, 12a
Matthew 15:21-28

Preface of Baptism

Kassiani is the only woman whose writings appear in the official liturgies of the Orthodox Church, and one of only two Byzantine women who is known as an author under her own name. Born to a wealthy family in Constantinople before 810, Kassiani received an excellent education in matters both secular and sacred, impressing bishops and monastic leaders such as Theodore the Studite with her literary style and knowledge while she was still a young girl.

According to three Byzantine chroniclers, when Emperor Michael II of Amorion died, his son Theophilos succeeded him. To find a suitable empress for Theophilos, a "bride show" of eligible maidens was arranged, Kassiani amongst six finalists. In an ancient custom involving the exchange of a golden apple, Theophilos approached Kassiani saying, "From woman [Eve] came our corruption." Kassiani coolly replied, "But from woman [the virgin Mary] also came our exaltation." Her bold response evidently proved too much for Theophilos, who then moved past her to offer the apple to Theodora.

After her rejection by Theophilos, Kassiani immediately embraced the monastic life—with what seemed more relief than disappointment at her narrow escape from becoming empress. Her pursuits as a nun included musical and literary accomplishments of distinction, courageous defenses of the veneration of icons, and the founding of a new convent. She was actively involved in the theological controversies of her day, and an iambic verse she penned denotes her bravery: "I hate silence, when it is time to speak."

By 843, Kassiani had built a convent on Xerólophos, the seventh hill of Constantinople, becoming its first abbess. Most notably, however, Kassiani was a prolific hymnographer and poet. Hundreds of poems and approximately fifty of her hymns are extant, including both her musical compositions and lyrics; of those, at least twenty-three hymns are included in Orthodox liturgical books. The most famous, the Hymn of Kassiani, is sung in the Orthodox Church on the eve of Holy Wednesday.

Kassiani

Poet and Hymnographer, 865

I O God of boundless mercy, whose handmaiden Kassiani brought forth poetry and song: Inspire in thy church a new song, that following her most excellent example, we may boldly proclaim the truth of thy Word; even Jesus Christ, our Savior and Deliverer. *Amen.*

II O God of boundless mercy, whose handmaiden Kassiani brought forth poetry and song: Inspire in your church a new song, that following her most excellent example, we may boldly proclaim the truth of your Word; even Jesus Christ, our Savior and Deliverer. *Amen.*

Lessons and Psalm

1 Samuel 2:1-10
Psalm 57:6-11
1 Corinthians 7:29-35
Mark 4:30-34

Preface of a Saint (3)

The gospels tell us little about the family and home of our Lord's mother. She is thought to have been of Davidic descent and to have been brought up in a devout Jewish family that cherished the hope of Israel for the coming kingdom of God, in remembrance of the promise to Abraham and the forefathers.

In the second century, a devout Christian sought to supply a fuller account of Mary's birth and family, to satisfy the interest and curiosity of believers. An apocryphal gospel, known as the *Protevangelium of James* or *The Nativity of Mary,* appeared. It included legendary stories of Mary's parents, Joachim and Anne. These stories were built out of Old Testament narratives of the births of Isaac and of Samuel (whose mother's name, Hannah, is the original form of Anne), and from traditions of the birth of John the Baptist. In these stories, Joachim and Anne—the childless, elderly couple who grieved that they would have no posterity—were rewarded with the birth of a girl, whom they dedicated in infancy to the service of God under the tutelage of the temple priests.

Many provinces of the Anglican Communion celebrate September 8 rather than August 15 as their primary Marian feast.

Although we do not know the truth of Mary's parentage or birth, we nevertheless rejoice for those who brought her into this world, and who raised her in such a way that even as a young woman she was able to give a courageous "yes" in response to her call from God.

The Nativity of the Blessed Virgin Mary

I Father in heaven, by whose grace the virgin mother of thy incarnate Son was blessed in bearing him, but still more blessed in keeping thy word: Grant us who honor the exaltation of her lowliness to follow the example of her devotion to thy will; through the same Jesus Christ our Lord, who liveth and reigneth with thee and the Holy Ghost, one God, for ever and ever. *Amen.*

II Father in heaven, by your grace the virgin mother of your incarnate Son was blessed in bearing him, but still more blessed in keeping your word: Grant us who honor the exaltation of her lowliness to follow the example of her devotion to your will; through Jesus Christ our Lord, who lives and reigns with you and the Holy Spirit, one God, for ever and ever. *Amen.*

Lessons and Psalm

1 Samuel 1:10-20
Psalm 27:1-5
Ephesians 1:3-14
Luke 1:26-38

Preface of the Incarnation

In August 1878, yellow fever invaded the city of Memphis, Tennessee, for the third time in ten years. By the month's end, the disease had become epidemic and a quarantine was ordered. While more than 25,000 citizens had fled in terror, nearly 20,000 more remained to face the pestilence. As cases multiplied, the death toll averaged 200 people per day. When the worst was over, ninety percent of the people who remained had contracted the fever and more than 5,000 people had died.

In that time of panic and flight, many brave men and women, both lay and ordained, remained at their posts of duty or came as volunteers to assist in spite of the terrible risk. Notable among these heroes were four Episcopal sisters from the Community of Saint Mary, and two of their clergy colleagues, all of whom died while tending to the sick. They have ever since been known as "The Martyrs of Memphis," as have those of other communions who ministered in Christ's name during this time of desolation.

The Sisters had come to Memphis in 1873, at Bishop Quintard's request, to found a school for girls adjacent to St. Mary's Cathedral. When the 1878 epidemic began, George C. Harris, the cathedral dean, and Sister Constance immediately organized relief work among the stricken. Helping were six of Constance's fellow Sisters of St. Mary, plus Sister Clare from St. Margaret's House, Boston, Massachusetts; the Reverend Charles C. Parsons, Rector of Grace and St. Lazarus Church, Memphis; and the Reverend Louis S. Schuyler, assistant at Holy Innocents, Hoboken, New Jersey. The cathedral group also included three physicians, two of whom were ordained Episcopal priests, the Sisters' two matrons, and several volunteer nurses from New York.

The cathedral buildings were located in the most infected region of Memphis. Here, amid sweltering heat and scenes of indescribable horror, these men and women of God gave relief to the sick, comfort to the dying, and homes to the many orphaned children. Only two of the workers escaped the fever. Among those who died were Sisters Constance, Thecla, Ruth, and Frances from the Community of Saint Mary, the Reverend Charles Parsons, and the Reverend Louis Schuyler. All six are buried at Elmwood Cemetery. The monument marking the joint grave of Fathers Parsons and Schuyler bears the inscription: "Greater Love Hath No Man." The high altar in St. Mary's Cathedral, Memphis, is a memorial to the four Sisters.

The Martyrs of Memphis: Constance, Thecla, Ruth, Frances, Charles Parsons, and Louis Schuyler

1878

I We give thee thanks and praise, O God of compassion, for the heroic witness of the Martyrs of Memphis, who, in a time of plague and pestilence, were steadfast in their care for the sick and dying, and loved not their own lives, even unto death; Inspire in us a like love and commitment to those in need, following the example of our Savior Jesus Christ; who with thee and the Holy Ghost liveth and reigneth, one God, now and for ever. *Amen.*

II We give you thanks and praise, O God of compassion, for the heroic witness of the Martyrs of Memphis, who, in a time of plague and pestilence, were steadfast in their care for the sick and dying, and loved not their own lives, even unto death; Inspire in us a like love and commitment to those in need, following the example of our Savior Jesus Christ; who with you and the Holy Spirit lives and reigns, one God, now and for ever. *Amen.*

Lessons and Psalm

Jeremiah 18:1-11
Psalm 17:6-10
2 Corinthians 1:3-5
John 12:24-28

Preface of a Saint (1)

Born March 3, 1819, in New York City, Alexander Crummell struggled against racism all his life. As a young man of color, he was driven out of an academy in New Hampshire, dismissed as a candidate for Holy Orders in New York, and rejected for admittance to General Seminary. Ordained in 1844 as a priest in the Diocese of Massachusetts, he left for England after being excluded from participating in diocesan convention.

After receiving a degree from Cambridge University, he went as a missionary to Liberia, where a model Christian republic seemed possible. The vision embraced by Crummell included European education and technology, traditional African communal culture, and a national Episcopal Church headed by a Black bishop. He traveled extensively in the United States, urging Black people to emigrate to Liberia and to support the work of the Episcopal Church there.

Upon returning to Liberia, he worked to establish a national Episcopal Church. Political opposition and a loss of funding finally forced him to return to the United States, where he concentrated his efforts on establishing a strong urban presence of independent Black congregations that would be centers of worship, education, and social service. When Southern bishops proposed that a separate missionary district be created for Black congregations, Crummell created a national convocation to defeat the proposal. The Union of Black Episcopalians is an outgrowth of that organization.

Crummell's ministry spanned more than half a century and three continents. Everywhere, at all times, he labored to prepare Black people and to build institutions that would serve them and provide scope for the exercises of their gifts in leadership and creativity. His faith in God, his perseverance in spite of repeated discouragement, his perception that the church transcended the racism and limited vision of its leaders, and his unfailing belief in the goodness and greatness of Black people are the legacy of this African American pioneer.

He died in Red Bank, New Jersey, in 1898.

Alexander Crummell

Priest, 1898

I Almighty and everlasting God, we give thanks to thee for thy servant Alexander Crummell, whom thou didst call to preach the gospel to those who were far off and to those who were near: Raise up, we beseech thee, in this and every land, evangelists and heralds of thy kingdom, that thy church may proclaim the unsearchable riches of our Savior Jesus Christ; who liveth and reigneth with thee and the Holy Ghost, one God, now and for ever. *Amen.*

II Almighty and everlasting God, we thank you for your servant Alexander Crummell, whom you called to preach the gospel to those who were far off and to those who were near: Raise up, in this and every land, evangelists and heralds of your kingdom, that your church may proclaim the unsearchable riches of our Savior Jesus Christ; who lives and reigns with you and the Holy Spirit, one God, now and for ever. *Amen.*

Lessons and Psalm

Ecclesiasticus 39:6-11
Psalm 19:7-11
James 1:2-5
Mark 4:21-25

Preface of a Saint (3)

John Henry Hobart was one of the leaders who revived the Episcopal Church, following the first two decades of its independent life after the American Revolution, a time that has been described as one of "suspended animation." Born in Philadelphia on September 14, 1775, Hobart was educated at the Universities of Pennsylvania and Princeton, graduating from the latter in 1793. Bishop William White, his longtime friend and adviser, ordained him as a deacon in 1798 and as a priest in 1801.

After serving parishes in Pennsylvania, New Jersey, and Long Island, Hobart became assistant minister of Trinity Church, New York City, in 1800. He was consecrated Assistant Bishop of New York on May 29, 1811. Five years later he succeeded Bishop Benjamin Moore, both as diocesan bishop and as rector of Trinity Church. He died at Auburn, New York, September 12, 1830, and was buried beneath the chancel of Trinity Church in New York City.

Within his first four years as bishop, Hobart doubled the number of his clergy and quadrupled the number of missionaries. Before his death, he had planted a church in almost every major town of New York State and had begun missionary work among the Oneida tribe of Native Americans. He was one of the founders of the General Theological Seminary, and the reviver of Geneva, now Hobart, College.

A strong and unbending upholder of church standards, Hobart established the Bible and Common Prayer Book Society of New York, and was one of the first American scholars to produce theological and devotional manuals for the laity. These "tracts," as they were called, and the personal impression he made on the occasion of a visit to Oxford, were an influence on the development of the Tractarian Movement in England. Both friends and foes respected Hobart for his staunch faith, his consuming energy, his personal integrity, and his missionary zeal.

John Henry Hobart

Bishop, 1830

I Revive thy church, Lord God of hosts, whenever it falls into complacency and sloth, by raising up devoted leaders like thy servant John Henry Hobart; and grant that their faith and vigor of mind may awaken thy people to thy message and their mission; through Jesus Christ our Lord, who liveth and reigneth with thee and the Holy Ghost, one God, for ever and ever. *Amen.*

II Revive your church, Lord God of hosts, whenever it falls into complacency and sloth, by raising up devoted leaders like your servant John Henry Hobart; and grant that their faith and vigor of mind may awaken your people to your message and their mission; through Jesus Christ our Lord, who lives and reigns with you and the Holy Spirit, one God, for ever and ever. *Amen.*

Lessons and Psalm

Job 38:1, 22-30
Psalm 92:1-7
Titus 1:7-9
Mark 8:1-13

Preface of a Saint (1)

Cyprian was a rich, aristocratic, and cultivated rhetorician in North Africa. He was converted to Christianity about 246, and by 248 was chosen Bishop of Carthage. A year later, in the persecution under the Emperor Decius, Cyprian went into hiding. For this he was severely criticized. Nonetheless, he kept in touch with his church by letter, and directed it with wisdom and compassion. In the controversy over what to do with those who had lapsed during the persecution, Cyprian held that they could be reconciled to the Church after suitable periods of penance, the gravity of the lapse determining the length of the penance. His moderate position was the one that generally prevailed in the church, over that of the rigorist Novatian, who led a group into schism at Rome and Antioch over this question. In another persecution, under the Emperor Valerian, Cyprian was placed under house arrest in Carthage, and, on September 14, 258, he was beheaded.

Many of Cyprian's writings have been preserved. His *Letter No. 63* contains one of the earliest affirmations that the priest, in offering the Eucharist ("the sacrifice"), acts in the place of Christ, imitating his actions.

In his treatise *On the Lord's Prayer,* he wrote: "We say 'Hallowed be thy Name,' not that we want God to be made holy by our prayers, but because we seek from the Lord that his Name may be made holy in us, . . . so that we who have been made holy in Baptism may persevere in what we have begun to be."

Although there is some question whether his book *On the Unity of the Catholic Church* affirms papal primacy, there is no question about the clarity of his statements on the unity of the college of bishops and the sin of schism. "The episcopate is a single whole," he wrote, "in which each bishop's share gives him a right to, and a responsibility for, the whole. So is the church a single whole, though she spreads far and wide into a multitude of churches . . . If you leave the church of Christ you will not come to Christ's rewards; you will be an alien, an outcast, an enemy. You cannot have God for your Father unless you have the church for your Mother."

Cypriam of Carthage

Bishop and Martyr, 258

I Almighty God, who gave to thy servant Cyprian boldness to confess the Name of our Savior Jesus Christ before the rulers of this world and courage to die for this faith: Grant that we may always be ready to give a reason for the hope that is in us and to suffer gladly for the sake of our Lord Jesus Christ; who liveth and reigneth with thee and the Holy Ghost, one God, for ever and ever. *Amen.*

II Almighty God, who gave to your servant Cyprian boldness to confess the Name of our Savior Jesus Christ before the rulers of this world and courage to die for this faith: Grant that we may always be ready to give a reason for the hope that is in us and to suffer gladly for the sake of our Lord Jesus Christ; who lives and reigns with you and the Holy Spirit, one God, for ever and ever. *Amen.*

Lessons and Psalm

Jeremiah 14:13-18
Psalm 116:10-17
James 4:11-17
John 10:11-16

Preface of a Saint (3)

The historian Eusebius, in his *Life of Constantine*, tells how that emperor ordered the erection of a complex of buildings in Jerusalem "on a scale of imperial magnificence," to set forth as "an object of attraction and veneration to all, the blessed place of our Savior's resurrection." The overall supervision of the work—on the site where the Church of the Holy Sepulchre now stands—was entrusted to Constantine's mother, the empress Helena.

In Jesus' time, the hill of Calvary had stood outside the city; but when the Roman city which succeeded Jerusalem, *Aelia Capitolina,* was built, the hill was buried under tons of fill. It was during the excavations directed by Helena that a relic, believed to be that of the true cross, was discovered.

Constantine's shrine included two principal buildings: a large basilica, used for the Liturgy of the Word, and a circular church, known as "The Resurrection"—its altar placed on the site of the tomb—which was used for the Liturgy of the Table, and for the singing of the Daily Office.

Toward one side of the courtyard which separated the two buildings, and through which the faithful had to pass on their way from Word to Sacrament, the exposed top of Calvary's hill was visible. It was there that the solemn veneration of the cross took place on Good Friday; and it was there that the congregation gathered daily for a final prayer and dismissal after Vespers.

The dedication of the buildings was completed on September 14, 335, the seventh month of the Roman calendar, a date suggested by the account of the dedication of Solomon's temple in the same city, in the seventh month of the Jewish calendar, hundreds of years before (2 Chronicles 7:8-10).

Holy Cross Day

I Almighty God, whose Son our Savior Jesus Christ was lifted high upon the cross that he might draw the whole world unto himself: Mercifully grant that we, who glory in the mystery of our redemption, may have grace to take up our cross and follow him; who liveth and reigneth with thee and the Holy Ghost, one God, in glory everlasting. *Amen.*

II Almighty God, whose Son our Savior Jesus Christ was lifted high upon the cross that he might draw the whole world to himself: Mercifully grant that we, who glory in the mystery of our redemption, may have grace to take up our cross and follow him; who lives and reigns with you and the Holy Spirit, one God, in glory everlasting. *Amen.*

Lessons and Psalm

Isaiah 45:21-25
Psalm 98 *or* 98:1-4
Philippians 2:5-11 *or* Galatians 6:14-18
John 12:31-36a

Preface of Holy Week

Catherine of Genoa is remembered both for her ministry of nursing the sick during repeated plagues, and also for the works that she wrote recounting her mystical experiences. Her writings became widely known when they were made the subject of Baron Friedrich von Hügel's classic work *The Mystical Element of Religion* (1908).

Catherine was born in Genoa, Italy, in 1447, the youngest of five children. As a teenager, Catherine wanted to become a nun, but her application to the convent was denied. Instead, she was married at the age of 16 to Giuliano Adorno as part of an attempt to end the feud between their two families. The couple were initially miserable together. Giuliano was angry, unfaithful, and lost most of their money through gambling and reckless spending. Catherine spent the first ten years of her marriage in a deep depression, praying that God would strike her with a great sickness so that she could remain in bed all day.

The trajectory of her life was changed on March 22, 1473, when she had a sudden mystical experience. While she was in church, in the middle of making her confession to a priest, she was suddenly struck with an overpowering sense of the overwhelming love of God. She was so stunned and dazed by this experience that she walked out of the church without even completing her confession. This was the beginning of a life of profound prayer.

Catherine combined a deep and intense contemplative life with an active dedication to caring for the sick in the local hospital. In time, her husband joined her in this work, and the couple became increasingly close to one another through their shared labor for those in need. They eventually moved together into the Pannatome, a large hospital in Genoa, in order to devote themselves completely to caring for the sick there. There Catherine also dictated a number of works of mystical theology, which were published some 40 years after her death.

Catherine insisted that God should be loved only for God's self, and not for anything that one might expect to receive from him, insisting that "Pure Love loves God without any *for*." She also wrote: "All that I have said is nothing compared to what I feel within, the witnessed correspondence of love between God and the soul; for when God sees the soul, as pure as it was in its origins, he tugs at it with a glance, draws it and binds it to himself with a fiery love that by itself could annihilate the immortal soul."

She died on September 15, 1510, while nursing the sick, and was buried in the hospital chapel.

Catherine of Genoa

Mystic and Nurse, 1510

I Gracious God, reveal to thy church the depths of thy love; that, like thy servant Catherine of Genoa, we might give ourselves in loving service, knowing that we have been perfectly loved by thee; through Jesus Christ our Lord. *Amen.*

II Gracious God, reveal to your church the depths of your love; that, like your servant Catherine of Genoa, we might give ourselves in loving service, knowing that we have been perfectly loved by you; through Jesus Christ our Lord. *Amen.*

Lessons and Psalm

Zephaniah 1:7-18
Psalm 86:3-12
James 5:1-6
Mark 9:43-50

Preface of a Saint (3)

The dates of Ninian's life, and the exact extent of his work, are much disputed. The earliest, and possibly the best, account is the brief one in Bede's *Ecclesiastical History.*

Ninian was a Romanized Briton, born in the latter half of the fourth century in southern Scotland. He is said to have been educated in Rome and to have received ordination as a bishop. But the main influence on his life was Martin of Tours, with whom he spent some time, and from whom he gained his ideals of an episcopal-monastic structure designed for missionary work.

Around the time of Martin's death in 397, Ninian established his base at a place called Candida Casa ("White House") or Whithorn in Galloway, which he dedicated to Martin. Traces of place names and church dedications suggest that his work covered the Solway Plains and the Lake District of England. Ninian seems also to have converted many of the Picts of northern Scotland, as far north as the Moray Firth.

Ninian, together with Patrick, is one of the links of continuity between the ancient Roman-British Church and the developing Celtic Christianity of Ireland and Scotland.

Ninian

Bishop, c. 430

I O God, who by the preaching of thy blessed servant and bishop Ninian didst cause the light of the Gospel to shine in the land of Britain: Grant, we beseech thee, that, having his life and labors in remembrance, we may show forth our thankfulness by following the example of his zeal and patience; through Jesus Christ our Lord, who liveth and reigneth with thee and the Holy Ghost, one God, for ever and ever. *Amen.*

II O God, who by the preaching of your blessed servant and bishop Ninian caused the light of the Gospel to shine in the land of Britain: Grant, we pray, that having his life and labors in remembrance we may show our thankfulness by following the example of his zeal and patience; through Jesus Christ our Lord, who lives and reigns with you and the Holy Spirit, one God, for ever and ever. *Amen.*

Lessons and Psalm

Numbers 22:21-33
Psalm 97
Acts 10:21-35
Matthew 28:16-20

Preface of Pentecost

Hildegard of Bingen, born in 1098 in the Rhineland Valley, was a mystic, poet, composer, dramatist, doctor, and scientist. Her parents' tenth child, she was tithed to the church and raised by the anchoress Jutta in a cottage near the Benedictine monastery of Disibodenberg.

Drawn by their life of silence and prayer, other women joined them, finding the freedom, rare outside of women's religious communities, to develop their intellectual gifts. They organized as a convent under the authority of the abbot of Disibodenberg, with Jutta as abbess. When Jutta died, Hildegard, then 38, became abbess. Later she founded independent convents at Bingen (1150) and Eibingen (1165), with the Archbishop of Mainz as her only superior.

From childhood, Hildegard experienced dazzling spiritual visions. When she was 43, a voice commanded her to tell what she saw. Thus began an outpouring of extraordinarily original writings, illustrated by unusual and wondrous illuminations. These works abound with feminine imagery for God and God's creative activity.

In 1147, Bernard of Clairvaux recommended her first book of visions, *Scivias,* to Pope Eugenius III, leading to papal authentication at the Synod of Trier. Hildegard quickly became famous, and was eagerly sought for counsel, becoming a correspondent of kings and queens, abbots and abbesses, archbishops and popes.

She carried out four preaching missions in northern Europe, which was an unprecedented activity for a woman. She also practiced medicine, focusing on women's needs; published treatises on natural science and philosophy; and wrote a liturgical drama, *The Play of the Virtues,* in which the personified virtues sing their parts and the devil, condemned to live without music, can only speak. For Hildegard, music was essential to worship. Her liturgical compositions, unusual in structure and tonality, were described by her contemporaries as "chant of surpassing sweet melody" and "strange and unheard-of music."

Hildegard lived in a world accustomed to male governance. Yet within her convents, and to a surprising extent outside of them, she exercised a commanding spiritual authority based on confidence in her visions and considerable political astuteness. When she died in 1179 at the age of 81, she left a rich legacy which speaks eloquently across the ages.

Hildegard of Bingen

Mystic and Scholar, 1179

I God of all times and seasons: Give us grace that we, after the example of thy servant Hildegard, may both know and make known the joy and jubilation of being part of thy creation, and show forth thy glory in the world; through Jesus Christ our Savior, who liveth and reigneth with thee and the Holy Ghost, one God, for ever and ever. *Amen.*

II God of all times and seasons: Give us grace that we, after the example of your servant Hildegard, may both know and make known the joy and jubilation of being part of your creation, and show forth your glory in the world; through Jesus Christ our Savior, who lives and reigns with you and the Holy Spirit, one God, for ever and ever. *Amen.*

Lessons and Psalm

Ecclesiasticus 43:1-12
Psalm 8
Colossians 3:14-17
John 3:16-21

Preface of the Epiphany

The revival of High Church teachings and practices in the Anglican Communion, known as the Oxford Movement, found its acknowledged leader in Edward Bouverie Pusey. Born near Oxford on August 22, 1800, Pusey spent all of his scholarly life in that University as Regius Professor of Hebrew and as Canon of Christ Church. At the end of 1833, he joined John Keble and John Henry Newman in producing the *Tracts for the Times,* which gave the Oxford Movement its popular name of Tractarianism.

His most influential activity, however, was his preaching—catholic in content, evangelical in his zeal for souls. But to many of his more influential contemporaries, it seemed dangerously innovative. A sermon preached before the University in 1843 on "The Holy Eucharist, a Comfort to the Penitent" was condemned without his being given an opportunity to defend it, and he himself was suspended from preaching for two years—a judgment he bore patiently.

His principles were thus brought before the public, and attention was drawn to the doctrine of the Real Presence of Christ in the Eucharist. The revival of private confession in the Anglican Communion may be dated from another University sermon, on "The Entire Absolution of the Penitent."

When John Henry Newman was received into the Roman Catholic Church in 1845, Pusey's adherence to the Church of England kept many other Anglicans from following, and he continued to defend the teachings and practices of the Oxford Movement as a legitimate expression of the Church of England.

After the death of his wife in 1839, Pusey devoted much of his family fortune to the establishment of churches for the poor, and much of his time and care to the revival of monasticism. His own daughter, Lucy, had longed to serve the church as a religious sister. While she died too young for her dream to be realized, Pusey dedicated himself to reviving the religious life for women so that other women would be able to respond to that sense of call even though his own daughter could not. In 1845, he established the first Anglican sisterhood since the Reformation. It was at this community's convent, Ascot Priory in Berkshire, that Pusey died on September 16, 1882. His body was brought back to Christ Church and buried in the cathedral nave. Pusey House, a house of studies founded after his death, perpetuates his name at Oxford University.

Edward Bouverie Pusey

Priest, 1882

I Grant unto us, O God, that in all time of our testing we may know thy presence and obey thy will; that, following the example of thy servant Edward Bouverie Pusey, we may with integrity and courage accomplish what thou givest us to do, and endure what thou givest us to bear; through Jesus Christ our Lord, who liveth and reigneth with thee and the Holy Ghost, one God, for ever and ever. *Amen.*

II Grant, O God, that in all time of our testing we may know your presence and obey your will; that, following the example of your servant Edward Bouverie Pusey, we may with integrity and courage accomplish what you give us to do, and endure what you give us to bear; through Jesus Christ our Lord, who lives and reigns with you and the Holy Spirit, one God, for ever and ever. *Amen.*

Lessons and Psalm

Ezekiel 36:24-28
Psalm 106:1-5
1 Peter 2:19-23
Matthew 18:12-24

Preface of a Saint (2)

Theodore was born in Asia Minor in 602 in Saint Paul's native city of Tarsus. He was ordained as Archbishop of Canterbury by Pope Vitalian on March 26, 668.

A learned monk of the East, Theodore was residing in Rome when the English church, decimated by plague and torn with strife over rival Celtic and Roman customs, was in need of strong leadership. Theodore provided this for a generation, beginning his episcopate at an age when most people are ready to retire.

When Theodore came to England, he established a school at Canterbury that gained a reputation for excellence in all branches of learning and where many leaders of both the Irish and the English churches were trained. His effective visitation of all England brought unity to the two strains of tradition among the Anglo-Saxon Christians. For example, he recognized Chad's worthiness and regularized his episcopal ordination.

Theodore gave definitive boundaries to English dioceses, so that their bishops could give better pastoral attention to their people. He presided over synods that brought about reforms, according to established rules of canon law. He also laid the foundations of the parochial organization that still persists in the English church.

According to Bede, Theodore was the first archbishop whom all the English obeyed, and possibly to no other leader does English Christianity owe so much. He died in his eighty-eighth year on September 19, 690, and was buried, with Augustine and the other early English archbishops, in the monastic Church of Saints Peter and Paul at Canterbury.

Theodore of Tarsus

Archbishop of Canterbury, 690

I Almighty God, who didst give thy servant Theodore of Tarsus gifts of grace and wisdom to establish unity where there had been division and order where there had been chaos: Create in thy church, we pray thee, by the operation of the Holy Ghost, such godly union and concord that it may proclaim, both by word and example, the Gospel of the Prince of Peace; who liveth and reigneth with thee and the Holy Ghost, one God, for ever and ever. *Amen.*

II Almighty God, who gave your servant Theodore of Tarsus gifts of grace and wisdom to establish unity where there had been division and order where there had been chaos: Create in your church, by the operation of the Holy Spirit, such godly union and concord that it may proclaim, both by word and example, the Gospel of the Prince of Peace; who lives and reigns with you and the Holy Spirit, one God, for ever and ever. *Amen.*

Lessons and Psalm

Malachi 2:5-7
Psalm 34:9-14
James 2:14-26
Matthew 24:42-47

Preface of a Saint (1)

The death of Bishop Patteson and his companions at the hands of Melanesian islanders, whom Patteson had sought to protect from slave-traders, aroused the British government to take serious measures to prevent piratical man-hunting in the South Seas. Their martyrdom was the seed that produced the strong and vigorous Church which flourishes in Melanesia today.

Patteson was born in London on April 1, 1827. He attended Balliol College, Oxford, where he took his degree in 1849. After travel in Europe and a study of languages, at which he was adept, he became a Fellow of Merton College in 1852 and was ordained the following year.

While serving as a curate of Alphington, Devonshire, near his family home, he responded to Bishop George Augustus Selwyn's call in 1855 for helpers in New Zealand. It is said that he learned to speak some twenty-three of the languages of the Melanesian people, and he established a school for boys on Norfolk Island to train native Christian workers. On February 24, 1861, he was consecrated Bishop of Melanesia.

On a visit to the island of Nakapu, Patteson was stabbed five times in the chest, in mistaken retaliation for the brutal outrages committed some time earlier by slave-traders. In the attack, several of Patteson's company were also killed or wounded. Bishop Selwyn later reconciled the natives of Melanesia to the memory of one who came to help and not to hurt.

John Coleridge Patteson
Bishop
and his companions
Martyrs, 1871

I Almighty God, who didst call thy faithful servant John Coleridge Patteson and his companions to witness to the gospel, and by their labors and sufferings didst raise up a people for thine own possession: Pour out thy Holy Ghost upon thy church in every land, that, by the service and sacrifice of many, thy holy Name may be glorified and thy kingdom enlarged; through Jesus Christ our Lord, who liveth and reigneth with thee and the Holy Ghost, one God, for ever and ever. *Amen.*

II Almighty God, who called your faithful servant John Coleridge Patteson and his companions to witness to the gospel, and by their labors and sufferings raised up a people for your own possession: Pour out your Holy Spirit upon your church in every land, that, by the service and sacrifice of many, your holy Name may be glorified and your kingdom enlarged; through Jesus Christ our Lord, who lives and reigns with you and the Holy Spirit, one God, for ever and ever. *Amen.*

Lessons and Psalm

1 Chronicles 21:1-13
Psalm 9:11-20
1 Peter 4:12-19
Mark 8:34-38

Preface of Holy Week

Matthew, one of Jesus' disciples, is probably to be identified with Levi, a tax collector ("publican") mentioned by Mark and Luke. In the Gospel according to Matthew, it is said that Matthew was seated in the custom-house when Jesus invited him, "Follow me." When Jesus called him, he at once left everything, followed Jesus, and later gave a dinner for him. Mark and Luke also note that Levi was a tax collector. In all three accounts, Jesus is severely criticized for eating at the same table with tax collectors and other disreputable persons.

Tax collectors were viewed as collaborators with the Roman State, extortioners who took money from their own people to further the cause of Rome and to line their own pockets. They were spurned as traitors and outcasts. The Jews so abhorred them that pious Pharisees refused to marry into a family that had a publican as a member. Clearly, Matthew was hardly the type of man that a devout Jew would have had among his closest associates. Yet Jesus noted that it was the publican rather than the proud Pharisee who prayed the acceptable prayer, "Lord, be merciful to me, a sinner." There are several favorable references to publicans in the sayings of Jesus in the Gospel according to Matthew.

According to the early Christian writers Irenaeus and Clement of Alexandria, Matthew converted many people to Christianity in Judea, and then traveled on to the East; however, there is no certain evidence for this. He has traditionally been venerated as a martyr, but the time and circumstances of his death are unknown.

Saint Matthew, Apostle and Evangelist

I We thank thee, heavenly Father, for the witness of thine apostle and evangelist Matthew to the Gospel of thy Son our Savior; and we pray that, after his example, we may with ready wills and hearts obey the calling of our Lord to follow him; through Jesus Christ our Lord, who liveth and reigneth with thee and the Holy Ghost, one God, now and for ever. *Amen.*

II We thank you, heavenly Father, for the witness of your apostle and evangelist Matthew to the Gospel of your Son our Savior; and we pray that, after his example, we may with ready wills and hearts obey the calling of our Lord to follow him; through Jesus Christ our Lord, who lives and reigns with you and the Holy Spirit, one God, now and for ever. *Amen.*

Lessons and Psalm

Proverbs 3:1-6
Psalm 119:33-40
2 Timothy 3:14-17
Matthew 9:9-13

Preface of Apostles and Ordinations

Born the youngest of fifteen children on December 14, 1775, in Cornish, New Hampshire, Philander Chase attended Dartmouth College, where he prepared to become a Congregationalist minister. While at Dartmouth, he happened upon a copy of the Book of Common Prayer. Next to the Bible, he thought it was the most excellent book he had ever studied, and believed that it was surely inspired by God. At the age of nineteen he was confirmed in the Episcopal Church.

Following his graduation from Dartmouth, Chase worked as a schoolteacher in Albany, New York, and read for Holy Orders. Ordained as a deacon in 1798, he began mission work on the northern and western frontiers among the pioneers and the Mohawk and Oneida peoples. The first of the many congregations he founded was at Lake George in New York State.

Ordained as a priest in 1799, at the age of twenty-three, Chase served as rector of Christ Church, Poughkeepsie, New York, until 1805. He then moved to New Orleans, where he organized the first Protestant congregation in Louisiana. That parish now serves as the cathedral church for the Diocese of Louisiana. In 1810, he returned north to Hartford, Connecticut, where he served for six years as rector of Christ Church, now the cathedral church of the Diocese of Connecticut. In 1817, he accepted a call to be the first rector of St. John's Church in Worthington, Ohio. A year later he was elected the first Bishop of Ohio. He immediately began founding congregations and organizing the diocese. He also established Kenyon College and Bexley Hall Seminary.

In 1831, Chase resigned as Bishop of Ohio and began ministering to Episcopalians and the unchurched in southern Michigan. In 1835, he was elected the first Bishop of Illinois and served in this office until he died on September 20, 1852. During his time in Illinois, he founded numerous congregations, together with Jubilee College, which included a seminary. As the senior bishop in the Episcopal Church, he served as the Presiding Bishop from 1843 until his death.

Philander Chase

Bishop, 1852

I Almighty God, whose Son Jesus Christ is the pioneer and perfecter of our faith: Grant that like thy servant Philander Chase, we might have the grace to minister in Christ's name in every place, led by bold witnesses to the Gospel of the Prince of Peace, even Jesus Christ our Lord, who liveth and reigneth with thee and the Holy Ghost, one God, for ever and ever. *Amen.*

II Almighty God, whose Son Jesus Christ is the pioneer and perfecter of our faith: Grant that like your servant Philander Chase, we might have the grace to minister in Christ's name in every place, led by bold witnesses to the Gospel of the Prince of Peace, Jesus Christ our Lord, who lives and reigns with you and the Holy Spirit, one God, for ever and ever. *Amen.*

Lessons and Psalm

Isaiah 44:1-8
Psalm 117
Acts 18:7-11
Luke 9:1-6

Preface of a Saint (1)

Thecla, who according to tradition was a disciple of the apostle Paul, was one of the most popular female saints in the early church. Her story is told in the second-century *Acts of Paul and Thecla*. According to this narrative, upon hearing Paul preach the gospel, Thecla abandoned her plans for marriage and followed Paul. Condemned to burn at the stake, her life was saved by a miraculous thunderstorm. As her adventures continued, she was thrown to the beasts in the local arena. There she was protected by a fierce lioness. Finally, thinking this was her last chance to be baptized, she threw herself into a pool of ravenous seals and baptized herself in the water, while the seals were struck dead by lightning. The governor then released her, and she went on to travel and preach the gospel.

Although the *Acts of Paul and Thecla* unabashedly incorporates many of the tropes and styles of ancient fiction, which makes it difficult to disentangle history from myth, Christians in late antiquity largely believed that there was indeed a historical Thecla behind all of the legends, and devotion to her was very widespread, especially among women. According to Tertullian (writing around the year 200), early Christian women appealed to Thecla's example to defend women's freedom to teach and to baptize.

A shrine to Thecla in Seleucia (Asia Minor) became a popular pilgrimage site in the fourth and fifth centuries. Devotion to Thecla from Gaul to Palestine is also evident in literature, art, and in the practice of naming children after her. Her image appeared on wall paintings, clay flasks, oil lamps, stone reliefs, textile curtains, and other materials.

In the Orthodox Church she is given the title "Proto-Martyr Among Women" because, just as Stephen is believed to have been the first male martyr, so Thecla is believed to have been the first female martyr.

Thecla of Iconium

Proto-Martyr Among Women, c. 70

I God of liberating power, who didst call Thecla to proclaim the gospel and didst not permit any obstacle or peril to inhibit her: Empower courageous evangelists among us, that men and women everywhere may know the freedom that thou dost offer us in Jesus Christ, who liveth and reigneth with thee and the Holy Ghost, one God, for ever and ever. *Amen.*

II God of liberating power, who called Thecla to proclaim the gospel and did not permit any obstacle or peril to inhibit her: Empower courageous evangelists among us, that men and women everywhere may know the freedom that you offer us in Jesus Christ, who lives and reigns with you and the Holy Spirit, one God, for ever and ever. *Amen.*

Lessons and Psalm

Judges 4:16-24
Psalm 123
2 Timothy 3:10-12
Luke 24:1-11

Preface of Apostles and Ordinations

Anna Ellison Butler Alexander was the youngest of 11 children, born to recently emancipated slaves Aleck and Daphne Alexander on Butler Plantation in MacIntosh County, Georgia, in 1865. Her parents were devout Episcopalians, and they also instilled in their children a love of learning. Anna became a teacher, and eventually the only African American to be consecrated as a deaconess in the Episcopal Church.

Anna dedicated herself to working for the education of African American children in poor communities. First she helped to found and to run St. Cyprian's School at St. Cyprian's Episcopal Church in Darien, and in 1902 she founded a school at Good Shepherd Church in rural Glynn County's Pennick community, where she taught children to read—by tradition, from the Book of Common Prayer and the Bible—in a one-room schoolhouse. The school was later expanded to two rooms with a loft where Anna lived.

In 1907, she was consecrated as a deaconess by Bishop C. K. Nelson. Deaconess Alexander served in difficult times, however. The Diocese of Georgia segregated its congregations in 1907 and African American congregations were not invited to another diocesan convention until 1947. However, her witness—wearing the distinctive dress of a deaconess, traveling by foot from Brunswick through Darien to Pennick, showing care and love for all whom she met—represents the best in Christian witness.

The poor white residents of Glynn County also trusted Deaconess Alexander. When the Depression hit the rural poor, she became the agent for government and private aid, and Good Shepherd Mission served as the distribution center. Locals remember that no one ever questioned her as she served the needs of both races in a segregated South. Strictly religious, strictly business, Deaconess Alexander commanded respect. White men took off their hats when she passed.

Deaconess Alexander wrote, "I am to see everyone gets what they need . . . some folk don't need help now and I know who they are. The old people and the children, they need the most . . . when I tell some they can't get help just now . . . that others come first, they get mad, a little, but I don't pay no mind and soon they forget to be mad."

She ministered in Pennick for 53 years, leaving a legacy of love and devotion that is still felt in Glynn County.

Anna Ellison Butler Alexander

Deaconess and Teacher, 1947

I Loving God, who didst call Anna Alexander as a deaconess in thy church: Grant unto us the wisdom to teach the gospel of Christ to whomever we meet, by word and by example, that all may come to the enlightenment thou dost intend for thy people; through Jesus Christ, our Teacher and Savior. *Amen.*

II Loving God, who called Anna Alexander as a deaconess in your church: Grant us the wisdom to teach the gospel of Christ to whomever we meet, by word and by example, that all may come to the enlightenment that you intend for your people; through Jesus Christ, our Teacher and Savior. *Amen.*

Lessons and Psalm

Deuteronomy 6:4-9
Psalm 78:1-7
2 Timothy 3:14—4:5
Matthew 11:25-30

Preface of Baptism

To the people of Russia, Sergius is a national hero and their patron saint. He was born in Rostov around 1314.

Civil war in Russia forced Sergius' family to leave the city and to live by farming at Radonezh near Moscow. At the age of twenty, he and his brother began a life of seclusion in a nearby forest, from which developed the Monastery of the Holy Trinity, a center of revival of Russian Christianity. There Sergius remained for the rest of his life, refusing higher advancement, including the see of Moscow in 1378.

Sergius' firm support of Prince Dimitri Donskoi helped to rally the Russians against their Tartar overlords. Dimitri won a decisive victory against them at the Kulikovo Plains in 1380 and laid the foundation of his people's independent national life.

Sergius was simple and gentle in nature, mystical in temperament, and eager to ensure that his monks should serve the needs of their neighbors. He was able to inspire intense devotion to the Orthodox faith. He died in 1392, and pilgrims still visit his shrine at the monastery of Sergiyev Posad, which he founded in 1340. The city, located some forty-three miles northwest of Moscow, contains several splendid cathedrals and is the residence of the Patriarch of Moscow.

The Russian Church observes Sergius' memory on September 25. His name is familiar to Anglicans from the Fellowship of St. Alban and St. Sergius, a society established to promote closer relations between the Anglican and Orthodox Churches.

Sergius of Radonezh

Monastic, 1392

I O God, whose blessed Son became poor that we, through his poverty, might be rich: Deliver us from an inordinate love of this world, that we, inspired by the devotion of thy servant Sergius, may serve thee with singleness of heart and attain to the riches of the age to come; through Jesus Christ our Lord, who liveth and reigneth with thee and the Holy Ghost, one God, for ever and ever. *Amen.*

II O God, whose blessed Son became poor that we, through his poverty, might be rich: Deliver us from an inordinate love of this world, that we, inspired by the devotion of your servant Sergius, may serve you with singleness of heart and attain to the riches of the age to come; through Jesus Christ our Lord, who lives and reigns with you and the Holy Spirit, one God, for ever and ever. *Amen.*

Lessons and Psalm

Ecclesiasticus 29:1-9
Psalm 39:4-8
1 John 2:15-17
Mark 2:23-28

Preface of a Saint (2)

Lancelot Andrewes, born in 1555, was the favorite preacher of King James I. He was the author of a great number of eloquent sermons, particularly on the Nativity and the Resurrection. They are witty, grounded in the Scriptures, and characterized by the kind of massive learning that the King loved. This makes them difficult reading for modern people, but they repay careful study. T. S. Eliot used the opening of one of Andrewes' Epiphany sermons as the inspiration for his poem "The Journey of the Magi":

> A cold coming we had of it,
> Just the worst time of the year
> For a Journey, and such a long journey:
> The way deep and the weather sharp,
> The very dead of winter.

Andrewes was also a distinguished biblical scholar, proficient in Hebrew and Greek, and was one of the translators of the Authorized (King James) Version of the Bible. He was Dean of Westminster and headmaster of the school there before he became a bishop and was influential in the education of a number of noted churchmen of his time, in particular, the poet George Herbert.

Andrewes was a very devout man, and one of his most admired works is his *Preces Privatae* ("Private Devotions"), an anthology from the Scriptures and the ancient liturgies, compiled for his own use. It illustrates his piety and throws light on the sources of his theology. He vigorously defended the catholicity of the Church of England against Roman Catholic critics. He was respected by many as an ideal model of a bishop at a time when bishops were generally held in low esteem. As his student, John Hacket, later Bishop of Lichfield, wrote about him: "Indeed he was the most Apostolical and Primitive-like Divine, in my Opinion, that wore a Rochet in his Age; of a most venerable Gravity, and yet most sweet in all Commerce; the most Devout that I ever saw, when he appeared before God; of such a Growth in all kind of Learning that very able Clerks were of a low Stature to him." He died in 1626.

Lancelot Andrewes

Bishop, 1626

I Perfect in us, Almighty God, whatever is lacking of thy gifts: of faith, to increase it; of hope, to establish it; of love, to kindle it; that like thy servant Lancelot Andrewes we may live in the life of thy grace and glory; through Jesus Christ thy Son our Lord, who liveth and reigneth with thee and the Holy Ghost, one God, now and for ever. *Amen.*

II Perfect in us, Almighty God, whatever is lacking of your gifts: of faith, to increase it; of hope, to establish it; of love, to kindle it; that like your servant Lancelot Andrewes we may live in the life of your grace and glory; through Jesus Christ your Son our Lord, who lives and reigns with you and the Holy Spirit, one God, now and for ever. *Amen.*

Lessons and Psalm

Isaiah 11:1-9
Psalm 63:1-7
1 Timothy 2:1-7
Luke 11:1-4

Preface of a Saint (1)

Euphrosyne was born in the fifth century, the beloved only child of a couple in Alexandria. She had a warm and loving family life, but her mother died when she was still a young girl. Her father, Paphnutius, instructed her in the Christian faith, and often used to take her to visit the monasteries outside of the city.

As she grew to adulthood, her father arranged what he thought was an excellent future for her—marriage to a wealthy and handsome young man from a prominent family. But Euphrosyne would have none of it. She and her father quarreled, and she ran away from home in anger without even saying goodbye. She cut her hair, changed her clothing for men's attire, and adopted the name of Smaragdus.

Smaragdus entered a monastic community outside of Alexandria, where he made great progress in prayer and in wisdom. Many years later, Paphnutius came to that same monastery, seeking consolation in his bereavement over the daughter he had lost, whom he believed to be dead. The abbot of the monastery (perhaps perceiving the situation more clearly than he had ever admitted) sent Paphnutius to Smaragdus for spiritual direction and guidance. Paphnutius was then instructed in the spiritual life by Smaragdus for years, coming weekly to the monastery for his wisdom and advice, but during all that time he failed to recognize his own child.

It was only as Smaragdus was ill and near to death that Paphnutius' eyes were finally opened, and he recognized that the beloved daughter he had mourned as dead and the monk who had guided him through his grief were in fact the same person. He nursed Smaragdus lovingly during his final illness, and then became a monk himself, occupying the same cell that his child had lived in for the rest of his life.

Euphrosyne/Smaragdus of Alexandria

Monastic, fifth century

I Merciful God, who lookest not with outward eyes but dost discern the heart of each: we confess that those whom we love the most are often strangers to us. Give to all parents and children, we pray, the grace to see one another as they truly are and as thou hast called them to be. All this we ask in the name of Jesus Christ, our only mediator and advocate. *Amen.*

II Merciful God, who looks not with outward eyes but discerns the heart of each: we confess that those whom we love the most are often strangers to us. Give to all parents and children, we pray, the grace to see one another as they truly are and as you have called them to be. All this we ask in the name of Jesus Christ, our only mediator and advocate. *Amen.*

Lessons and Psalm

Judges 11:32-40
Psalm 19
1 Corinthians 13:8-13
Luke 14:25-33

Preface of a Saint (3)

Paula (b. 347) was descended from Cornelia Africana, the mother of the Gracchi. As Cornelia was the model of a Roman Matron whose sons were her only jewels, so Paula became the model of the Desert Mother whose wealth was surrendered to the service of God. Married at a young age, she had five children and was widowed at age 32. Though she had lived in patrician luxury, after being widowed she was inspired by the example of Marcella (January 31) and devoted her life to the worship of God, rigorous asceticism, and service to the needy. Both Marcella and Paula converted their palaces into monasteries and gathered to them many windows and virgins.

In 382 Paula met Jerome, who had come to Rome at the invitation of Bishop Damasus, and was residing in the home of Marcella. Paula and her daughter Eustochium (b. 386) took to the irascible scholar and preacher of asceticism. They became Jerome's dearest companions and the only antidotes to his infamous wrath. They restrained his temper and frequently recalled him to the mildness and humility that Christ enjoins. While urged by her noble family to marry, Eustochium, under the guidance of Jerome, made a vow of perpetual virginity. Jerome's famous *De custodia virginitatis* was written for her instruction.

Fluent in Greek, Paula and Eustochium were ardent students of the scriptures and they quickly mastered Hebrew under Jerome's tutelage. When he left to return to the East, Paula and Eustochium followed after him, making a pilgrimage of the Holy Land. The three of them settled in Bethlehem and there Paula had four monasteries erected—one for men, over which Jerome presided, and three for women.

In Bethlehem, their passion for the study of scripture only grew, and their challenging questions led Jerome to write many of his commentaries. Under Paula's persuasive and persistent influence, Jerome undertook a new Latin translation of the Bible from the original languages, which came to be known as the Vulgate. Paula also provided the books that were essential to Jerome's work. She and Eustochium suggested revisions to his translation drafts and edited all his works, and the women of their convents were the scribes who made copies of the finished work available. Paula and Eustochium were Jerome's colleagues in this work and without them there would be no Vulgate.

Paula presided over the Bethlehem monasteries for twenty years until her death in 404. In his eulogy for her, Jerome wrote: "If all the members of my body were turned into tongues and all my joints were to utter human voices, I should be unable to say anything worthy of the holy and venerable Paula." After the death of her mother, Eustochium assumed direction of the monasteries. Eustochium died in 419 or 420, her eyes closed by her niece Paula, who took over direction of the monasteries after her death.

Paula and Eustochium of Rome

Monastics and Scholars, 404 and c. 419

I Compel us, O God, to attend diligently to thy Word, as didst thy faithful servants Paula and Eustochium; that, by the inspiration of the Holy Ghost, we may find it profitable for doctrine, for reproof, for correction, and for instruction in righteousness; and that thereby we may be made wise unto salvation through faith in Christ Jesus our Lord. *Amen.*

II Compel us, O God, to attend diligently to your Word, as did your faithful servants Paula and Eustochium; that, by the inspiration of the Holy Spirit, we may find it profitable for doctrine, for reproof, for correction, and for instruction in righteousness; and that thereby we may be made wise unto salvation through faith in Christ Jesus our Lord. *Amen.*

Lessons and Psalm

Judith 8:9-17
Psalm 111
James 4:1-10
Luke 8:1-3

Preface of a Saint (3)

The biblical word "angel" (Greek: *angelos*) means, literally, a messenger. Messengers from God can be visible or invisible, and may assume human or non-human forms. Christians have always felt themselves to be attended by helpful spirits—swift, powerful, and enlightening. Those beneficent spirits are often depicted in Christian art in human form, with wings to signify their swiftness and spacelessness, with swords to signify their power, and with dazzling raiment to signify their ability to enlighten. Unfortunately, this type of pictorial representation has led many to dismiss the angels as "just another mythical beast, like the unicorn, the griffin, or the sphinx."

Of the many angels spoken of in the Bible, only four are called by name: Michael, Gabriel, Uriel, and Raphael. The Archangel Michael is the powerful agent of God who wards off evil from God's people, and delivers peace to them at the end of this life's mortal struggle. "Michaelmas," as his feast is called in England, has long been one of the popular celebrations of the Christian Year in many parts of the world.

Michael is the patron saint of countless churches, including Mont Saint-Michel, the monastery fortress off the coast of Normandy that figured so prominently in medieval English history, and Coventry Cathedral, England's most famous modern church building, rising from the ashes of the Second World War.

Saint Michael and All Angels

I O Everlasting God, who hast ordained and constituted the ministries of angels and men in a wonderful order: Mercifully grant that, as thy holy angels always serve and worship thee in heaven, so by thy appointment they may help and defend us on earth; through Jesus Christ our Lord, who liveth and reigneth with thee and the Holy Ghost, one God, for ever and ever. *Amen.*

II Everlasting God, who has ordained and constituted in a wonderful order the ministries of angels and mortals: Mercifully grant that, as your holy angels always serve and worship you in heaven, so by your appointment they may help and defend us here on earth; through Jesus Christ our Lord, who lives and reigns with you and the Holy Spirit, one God, for ever and ever. *Amen.*

Lessons and Psalm

Genesis 28:10-17
Psalm 103 *or* 103:19-22
Revelation 12:7-12
John 1:47-51

Preface of Trinity Sunday

Jerome was the foremost biblical scholar of early Latin Christianity. His Latin translation of the Bible from early Hebrew and Greek texts, known as the Vulgate version, along with his commentaries and homilies on the biblical books, have made him a major intellectual force in the Western church.

Jerome was born in Stridon, in the Roman province of Dalmatia, around 347, and was converted and baptized during his days as a student in Rome. On a visit to Trier, in the Rhineland, he found himself attracted to the monastic life, which he tested in a brief but unhappy experience as a hermit in the Syrian desert. At Antioch in 378, he reluctantly allowed himself to be ordained as a priest, and there continued his studies in Hebrew and Greek. The following year, he was in Constantinople as a student of Gregory of Nazianzus. From 382 to 384, he served as secretary to Pope Damasus I in Rome, who set him to the task of making a new translation of the Bible into Latin—the *vulgus* tongue used by the common people, as distinguished from the classical Greek—hence the name of his translation, the Vulgate.

After the Pope's death, Jerome returned to the East and established a monastery at Bethlehem, where he lived and worked until his death on September 30, 420. He was buried in a chapel beneath the Church of the Nativity, near the traditional place of our Lord's birth.

Jerome's irascible disposition, pride of learning, and extravagant promotion of asceticism involved him in many bitter controversies over both theological and exegetical questions. Yet he was candid at times in admitting his failings, never ambitious for churchly honors, a militant champion of orthodoxy, an indefatigable worker, and a literary stylist with rare gifts.

Jerome

Priest and Scholar, 420

I O God, who didst give us the holy Scriptures as a light to shine upon our path: Grant us, after the example of thy servant Jerome, so to learn of thee according to thy holy Word, that we may find the Light that shines more and more to the perfect day; even Jesus Christ our Lord, who liveth and reigneth with thee and the Holy Ghost, one God, now and ever. *Amen.*

II O God, who gave us the holy Scriptures as a light to shine upon our path: Grant us, after the example of your servant Jerome, so to learn of you according to your holy Word, that we may find the Light that shines more and more to the perfect day; even Jesus Christ our Lord, who lives and reigns with you and the Holy Spirit, one God, now and ever. *Amen.*

Lessons and Psalm

Numbers 9:15-23
Psalm 19:7-14
Colossians 3:1-11
Luke 24:44-48

Preface of Pentecost

Called "the greatest saint in modern times" by Pope Pius X, canonized by Pope Pius XI just twenty-eight years after her death, and named a Doctor of the Church by Pope John Paul II, Thérèse of Lisieux has become one of the most beloved saints of the Roman Catholic Church.

From an early age, Thérèse felt called to the religious life; even as a little girl she played at being a nun. On Christmas Eve 1886, at age fourteen, she experienced a vision of the infant Christ and what she called a "complete conversion." Thereafter she understood her vocation to be prayer for priests, and she began seeking admittance to the Carmelite convent in Lisieux. When she entered the order at age 17 as a Discalced Carmelite, she assumed the name Thérèse of the Child Jesus and the Holy Face.

Dedicated to what she called her "little way," she led a simple, quiet life of prayer—in particular for priests—and small acts of charity. She struggled with illness throughout her life and suffered greatly from tuberculosis before her death in 1897 at age twenty-four. At age twenty-two, just two years before her death, her prioress instructed her to write her memoirs. *The Story of a Soul,* as it came to be called, commended a life of "great love" rather than "great deeds," echoing the insight of *The Imitation of Christ* by Thomas à Kempis, a book that had helped her to discover her vocation and develop her spiritual life. She corresponded with Roman Catholic missionaries to China and Indonesia as well as with young priests, pursuing what she saw as the mission of the Carmelites, "to form evangelical workers who will save thousands of souls whose mothers we shall be."

Toward the end of her short life, Thérèse experienced a profound sense of abandonment by God, but even this did not shake her love for God. On the verge of death, Thérèse confessed that she had "lost her faith" and all her certainty, and was now "only capable of loving." She experienced her sense of separation from God as something to be borne in solidarity with unbelievers. She "no longer saw" God in the light of faith, but nevertheless responded to him with a passionate love. In this experience, her youthful decision that her vocation was "to be love in the heart of the church" lost all hint of sentimentality. Her last words epitomize her "little way": "My God, I love you."

Thérèse of Lisieux

Monastic, 1897

I O Gracious Father, who didst call thy servant Thérèse to a life of fervent prayer: Give unto us that spirit of prayer and zeal for the ministry of the Gospel, that the love of Christ may be known throughout all the world; through the same, Jesus Christ our Lord. *Amen.*

II Gracious Father, who called your servant Thérèse to a life of fervent prayer: Give to us that spirit of prayer and zeal for the ministry of the Gospel, that the love of Christ may be known throughout all the world; through the same Jesus Christ, our Lord. *Amen.*

Lessons and Psalm

Judith 8:1-8
Psalm 119:57-64
Colossians 3:1-4
Luke 21:1-4

Preface of a Saint (2)

Remigius, also known as Remi, one of the patron saints of France, was born around 438, the son of the Count of Laon. At the age of twenty-two he became Bishop of Rheims.

Noted for his learning and holiness of life, Remigius is chiefly remembered because he converted and baptized King Clovis of the Franks on Christmas Day, 496. This event changed the religious history of Europe. By becoming Catholic instead of Arian, as most of the Germanic people were at the time, Clovis was able to unite the Gallo-Roman population and their Christian leaders behind his expanding hegemony over the Germanic rulers of the West and to liberate Gaul from Roman domination. His conversion also made possible the cooperation the Franks gave later to Pope Gregory the Great in his evangelistic efforts for the English.

Certainly, Clovis' motives in accepting Catholic Christianity were mixed, but there is no doubt of the sincerity of his decision, nor of the important role of Remigius in bringing it to pass. When Clovis was baptized, together with 3,000 of his followers, Remigius gave him the well-known charge: "Worship what you have burned, and burn what you have worshiped."

The feast of Remigius is observed at Rheims on January 13, possibly the date of his death. The later date of October 1 is derived from the translation of his relics to a new abbey church by Pope Leo IX in 1049.

Remigius of Rheims

Bishop, c. 530

I Almighty God, who by thy servant Remigius spread the truth of the gospel and the fullness of the catholic faith: Grant that we who glory in the name of Christian may show forth our faith in worthy deeds; through Jesus Christ our Lord, who liveth and reigneth with thee and the Holy Ghost, one God, for ever and ever. *Amen.*

II Almighty God, who by your servant Remigius spread the truth of the gospel and the fullness of the catholic faith: Grant that we who glory in the name of Christian may show forth our faith in worthy deeds; through Jesus Christ our Lord, who lives and reigns with you and the Holy Spirit, one God, for ever and ever. *Amen.*

Lessons and Psalm

Jeremiah 10:1-11
Psalm 135:13-21
1 John 4:1-6
John 14:3-7

Preface of a Saint (1)

A dedicated missionary for the worldwide spread of the gospel, John Raleigh Mott connected ecumenism and evangelism as related tasks for modern Christianity.

John Mott was born in Livingston Manor, New York, on May 25, 1865, and moved with family to Iowa in September of that same year. After graduating from Cornell University in 1888, Mott became student secretary of the International Committee of the YMCA and chairman of the executive committee of the Student Volunteer Movement. In 1895, he became General Secretary of the World Student Christian Federation, and, in 1901, he was appointed the Assistant General Secretary of the YMCA. During World War I, President Woodrow Wilson appointed him to the National War Work Council, for which he received the Distinguished Service Medal.

His ecumenical work was rooted in the missionary slogan "The Evangelization of the World in This Generation." Convinced of the need for better cooperation among Christian communions in the global mission field, he served as chairman of the committee that organized the International Missionary Conference in Edinburgh in 1910, over which he also presided. Considered to be the broadest gathering of Christians up to that point, the Conference marked the beginning of the modern ecumenical movement.

Speaking before that Conference, Mott summed up his view of Christian missions: "It is a startling and solemnizing fact that even as late as the twentieth century, the Great Command of Jesus Christ to carry the Gospel to all mankind is still so largely unfulfilled . . . The church is confronted today, as in no preceding generation, with a literally worldwide opportunity to make Christ known." Mott continued his involvement in the developing ecumenical movement, participating in the Faith and Order Conference at Lausanne in 1927, and was Vice-President of the Second World Conference on Faith and Order in Edinburgh (1937). He also served as Chairman of the Life and Work Conference in Oxford, also held in 1937.

In 1946, he received the Nobel Peace Prize for his work in establishing and strengthening international organizations which worked for peace. The World Council of Churches, the founding of which was largely driven by Mott's efforts, elected him its life-long Honorary President in 1948. Although Mott was a Methodist, the Episcopal Church recognized his work by making him an honorary canon of the National Cathedral. Mott died in 1955.

John Raleigh Mott

Ecumenist and Missionary, 1955

I Everlasting God, who dost lead thy people's feet into the ways of peace; Raise up, we beseech thee, heralds and evangelists of thy kingdom like thy servant John Mott, that thy church may make known to all the world the unsearchable riches and unsurpassed peace of thy Son, Jesus Christ our Lord; to whom with thee and the Holy Ghost be all honor and glory, now and for ever. *Amen.*

II Everlasting God, who leads your people's feet into the ways of peace; Raise up heralds and evangelists of your kingdom like your servant John Mott, that your church may make known to all the world the unsearchable riches and unsurpassed peace of your Son, Jesus Christ our Lord; to whom with you and the Holy Spirit be all honor and glory, now and for ever. *Amen.*

Lessons and Psalm

Isaiah 60:1-5
Psalm 133
1 John 2:12-14
Luke 7:11-17

Preface of All Saints

Francis, the son of a prosperous merchant of Assisi, was born in 1182. His early youth was spent in harmless revelry and fruitless attempts to win military glory. Various encounters with beggars and lepers pricked the young man's conscience, however, and he decided to embrace a life devoted to Lady Poverty. Despite his father's intense opposition, Francis totally renounced all material values and devoted himself to serve the poor. In 1210, Pope Innocent III confirmed the simple Rule for the Order of Friars Minor, a name Francis chose to emphasize his desire to be numbered among the "least" of God's servants.

The order grew rapidly all over Europe. But, by 1221, Francis had lost control of it, since his ideal of strict and absolute poverty, both for the individual friars and for the order as a whole, was found to be too difficult to maintain. His last years were spent in much suffering of body and spirit, but his unconquerable joy never failed. In his later years he was ordained as a deacon, but he resisted all efforts to persuade him to become a priest.

Not long before his death, during a retreat on Mount La Verna, Francis received, on September 14, Holy Cross Day, the marks of the Lord's wounds, the stigmata, in his own hands and feet and side. Pope Gregory IX, a former patron of the Franciscans, canonized Francis in 1228 and began the erection of the great basilica in Assisi where Francis is buried.

Of all the saints, Francis is perhaps the most popular and admired but probably the least imitated; few have attained to his total identification with the poverty and suffering of Christ. Francis left few writings; but, of these, his spirit of joyous faith comes through most truly in the "Canticle of the Sun," which he composed at Clare's convent of St. Damian's. The version in *The Hymnal* begins (*The Hymnal 1982*, #406; #407):

> Most High, omnipotent, good Lord,
> To thee be ceaseless praise outpoured,—
> And blessing without measure.
> Let creatures all give thanks to thee
> And serve in great humility.

Francis of Assisi

Friar and Deacon, 1226

I Most high, omnipotent, good Lord, grant thy people grace to renounce gladly the vanities of this world; that, following the way of blessed Francis, we may, for love of thee, delight in thy whole creation with perfectness of joy; through Jesus Christ our Lord, who lives and reigns with thee and the Holy Ghost, one God, for ever and ever. *Amen.*

II Most high, omnipotent, good Lord, grant your people grace to renounce gladly the vanities of this world; that, following the way of blessed Francis, we may, for love of you, delight in your whole creation with perfectness of joy; through Jesus Christ our Lord, who lives and reigns with you and the Holy Spirit, one God, for ever and ever. *Amen.*

Lessons and Psalm

Job 39:1-18
Psalm 121
Acts 4:32-35, 5:1-11
Luke 12:13-21

Preface of a Saint (3)

William Tyndale was born about 1495 at Slymbridge near the Welsh border. He received his B.A. and M.A. degrees at Magdalen College, Oxford, and also spent some time in study at Cambridge. After his ordination, about 1521, he entered the service of Sir John Walsh at Little Sodbury, Gloucestershire, as domestic chaplain and tutor. In 1523 he went to London and obtained a similar position with a rich cloth merchant, Humphrey Monmouth.

Tyndale was determined to translate the Scriptures into English, but, despairing of official support, he left for Germany in 1524. From this point on, his life reads like a cloak-and-dagger story, as King Henry VIII, Cardinal Wolsey, and others, sought to destroy his work of translation and put him to death. He was finally betrayed by one whom he had befriended, and in Brussels, on October 6, 1536, he was strangled at the stake, and his body was burned.

William Tyndale was a man of a single passion, to translate the Bible into English; so that, as he said to a prominent Churchman, "If God spare my life, ere many years I will cause a boy that driveth the plough shall know more scripture than thou dost." His accomplished work is his glory. Before his betrayal and death, he had finished and revised his translation of the New Testament, and had completed a translation of the Pentateuch and of Jonah and, though he did not live to see them published, of the historical books from Joshua through 2 Chronicles. His work has been called "a well of English undefiled." Some eighty percent of his version has survived in the language of later and more familiar versions, such as the Authorized (King James) Version of 1611.

After the fashion of his time, Tyndale could be a bitter controversialist, and his translations sometimes had a polemical purpose. He was a lonely and desperate man, constantly hunted and hounded. In his personal life he was amiable and self-denying. His last words were prophetic: "Lord, open the King of England's eyes."

William Tyndale

Priest, 1536

I Reveal to us thy saving word, O God, that like thy servant William Tyndale we might hear its call to repentance and new life. Plant in our hearts that same consuming passion to bring the scriptures to all people in their native tongue, and the strength to endure amidst all obstacles; through Jesus Christ our Lord, who liveth and reigneth with thee and the Holy Ghost, one God, for ever and ever. *Amen.*

II Reveal to us your saving word, O God, that like your servant William Tyndale we might hear its call to repentance and new life. Plant in our hearts that same consuming passion to bring the scriptures to all people in their native tongue, and the strength to endure amidst all obstacles; through Jesus Christ our Lord, who lives and reigns with you and the Holy Spirit, one God, for ever and ever. *Amen.*

Lessons and Psalm

Proverbs 8:10-17
Psalm 15
James 1:19-27
John 12:44-50

Preface of the Epiphany

Birgitta Birgersdotter came from a noble Swedish family and was born in 1303. Early in her life she discerned a religious vocation, but was married against her will at the age of 13 to a member of the Swedish nobility. The couple had eight children. Birgitta sought to live a holy, religious life. When her husband was absent, she openly practiced a strict asceticism, and when he was home, she did so secretly. Both she and her husband became members of the Franciscan Third Order, which admitted laypeople.

From childhood, Birgitta had experienced visions. Christ, Mary, and the saints spoke with her often in Swedish and shared with her warnings intended for others, which Birgitta would write down or dictate to her confessor. Eventually these messages became increasingly political, which caused her great discomfort. Although Birgitta enjoyed a good relationship with the royal family, she sharply criticized the king, becoming a symbolic leader for the aristocratic Swedish opposition.

Birgitta advised popes and rulers throughout Europe, and criticized the extravagant lifestyles of the clergy, monastic orders, and laity, challenging four popes to return to Rome from Avignon. She also tried to persuade the rulers of England and France to negotiate peace and end the war that would later be called the Hundred Years' War. Because of her struggles, she was recognized throughout Europe as an uncomfortable counselor and a visionary.

After the death of her husband in 1344, Birgitta devoted herself entirely to the religious life. The Order she founded, the Brigittines, was based on the revelations she had received earlier in her life. Her monastery would always have a women's and men's cloister next to one another, joined by a shared church, in which the monks, nuns, and laity would pray together. The abbess would be in charge of both the men's and women's cloister. To get papal approval for her order's founding, Birgitta traveled to Rome. In 1370, Urban V recognized the new order and allowed its foundation at Vadstena, Sweden. Birgitta was, in fact, not the first abbess there, but rather her daughter Catherine.

Except for several pilgrimages, Birgitta remained in Rome for the rest of her life. She ministered to both rich and poor, sheltered the homeless, and worked untiringly for the return of the pope from Avignon to Rome. In 1372, she was spurred by a vision to visit the Holy Land. On the return trip from Jerusalem Birgitta fell ill and entered eternal life on July 23, 1373. In Sweden she is celebrated on October 7, which is the anniversary of her canonization.

Birgitta of Sweden

Mystic, 1373

I O God, who beholdest all things and whose judgment is always mercy; by the example of thy servant Birgitta of Sweden, give to us in this life the vision of thy kingdom, where Jesus Christ is all and in all, that we might pattern our earthly lives on things heavenly, where our lives art hid with the same Christ in thee; who with him and the Holy Ghost livest and reignest for ever and ever. *Amen.*

II O God, who beholds all things and whose judgment is always mercy; by the example of your servant Birgitta of Sweden, give to us in this life the vision of your kingdom, where Jesus Christ is all and in all, that we may pattern our earthly lives on things heavenly, where our lives are hidden with Christ in you; who with him and the Holy Spirit live and reign for ever and ever. *Amen.*

Lessons and Psalm

1 Samuel 28:3-19
Psalm 12
1 Corinthians 14:6-12
Matthew 11:2-15

Preface of a Saint (1)

Robert Grosseteste, one of the outstanding English bishops of the thirteenth century, rose to preeminence in the church from humble beginnings in Suffolk. He distinguished himself as a scholar in all branches of study—law, medicine, languages, sciences, and theology.

He was appointed Master of the Oxford School, and teacher of theology to the Franciscans when they established a house at Oxford. Grosseteste translated Aristotle's works from the Greek, wrote commentaries on them, and sought to refute the philosopher's views by developing a scientific method based on Augustine's theories. Because of Grosseteste, Oxford began to emphasize the study of the sciences, especially physics, geometry, and mathematics. One notable pupil of Grosseteste was Roger Bacon, a brilliant proponent of the scientific method. Both as a teacher and as a bishop, Grosseteste had a strong influence on John Wycliffe.

In 1235, Grosseteste was consecrated as Bishop of Lincoln. He exercised his office with efficiency and conscientiousness, remarking that a bishop's pastoral responsibility was not merely to give instructions but to see that they were carried out. "I am obligated to visit the sheep committed to me with all diligence, as Scripture prescribes," he said.

He traveled regularly to each rural deanery, called together the clergy and laity, preached, confirmed, and dealt with questions of doctrine. "My lord, you are doing something new and exceptional," remarked some of the people during his first visitation. He replied, "Every new thing which implants and promotes and perfects the new man, corrupts and destroys the old. Blessed is the new, and in every way welcome to him who comes to re-create the old man in newness."

Grosseteste actively opposed royal infringements on church liberties and he did not fear to protest even papal abuses of local prerogatives. He once refused to accept the appointment of the pope's nephew to a living in his diocese, saying, "As an obedient son, I disobey, I contradict, I rebel . . . my every word and act is not rebellion, but filial honor due by God's blessed command to father and mother."

Robert Grosseteste

Bishop, 1253

I O God, our heavenly Father, who didst raise up thy faithful servant Robert Grosseteste to be a bishop and pastor in thy church and to feed thy flock: Give abundantly to all pastors the gifts of thy Holy Ghost, that they may minister in thy household as true servants of Christ and stewards of thy divine mysteries; through the same Jesus Christ our Lord, who liveth and reigneth with thee and the Holy Ghost, one God, for ever and ever. *Amen.*

II O God, our heavenly Father, who raised up your faithful servant Robert Grosseteste to be a bishop and pastor in your church and to feed your flock: Give abundantly to all pastors the gifts of your Holy Spirit, that they may minister in your household as true servants of Christ and stewards of your divine mysteries; through Jesus Christ our Lord, who lives and reigns with you and the Holy Spirit, one God, for ever and ever. *Amen.*

Lessons and Psalm

Ezekiel 1:1-14
Psalm 90:13-17
Titus 2:11-15
Luke 16:10-15

Preface of a Saint (1)

Vida Dutton Scudder exemplifies the marriage of contemplation and action within an engaged Christian spirituality. As a contemplative laywoman, Scudder was a champion for peace, social action, and women throughout her life.

Scudder was born on December 15, 1861, the child of Congregationalist missionaries in India. In the 1870s, Vida and her mother were prepared for confirmation in the Episcopal Church by Phillips Brooks, then Rector of Trinity Church, Copley Square, Boston, and later Bishop of Massachusetts. After studying English literature at Smith College and Oxford University, Scudder began teaching at Wellesley College. Her love of scholarship was matched by her social conscience and deep spirituality. As a young woman, Scudder founded the College Settlements Association, joined the Society of Christian Socialists, and, in 1889, began a lifelong association with the Society of the Companions of the Holy Cross, a community living in the world and devoted to intercessory prayer.

In 1893, Scudder took a leave of absence from Wellesley to work with Helena Stuart Dudley in founding Denison House in Boston, a "college settlement," where wealthy college-educated women provided social services to poor immigrant neighbors, in conversation with the local parish priest. Stresses from teaching and her activism led to a breakdown in 1901. After two years' recuperation in Italy, she returned renewed and became even more active in church and socialist groups; she started a group for Italian immigrants at Denison House and took an active part in organizing the Women's Trade Union League. In 1911, Scudder founded the Episcopal Church Socialist League, and formally joined the Socialist party. Her support of the Lawrence, Massachusetts, textile workers' strike in 1912 drew a great deal of criticism and threatened her teaching position. Though she initially supported World War I, she joined the Fellowship of Reconciliation in 1923, and by the 1930s was a firm pacifist.

Throughout her life, Scudder's primary relationships and support network were women. After retirement, she authored 16 books on religious and political subjects, combining her intense activism with an equally vibrant spirituality. "If prayer is the deep secret creative force that Jesus tells us it is, we should be very busy with it," she wrote characteristically, adding that there was one sure way "of directly helping on the Kingdom of God. That way is prayer. Social intercession may be the mightiest force in the world." Vida Scudder died on October 9, 1954.

Vida Dutton Scudder

Educator, 1954

I Most gracious God, who didst send thy beloved Son to preach peace to those who are far off and to those who are near: Raise up in thy church witnesses who, after the example of thy servant Vida Dutton Scudder, stand firm in proclaiming the power of the gospel of Jesus Christ; who liveth and reigneth with thee and the Holy Ghost, one God, now and for ever. *Amen.*

II Most gracious God, you sent your beloved Son to preach peace to those who are far off and to those who are near: Raise up in your church witnesses who, after the example of your servant Vida Dutton Scudder, stand firm in proclaiming the power of the gospel of Jesus Christ; who lives and reigns with you and the Holy Spirit, one God, now and for ever. *Amen.*

Lessons and Psalm

Job 38:1, 34-41
Psalm 25:1-14
Romans 12:1-2, 14-21
John 6:37-51

Preface of a Saint (3)

Philip, who has been traditionally referred to as a deacon and an evangelist, was one of the seven honest men appointed or ordained by the apostles to distribute bread and alms to the widows and the poor in Jerusalem.

After the martyrdom of Stephen, Philip went to Samaria to preach the gospel. In his travels south to Gaza, he encountered an Ethiopian eunuch, a servant of the Ethiopian queen, reading the Isaiah text on the Suffering Servant. They traveled together, and, in the course of their journey, the Ethiopian was converted and baptized by Philip.

Subsequently, Philip traveled as a missionary from Ashdod northwards and settled in Caesarea, where he hosted the apostle Paul.

Philip

Deacon and Evangelist

I O God, who hast made of one blood all the peoples of the earth and sent thy Son to preach peace to those who are far off and to those who are near: Grant that we, following the example of thy servant Philip, may bring thy Word to those who seek thee, for the glory of thy Name; through Jesus Christ our Lord, who liveth and reigneth with thee in the unity of the Holy Ghost, one God, now and for ever. *Amen.*

II O God, who has made of one blood all the peoples of the earth and sent your Son to preach peace to those who are far off and to those who are near: Grant that we, following the example of your servant Philip, may bring your Word to those who seek you, for the glory of your Name; through Jesus Christ our Lord, who lives and reigns with you in the unity of the Holy Spirit, one God, now and for ever. *Amen.*

Lessons and Psalm

Leviticus 19:9-16
Psalm 67
Acts 8:26-40
Luke 24:13-27

Preface of Apostles and Ordinations

Edith Cavell was born the eldest of four children on December 4, 1865, in a small village near Norwich, England, where her father held a long tenure as vicar. Edith received a classical English boarding school education and spent a period after her schooling serving as a governess in Brussels.

After caring for her father following a grave illness, Edith became a nurse at the London Hospital in 1896. In addition to working at hospitals and infirmaries throughout England, Edith served as a private traveling nurse, visiting and caring for patients in their own homes. In 1907, Edith assumed a position as matron at the newly founded L'École Belge d'Infirmières Diplômées (known in English as the Berkendael Medical Institute) in Brussels. While serving as matron at the Berkendael Medical Institute, Edith launched a nursing journal, *L'infirmière,* and taught nursing in many schools throughout Belgium.

World War I broke out while Edith was in England visiting family, which precipitated an immediate return to Belgium where she began serving as a Red Cross nurse. Following the German occupation of Brussels in 1914, Cavell began collaborating with others to shelter and smuggle Allied soldiers out of Belgium and into the Netherlands. Motivated by deeply held Christian faith, Edith insisted on treating wounded soldiers on both sides of the war effort, which, combined with her outspokenness against the war and the occupation, placed her in violation of German military law. Edith Cavell was arrested on August 3, 1915. During her depositions to the German police, Edith confessed to smuggling more than 60 British and 15 French soldiers, as well as 100 French and British draftable civilians out of Belgium and into neutral countries.

The evening before she was executed, Edith spoke to Father Stirling Gahan, the Anglican prison chaplain, these words which are inscribed on her memorial near Trafalgar Square in London: "Patriotism is not enough. I must have no hatred or bitterness towards anyone." On the morning of her execution, she asked Pastor Paul Le Seur, the Lutheran prison chaplain, to ask "Father Gahan to tell my loved ones later on that my soul, as I believe, is safe, and that I am glad to die for my country." Edith Cavell was executed by the German government on October 12, 1915.

Edith Cavell

Nurse, 1915

I Living God, who art the source of all healing and wholeness: we bless thee for the compassionate witness of thy servant Edith Cavell. Inspire us, we beseech thee, to be agents of peace and reconciliation in a world beset by injustice, poverty, and war. We ask this through Jesus Christ, the Prince of Peace, who livest and reignest with thee and the Holy Ghost, one God, unto the ages of ages. *Amen.*

II Living God, the source of all healing and wholeness: we bless you for the compassionate witness of your servant Edith Cavell. Inspire us to be agents of peace and reconciliation in a world beset by injustice, poverty, and war. We ask this through Jesus Christ, the Prince of Peace, who lives and reigns with you and the Holy Spirit, one God, to the ages of ages. *Amen.*

Lessons and Psalm

Joshua 2:1-21
Psalm 46
Romans 2:1-4
Matthew 18:21-35

Preface of a Saint (1)

Joseph Schereschewsky was born on May 6, 1831, of Jewish parents, in the Lithuanian town of Tauroggen. His early education was directed toward the rabbinate but, during graduate studies in Germany, he became interested in Christianity, both through contact with missionaries and through his own reading of a Hebrew translation of the New Testament. In 1854, Schereschewsky immigrated to America and entered the Western Theological Seminary in Pittsburgh to train for the ministry of the Presbyterian Church. After two years, he decided to become an Episcopalian and to finish his theological studies at the General Theological Seminary in New York City, from which he graduated in 1859.

After ordination, and in response to Bishop Boone's call for helpers in China, Schereschewsky left for Shanghai. Being a talented linguist, he learned to write Chinese during the voyage. From 1862 to 1875, he lived in Peking and translated the Bible and parts of the Prayer Book into Mandarin. Schereschewsky was elected Bishop of Shanghai in 1877 and was consecrated in Grace Church, New York City. He established St. John's University in Shanghai, and began his translation of the Bible and other works into classical Chinese.

After some years, however, he became seriously ill. Stricken with paralysis, he resigned his see in 1883. Schereschewsky was determined to continue his translation work, however, and after many difficulties in finding support, he was able to return to Shanghai in 1895. Two years later, he moved to Tokyo, where he died on October 15, 1906. With heroic perseverance, Schereschewsky completed his translation of the Bible, typing some 2,000 pages with the middle finger of his partially crippled hand. Four years before his death, he said, "I have sat in this chair for over twenty years. It seemed very hard at first. But God knew best. He kept me for the work for which I am best fitted." He is buried in the Aoyama Cemetery in Tokyo, next to his wife, Susan Mary Waring, who supported him constantly during his labors and illness.

Samuel Isaac Joseph Schereschewsky

Bishop and Missionary, 1906

I O God, who in thy providence didst call Joseph Schereschewsky to the ministry of this church and gave him the gifts and the perseverance to translate the Holy Scriptures: Inspire us, by his example and prayers, to commit our talents to thy service, confident that thou dost uphold those whom thou dost call; through Jesus Christ our Lord, who liveth and reigneth with thee and the Holy Ghost, one God, for ever and ever. *Amen.*

II O God, who in your providence called Joseph Schereschewsky to the ministry of this church and gave him the gifts and the perseverance to translate the Holy Scriptures: Inspire us, by his example and prayers, to commit our talents to your service, confident that you uphold those whom you call; through Jesus Christ our Lord, who lives and reigns with you and the Holy Spirit, one God, for ever and ever. *Amen.*

Lessons and Psalm

Isaiah 12:1-6
Psalm 90:1-12
2 Corinthians 4:11-18
Luke 15:1-7

Preface of Pentecost

Teresa was born in Spain, near Avila. Even in her childhood, she took much pleasure in the study of saints' lives, and she used to delight in spending times of contemplation, repeating over and over, "For ever, for ever, for ever, for ever, they shall see God."

In her autobiography, Teresa tells that following her mother's death, she became quite worldly. To offset this, her father placed her in an Augustinian convent to be educated, but serious illness ended her studies. During convalescence, she determined to enter the religious life and, though opposed by her father, she became a postulant at a Carmelite convent. Again, illness forced her to return home, but after three years, she returned to the convent.

Her prayer life during this period was difficult. She wrote: "I don't know what heavy penance could have come to mind that I would not have gladly and frequently undertaken rather than recollect myself in the practice of prayer." This early difficult experience would shape her later writings on prayer, in which she insisted that the spiritual life cannot be grounded in feelings and consolations.

In time, frustrated by the laxity of life in her community, Teresa set out to establish a reformed Carmelite order of "discalced" religious, who wore sandals or went barefoot. Despite many setbacks, she traveled for 25 years throughout Spain. Energetic, practical, and efficient, as well as being a mystic and ascetic, she established 17 convents of Reformed Carmelites. Even imprisonment did not deter her. Her younger contemporary John of the Cross became a close personal and spiritual friend.

Her sisters urged her to write down some of her teachings on prayer for them, which is how we came to have her works *The Interior Castle* and *The Way of Perfection*. Many people at the time felt that mental prayer (as opposed to reciting the vocal prayer of the liturgy) was too difficult and too dangerous for women, but Teresa insisted that "Mental prayer is nothing else than an intimate sharing between friends. It means taking time frequently to be alone with him whom we know loves us."

Despite the demands of her administrative and missionary work, Teresa found time to write the numerous letters that give us rare insights into her personality and concerns. Her extensive correspondence often kept her awake at night until 3:00 in the morning, after which she would awaken at 5:00 for morning prayer with the community. Teresa found writing to be burdensome, and often protested that she would be much happier spinning or working in the kitchen. Once she sat down to write, however, she was eloquent and efficient. Her great work *The Interior Castle* was written in less than two months.

Her death in 1582, following two years of illness, was peaceful. Her last sight was of the Sacrament, brought for her comfort; her last words, "O my Lord! Now is the time that we may see each other."

Teresa of Avila

Mystic and Monastic Reformer, 1582

I O God, who by the Holy Ghost didst move Teresa of Avila to manifest to thy church the way of perfection: Grant us, we beseech thee, to be nourished by her teaching, and enkindle within us a lively and unquenchable longing for true holiness; through Jesus Christ, the joy of loving hearts, who with thee and the Holy Ghost liveth and reigneth, one God, for ever and ever. *Amen.*

II O God, who by your Holy Spirit moved Teresa of Avila to manifest to your church the way of perfection: Grant us, we pray, to be nourished by her teaching, and enkindle within us a keen and unquenchable longing for true holiness; through Jesus Christ, the joy of loving hearts, who with you and the Holy Spirit lives and reigns, one God, for ever and ever. *Amen.*

Lessons and Psalm

1 Samuel 3:1-18
Psalm 42:1-7
Romans 8:22-27
Mark 1:35-39

Preface of Baptism

Hugh Latimer, Nicholas Ridley, and Thomas Cranmer were among the early Anglican bishops who were executed during the reign of the Roman Catholic Queen Mary I. Hugh Latimer was born around 1490 and graduated from Clare College, Cambridge. King Henry VIII made him a royal chaplain in 1530, and five years later appointed him to the See of Worcester, a position he relinquished in 1539 in opposition to the king's reactionary policies against the progress of the Reformation. With the accession of Queen Mary in 1553 he was imprisoned, and, on October 16, 1555, he was burned at the stake in Oxford alongside Bishop Nicholas Ridley.

Nicholas Ridley was made Bishop of Rochester and participated with Cranmer in the preparation of the first Book of Common Prayer. He was transferred to the See of London in 1550, where he was a strong advocate for and administrator of the principles of the Reformation. His unwillingness to recant of his Protestant theology and his opposition to the accession of Queen Mary led to his condemnation and his execution in 1555.

Thomas Cranmer was born in Nottinghamshire, England, on July 2, 1489, and studied theology at Cambridge University, where he subsequently taught. During his years at Cambridge, he diligently studied the Bible and the new doctrines emanating from the continental Reformation. A chance meeting with King Henry VIII in 1529 led to his involvement in the "King's Affair"—the annulment of Henry's marriage to Catherine of Aragon. Cranmer prepared the King's defense and presented it to the universities in England and Germany, and to Rome. While in Germany, Cranmer associated with the Lutheran reformers, especially with Andreas Osiander, whose daughter he married. When Archbishop Warham died, the King obtained papal confirmation of Cranmer's appointment to the See of Canterbury, and he was consecrated on March 30, 1533. Among his earliest acts was to declare the King's marriage null and void. He then validated the King's marriage to Anne Boleyn. Her child, the future Queen Elizabeth I, was Cranmer's godchild.

During the reign of Edward VI, Cranmer had a free hand in reforming the worship, doctrine, and practice of the Church. He was principally responsible for the first Book of Common Prayer of 1549, and for the second Book, in 1552. But at Edward's death he subscribed to the dying King's will that the succession should pass to his cousin, Lady Jane Grey. For this, and also for his reforming work, he was arrested, deprived of his office and authority, and condemned by Queen Mary I, a staunch Roman Catholic. He was burned at the stake on March 21, 1556.

Cranmer wrote two recantations during his imprisonment, but ultimately denied his recantations and died heroically, saying, "Forasmuch as my hand offended in writing contrary to my heart, there my hand shall first be punished; for if I may come to the fire, it shall first be burned."

Hugh Latimer and Nicholas Ridley

Bishops and Martyrs, 1555

and Thomas Cranmer

Archbishop of Canterbury, 1556

I Keep us, O Lord, constant in faith and zealous in witness, that, like thy servants Hugh Latimer, Nicholas Ridley, and Thomas Cranmer we may live in thy fear, die in thy favor, and rest in thy peace; for the sake of Jesus Christ, thy Son our Lord, who liveth and reigneth with thee and the Holy Ghost, one God, now and for ever. *Amen.*

II Keep us, O Lord, constant in faith and zealous in witness, that, like your servants Hugh Latimer, Nicholas Ridley, and Thomas Cranmer we may live in your fear, die in your favor, and rest in your peace; for the sake of Jesus Christ, your Son our Lord, who lives and reigns with you and the Holy Spirit, one God, now and for ever. *Amen.*

Lessons and Psalm

Zephaniah 3:1-5
Psalm 142
1 Corinthians 3:9-14
John 15:18-20

Preface of a Saint (1)

Ignatius of Antioch, martyred in 115, had a profound sense of two ends—his own, and the consummation of history in Jesus Christ. In ecstasy, he saw his impending martyrdom as the fitting conclusion to a long episcopate.

Seven letters, which Ignatius wrote to churches while he journeyed across Asia Minor in the custody of ten soldiers ("my leopards," he called them), give valuable insights into the life of the early church and the controversies that it faced. Of certain Gnostic teachings that exalted the divinity of Jesus at the expense of his humanity, Ignatius wrote: "Be deaf . . . to any talk that ignores Jesus Christ, of David's lineage, of Mary; who was really born, ate, and drank; was really persecuted under Pontius Pilate; was really crucified and died in the sight of heaven and earth and the underworld. He was really raised from the dead."

In another letter, he condemned a form of biblicism espoused by some as the method of historical interpretation and the only rule of church practice. He wrote: "When I heard some people saying, 'If I don't find it in the ancient documents, I don't believe it in the Gospel,' I answered them, 'But it is written there.' They retorted, 'That has got to be proved.' But to my mind it is Jesus Christ who is the ancient documents."

Ignatius maintained that the church's unity would always spring from that liturgy by which all are initiated into Christ through baptism. He exhorted: "Try to gather more frequently to celebrate God's Eucharist and to praise him . . . At these meetings you should heed the bishop and presbyters attentively and break one loaf, which is the medicine of immortality."

Ignatius regarded the church as God's holy order in the world. He was, therefore, concerned for the proper ordering of the church's teaching and worship. He wrote: "Flee from schism as the source of mischief. You should all follow the bishop as Jesus Christ did the Father. Follow, too, the priests as you would the apostles; and respect the deacons as you would God's law . . . Where the bishop is present, there let the congregation gather, just as where Jesus Christ is, there is the catholic church."

Ignatius of Antioch

Bishop and Martyr, c. 115

I Almighty God, we praise thy Name for thy bishop and martyr Ignatius of Antioch, who offered himself as grain to be ground by the teeth of wild beasts that he might present to thee the pure bread of sacrifice. Accept, we pray, the willing tribute of our lives and give us a share in the pure and spotless offering of thy Son Jesus Christ; who liveth and reigneth with thee and the Holy Ghost, one God, for ever and ever. *Amen.*

II Almighty God, we praise your Name for your bishop and martyr Ignatius of Antioch, who offered himself as grain to be ground by the teeth of wild beasts that he might present to you the pure bread of sacrifice. Accept, we pray, the willing tribute of our lives and give us a share in the pure and spotless offering of your Son Jesus Christ; who lives and reigns with you and the Holy Spirit, one God, for ever and ever. *Amen.*

Lessons and Psalm

Jeremiah 9:1-9
Psalm 28
Romans 8:18-25
John 12:23-26

Preface of a Saint (3)

According to tradition, Luke was a physician, and one of Paul's fellow missionaries in the early spread of Christianity throughout the Roman world. He has been identified as the writer of both the Gospel that bears his name, and its sequel, the Acts of the Apostles.

Luke seems to have either been a Gentile or a Hellenistic Jew and, like the other New Testament writers, he wrote in Greek, so that Gentiles might learn about the Lord whose life and deeds so impressed him. In the first chapter of his Gospel, he makes clear that he is offering authentic information about Jesus' birth, ministry, death, and resurrection, as it had been handed down to him from those who had firsthand knowledge.

Only Luke provides the very familiar stories of the annunciation to Mary, of her visit to Elizabeth, of the child in the manger, the angelic host appearing to shepherds, and the meeting with the aged Simeon. Luke also includes in his work six miracles and eighteen parables not recorded in the other Gospels. In Acts he tells about the coming of the Holy Spirit, the struggles of the apostles and their triumphs over persecution, of their preaching of the Good News, and of the conversion and baptism of other disciples, who would extend the church in future years.

Luke was with Paul apparently until the latter's martyrdom in Rome. What happened to Luke after Paul's death is unknown, but early tradition has it that he wrote his Gospel in Greece, and that he died at the age of eighty-four in Boeotia. Gregory of Nazianzus says that Luke was martyred, but this testimony is not corroborated by other sources. In the fourth century, the Emperor Constantius ordered the relics of Luke to be removed from Boeotia to Constantinople, where they could be venerated by pilgrims.

According to Orthodox Christian tradition, Luke was also the first iconographer. He is traditionally regarded as the patron saint of artists and physicians.

Saint Luke the Evangelist

I Almighty God, who didst inspire thy servant Luke the physician to set forth in the Gospel the love and healing power of thy Son: Graciously continue in thy church the like love and power to heal, to the praise and glory of thy Name; through the same thy Son Jesus Christ our Lord, who liveth and reigneth with thee, in the unity of the Holy Ghost, one God, now and for ever. *Amen.*

II Almighty God, who inspired your servant Luke the physician to set forth in the Gospel the love and healing power of your Son: Graciously continue in your church this love and power to heal, to the praise and glory of your Name; through Jesus Christ our Lord, who lives and reigns with you, in the unity of the Holy Spirit, one God, now and for ever. *Amen.*

Lessons and Psalm

Ecclesiasticus 38:1-4, 6-10, 12-14
Psalm 147 *or* 147:1-7
2 Timothy 4:5-13
Luke 4:14-21

Preface of All Saints

Henry Martyn, an English missionary and translator, died when he was only thirty-one years old. Though his life was brief, it was a remarkable one.

Martyn was educated at Cambridge. He had intended to become a lawyer, but Charles Simeon, the rector of Holy Trinity, Cambridge, inspired him to go to India as a missionary. After serving as Simeon's curate for a short time, Martyn traveled to Calcutta in 1806 as chaplain of the East India Company.

During his five years in India, Martyn preached the gospel, organized private schools, and founded churches. In addition to his work as a missionary, Martyn translated the New Testament and the Book of Common Prayer into Hindi, which was a valuable missionary aid to the young Anglican Church in India. He also began the study of Persian, and translated the New Testament into that language as well.

Martyn longed to go to Persia, and in 1811, his persistence brought him to Shiraz, as the first English clergyman in that city. He engaged in theological discussions with learned Muslims and corrected his Persian translations of the New Testament. Martyn hoped eventually to visit Arabia and to translate the New Testament into Arabic.

While on his way to Constantinople in 1812, however, Martyn died in the Turkish city of Tokat. The Armenian Orthodox Christians of the city buried him with the honors usually accorded to one of their own bishops. Very soon afterwards, his life of energetic devotion and remarkable accomplishment became widely known. He is remembered as one of the founders of the modern Christian church in both India and Iran.

Henry Martyn

Priest and Missionary, 1812

I O God of the nations, who gave to thy servant Henry Martyn a longing to share thy Gospel with all peoples; Inspire the church in our own day, we beseech thee, with that same desire, that we may be eager to commit both life and talents to thee who didst bestow them; through Jesus Christ our Lord, who liveth and reigneth with thee and the Holy Ghost, one God, for ever and ever. *Amen.*

II O God of the nations, who gave to your servant Henry Martyn a longing to share your Gospel with all peoples; Inspire the church in our own day with that said desire, that we may be eager to commit both life and talents to you who gave them; through Jesus Christ our Lord, who lives and reigns with you and the Holy Spirit, one God, for ever and ever. *Amen.*

Lessons and Psalm

Isaiah 49:1-7
Psalm 98
Romans 1:8-15
John 4:21-26

Preface of a Saint (2)

All that we know about Cornelius is contained in the Acts of the Apostles (chapters 10-11). He was the first Gentile converted to the Christian faith, along with his household. A centurion was commander of a company of one hundred men in the Roman army, responsible for their discipline, both on the field of battle and in camp. A centurion was a Roman citizen, a military career man, well paid, and generally noted for courage and competence. Some centurions, such as Cornelius and those whom we know about from the gospel narratives, were men of deep religious piety.

The author of Acts considered Cornelius' conversion very momentous for the future of Christianity. He records that it occurred as the result of divine intervention and revelation, and as a response to the preaching of Peter, the chief apostle. The experience of Cornelius' household was regarded as comparable to a new Pentecost, and it was a primary precedent for the momentous decision of the apostolic council, held in Jerusalem a few years later, to admit Gentiles to full and equal partnership with Jewish converts in the household of faith.

According to tradition, Cornelius became a missionary and eventually the bishop of Caesarea. Cornelius and his household likely formed the nucleus of the first church in this important city, a church that was gathered by Philip the Evangelist (Acts 8:40 and 21:8).

Cornelius the Centurion

I O God, who by thy Spirit didst call Cornelius the Centurion to be the first Christian among the Gentiles: Grant to thy church, we beseech thee, such a ready will to go where thou dost send and to do what thou dost command that the prejudices that blind us might cease, and that we might welcome all who turn to thee in love through Jesus Christ our Lord, who liveth and reigneth with thee and the Holy Ghost, one God, for ever and ever. *Amen.*

II O God, who by your Spirit called Cornelius the Centurion to be the first Christian among the Gentiles: Grant to your church such a ready will to go where you send and to do what you command that the prejudices that blind us might cease, and that we might welcome all who turn to you in love; through Jesus Christ our Lord, who lives and reigns with you and the Holy Spirit, one God, for ever and ever. *Amen.*

Lessons and Psalm

Isaiah 56:6-8
Psalm 67
Acts 11:1-18
Luke 13:22-29

Preface of Pentecost

In the Gospel according to Matthew and in the Epistle to the Galatians, the James whom we commemorate today is called the Lord's brother. Other writers, following Mark's tradition, believe him to have been a cousin of Jesus. Certain apocryphal writings speak of him as a son of Joseph's first wife. Whatever his relationship to Jesus—brother, half-brother, or cousin—James was converted after the resurrection. Eventually, he became Bishop of Jerusalem.

In the first letter to the Corinthians (15:7), Paul says that James was favored with a special appearance of the Lord before the ascension. Later, James dealt cordially with Paul at Jerusalem, when the latter came there to meet Peter and the other apostles. During the Council of Jerusalem, when there was disagreement about whether Gentile converts should be circumcised, James summed up the momentous decision with these words: "My judgment is that we should impose no irksome restrictions on those Gentiles who are turning to God" (Acts 15:19).

Eusebius, quoting from an earlier church history by Hegesippus, declares that James was surnamed "the Just." He was holy, abstemious, did not cut his hair nor oil his body, and was continually on his knees in prayer, interceding for his people. "As many as came to believe did so through James," says Hegesippus.

James' success in converting many to Christ greatly perturbed some factions in Jerusalem. According to Hegesippus, they begged him to "restrain the people, for they have gone astray to Jesus, thinking him to be the Messiah . . . We bear you witness that you are just . . . Persuade the people that they do not go astray . . . we put our trust in you." They then set James on the pinnacle of the temple, bidding him to preach to the multitude and turn them from Jesus. James, however, testified for the Lord. Thereupon, they hurled him from the roof to the pavement, and cudgeled him to death.

Saint James of Jerusalem

Brother of Our Lord Jesus Christ, and Martyr, c. 62

I Grant, we beseech thee, O God, that after the example of thy servant James the Just, brother of our Lord, thy church may give itself continually to prayer and to the reconciliation of all who are at variance and enmity; through the same our Lord Jesus Christ, who liveth and reigneth with thee and the Holy Ghost, one God, now and for ever. *Amen.*

II Grant, O God, that, following the example of your servant James the Just, brother of our Lord, your church may give itself continually to prayer and to the reconciliation of all who are at variance and enmity; through Jesus Christ our Lord, who lives and reigns with you and the Holy Spirit, one God, now and for ever. *Amen.*

Lessons and Psalm

Acts 15:12-22a
Psalm 1
1 Corinthians 15:1-11
Matthew 13:54-58

Preface of All Saints

Tabitha, also known by her Greek name Dorcas, already had a reputation for being a woman of good works and charity before Peter arrived in Joppa to preach the Gospel (Acts 9:36). The Scriptures mention that many widows had benefitted from her work in making them clothes. Their desire to show Peter examples was both a testament to her charity and perhaps also the level of craftsmanship with which she made them.

Perhaps due to the reputation that the apostles had as wonder workers, when Tabitha died her friends called for Peter to come see her. This story is likely intended to recall the story of Jesus healing the young girl in Luke 8:41-56 when Jesus performed a similar miracle. This miracle of life performed for Tabitha through Peter caused many in the town to believe in Jesus. It, like many miracles recorded in Acts, was a confirmation that the message was true and that the apostles did indeed speak for God.

She is also mentioned by Basil of Caesarea as an example of charity and good works, and as a role model for other widows: "A widow who enjoys sufficiently robust health should spend her life in works of zeal and solicitude, keeping in mind the words of the Apostle and the example of Dorcas."

Tabitha (Dorcas) of Joppa

I Most Holy God, who didst raise from the dead thy servant Tabitha to display thy power and confirm that thy Son is Lord; Grant unto us thy grace, that, aided by her prayers and example, we may be given a new life in thee, to do works pleasing in thy sight; through Jesus Christ thy Son our Lord; who liveth and reigneth with thee, in the unity of the Holy Ghost, one God, for ever and ever. *Amen.*

II Most Holy God, who did raise from the dead your servant Tabitha to display your power and confirm that your Son is Lord; Grant unto us your grace, that, aided by her prayers and example, we may be given a new life in you, to do works pleasing in your sight; through Jesus Christ your Son our Lord; who lives and reigns with you, in the unity of the Holy Spirit, one God, for ever and ever. *Amen.*

Lessons and Psalm

Leviticus 19:32-37
Psalm 101:1-4
Acts 9:36-42
Matthew 25:1-13

Preface of God the Son

Alfred, alone of all English rulers, has been called "the Great," because of his courage and Christian virtues. Born in 849 at Wantage, the youngest of five sons of King Aethelwulf, Alfred spent his life in a time of "battle, murder, and sudden death" during the Viking invasions and settlement in Britain. He was deeply impressed when, on a visit to Rome at the age of four, he was blessed by Pope Leo IV, and two years later, when he witnessed the marriage of Aethelwulf to a young princess of the Frankish court. Following his father's death and the short reigns of his brothers, Alfred became King in 871.

In heroic battles and by stratagems against the Danes, Alfred halted the tide of their invasion and secured control of the southern, and part of the midland, regions of England. After a decisive victory in 878 at Edington over the Danish leader Guthrum, he persuaded his foe to accept baptism.

A man of deep piety, Alfred's leadership in battle and administration was grounded by his faith. His biographer Asser wrote of his commitment to a life of prayer influenced by monasticism. "He learned the daily course, that is, the celebrations of the Hours, and after that certain psalms and many prayers, gathered together in one book for the sake of prayer, which he carried around with him everywhere on his person by day and night, just as we have seen, inseparable from himself, in all of the doings of this present life."

In his later years, Alfred sought to repair the damage that the Viking invasions had inflicted upon culture and learning, especially among the parish clergy. With the help of scholars from Wales and the European continent, he supervised translations into English of important classics of theology and history, including works by Gregory the Great, Augustine of Hippo, and Bede. In one of them he commented: "He seems to me a very foolish man, and very wretched, who will not increase his understanding while he is in the world, and ever wish and long to reach that endless life where all shall be made clear."

Alfred died on October 26, 899, and was buried in Winchester.

Alfred

King, 899

I O God, who didst call thy servant Alfred to an earthly throne that he might advance thy heavenly kingdom and didst give him zeal for thy church and love for thy people: Grant that we, inspired by his example and prayers, may remain steadfast in the work thou hast given us to do for the building up of thy reign of love; through Jesus Christ our Lord, who liveth and reigneth with thee and the Holy Ghost, one God, for ever and ever. *Amen.*

II O God, who called your servant Alfred to an earthly throne that he might advance your heavenly kingdom and gave him zeal for your church and love for your people: Grant that we, inspired by his example and prayers, may remain steadfast in the work you have given us to do for the building up of your reign of love; through Jesus Christ our Lord, who lives and reigns with you and the Holy Spirit, one God, for ever and ever. *Amen.*

Lesson and Psalms

Wisdom 6:1-11
Psalm 21:1-7
2 Thessalonians 2:13-17
Luke 6:43-49

Preface of Baptism

Little is known about Simon and Jude, both named in New Testament lists of the twelve disciples, but tradition has consistently associated both apostles with one another, and with missionary work in Persia and Armenia. According to most ancient authorities they were martyred together, possibly in Beirut, but accounts vary.

There are other scholarly questions about both men. One involves Simon's appellation "Zelotes" or "the Zealot." Whether in fact he had been a member before his conversion of one of the several Jewish factions called "Zealots," or whether this title refers to his zeal for the Jewish law, is not known, but he has consistently been identified by it.

Jude has long been regarded in popular devotion as the patron of desperate or lost causes. The Epistle of Jude, which is attributed to the disciple, concludes with this striking doxology: "Now to him who is able to keep you from falling, and to present you without blemish before the presence of his glory with rejoicing, to the only God our Savior, be glory, majesty, dominion, and authority, through Jesus Christ our Lord, before all time and now and forever" (Jude 24-25).

Saint Simon and Saint Jude, Apostles

I O God, we thank thee for the glorious company of the apostles, and especially on this day for Simon and Jude; and we pray that, as they were faithful and zealous in their mission, so we may with ardent devotion make known the love and mercy of our Lord and Savior Jesus Christ; who liveth and reigneth with thee and the Holy Ghost, one God, for ever and ever. *Amen.*

II O God, we thank you for the glorious company of the apostles, and especially on this day for Simon and Jude; and we pray that, as they were faithful and zealous in their mission, so we may with ardent devotion make known the love and mercy of our Lord and Savior Jesus Christ; who lives and reigns with you and the Holy Spirit, one God, for ever and ever. *Amen.*

Lessons and Psalm

Deuteronomy 32:1-4
Psalm 119:89-96
Ephesians 2:13-22
John 15:17-27

Preface of Apostles and Ordinations

James Hannington was born in Sussex on September 3, 1847, and was educated at Temple School in Brighton. For six years, he assisted his father in the warehouse business. The family became members of the Church of England in 1867, and the following year, Hannington entered St. Mary Hall, Oxford, where he obtained his B.A. and M.A. degrees.

Following his ordination at Exeter, Hannington served as a curate in his native town until, in 1882, he offered himself to the Church Missionary Society for its mission in Victoria, Nyanza, Africa. Serious illness soon required his return to England, but he went out again to Africa in 1884, as Bishop of Eastern Equatorial Africa.

Hannington's mission field was on the shores of Lake Victoria. He dreamed of creating a shorter and more efficient route directly from Mombasa, in Kenya, to Buganda. Ignoring the advice of his local guides and porters that the venture would be politically sensitive, and failing to heed a warning from emissaries of King Mwanga to stop, he and his party were apprehended and imprisoned. After a week of cruel privations and suffering, he and the remaining members of his company were executed on October 29, 1885, on the orders of King Mwanga.

Hannington's last words were: "Go, tell Mwanga I have purchased the road to Uganda with my blood." Other martyrs of Uganda shared his fate before the gospel was firmly planted in this heartland of Africa, where today the church has a vigorous life under an indigenous ministry. Mwanga was eventually exiled to Seychelles in 1899, where he was received into the Anglican Church and baptized. He died there in 1903.

James Hannington

Bishop

and his Companions

Martyrs, 1885

I O God, by whose providence the blood of the martyrs is the seed of the church: Grant that we who remember before thee James Hannington and his companions, may, like them, be steadfast in our faith in Jesus Christ, to whom they gave obedience unto death, and by their sacrifice brought forth a plentiful harvest; through Jesus Christ our Lord, who liveth and reigneth with thee and the Holy Ghost, one God, for ever and ever. *Amen.*

II O God, by whose providence the blood of the martyrs is the seed of the church: Grant that we who remember before you James Hannington and his companions, may, like them, be steadfast in our faith in Jesus Christ, to whom they gave obedience even to death, and by their sacrifice brought forth a plentiful harvest; through Jesus Christ our Lord, who lives and reigns with you and the Holy Spirit, one God, for ever and ever. *Amen.*

Lessons and Psalm

Ecclesiasticus 3:17-24
Psalm 124
1 Peter 3:14-22
Matthew 10:37-42

Preface of Holy Week

Maryam of Qidun is one of the most popular Syriac Christian saints. The drama of her life story easily lends itself to fictionalized interpretations, and multiple accounts of her life were produced. There nevertheless does seem to be a historical person in the background of all of these accounts, who became the inspiration for all of these legends.

Maryam grew up in a Christian family and was orphaned at the age of seven. Her only living relative was an uncle named Abraham who lived as a hermit in the desert near Qidun, a village outside of Edessa. Despite the seeming oddity of an anchorite serving as the guardian for a young girl, therefore, she was given to him to raise. For twenty years, she lived an ascetic life in her own room in his dwelling, growing deeply in holiness and prayer, teaching those who came to seek her wisdom through a window, and being praised and admired by all who met her.

However, there was a monk who desired her, and who used to come to the hermitage every day on the pretext of speaking with Abraham in order to see her. One day, when Maryam's uncle was away, the monk raped her. Maryam fell into despair about the possibility of her salvation, for she had always been admired for her purity and holiness. Deeply shaken, she questioned, "How can I ever again raise my eyes up to heaven when I cannot even bring myself to look at my uncle?" Rather than face him and confess to him what she believed to be a sin, she ran away to the city, trapped by societal judgment and working as a prostitute in a tavern.

After two years of frantic searching, her uncle discovered where she was living, and he borrowed a soldier's uniform and a horse. He covered his face with the helmet and set off for the tavern. When he saw her dressed as a prostitute and flirting with the customers he nearly wept, but he concealed his emotions lest she recognize him and run away. Although he had not touched wine or cooked food in nearly fifty years, he feasted and drank and joked as though he were truly a soldier. But when the girl led him back to her bedroom he took off his helmet and said, "My daughter Maryam, don't you know me? Whatever has happened to you? Why did you not just tell me when you had sinned? I would not have been angry with you, for who is without sin, except for God alone? I would have done penance for you myself, yet instead you have left me all alone in unspeakable sadness and grief."

As he spoke these words, she was motionless like a stone, too ashamed and afraid to speak or even to raise her eyes to his. But he spoke words of comfort and compassion to her all night, and in the morning, she allowed him to lead her home.

In one way, Maryam's story demonstrates that, regardless of how she first perceived the value of her virginity, God's grace proved to be far wider than she imagined. And in another way, Maryam's story demonstrates that "neither death, nor life . . . nor things present, nor things to come . . . nor anything else in all creation," including the evils that ensnared her and defamed her, could separate her from "the love of God in Christ Jesus our Lord" (Romans 8:38).

Maryam of Qidun

Monastic, fourth century

I O God of holiness and strength, rescue us from the sins that ensnare us and destroy the evils that defame us, that, like thy servant Maryam of Qidun, we may find our own selves inseparable from thy love made known in Christ Jesus our Lord; who with thee and the Holy Ghost liveth and reigneth, one God, in glory everlasting. *Amen.*

II O God of holiness and strength, rescue us from the sins that ensnare us and destroy the evils that defame us, that, like your servant Maryam of Qidun, we may find our own selves inseparable from your love made known in Christ Jesus our Lord; who with you and the Holy Spirit lives and reigns, one God, in glory everlasting. *Amen.*

Lessons and Psalm

Hosea 11:1-4, 8-9
Psalm 31:15-24
Romans 8:31-39
John 8:1-11

Preface of Holy Week

It is believed that the commemoration of all the saints on November 1 originated in Ireland, spread from there to England, and then to the European continent. That it had reached Rome and had been adopted there early in the ninth century is attested by a letter of Pope Gregory IV, who reigned from 828 to 844, to Emperor Louis the Pious, urging that such a festival be observed throughout the Holy Roman Empire.

However, the desire of Christian people to express the intercommunion of the living and the dead in the Body of Christ by a commemoration of those who, having professed faith in the living Christ during their lives, had entered into the nearer presence of their Lord, and especially of those who had crowned their profession with heroic deaths, was far older than the early Middle Ages. Gregory Thaumaturgus (the "Wonder Worker"), writing before the year 270, refers to the observance of a festival of all martyrs, though he does not date it. A hundred years later, Ephrem the Deacon mentions such an observance in Edessa on May 13; and the patriarch John Chrysostom, who died in 407, says that a festival of All Saints was observed on the first Sunday after Pentecost in Constantinople at the time of his episcopate. The lectionary of the East Syrians set a commemoration of all the saints on Friday in Easter week. On May 13, in the year 610, the Pantheon in Rome—originally a pagan temple dedicated to "all the gods"—was dedicated as the Church of St. Mary and All Martyrs.

All Saints' Day is classified in the Prayer Book as a Principal Feast, taking precedence over any other day or observance. Among the seven Principal Feasts, All Saints' Day alone may be observed on the following Sunday, in addition to its observance on its fixed date. It is also one of the four days particularly recommended in the Prayer Book (page 312) for the administration of Holy Baptism.

All Saints

I O Almighty God, who hast knit together thine elect in one communion and fellowship in the mystical body of thy Son Christ our Lord: Grant us grace so to follow thy blessed saints in all virtuous and godly living, that we may come to those ineffable joys which thou hast prepared for those who unfeignedly love thee; through the same Jesus Christ our Lord, who with thee and the Holy Ghost liveth and reigneth, one God, in glory everlasting. *Amen.*

II Almighty God, you have knit together your elect in one communion and fellowship in the mystical body of your Son Christ our Lord: Give us grace so to follow your blessed saints in all virtuous and godly living, that we may come to those ineffable joys that you have prepared for those who truly love you; through Jesus Christ our Lord, who with you and the Holy Spirit lives and reigns, one God, in glory everlasting. *Amen.*

Lessons and Psalm

Year A:
Revelation 7:9-17
Psalm 34:1-10, 22
1 John 3:1-3
Matthew 5:1-12

Year B:
Wisdom of Solomon 3:1-9 *or* Isaiah 25:6-9
Psalm 24
Revelation 21:1-6a
John 11:32-44

Year C:
Daniel 7:1-3, 15-18
Psalm 149
Ephesians 1:11-23
Luke 6:20-31

Preface of All Saints

In the New Testament, the word "saints" is used to describe the entire membership of the Christian community, and in the Collect for All Saints' Day the word "elect" is used in a similar sense. From very early times, however, the word "saint" came to be applied primarily to persons of heroic sanctity, whose deeds were recalled with gratitude and admiration by later generations.

Beginning in the tenth century, it became customary to set aside another day on which the church remembered that vast body of the faithful who, though no less members of the company of the redeemed, are unknown in the wider fellowship of the church. It was also a day for particular remembrance of family members and friends. Although those in this wider body of the faithful are no less part of the communion of saints than those persons whose particular sanctity is celebrated on All Saints' Day, the liturgical mood of the two days is nevertheless quite different, as the joy and exultation of All Saints' Day transitions to the much more personal remembrances and griefs of All Souls' Day.

Although the observance of All Souls' Day was abolished at the Reformation because of abuses connected with masses for the dead, a renewed understanding of its meaning has led to a widespread acceptance of this commemoration among Anglicans, and to its inclusion as an optional observance in the calendar of the Episcopal Church.

All Souls/All the Faithful Departed

I O God, the Maker and Redeemer of all believers: Grant to the faithful departed the unsearchable benefits of the passion of thy Son; that on the day of his appearing they may be manifested as thy children; through Jesus Christ our Lord, who liveth and reigneth with thee and the Holy Ghost, one God, now and for ever. *Amen.*

II O God, the Maker and Redeemer of all believers: Grant to the faithful departed the unsearchable benefits of the passion of your Son; that on the day of his appearing they may be manifested as your children; through Jesus Christ our Lord, who lives and reigns with you and the Holy Spirit, one God, now and for ever. *Amen.*

Lessons and Psalm

Wisdom 3:1-9
Psalm 130
1 Thessalonians 4:13-18
John 5:24-27

Preface of the Commemoration of the Dead

In any list of Anglican theologians, Richard Hooker's name would stand high, if not first. He was born in 1553 near Exeter, and was admitted in 1567 to Corpus Christi College, Oxford, of which he became a Fellow ten years later. After ordination and marriage in 1581, he held a living in Buckinghamshire. In 1586, he became Master of the Temple in London. Later, he served country parishes in Boscombe, Salisbury, and Bishopsbourne near Canterbury.

A controversy with a noted Puritan led Hooker to prepare a comprehensive defense of the Reformation settlement under Queen Elizabeth I. This work, his masterpiece, was entitled *The Laws of Ecclesiastical Polity*. Its philosophical base is Aristotelian, with a strong emphasis upon the natural law eternally planted by God in creation. On this foundation, all positive laws of church and state are grounded—upon Scriptural revelation, tradition, and reason.

Book Five of the *Laws* is a massive defense of the Book of Common Prayer, directed primarily against Puritan detractors. Hooker's arguments are buttressed by enormous patristic learning, but the needs of the contemporary worshiper are paramount, and he draws effectively on his twenty-year experience of using the Prayer Book.

Concerning the nature of the church, Hooker wrote: "The church is always a visible society of men; not an assembly, but a society. For although the name of the church be given unto Christian assemblies, although any multitude of Christian men congregated may be termed by the name of a church, yet assemblies properly are rather things that belong to a church. Men are assembled for performance of public actions; which actions being ended, the assembly dissolveth itself and is no longer in being, whereas the church which was assembled doth no less continue afterwards than before."

Pope Clement VIII is reported to have said that Hooker's work "had in it such seeds of eternity that it would abide until the last fire shall consume all learning."

Richard Hooker

Priest and Theologian, 1600

I O God of truth and peace, who didst raise up thy servant Richard Hooker in a day of bitter controversy to defend with sound reasoning and great charity the catholic and reformed religion: Grant that we may maintain that middle way, not as a compromise for the sake of peace, but as a comprehension for the sake of truth; through Jesus Christ our Lord, who liveth and reigneth with thee and the Holy Ghost, one God, for ever and ever. *Amen.*

II O God of truth and peace, you raised up your servant Richard Hooker in a day of bitter controversy to defend with sound reasoning and great charity the catholic and reformed religion: Grant that we may maintain that middle way, not as a compromise for the sake of peace, but as a comprehension for the sake of truth; through Jesus Christ our Lord, who lives and reigns with you and the Holy Spirit, one God, for ever and ever. *Amen.*

Lessons and Psalm

Ecclesiasticus 44:10-15
Psalm 37:1-9
1 Corinthians 2:6-16
John 17:18-23

Preface of Baptism

Adeline Blanchard Tyler (1805-1875) was the first Episcopal deaconess. Along with Caroline (Carrie) Elizabeth Guild (1827-1880), Eveline Black (1825-1875), and Catherine Minard (1837-1917), she was admitted to the office of deaconess on the 4th of November 1856. Accepting the threefold charge to be "servants of the Lord Jesus; servants to the sick and poor and needy, of every class, for Jesus' sake; and servants to one another," they provided nursing care, religious and practical education, material support, and advocacy at the newly established St. Andrew's Infirmary in Baltimore. They cared for men, women, and children, Black and white, from near and far, and would become known as the United Deaconesses of Maryland.

Previously, Adeline had been a member of Boston's Trinity Church, where she was among the founders of Trinity Hall, a Sunday School for poor children; the Episcopal City Mission; and St. Stephen's Chapel. After joining the Church of the Advent in 1846 (where she would later sponsor Carrie Guild for baptism), Adeline continued in her works of Christian charity, becoming Matron of the Parish School, which the rector described as "a place of instruction for children of the Parish especially those who are poor and uncared for. We have about 50 children...10 are the children of colored Parishioners."

In 1856, the Rev. Horace Stringfellow, rector of St. Andrew's Church in Baltimore, invited Adeline to head his new infirmary, the fulfillment of his vision to emulate the nursing Sisterhoods and Deaconess hospitals he had seen in England and France. Adeline and Carrie arrived in Baltimore from Boston that September. They joined Eveline Black and Catherine Minard, who had been working with Stringfellow since 1855 at St. Andrew's Church, but did not become deaconesses until Bishop Whittingham formally assumed "Pastoral Supervision and Visitorial care of your Sisterhood and of the Infirmary and Schools" on November 4, 1856. Soon the four original Deaconesses were joined by two associates, identified as Miss Hickey and Miss Martin. The report of the Infirmary's first year notes 53 patients admitted, 88 out-door patients, 756 visits made, 93 children in the Charity School, 500 garments and 85 pairs of shoes distributed, 5 patients baptized, 4 confirmed, 8 admitted to their "first reception of the Holy Communion."

During and after the Civil War, Adeline and her companions provided nursing care to the wounded on both sides of the conflict. At the Camden Street Hospital in Baltimore and the military hospital in Chester, Pennsylvania, and, somewhat later at the Naval Hospital at Annapolis, Maryland, often as many as one thousand wounded soldiers were under her care.

She died on January 9, 1875.

[Adeline Blanchard Tyler and her Companions]

I Merciful God, who didst endow Adeline and her companions with faith and courage, wisdom and humility, and called them to serve thee as deaconesses, ministering to the sick, the oppressed, and the poor: by thy grace, grant that we, following their example, may live to serve thee as they did, revealing thy steadfast love to the world, though our Lord Jesus Christ. *Amen.*

II Merciful God, who endowed Adeline and her companions with faith and courage, wisdom and humility, and called them to serve you as deaconesses, ministering to the sick, the oppressed, and the poor: by your grace, grant that we, following their example, may live to serve you as they did, revealing your steadfast love to the world, though our Lord Jesus Christ. *Amen.*

Lessons and Psalm

Isaiah 58:1-12
Psalm 103:1-6
Romans 16:1-2, 25-27
Matthew 14:13-21

Preface of a Saint (1)

William Temple was a renowned teacher and preacher who served as Archbishop of Canterbury during the difficult days of the Second World War. His writings reflect a robust social theology that engaged the challenges of modern industrialized society.

Temple was born on October 15, 1881. His father, Dr. Frederick Temple, Bishop of Exeter and then of London, became Archbishop of Canterbury when William was fifteen. Growing up at the heart of the Church of England, William's love for it was deep and lifelong. Endowed with a brilliant mind, Temple took a first-class honors degree in classics and philosophy at Oxford, where he was then elected Fellow of Queen's College. At the age of twenty-nine he became headmaster of Repton School, and then, in quick succession, rector of St. James's Church, Piccadilly, Bishop of Manchester, and Archbishop of York.

Although he was never subject to poverty himself, he developed a passion for social justice which shaped his words and his actions. He owed this passion to a profound belief in the Incarnation. He wrote that in Jesus Christ God took flesh and dwelt among us, and, as a consequence, "the personality of every man and woman is sacred." In 1917, Temple resigned from St. James's, Piccadilly, to devote his energies to the "Life and Liberty" movement for reform within the Church of England. Two years later, an Act of Parliament led to the setting up of the Church Assembly, which for the first time gave the laity a voice in church governance.

As bishop, and later as archbishop, Temple committed himself to seeking "the things which pertain to the Kingdom of God." He understood the Incarnation as giving worth and meaning not only to individuals but to all of life. He therefore took the lead in establishing the Conference on Christian Politics, Economics, and Citizenship (COPEC), held in 1924. In 1940, he convened the great Malvern Conference to reflect on the social reconstruction that would be needed in Britain once the Second World War was over. At the same time, he was a prolific writer on theological, ecumenical, and social topics, and his two-volume *Readings in St. John's Gospel,* written in the early days of the war, rapidly became a spiritual classic.

In 1942, Temple was appointed Archbishop of Canterbury and reached an even wider audience through his wartime radio addresses and newspaper articles. However, the scope of his responsibilities and the pace he set himself took their toll. On October 26, 1944, he died at Westgate-on-Sea, Kent, after only two and a half years at Canterbury.

William Temple

Archbishop of Canterbury, 1944

I O God of light and love, who illumined thy church through the witness of thy servant William Temple: Inspire us, we pray, by his teaching and example, that we may rejoice with courage, confidence, and faith in the Word made flesh, and may be led to establish that city which has justice for its foundation and love for its law; through Jesus Christ, the light of the world, who liveth and reigneth with thee and the Holy Ghost, one God, now and for ever. *Amen.*

II O God of light and love, you illumined your church through the witness of your servant William Temple: Inspire us, we pray, by his teaching and example, that we may rejoice with courage, confidence, and faith in the Word made flesh, and may be led to establish that city which has justice for its foundation and love for its law; through Jesus Christ, the light of the world, who lives and reigns with you and the Holy Spirit, one God, now and for ever. *Amen.*

Lessons and Psalm

Exodus 22:21-27
Psalm 119:97-104
Philippians 2:12-13
John 1:1-14

Preface of the Epiphany

We know about Willibrord's life and missionary labors through a notice in Bede's *Ecclesiastical History* and a biography by his younger kinsman, Alcuin. He was born in Northumbria around 658, and, from the age of seven, was brought up and educated at Bishop Wilfrid's monastery in Ripon. For twelve years, from 678 to 690, he studied in Ireland, where he acquired his thirst for missionary work.

In 690, with twelve companions, he set out for Frisia, a pagan area that was increasingly coming under the domination of the Christian Franks. There, Bishop Wilfrid and a few other Englishmen had made short missionary visits, but with little success. With the aid of the Frankish rulers, Willibrord established his base at Utrecht, and in 695 Pope Sergius ordained him as a bishop and gave him the name of Clement.

In 698, he founded the monastery of Echternach, near Trier. His work was frequently disturbed by the conflict of the pagan Frisians with the Franks, and for a time he left the area to work among the Danes. For three years, from 719 to 722, he was assisted by Boniface, who at a later time came back to Frisia to strengthen the mission. In a very real sense, Willibrord prepared the way for Boniface's more successful achievements by his relations with the Frankish rulers and the papacy, who thus became joint sponsors of missionary work. He died at Echternach, November 7, 739.

Willibrord

Bishop and Missionary, 739

I O Lord our God, who dost call whom thou willest and send them where thou choosest: We thank thee for sending thy servant Willibrord to be an apostle to the Low Countries, to turn them from the worship of idols to serve thee, the living God; and we entreat thee to preserve us from the temptation to exchange the perfect freedom of thy service for servitude to false gods and to idols of our own devising; through Jesus Christ our Lord, who liveth and reigneth with thee and the Holy Spirit, one God, for ever and ever. *Amen.*

II O Lord our God, you call whom you will and send them where you choose: We thank you for sending your servant Willibrord to be an apostle to the Low Countries, to turn them from the worship of idols to serve you, the living God; and we entreat you to preserve us from the temptation to exchange the perfect freedom of your service for servitude to false gods and to idols of our own devising; through Jesus Christ our Lord, who lives and reigns with you and the Holy Spirit, one God, for ever and ever. *Amen.*

Lessons and Psalm

2 Kings 2:19-25
Psalm 105:1-5
Acts 1:1-9
Luke 18:1-8

Preface of Apostles and Ordinations

The most popular story that is related about Ammonius would seem quite unbelievable if it were not recorded in such a large number of historical sources, including many that were contemporary with his life. Although praised for his learning and his asceticism, he is most vividly remembered for the vehemence with which he resisted ordination.

Ammonius was one of four brothers who became monastic hermits in Scete in northern Egypt, disciples of the great ascetic Pambo. Although most of the monks in that settlement were illiterate, Ammonius had been exceptionally well educated. He is said to have had the entire Old and New Testament memorized, as well as the works of many early Christian theologians. Although he left no writings, many of his students and colleagues did, perhaps the most famous of whom is Evagrius of Pontus.

In addition to his great knowledge, Ammonius was also very strict in his spiritual practice and was well loved as a spiritual director and guide. Because of all of this, the inhabitants of a nearby village wanted him to be their bishop. Forcible ordination was not unusual in the early church, and so Bishop Timothy of Alexandria told the people that if they were able to bring this holy man to him, he would absolutely ordain him.

Ammonius pleaded with them not to do this thing, but they would not hear it, and a large crowd of them gathered to drag him back to Alexandria by force. Seeing that they were too numerous for him to resist or to flee, Ammonius seized a sword and chopped off his ear in front of the shocked observers. He then calmly replied that he was now utterly disqualified for ecclesiastical office since the law forbids a man who is mutilated to become a priest (Leviticus 21:16-24). Deeply shaken, the people returned to Bishop Timothy, who told them: "This law is only observed by the Jews. If you bring him to me, I will ordain him even if he chops off his nose too!"

Therefore, they returned, but when they attempted to drag Ammonius off again, this time he said to them, "I swear to you that if you do such a thing to me, I shall cut out my tongue as well!" Alarmed by the prospect of losing his preaching and exhortation, they finally left him in peace. This story was as striking in antiquity as it is today, and is recounted by a number of writers (including his disapproving bishop). Most sources refer to him as "Ammonius the Earless" from that time forth.

Despite his strident refusal of the episcopate, Ammonius was by no means anti-clerical. His own brother Dioscorus had become a bishop, his other two brothers were both priests, and when he left Egypt toward the end of his life during the theological controversies that had embroiled Scete, he sought out the company of his close friend John Chrysostom. He was also a close companion and associate of Melania the Elder, welcoming her as a guest to his monastic settlement, visiting her in Jerusalem at hers, and welcoming her protege Evagrius to his community. He died while visiting John Chrysostom sometime around the year 403.

Ammonius

Hermit, c. 403

I Drive far from thy church, O God, every vain spirit of clerical ambition, that, like thy servant Ammonius, we may refuse to conflate ordination and leadership, and may never confuse rank with holiness; in the name of thy son Jesus Christ our Lord, who alone is our great High Priest. *Amen.*

II Drive far from your church, O God, every vain spirit of clerical ambition, that, like your servant Ammonius, we may refuse to conflate ordination and leadership, and may never confuse rank with holiness; in the name of your son Jesus Christ our Lord, who alone is our great High Priest. *Amen.*

Lessons and Psalm

1 Samuel 10:20-27
Psalm 24
James 3:1-12
Matthew 23:1-12

Preface of Baptism

Richard Rolle, Walter Hilton, and Margery Kempe were three prominent figures associated with the development of Christian mysticism in England.

Richard Rolle, born in 1290, was an English hermit about whose early life we know little. Although he grew up in a poor farming family, he was sponsored for education at Oxford by the Archdeacon of Durham. At the age of 18, however, he dropped out of Oxford to live as a hermit, out of which grew a ministry of prayer, writing, and spiritual direction. His writings were among the most widely read works of spirituality in England in the fifteenth century and include several scriptural commentaries, some theological writings, and many poems. Rolle spent his final years near the Cistercian convent near Hampole, a village in south Yorkshire, where he served as a spiritual director for the nuns.

We likewise know little about the early life of Walter Hilton beyond his birth in 1340, but evidence suggests that he studied at Cambridge. Hilton spent time as a hermit before becoming an Augustinian canon at Thurgarton Priory in Nottinghamshire in the late fourteenth century. In his great work, *The Scale of Perfection,* he develops his understanding of the "luminous darkness" which marks the transition between self-love and the love of God. His writings were influential in England not only in the years leading up to the Reformation, but also during the Oxford Movement. Evelyn Underhill was greatly drawn to his works and published an updated translation of *The Scale of Perfection* in modern English in 1923.

Born around 1373, Margery Kempe and her husband John had at least 14 children. She seems to have had no formal education. Though illiterate, she dictated the *Book of Margery Kempe,* from which we learn most of our knowledge of her. A mystic who experienced intense visions, she went on pilgrimages to Canterbury, the Holy Land, and to Santiago de Compostela. She also visited Julian of Norwich and was encouraged by her. Her book describes her travels as well as her mystical experiences and her deep compassion for sinners.

These three writers of vernacular English mysticism, together with the anonymous authors of *The Cloud of Unknowing* and the *Ancrene Wisse,* all exerted a great influence on later English and Anglican spiritual writings.

Richard Rolle, Walter Hilton, and Margery Kempe

Mystics, 1349, 1396, and c. 1440

I Direct our hearts, O Gracious God, and inspire our minds; that, like thy servants Richard Rolle, Walter Hilton, and Margery Kempe, we might pass through the cloud of unknowing until we behold thy glory face to face; in the Name of Jesus Christ our Lord who with thee and the Holy Ghost liveth and reigneth, one God, for ever and ever. *Amen.*

II Direct our hearts, O Gracious God, and inspire our minds; that like your servants Richard Rolle, Walter Hilton, and Margery Kempe, we might pass through the cloud of unknowing until we behold your glory face to face; in the Name of Jesus Christ our Lord; who with you and the Holy Spirit lives and reigns, one God, for ever and ever. *Amen.*

Lessons and Psalm

Job 26:1-14
Psalm 63:1-8
Romans 11:33-36
Mark 4:35-41

Preface of a Saint (3)

When Leo was born, around the year 400, the Western Roman Empire was almost in shambles. Weakened by barbarian invasions and by a totally inefficient economic and political system, the structure that had been carefully built by Augustus had become a chaos of internal warfare, subversion, and corruption.

The social and political situation notwithstanding, Leo received a good education, and was ordained as a deacon, with the responsibility of looking after church possessions, managing the distribution of food, and generally administering the finances. He won considerable respect for his abilities, and a contemporary of his, Cassian, described him as "the ornament of the Roman Church and the divine ministry."

In 440, Leo was unanimously elected Pope, despite the fact that he was absent at the time on a mission in Gaul. His ability as a preacher shows clearly in the 96 sermons still extant, in which he expounds doctrine, encourages almsgiving, and refutes various heresies.

In Gaul, Africa, and Spain, Leo's strong hand was felt, as he issued orders to limit the powers of one over-presumptuous bishop, confirmed the rights of another bishop over his vicars, and selected candidates for holy orders. Leo's letter to the Council of Chalcedon in 451 dealt so effectively with the doctrine of the human and divine natures of the One Person of Christ that the assembled bishops declared, "Peter has spoken by Leo," and affirmed his definition as orthodox teaching.

With similar strength of spirit and wisdom, Leo negotiated with Attila when the Huns were about to sack Rome. He persuaded them to withdraw from Italy and to accept an annual tribute. Three years later, Genseric led the Vandals against Rome. Again Leo negotiated. Unable to prevent pillaging by the barbarians, he did dissuade them from burning the city and slaughtering its inhabitants. He worked, thereafter, to repair the damage, to replace the holy vessels in the desecrated churches, and to restore the morale of the Roman people. Leo died in Rome in 461.

Leo of Rome

Bishop, 461

I O Lord our God, grant that thy church, following the teaching of thy servant Leo of Rome, may hold fast the great mystery of our redemption and adore the one Christ, true God and true Man, neither divided from our human nature nor separate from thy divine Being; through the same Jesus Christ our Lord, who liveth and reigneth with thee and the Holy Ghost, one God, now and for ever. *Amen.*

II O Lord our God, grant that your church, following the teaching of your servant Leo of Rome, may hold fast the great mystery of our redemption and adore the one Christ, true God and true Man, neither divided from our human nature nor separate from your divine Being; through the same Jesus Christ our Lord, who lives and reigns with you and the Holy Spirit, one God, now and for ever. *Amen.*

Lessons and Psalm

Jeremiah 38:1-6
Psalm 77:11-15
2 Timothy 1:6-12
Matthew 5:13-19

Preface of the Epiphany

Martin, one of the patron saints of France, was born about 330 at Sabaria, the modern Szombathely in Hungary. His early years were spent in Pavia in Italy. After a term of service in the Roman army, he traveled around Europe and finally settled in Poitiers, whose bishop, Hilary, he had come to admire.

According to an old legend, while Martin was still a catechumen, he was approached by a poor man, who asked for alms in the name of Christ. Martin, drawing his sword, cut off part of his military cloak and gave it to the beggar. On the following night, Jesus appeared to Martin, clothed in half a cloak, and said to the saints and angels surrounding him, "Martin, a simple catechumen, covered me with this garment."

Martin was baptized, but believed that his commitment as a Christian required him to leave the army, saying famously: "I am a soldier of Christ. I cannot fight." Martin pursued the vocation of a hermit for some years until, to his dismay, he was elected as Bishop of Tours in 372. He agreed to serve only if he were allowed to continue his strict, ascetic way of life. His monastery of Marmoutier, near Tours, had a great influence on the development of Celtic monasticism in Britain, where Ninian, among others, promoted Martin's ascetic and missionary ideals.

Martin was unpopular with many of his episcopal colleagues, both because of his manner of life and because of his strong opposition to their violent repression of heresy. Martin believed that heretics should be persuaded by sound preaching and by the testimony of holy lives rather than by force. He was a diligent missionary to the pagans in the countryside near his hermitage and was always a staunch defender of the poor and the marginalized.

Martin died on November 8, 397, but he has long been commemorated on November 11, the date of his burial. His shrine at Tours became a popular site for pilgrimages and a secure sanctuary for those seeking protection and justice.

Martin of Tours

Bishop, 397

I Lord God of hosts, who didst clothe thy servant Martin the soldier with the spirit of sacrifice and set him as a bishop in thy church to be a defender of the catholic faith: Give us grace to follow in his holy steps, that, at the last, we may be found clothed with righteousness in the dwellings of peace; through Jesus Christ our Lord, who liveth and reigneth with thee and the Holy Ghost, one God, for ever and ever. *Amen.*

II Lord God of hosts, you clothed your servant Martin the soldier with the spirit of sacrifice and set him as a bishop in your church to be a defender of the catholic faith: Give us grace to follow in his holy steps, that, at the last, we may be found clothed with righteousness in the dwellings of peace; through Jesus Christ our Lord, who lives and reigns with you and the Holy Spirit, one God, for ever and ever. *Amen.*

Lessons and Psalm

Hosea 2:18-23
Psalm 11
Galatians 6:1-2
Matthew 25:31-46

Preface of a Saint (2)

The historian Thomas Macaulay said about Charles Simeon, "If you knew what his authority and influence were, and how they extended from Cambridge to the most remote corners of England, you would allow that his real sway in the Church was far greater than that of any primate."

Simeon's conversion in 1779, while he was still a student, occurred as he was preparing himself to receive Holy Communion, an act required of undergraduates at the University. His first Communion had been a deeply depressing and discouraging experience because of his use of the popular devotional tract, *The Whole Duty of Man,* which emphasized law and obedience as the means of receiving the Sacrament worthily. When he was again preparing for Communion before Easter, he was given a copy of Bishop Thomas Wilson's *Instructions for the Lord's Supper.* Here was a very different approach, which recognized that the law could not make one righteous and that only the sacrifice of Christ, perceived by faith, could enable one to communicate worthily. This time, the experience of Holy Communion was one of peace and exhilaration, a new beginning in a Christian life whose influence would be difficult to exaggerate.

In 1782, the year of his graduation from King's College, Cambridge, he was placed in charge of Trinity Church in that city, while still a deacon. He remained as rector there for 54 years, despite intense early opposition from the churchwardens and congregation over his evangelical preaching.

Simeon's influence and authority developed slowly, but he eventually became the recognized leader of the evangelical movement in the Church of England. He helped to found the Church Missionary Society and was active in recruiting and supporting missionaries, including Henry Martyn. As a preacher, he ranks high in the history of Anglicanism. His sermons were unfailingly biblical, simple, and passionate.

The influence of Simeon and his friends was thus described by the historian William Edward Hartpole Lecky: "They gradually changed the whole spirit of the English Church. They infused into it a new fire and passion of devotion, kindled a spirit of fervent philanthropy, raised the standard of clerical duty, and completely altered the whole tone and tendency of the preaching of its ministers."

Simeon died on November 13, 1836, in Cambridge, and was buried at King's College.

Charles Simeon

Priest, 1836

I Loving God, whose unerring wisdom and unbounded love doth order all things: Grant us in all things to see thy hand; that, following the example and teaching of thy servant Charles Simeon, we may walk with Christ in all simplicity and serve thee with a quiet and contented mind; through Jesus Christ our Lord, who liveth and reigneth with thee and the Holy Ghost, one God, for ever and ever. *Amen.*

II Loving God, whose unerring wisdom and unbounded love order all things: Grant us in all things to see your hand; that, following the example and teaching of your servant Charles Simeon, we may walk with Christ in all simplicity and serve you with a quiet and contented mind; through Jesus Christ our Lord, who lives and reigns with you and the Holy Spirit, one God, for ever and ever. *Amen.*

Lessons and Psalm

Amos 6:1-7
Psalm 108:1-6
Ephesians 3:7-12
Matthew 22:1-14

Preface of a Saint (1)

Samuel Seabury, the first bishop of the Episcopal Church, was born in Groton, Connecticut on November 30, 1729. After ordination in England in 1753, he was assigned, as a missionary of the Society for the Propagation of the Gospel, to Christ Church, New Brunswick, New Jersey. In 1757, he became rector of Grace Church, Jamaica, Long Island, and in 1766, rector of St. Peter's, Westchester County. During the American Revolution, he remained loyal to the British crown and served as a chaplain in the British army.

After the Revolution, a secret meeting of Connecticut clergy in Woodbury, held on March 25, 1783, named Seabury or the Rev. Jeremiah Leaming, whichever would be able or willing, to seek episcopal consecration in England. They extended the call first to Leaming, who declined; Seabury then accepted, and sailed for England.

After a year of negotiation, Seabury found it impossible to obtain episcopal orders from the Church of England because, as an American citizen, he could not swear allegiance to the crown. He then turned to the Non-Juring bishops of the Episcopal Church in Scotland. On November 14, 1784, in Aberdeen, he was consecrated by the Bishop and the Bishop Coadjutor of Aberdeen and the Bishop of Ross and Caithness in the presence of many people.

Upon his return home, Seabury was recognized as Bishop of Connecticut in Convocation on August 3, 1785, at Middletown. With Bishop William White, he was active in the organization of the Episcopal Church at the General Convention of 1789. Seabury kept his promise, made in a concordat with the Scottish bishops, to persuade the American Church to adopt the Scottish form for the celebration of the Holy Eucharist.

In 1790, Seabury became responsible for episcopal oversight of the churches in Rhode Island; and, at the General Convention of 1792, he participated in the first consecration of a bishop on American soil, that of John Claggett of Maryland. Seabury died on February 25, 1796, and is buried beneath St. James Church, New London.

The Consecration of Samuel Seabury

1784

I We give thanks to thee, O Lord our God, for thy goodness in bestowing upon this church the gift of the episcopate; and we pray that, joined together in unity with our bishops and nourished by thy holy sacraments, we may proclaim the Gospel of redemption with apostolic zeal; through Jesus Christ our Lord, who liveth and reigneth with thee and the Holy Ghost, one God, now and for ever. *Amen.*

II We give you thanks, O Lord our God, for your goodness in bestowing upon this church the gift of the episcopate; and we pray that, joined together in unity with our bishops and nourished by your holy sacraments, we may proclaim the Gospel of redemption with apostolic zeal; through Jesus Christ our Lord, who lives and reigns with you and the Holy Spirit, one God, now and for ever. *Amen.*

Lessons and Psalm

1 Samuel 8:1-22
Psalm 110:1-4
Acts 1:15-26
Matthew 9:35-38

Preface of Apostles and Ordinations

Herman of Alaska, known in the Russian Orthodox Church as "St. Herman: Wonderworker of All America," was the first saint to be canonized by the Orthodox Church in America.

Herman was born in Russia, near Moscow, in 1756. His baptismal and family names are unknown, and he is known only by his monastic name. Naturally pious from an early age, Herman entered the Trinity-St. Sergius Hermitage near St. Petersburg at the age of 16 and, drawn to the spiritual charism of Abbot Nasarios, eventually transferred to the Valaam Monastery. He was never ordained, although his Metropolitan suggested it several times. For many years he secured permission to live as a hermit, attending the liturgies of the monastery only on holy days.

In 1793, with a small group of colleagues, Herman set out to do missionary work in Alaska. They settled on Spruce Island, near Kodiak, and named their community "New Valaam" in honor of their home monastery. Herman lived and worked in the area for the remainder of his life.

Herman advocated for and defended the native Aleut against sometimes-oppressive authorities, particular Russian and European colonists with commercial interests. He cared lovingly and sacrificially for all who came to him, counseling and teaching them, and tirelessly nursing the sick. He especially loved children, for whom he often baked biscuits and cookies.

Even though Herman had minimal formal education outside of the monastic life, he was regarded among the native Alaskans as a great and compelling teacher. Over time he also developed a reputation as a teacher and sage among the Russian and European settlers in the area. He so captivated his listeners that many would listen to him through the long hours of the night and not leave his company until morning. The people he served often referred to Herman as their North Star.

Herman died at Spruce Island on November 15, 1837.

Herman of Alaska

Missionary, 1837

I Almighty God, who didst raise up thy servant Herman to be a light in the world, and to preach the Gospel to the people of Alaska: Illuminate our hearts, that we also in our own generation may show forth thy praise, who hast called us out of darkness and into thy marvelous light; through Jesus Christ our Lord, who liveth and reigneth with thee and the Holy Ghost, one God, now and for ever. *Amen.*

II Almighty God, who raised up your servant Herman to be a light in the world, and to preach the Gospel to the people of Alaska: Illuminate our hearts, that we also in our own generation may show forth your praise, who called us out of darkness and into your marvelous light; through Jesus Christ our Lord, who lives and reigns with you and the Holy Spirit, one God, now and for ever. *Amen.*

Lessons and Psalm

2 Kings 4:38-41
Psalm 148:7-14
2 Timothy 1:3-7
Luke 9:46-48

Preface of Apostles and Ordinations

Shakespeare made familiar the names of Macbeth and Macduff, Duncan, and Malcolm; but it is not always remembered that Malcolm married an English princess, Margaret, about 1070.

With considerable zeal, Margaret sought to change what she considered to be old-fashioned and careless practices among the Scottish clergy. She insisted that the observance of Lent, for example, was to begin on Ash Wednesday, rather than on the following Monday, and that the Mass should be celebrated according to the accepted Roman Rite. The Lord's Day was to be a day when, she said, "we apply ourselves only to prayers." She argued vigorously, though not always with success, against an exaggerated sense of unworthiness that made many of the pious Scots unwilling to receive communion regularly.

Margaret's energies were not limited to reformation of formal church practices. She encouraged the founding of schools, hospitals, and orphanages, and used her influence with King Malcolm to help her improve the quality of life among the isolated Scottish clans. Together, Margaret and her husband rebuilt the monastery of Iona and founded Dunfermline Abbey, under the direction of Benedictine monks.

In addition to her zeal for the church and her people, Margaret was a conscientious wife and the mother of eight children. Malcolm, a strong-willed man, came to trust her judgment even in matters of politics. She also saw to the spiritual welfare of her large household.

Margaret was not as successful as she wished to be in creating greater unity in faith and works between her own native England and the Scots. She was unable, for example, to bring an end to the warfare among the highland clans, and, after her death in 1093, there was a brief return to the earlier isolation of Scotland from England. Nevertheless, her work among the people and her reforms in the Church made her Scotland's most beloved saint. She died on November 16, 1093, and was buried at Dunfermline Abbey.

Margaret of Scotland

Queen, 1093

I O God, who didst call thy servant Margaret to an earthly throne that she might advance thy heavenly kingdom, and gave her zeal for thy church and love for thy people: Mercifully grant that we also may be fruitful in good works and attain to the glorious crown of thy saints; through Jesus Christ our Lord, who liveth and reigneth with thee and the Holy Ghost, one God, for ever and ever. *Amen.*

II O God, who called your servant Margaret to an earthly throne that she might advance your heavenly kingdom, and gave her zeal for your church and love for your people: Mercifully grant that we also may be fruitful in good works, and attain to the glorious crown of your saints; through Jesus Christ our Lord, who lives and reigns with you and the Holy Spirit, one God, for ever and ever. *Amen.*

Lessons and Psalm

Proverbs 31:10-20
Psalm 139:10-17
2 John 1-9
Matthew 13:44-46

Preface of Baptism

Hugh was born into a noble family in Burgundy, France. His mother died when he was eight years old, and his father then entered a monastic community.

Hugh entered the monastic life himself at the age of fifteen. Around 1160, he transferred his membership from the Benedictine order to the Carthusians, who practiced a more austere form of monasticism, becoming the procurator of their major house, the Grande Chartreuse.

With reluctance, he accepted the invitation of King Henry II to become prior of a new foundation of Carthusians in England at Witham, Somerset. With even greater hesitation, Hugh accepted the King's appointment to the See of Lincoln in 1186. He died in London on November 16, 1200, and is buried in Lincoln Cathedral, of which he laid the foundation.

As a bishop, Hugh continued to live as much as possible under the strict discipline of his order. His humility and tact, his total lack of self-regard, and his cheerful disposition made it difficult to oppose him. His people loved him for his unrelenting care of the poor and oppressed. He worked to improve education in the cathedral school, served as a diplomat in sensitive political negotiations, and strove to protect the Jews of his diocese from persecution.

Steadfastly independent of secular influences, he was never afraid to reprove his king for unjust treatment of the people. Hugh refused to raise money for King Richard's foreign wars. Yet Richard said of him, "If all bishops were like my Lord of Lincoln, not a prince among us could lift his head against them."

Hugh of Lincoln

Bishop, 1200

I Holy God, who didst endow thy servant Hugh of Lincoln with wise and cheerful boldness, and taught him to commend the discipline of holy life to kings and princes: Grant that we also, rejoicing in the Good News of thy mercy, and fearing nothing but the loss of thee, may be bold to speak the truth in love, in the name of Jesus Christ our Redeemer; who liveth and reigneth with thee and the Holy Ghost, one God, for ever and ever. *Amen.*

II Holy God, who endowed your servant Hugh of Lincoln with wise and cheerful boldness, and taught him to commend the discipline of holy life to kings and princes: Grant that we also, rejoicing in the Good News of your mercy, and fearing nothing but the loss of you, may be bold to speak the truth in love, in the name of Jesus Christ our Redeemer; who lives and reigns with you and the Holy Spirit, one God, for ever and ever. *Amen.*

Lessons and Psalm

Tobit 6:1-6
Psalm 15
Titus 2:7-8, 11-14
Mark 13:32-37

Preface of a Saint (2)

"Hilda's career falls into two equal parts," wrote Bede, "for she spent thirty-three years nobly in secular habit, while she dedicated an equal number of years still more nobly to the Lord, in the monastic life."

Hilda, born in 614, was the grandniece of King Edwin. She was instructed by Paulinus (one of the companions of Augustine of Canterbury) in the doctrines of Christianity in preparation for her baptism at the age of thirteen. She lived at the King's court for twenty years and then decided to enter the monastic life. She had hoped to join the convent of Chelles in Gaul, but Bishop Aidan was so impressed by her holiness of life that he recalled her to her home country, in East Anglia, to live in a small monastic settlement.

One year after her return, she was appointed Abbess of Hartlepool. There, Hilda established the rule of life that she had been taught by Paulinus and Aidan. She became renowned for her wisdom, her eagerness for learning, and her devotion to God's service.

Some years later, she founded the abbey at Whitby, where both nuns and monks lived in strict obedience to Hilda's rule of justice, devotion, chastity, peace, and charity. Known for her prudence and good sense, Hilda was sought out by kings and other public figures for advice and counsel. Several of her monks became bishops, and at least one pursued further studies in Rome. She encouraged the poet Caedmon, a servant at Whitby, to become a monk and to continue his inspired writing. All who knew her, Bede remarks, called her "mother."

In 663, Whitby was the site of the famous synod convened to decide divisive questions involved in the differing traditions of Celtic Christians and the followers of Roman order. Hilda favored the Celtic position, but, when the Roman position prevailed, she was obedient to the synod's decision. Hilda died on November 17, 680, surrounded by her nuns and monks, whom, in her last hour, she urged to preserve the gospel of peace.

Hilda of Whitby

Abbess, 680

I O God of peace, by whose grace the abbess Hilda was endowed with gifts of justice, prudence, and strength to rule as a wise mother over the nuns and monks of her household: Raise up these gifts in us, that we, following her example and prayers, might build up one another in love to the benefit of thy church; through Jesus Christ our Lord, who liveth and reigneth with thee and the Holy Ghost, one God, now and for ever. *Amen.*

II O God of peace, by whose grace the abbess Hilda was endowed with gifts of justice, prudence, and strength to rule as a wise mother over the nuns and monks of her household: Raise up these gifts in us, that we, following her example and prayers, may build up one another in love to the benefit of your church; through Jesus Christ our Lord, who lives and reigns with you and the Holy Spirit, one God, now and for ever. *Amen.*

Lessons and Psalm

Proverbs 6:20-23
Psalm 122
Ephesians 4:1-6
Matthew 19:27-29

Preface of a Saint (1)

Elizabeth's charity is remembered in numerous hospitals that bear her name throughout the world. She was born in 1207 at Pressburg (now Bratislava), daughter of King Andrew II of Hungary, and was married in 1221 to Louis IV, Landgrave of Thuringia, to whom she bore three children.

At an early age she showed concern for the poor and the sick, and was thus attracted to the Franciscans who came to the Wartburg in 1223. From them she received spiritual direction. Her husband was sympathetic to her almsgiving and allowed her to use her dowry for this purpose. During a famine and epidemic in 1226, when her husband was in Italy, she sold her jewels and established a hospital, where she cared for the sick and the poor. To supply their needs, she opened the royal granaries. After her husband's death in 1227, however, the opposition of the court to such "extravagances" compelled her to leave the Wartburg with her children.

For some time, Elizabeth lived in great distress. She then took the habit of the Franciscans—the first of the Franciscan Tertiaries, or Third Order, in Germany. Finally, arrangements with her family gave her a subsistence, and she spent her remaining years in Marburg, living in self-denial and caring for the sick and needy. She died from exhaustion, November 17, 1231, and was canonized by Pope Gregory IX four years later. With Louis of France she shares the title of patron of the Third Order of St. Francis.

Elizabeth of Hungary

Princess, 1231

I Almighty God, by whose grace thy servant Elizabeth of Hungary recognized and honored Jesus in the poor of this world: Grant that we, following her example, may with love and gladness serve those in any need or trouble, in the name and for the sake of Jesus Christ; who liveth and reigneth with thee and the Holy Ghost, one God, for ever and ever. *Amen.*

II Almighty God, by your grace your servant Elizabeth of Hungary recognized and honored Jesus in the poor of this world: Grant that we, following her example, may with love and gladness serve those in any need or trouble, in the name and for the sake of Jesus Christ; who lives and reigns with you and the Holy Spirit, one God, for ever and ever. *Amen.*

Lessons and Psalm

Tobit 12:8-10
Psalm 112
2 Corinthians 8:7-15
Luke 12:32-34

Preface of a Saint (2)

Edmund ascended the throne of East Anglia at the age of fifteen, one of several monarchs who ruled various parts of England at that period of its history. The principal source of information about the martyrdom of the young king is an account by Dunstan, who became Archbishop of Canterbury ninety years after Edmund's death. Dunstan had heard the story many years before from a man who claimed to have been Edmund's armor bearer.

Edmund had reigned as a Christian king for nearly fifteen years when Danish armies invaded England in 870. Led by two brothers, Hinguar and Hubba, the Danes moved south, burning monasteries and churches, plundering and destroying entire villages, and killing hundreds. Upon reaching East Anglia, the brothers confronted Edmund and offered to share their treasure with him if he would acknowledge their supremacy, forbid all practice of the Christian faith, and become a figurehead ruler. Edmund's bishops advised him to accept the terms and avoid further bloodshed, but the king refused. He declared that he would not forsake Christ by surrendering to pagan rule, nor would he betray his people by consorting with the enemy.

Edmund's small army fought bravely against the Danes, but the king was eventually captured. According to Dunstan's account, Edmund was tortured, beaten, shot through with arrows, and finally beheaded. By tradition, the date of his death is November 20, 870.

The cult of the twenty-nine-year-old martyr grew very rapidly, and his remains were eventually enshrined in a Benedictine monastery in Bedericesworth—now called Bury St. Edmunds. Over the centuries, Edmund's shrine became a traditional place of pilgrimage for England's kings, who came to pray at the grave of a man who remained steadfast in the Christian faith and loyal to the integrity of the English people.

Edmund

King, 870

I Merciful God, who didst give grace and fortitude to Edmund to die nobly for thy Name: Bestow on us thy servants, we beseech thee, the shield of faith, wherewith we may withstand the assaults of our ancient enemy; through Jesus Christ our Redeemer, who liveth and reigneth with thee and the Holy Ghost, one God, now and for ever. *Amen.*

II Merciful God, who gave grace and fortitude to Edmund to die nobly for your Name: Bestow on us your servants the shield of faith, with which we can withstand the assaults of our ancient enemy; through Jesus Christ our Redeemer, who lives and reigns with you and the Holy Spirit, one God, now and for ever. *Amen.*

Lessons and Psalm

2 Kings 11:1-8
Psalm 7:1-10
Ephesians 6:10-17
Matthew 10:16-22

Preface of Baptism

Mechthilde of Hackeborn and Gertrude the Great were both Benedictine nuns at St. Mary's Monastery in Helfta, which was renowned for fostering the intellectual gifts of its sisters.

Mechthilde was born to a pious and noble family in Germany around 1240. Her older sister was already the abbess of a convent, and when Mechthilde was seven years old the family went to visit her. Mechthilde was so enchanted with the convent, particularly its extensive library, that she refused to go home again, and her parents eventually yielded to her pleas. In the convent, Mechthilde received a superb education, and eventually directed both the convent choir and its library, illuminating manuscripts and writing her own original works. In time, the convent was transferred to her family's estate at Helfta as it continued to grow.

Mechthilde's most famous work is her *Book of Special Grace*. Only translated into English in 2017, it is an account of how she was consoled after going through a spiritually difficult time in her fifties.

Gertrude was also a nun at Helfta, but seems to have come from a very different social background. She came to the convent as a five-year-old child of unknown parentage. Although the nuns were not willing to accept a child so young as a sister, she was given to Mechthilde to raise, and would formally enter the community several years later.

Gertrude's writings indicate how thorough an education she must have received. She writes in fluent Latin, and shows extensive familiarity with the Scriptures, early Christian authorities such as Augustine and Gregory the Great, and even more contemporary theologians, including Bernard of Clairvaux, Richard and Hugh of St. Victor, and William of St. Thierry. She was given the title "Gertrude the Great" because she was among the most prominent theological writers of her age, either male or female.

Gertrude wrote a number of works, touching on both mysticism and theology. Her most famous book is *The Herald of Divine Love*. Gertrude died in 1302, but the exact date is unknown. She is therefore often commemorated together with her foster mother and teacher Mechthilde.

Mechthilde of Hackeborn and Gertrude the Great

Mystics and Theologians, 1298 and 1302

I Almighty God, who didst give to thy servants Mechthilde and Gertrude special gifts of grace to understand and teach the truth in Christ Jesus: Grant, we beseech thee, that by their teachings we may know thee, the one true God, and Jesus Christ thy Son, who liveth and reigneth with thee and the Holy Ghost, one God, for ever and ever. *Amen.*

II Almighty God, who gave to your servants Mechthilde and Gertrude special gifts of grace to understand and teach the truth in Christ Jesus: Grant that by their teachings we may know you, the one true God, and Jesus Christ your Son; who lives and reigns with you and the Holy Spirit, one God, for ever and ever. *Amen.*

Lessons and Psalm

1 Samuel 1:21-28
Psalm 119:41-48
Acts 2:42-47
Luke 10:38-42

Preface of a Saint (3)

"You must make your choice," C. S. Lewis wrote in *Mere Christianity*. "Either this man was, and is, the Son of God, or else a madman or something worse. You can shut Him up as a fool, you can spit at Him and kill Him as a demon, or you can fall at His feet and call Him Lord and God."

Lewis did not always believe this. Born in Belfast on November 29, 1898, Lewis was raised as an Anglican but rejected Christianity during his adolescent years. After serving in World War I, he started a long academic career as a scholar in medieval and Renaissance literature at both Oxford and Cambridge. He also began an inner journey that led him from atheism to agnosticism to theism and finally to faith in Jesus Christ.

"Really, a young Atheist cannot guard his faith too carefully," he later wrote of his conversion to theism in *Surprised by Joy*. "Dangers lie in wait for him on every side . . . Amiable agnostics will talk cheerfully about 'man's search for God'. To me, as I then was, they might as well have talked about the mouse's search for the cat. You must picture me all alone in that room at Magdalen, night after night, feeling, whenever my mind lifted even for a second from my work, the steady, unrelenting approach of Him whom I so earnestly desired not to meet. That which I greatly feared had at last come upon me. In the Trinity Term of 1929 I gave in, and admitted that God was God, and knelt and prayed: perhaps, that night, the most dejected and reluctant convert in all England." Two years later, his conversion was completed: "I know very well when, but hardly how, the final step was taken. I was driven to Whipsnade one sunny morning. When we set out, I did not believe that Jesus Christ is the Son of God, and when we reached the zoo, I did."

Lewis' conversion inaugurated a wonderful outpouring of Christian apologetics in media as varied as popular theology, children's literature, fantasy and science fiction, and correspondence on spiritual matters with friends and strangers alike.

In 1956 Lewis married Joy Davidman, a recent convert to Christianity. Her death four years later led him to a transforming encounter with the Mystery of which he had written so eloquently before. Lewis died at his home in Oxford on November 22, 1963. The inscription on his grave reads: "Men must endure their going hence."

Clive Staples Lewis

Apologist and Spiritual Writer, 1963

I O God of searing truth and surpassing beauty, we give thanks to thee for Clive Staples Lewis, whose sanctified imagination lit fires of faith in young and old alike; Surprise us also with thy joy and draw us into that new and abundant life which is ours in Christ Jesus, who liveth and reigneth with thee and the Holy Ghost, one God, now and for ever. *Amen.*

II O God of searing truth and surpassing beauty, we give you thanks for Clive Staples Lewis, whose sanctified imagination lit fires of faith in young and old alike; Surprise us also with your joy and draw us into that new and abundant life which is ours in Christ Jesus, who lives and reigns with you and the Holy Spirit, one God, now and for ever. *Amen.*

Lessons and Psalm

Proverbs 23:15-18
Psalm 139:1-9
1 Peter 1:3-9
John 16:7-15

Preface of a Saint (3)

According to early traditions, Clement was a disciple of the Apostles and the third Bishop of Rome. He is generally regarded as the author of a letter written about the year 96 from the Church in Rome to the Church in Corinth, and known as "First Clement" in the collection of early documents called "The Apostolic Fathers."

The occasion of the letter was the action of a younger group at Corinth, who had deposed the elder clergy because of dissatisfaction with their ministrations. The unity of the Church was being jeopardized by a dispute over its ministry. Clement's letter sets forth a hierarchical view of Church authority. It insists that God requires due order in all things, that the deposed clergy must be reinstated, and that the legitimate superiors must be obeyed.

The letter used the terms "bishop" and "presbyter" interchangeably to describe the higher ranks of clergy, but refers to some of them as "rulers" of the Church. It is they who lead its worship and "offer the gifts" of the Eucharist, just as the duly appointed priests of the Old Testament performed the various sacrifices and liturgies in their time.

Many congregations of the early Church read this letter in their worship, and several ancient manuscripts include it in the canonical books of the New Testament, along with a second letter, which is actually an early homily of unknown authorship. The text of First Clement was lost to the western Church in the Middle Ages, and was not rediscovered until 1628.

Clement writes: "The apostles received the Gospel for us from the Lord Jesus Christ; Jesus the Christ was sent from God. Thus Christ is from God and the apostles from Christ. In both instances, the orderly procedure depends on God's will. So thereafter, when the apostles had been given their instructions, and all their doubts had been set at rest by the resurrection of our Lord Jesus Christ, they went forth in the confidence of the Holy Spirit to preach the Good News of the coming of God's kingdom. They preached in country and city, and appointed their first converts, after testing them by the Spirit, to be the bishops and deacons of future believers."

Clement of Rome

Bishop, c. 100

I Almighty God, who didst choose thy servant Clement of Rome to recall the church in Corinth to obedience and stability: Grant that thy church may be grounded and settled in thy truth by the indwelling of the Holy Ghost; reveal to it what is not yet known; fill up what is lacking; confirm what has already been revealed; and keep it blameless in thy service; through Jesus Christ our Lord, who liveth and reigneth with thee and the Holy Ghost, one God, for ever and ever. *Amen.*

II Almighty God, who chose your servant Clement of Rome to recall the church in Corinth to obedience and stability: Grant that your church may be grounded and settled in your truth by the indwelling of the Holy Spirit; reveal to it what is not yet known; fill up what is lacking; confirm what has already been revealed; and keep it blameless in your service; through Jesus Christ our Lord, who lives and reigns with you and the Holy Spirit, one God, for ever and ever. *Amen.*

Lessons and Psalm

1 Chronicles 23:28-32
Psalm 78:1-7
Colossians 2:6-15
Luke 6:37-45

Preface of a Saint (2)

Catherine of Alexandria, Barbara of Nicomedia, and Margaret of Antioch were three of the most popular ancient and medieval saints, and they even attracted widespread devotion among Anglicans after the Reformation. In the mid-twentieth century, however, their popularity waned significantly as doubts about this historicity grew. The lives of all three virgin martyrs contain many elements that are indisputably either legendary or metaphorical. In recent decades, however, martyrdom accounts written in such a style have attracted increased scholarly attention as we have started to ponder the particular ways in which communities choose to remember trauma. It is striking, for example, that virtually no female martyrdom accounts include sexual violence, even though we know from other genres of writing that it was historically very common. Whatever is happening in these accounts, it is clearly not a straightforward description of the facts, but seems to be rather a recasting of trauma into something that one might actually *want* to remember and feel inspired by, and the kind of stories that one could pass on to one's children. If the purpose of such narratives is not to convey the literal truth of what happened, but rather to portray the unvanquished spirits of these early Christian martyrs in the face of trauma, then perhaps there may be a kind of truth behind the legends after all.

According to the life of Catherine of Alexandria, she was a young scholar and the daughter of an Egyptian government official who converted to Christianity as a teenager. When she rebuked the emperor for his cruelty in inciting persecution against the Christians, he summoned 50 of his best philosophers and orators to debate with her, but she won every single argument and many of them were converted to Christianity. The emperor then condemned her to be tortured to death on a spiked wheel, but it shattered at her touch. Finally, he had her beheaded.

Barbara's life states that because of her beauty, her father locked her up in a tower where only her pagan tutors were granted access to her. From them she became highly educated and began to consider the nature of the physical and metaphysical world, and eventually decided that there was only one true God, and that it might be the God of the Christians. She had a third window added to her prison, and thus created a place of personal prayer where she could contemplate the Trinity as the light moved across the three windows. When her father questioned this action, she professed her Christian faith to him and was executed.

The life of Margaret of Antioch recounts that she was the daughter of a pagan priest named Aedesius. Her mother died in childbirth, and so she was given to a Christian woman to nurse, and as she grew up she embraced the Christian religion. When her religion became known, she was subjected to severe persecutions; the most famous trial included being swallowed by Satan in the form of a dragon. The cross that she was holding in her hand irritated the dragon's stomach, however, and caused it to immediately explode. Eventually, after prevailing through many trials, she was executed. Margaret was one of the most popular English saints, both before and after the Reformation. Many Anglican parishes have been dedicated to her, as has the women's religious community, the Society of Saint Margaret.

Catherine of Alexandria, Barbara of Nicomedia, and Margaret of Antioch

Martyrs, c. 305

I Embolden thy church, O God, with the stories of thy saints Catherine, Barbara, and Margaret, that we might face all trials and adversities with a fearless mind and an unbroken spirit, knowing that we are more than conquerors through Jesus Christ who strengthens us. Through the same Jesus Christ our Lord. *Amen.*

II Embolden your church, O God, with the stories of your saints Catherine, Barbara, and Margaret, that we might face all trials and adversities with a fearless mind and an unbroken spirit, knowing that we are more than conquerors through Jesus Christ who strengthens us. Through the same Jesus Christ our Lord. *Amen.*

Lessons and Psalm

Judith 12:16—13:10
Psalm 43
Romans 8:31-39
Matthew 5:1-12

Preface of Epiphany

In the Rule for the Order of the Holy Cross, James Huntington wrote: "Holiness is the brightness of divine love, and love is never idle; it must accomplish great things." Commitment to active ministry rooted in the spiritual life was the guiding principle for the founder of the first permanent Episcopal monastic community for men in the United States.

James Otis Sargent Huntington was born in Boston in 1854. After graduation from Harvard, he studied theology at St. Andrew's Divinity School in Syracuse, New York, and was ordained as a deacon and as a priest by his father, the first Bishop of Central New York. In 1880 and 1881, he ministered in a working-class congregation at Calvary Mission, Syracuse.

While attending a retreat at St. Clement's Church in Philadelphia, Huntington discerned a call to the religious life. He considered joining the Society of St. John the Evangelist, which had by that time established a province in the United States, but he perceived a need to found an indigenous American community.

Huntington and two other priests began their common life at Holy Cross Mission on New York's Lower East Side, ministering with the Sisters of St. John Baptist among poor immigrants. The taxing daily regimen of Eucharist, prayer, and long hours of pastoral work soon forced one priest to leave for reason of health. The other discerned that this was not his vocation. Despite these setbacks, Huntington went on alone, and on November 25, 1884, his life vow was received by Bishop Potter of New York.

As Huntington continued his work among the immigrants, with emphasis on helping young people, he became increasingly committed to the social witness of the church. His early involvements in the single-tax movement and the labor union movement were instrumental in the eventual commitment of the Episcopal Church to social ministries. The order gradually attracted vocations and, as it grew in the ensuing years, the community moved, first to Maryland, and, in 1902, to West Park, New York, where it established the monastery which is its mother house. Huntington served as Superior on several occasions, continuing his energetic round of preaching, teaching, and spiritual counsel until his death on June 28, 1935. He is commemorated on November 25 in honor of his profession of life vows.

James Otis Sargent Huntington

Monastic and Priest, 1935

I Preserve thy people, O God, from discouragement in the face of adversity, as thou didst thy servant James Huntington, knowing that when thou hast begun a good work thou wilt bring it to completion. Through Jesus Christ our Lord, who with thee and the Holy Ghost liveth and reigneth, one God, for ever and ever. *Amen.*

II Preserve your people, O God, from discouragement in the face of adversity, as you did your servant James Huntington, knowing that when you have begun a good work you will bring it to completion. Through Jesus Christ our Lord, who with you and the Holy Spirit lives and reigns, one God, for ever and ever. *Amen.*

Lessons and Psalm

Nehemiah 5:1-12
Psalm 34:1-8
Galatians 6:14-18
John 6:34-38

Preface of a Saint (2)

Within a year of ascending the throne in 1855, the twenty-year-old King Kamehameha IV and his spouse, Emma Rooke, embarked on the path of altruism and unassuming humility for which they have been revered by their people. The year before, Honolulu, and especially its native Hawaiians, had been horribly afflicted by smallpox. The people, accustomed to a royalty which ruled with pomp and power, were confronted instead by a king and queen who went about, "with notebook in hand," soliciting from rich and poor the funds to build a hospital. Queen's Hospital, named for Emma, is now the largest civilian hospital in Hawai'i.

In 1860, the king and queen petitioned the Bishop of Oxford to send missionaries to establish the Anglican Church in Hawai'i. The king's interest came through a boyhood tour of England where he had seen, in the stately beauty of Anglican liturgy, a quality that seemed attuned to the gentle beauty of the Hawaiian spirit. England responded by sending the Rt. Rev. Thomas N. Staley and two priests. They arrived on October 11, 1862, and the king and queen were confirmed a month later, on November 28, 1862. They then began preparations for a cathedral and school, and the king set about to translate the Book of Common Prayer and much of the hymnal.

Kamehameha's and Emma's lives were marred by the tragic death of their only child, a four-year-old son, in 1862. Kamehameha seemed unable to survive his sadness, although a sermon he preached after his son's death expresses a hope and faith that is eloquent and profound. His own death took place only a year after his son's, in 1863. Emma declined to rule; instead, she committed her life to good works. She was responsible for schools, churches, and efforts on behalf of the poor and sick. She traveled several times to England and the European continent to raise funds and became a favorite of Queen Victoria's. Archbishop Longley of Canterbury remarked upon her visit to Lambeth: "I was much struck by the cultivation of her mind . . . But what excited my interest most was her almost saintly piety."

The cathedral was completed after Emma died. It was named St. Andrew's in memory of the king, who died on that saint's day. Among the Hawaiian people, Emma is still referred to as "our beloved Queen."

Kamehameha and Emma of Hawai‘i

King and Queen, 1863 and 1885

I O God, who didst call thy servants Kamehameha and Emma to an earthly throne that they might advance thy heavenly kingdom, and gave them zeal for thy church and love for thy people: Mercifully grant that we also may be fruitful in good works and attain to the glorious crown of thy saints; through Jesus Christ our Lord, who liveth and reigneth with thee and the Holy Ghost, one God, for ever and ever. *Amen.*

II O God, who called your servants Kamehameha and Emma to an earthly throne that they might advance your heavenly kingdom, and gave them zeal for your church and love for your people: Mercifully grant that we also may be fruitful in good works, and attain to the glorious crown of your saints; through Jesus Christ our Lord, who lives and reigns with you and the Holy Spirit, one God, for ever and ever. *Amen.*

Lessons and Psalm

Micah 4:1-4
Psalm 33:12-22
Acts 17:22-31
Matthew 25:14-29

Preface of Baptism

Agricultural festivals are of great antiquity and common to many religions. Among the Jews, the three pilgrimage feasts—Passover, Pentecost, and Tabernacles—each had agricultural significance. Medieval Christianity also developed a number of such observances, none of which, however, were incorporated into the Book of Common Prayer.

Thanksgiving Day in the United States finds its roots in observances begun by colonists in Massachusetts and Virginia, a tradition later taken up and extended to the whole of the new American nation by action of the Continental Congress. The celebration continued intermittently during the nineteenth century, and in 1863 President Abraham Lincoln issued a proclamation establishing Thanksgiving Day on the last Thursday in November. Following an act of Congress, in 1941 President Franklin Delano Roosevelt officially designated the fourth Thursday in November as Thanksgiving Day.

Thanksgiving Day

I Almighty and gracious Father, we give thee thanks for the fruits of the earth in their season and for the labors of those who harvest them. Make us, we beseech thee, faithful stewards of thy great bounty, for the provision of our necessities and the relief of all who are in need, to the glory of thy Name; through Jesus Christ our Lord, who liveth and reigneth with thee and the Holy Spirit, one God, now and for ever. *Amen.*

II Almighty and gracious Father, we give you thanks for the fruits of the earth in their season and for the labors of those who harvest them. Make us, we pray, faithful stewards of your great bounty, for the provision of our necessities and the relief of all who are in need, to the glory of your Name; through Jesus Christ our Lord, who lives and reigns with you and the Holy Spirit, one God, now and for ever. *Amen.*

Lessons and Psalm

Deuteronomy 8:1-3, 6-10 (17-20)
Psalm 65 *or* 65:9-14
James 1:17-18, 21-27
Matthew 6:25-33

Preface of Trinity Sunday

Most biographical notes on this Apostle begin "Andrew was Simon Peter's brother," and he is so described in the Gospels. Identifying Andrew as Peter's brother makes it easy to know who he is, but it also makes it easy to overlook the fact of Andrew's own special gift to the company of Christ. The Gospel according to John tells how Andrew, a disciple of John the Baptist, was one of two disciples who followed Jesus after John had pointed him out, saying, "Behold the Lamb of God" (John 1:29). Andrew and the other disciple went with Jesus and stayed with him, and Andrew's first act afterward was to find his brother and bring him to Jesus. We might call Andrew the first missionary in the company of disciples.

Though Andrew was not a part of the inner circle of disciples (Peter, James, and John), he is always named in the list of disciples, and the Gospel of Matthew records Jesus' calling them from their occupation, and their immediate response to his call. Andrew was also the disciple who brought the boy with the loaves and fishes to Jesus for the feeding of the multitude.

We hear little of Andrew as a prominent leader, and he seems always to be in the shadow of Peter. Eusebius, the early church historian, records his going to Scythia, but there is no reliable information about the end of his life. Tradition has it that he was fastened to an X-shaped cross and suffered death at the hands of angry pagans. Andrew is the patron saint of Scotland.

Saint Andrew the Apostle

I Almighty God, who didst give such grace to thine apostle Andrew that he readily obeyed the call of thy Son Jesus Christ, and brought his brother with him: Give unto us, who are called by thy Word, grace to follow him without delay, and to bring those near to us into his gracious presence; who liveth and reigneth with thee and the Holy Ghost, one God, now and for ever. *Amen.*

II Almighty God, who gave such grace to your apostle Andrew that he readily obeyed the call of your Son Jesus Christ, and brought his brother with him: Give unto us, who are called by your Word, grace to follow him without delay, and to bring those near to us into his gracious presence; who lives and reigns with you and the Holy Spirit, one God, now and for ever. *Amen.*

Lessons and Psalm

Deuteronomy 30:11-14
Psalm 19 *or* 19:1-6
Romans 10:8b-18
Matthew 4:18-22

Preface of Apostles and Ordinations

Charles de Foucauld, sometimes referred to as Brother Charles of Jesus, is often credited with the revival of desert spirituality in the early twentieth century and was the inspiration behind the founding of new religious communities for men and women.

Born in Strasbourg, France in 1858, Charles was orphaned at age six and raised by his grandparents. As a young man, he lost his faith and, in spite of the discipline of his grandfather, whom he deeply respected, Charles lived a life that was a mix of laxity and stubbornness. After training as a career army officer, Charles served in Algeria and Tunisia until he resigned his commission in 1882. He then became an explorer in Morocco. There he encountered devout Muslims, whose practice of their faith inspired Charles to begin a search for the faith that was his own. Upon returning to France, he continued his quest, and, in 1886, at age 28, re-discovered God and made a new commitment that would guide the rest of his life.

Charles entered the Cistercian Order of Strict Observance, the Trappists, first in France and then in Syria, for a commitment of seven years. He then went to Nazareth and lived as a servant to a convent of the Poor Clares. It was there that he began to develop a life of solitude, prayer, and adoration. The Poor Clares saw in him a vocation to the priesthood, encouraged him in spite of his reluctance, and he was ordained a priest in 1901.

Charles then moved to the Sahara, where his desire was to live a "ministry of presence" among "the furthest removed, the most abandoned." He believed his call was to live among those whose faith and culture differed from his own. To witness to Christ among them was not to be eloquent preaching or missionary demands, but "to shout the Gospel with his life." Charles sought to live so that those who saw his life would ask, "If such is the servant, what must the Master be like?"

Charles lived among the Tuareg people, learning their language and culture as he ministered to them. He was shot to death outside his refuge by bandits on December 1, 1916. He is considered a martyr by the Roman Catholic Church and was beatified in 2005.

Charles de Foucauld

Monastic and Martyr, 1916

I Loving God, help us to know thee wherever we find thee and seek to serve thee in all people, that with thy servant Charles de Foucauld, we may be faithful even unto death; through Jesus Christ our Lord, who liveth and reigneth with thee and the Holy Ghost, one God, now and for ever. *Amen.*

II Loving God, help us to know you wherever we find you and seek to serve you in all people, that with your servant Charles de Foucauld, we may be faithful even unto death; through Jesus Christ, who lives and reigns with you and the Holy Spirit, one God, now and for ever. *Amen.*

Lessons and Psalm

Habakkuk 3:17-19
Psalm 73:24-29
James 1:1-11
John 16:25-33

Preface of a Saint (3)

Channing Moore Williams, a farmer's son, was born in Richmond, Virginia, on July 18, 1829, and was brought up in straitened circumstances by his widowed mother. He attended the College of William and Mary and the Virginia Theological Seminary.

Ordained as a deacon in 1855, he offered himself for work in China, where he was ordained as a priest in 1857. Two years later, he was sent to Japan and opened work in Nagasaki. His first convert was baptized in 1866, the year that he was chosen as bishop for both China and Japan.

After 1868, he decided to concentrate all his work in Japan, following the revolution that opened the country to renewed contact with the western world. Relieved of his responsibility for China in 1874, Williams made his base at Yedo (now Tokyo), where he founded a divinity school, later to become St. Paul's University. At a synod in 1887, he helped bring together the English and American Anglican missions to form the Nippon Sei Ko Kai, the Holy Catholic Church of Japan, when the church there numbered fewer than a thousand communicants.

Williams translated parts of the Prayer Book into Japanese, and he was a close friend and warm supporter of Bishop Schereschewsky, his successor in China, in the latter's arduous work of translating the Bible into Chinese.

After resigning his jurisdiction in 1889, Bishop Williams stayed in Japan to help his successor there, Bishop John McKim, who was consecrated in 1893. Williams lived in Kyoto and continued to work in the opening of new mission stations until his return to the United States in 1908. He died in Richmond, Virginia, on December 2, 1910.

Channing Moore Williams

Bishop and Missionary, 1910

I O God, who in thy providence didst call Channing Moore Williams to the ministry of this church and gave him the gifts and the perseverance to preach the Gospel in new lands: Inspire us, by his example and prayers, to commit our talents to thy service, confident that thou dost uphold those whom thou dost call; through Jesus Christ our Lord, who liveth and reigneth with thee and the Holy Ghost, one God, for ever and ever. *Amen.*

II O God, who in your providence called Channing Moore Williams to the ministry of this church and gave him the gifts and the perseverance to preach the Gospel in new lands: Inspire us, by his example and prayers, to commit our talents to your service, confident that you uphold those whom you call; through Jesus Christ our Lord, who lives and reigns with you and the Holy Spirit, one God, for ever and ever. *Amen.*

Lessons and Psalm

Isaiah 49:22-23
Psalm 96:1-7
Acts 1:1-9
Luke 10:1-12

Preface of Pentecost

Francis Xavier was one of the great missionaries of the church. Born in Spain in 1506, he studied locally before taking up university studies in Paris in 1526, receiving a master's degree in 1530. While in Paris he met Ignatius Loyola and, with a small group of companions, they bound themselves together for the service of God on August 15, 1534, the beginning of what would later become the Society of Jesus, or the Jesuits. After further theological study, Francis and Ignatius were ordained together in 1537.

Francis went to India as the nuncio to the east for King John III of Portugal, arriving at Goa on the western coast in 1542. He later moved south and traveled to Sri Lanka and the Molucca Islands, now Indonesia. For seven years, he labored among the people there, winning many converts to the faith, baptizing, teaching, and trying to ease the suffering of the people. His efforts were not always well received. New Christians were often abused and enslaved and sometimes killed.

In 1549, Francis moved on to the southern region of Japan and immediately set about learning the language and preparing a catechism to support his missionary efforts. In time, he moved north to the imperial capital, Kyoto, and made an effort to see the Mikado, the Japanese emperor. Civil strife and localized resistance made Francis' Japanese efforts difficult, but he came away from the experience with a deep sense of respect for the people and their culture.

After returning to India in 1551, Francis was appointed the Jesuit Provincial for India, but he was not satisfied only to maintain the work already begun. He immediately set out for China, at the time closed to foreigners, in hopes of launching new missionary efforts there. He set up camp near the mouth of the Canton River in August 1552, hoping to secure passage into the country. Later that year he took ill and died, at age forty-six, on December 3, 1552. His remains were later transferred back to Goa, India.

Francis Xavier

Priest and Missionary, 1552

I God of all nations; Raise up, we beseech thee, in this and every land, evangelists and heralds of thy kingdom, that like thy servant Francis Xavier we may proclaim the unsearchable riches of our Savior Jesus Christ; who liveth and reigneth with thee and the Holy Ghost, one God, now and for ever. *Amen.*

II God of all nations; Raise up in this and every land, evangelists and heralds of your kingdom, that like your servant Francis Xavier we may proclaim the unsearchable riches of our Savior Jesus Christ; who lives and reigns with you and the Holy Spirit, one God, now and for ever. *Amen.*

Lessons and Psalm

Ecclesiasticus 2:1-7
Psalm 62
1 Corinthians 9:16-23
Mark 16:15-20

Preface of a Saint (2)

John of Damascus was the son of a Christian government official for the Muslim Caliph of Damascus. At an early age, he succeeded his father in this office, but in about 715, he entered the monastery of St. Sabas near Jerusalem. There he devoted himself to an ascetic life and to the study of theology.

In the same year that John was ordained as a priest, 726, the Byzantine Emperor Leo the Isaurian published his first edict against the Holy Images, which signaled the formal outbreak of the iconoclastic controversy. The edict forbade the veneration of sacred images, or icons, and ordered their destruction. In 729–730, John wrote three "Apologies (or Treatises) against the Iconoclasts and in Defense of the Holy Images." He argued that such images were not idols, for they represented neither false gods nor even the true God in his divine nature; but only saints, or our Lord as a man. He further distinguished between the respect, or veneration (*proskynesis*), that is properly paid to created beings, and the worship (*latreia*), that is properly given only to God.

The Seventh Ecumenical Council, in 787, decreed that crosses, icons, the book of the gospels, and other sacred objects were to receive reverence or veneration, expressed by salutations, incense, and lights, because the honor paid to them passed on to that which they represented. True worship (*latreia*), however, was due to God alone.

John also wrote a great synthesis of theology, *The Fount of Knowledge,* of which the last part, "On the Orthodox Faith," is best known. To Anglicans, John is perhaps best known as the author of the Easter hymns "Thou hallowed chosen morn of praise" (*The Hymnal 1982,* #198), "Come, ye faithful, raise the strain" (#199; #200), and "The day of resurrection" (#210).

John of Damascus

Priest and Theologian, c. 760

I Confirm our minds, O Lord, in the mysteries of the true faith, set forth with power by thy servant John of Damascus; that we, with him, confessing Jesus to be true God and true Man and singing the praises of the risen Lord, may, by the power of the resurrection, attain to eternal joy; through Jesus Christ our Lord, who liveth and reigneth with thee and the Holy Ghost, one God, now and for ever. *Amen.*

II Confirm our minds, O Lord, in the mysteries of the true faith, set forth with power by your servant John of Damascus; that we, with him, confessing Jesus to be true God and true Man and singing the praises of the risen Lord, may, by the power of the resurrection, attain to eternal joy; through Jesus Christ our Lord, who lives and reigns with you and the Holy Spirit, one God, now and for ever. *Amen.*

Lessons and Psalm

Wisdom 16:20-26
Psalm 118:14-21
Romans 6:1-11
Luke 17:20-21

Preface of Easter

Clement was born in the middle of the second century. He was a cultured Greek philosopher who sought truth in many schools until he met Pantaenus, founder of the Christian catechetical school at Alexandria in Egypt. Clement succeeded Pantaenus as head of that school in about 190, and was for many years an apologist for the Christian faith to both pagans and Christians. His learning and allegorical exegesis of the Bible helped to commend Christianity to the intellectual circles of Alexandria. His work prepared the way for his pupil Origen, the most eminent theologian of early Greek Christianity. During the persecution under the Emperor Severus in 202, he left Alexandria, possibly for Jerusalem or Cappadocia. The exact time and place of his death are unknown.

Clement lived in the age of "Gnosticism," a comprehensive term for many theories or ways of salvation current in the second and third centuries, all emphasizing "Gnosis" or "knowledge." Salvation, for Gnostics, was to be had through a secret and rather esoteric knowledge accessible only to a few. It was salvation from the world, rather than the salvation of the world. Clement asserted that there was a true Christian Gnosis, to be found in the Scriptures, available to all. Although his understanding of this Christian knowledge—ultimately knowledge of Christ—incorporated several tenets of Greek philosophy that the Gnostics also held, Clement dissented from their negative view of the world and their denial of the role of free will.

Among Clement's writings are the hymns "Sunset to sunrise changes now" (*The Hymnal 1982,* #163) and "Jesus our mighty Lord" (#478).

Clement of Alexandria

Priest and Theologian, c. 210

I O God of unsearchable wisdom, who didst give thy servant Clement grace to understand and teach the truth as it is in Jesus Christ, the source of all truth: Grant to thy church the same grace to discern thy Word wherever truth is found; through Jesus Christ our unfailing light, who liveth and reigneth with thee and the Holy Ghost, one God, for ever and ever. *Amen.*

II O God of unsearchable wisdom, you gave your servant Clement grace to understand and teach the truth as it is in Jesus Christ, the source of all truth: Grant to your church the same grace to discern your Word wherever truth is found; through Jesus Christ our unfailing light, who lives and reigns with you and the Holy Spirit, one God, for ever and ever. *Amen.*

Lessons and Psalm

1 Samuel 12:20-25
Psalm 34:9-14
Colossians 1:11-20
John 6:57-63

Preface of Baptism

Very little is known about the life of Nicholas, except that he suffered torture and imprisonment during the persecution under the Emperor Diocletian. It is probable that he was one of the bishops attending the Council of Nicaea in 325. According to popular tradition, he famously lost his temper at the council and punched the heretic Arius, but this story dates to more than 1,000 years after his death and is almost certainly apocryphal.

He was honored as a saint in Constantinople in the sixth century by the Emperor Justinian. His veneration also became immensely popular in the West after the supposed removal of his body to Bari, Italy, in the late eleventh century. In England, almost 400 churches were dedicated to him.

Nicholas is famed as the traditional patron of seafarers and sailors, and, more especially, of children. Many of the accounts of Nicholas' life recount his habit of secret gift-giving to those in need, a tradition that many Christians have felt inspired to continue in his honor.

As a bearer of gifts to children, his name was brought to America by the Dutch colonists in New York, from whom he is popularly known as Santa Claus.

Nicholas of Myra

Bishop, c. 342

I Grant, Almighty God, that thy church may be so inspired by the example of thy servant Nicholas of Myra, that it may never cease to work for the welfare of children, the safety of sailors, the relief of the poor, and the help of those tossed by tempests of doubt or grief; through Jesus Christ our Lord, who liveth and reigneth with thee and the Holy Ghost, one God, now and for ever. *Amen.*

II Grant, Almighty God, that your church may be so inspired by the example of your servant Nicholas of Myra, that it may never cease to work for the welfare of children, the safety of sailors, the relief of the poor, and the help of those tossed by tempests of doubt or grief; through Jesus Christ our Lord, who lives and reigns with you and the Holy Spirit, one God, now and for ever. *Amen.*

Lessons and Psalm

1 Kings 17:7-16
Psalm 145:8-13
1 John 4:7-14
Mark 10:13-16

Preface of a Saint (1)

Ambrose was the son of a Roman governor in Gaul, and in 373, he himself became governor in Upper Italy. Though brought up in a Christian family, Ambrose had not been baptized. He became involved in the election of a Bishop of Milan only as mediator between the battling factions of Arians and Nicene Christians. The election was important, because the victorious party would control the powerful see of Milan.

Ambrose exhorted the nearly riotous mob to keep the peace and to obey the law. Suddenly both sides raised the cry, "Ambrose shall be our bishop!" He protested, but the people persisted. Hastily baptized, he was ordained as a bishop on December 7, 373.

Ambrose rapidly won renown as a defender of orthodoxy against Arianism and as a statesman of the church. He was also a skillful hymnodist. He introduced antiphonal chanting to enrich the liturgy and wrote straightforward, practical discourses to educate his people in such matters of doctrine as Baptism, the Trinity, the Eucharist, and the Person of Christ. His persuasive preaching was an important factor in the conversion of Augustine of Hippo.

Ambrose did not fear to rebuke emperors, including the hot-headed Theodosius, whom he forced to do public penance for the slaughter of several thousand citizens of Thessalonica. He also preached passionate sermons in defense of the poor and the needy. In a homily on Naboth's vineyard (1 Kings 21) he declares: "The story of Naboth is an old one, but it is repeated every day. Who among the rich does not daily covet the goods of others? Who among the wealthy does not make every effort to drive the poor person out from his little plot and turn the needy out from the boundaries of his ancestral fields? Who is satisfied with what is his? What rich person's thoughts are not preoccupied with his neighbor's possessions? It is not one Ahab who was born, therefore, but—what is worse—Ahab is born every day, and never does he die as far as this world is concerned. For each one who dies there are many others who rise up; there are more who steal property than who lose it . . . How far, O rich, will you extend your mad greed?"

A meditation attributed to him includes these words: "Lord Jesus Christ, you are for me medicine when I am sick; you are my strength when I need help; you are life itself when I fear death; you are the way when I long for heaven; you are light when all is dark; you are my food when I need nourishment." Among hymns attributed to Ambrose are "The eternal gifts of Christ the King" (*The Hymnal 1982*, #233; #234), "O Splendor of God's glory bright" (#5), and a series of hymns for the daily office.

Ambrose of Milan

Bishop and Theologian, 397

I O God, who didst give thy servant Ambrose grace eloquently to proclaim thy righteousness in the great congregation and fearlessly to bear reproach for the honor of thy Name: Mercifully grant to all bishops and pastors such excellence in preaching and faithfulness in ministering thy Word, that thy people may be partakers with them of the glory that shall be revealed; through Jesus Christ our Lord, who liveth and reigneth with thee and the Holy Ghost, one God, now and for ever. *Amen.*

II O God, who gave your servant Ambrose grace eloquently to proclaim your righteousness in the great congregation and fearlessly to bear reproach for the honor of your Name: Mercifully grant to all bishops and pastors such excellence in preaching and faithfulness in ministering your Word, that your people may be partakers with them of the glory that shall be revealed; through Jesus Christ our Lord, who lives and reigns with you and the Holy Spirit, one God, now and for ever. *Amen.*

Lessons and Psalm

1 Kings 21:17-29
Psalm 27:5-11
Acts 4:23-31
Luke 12:35-46

Preface of a Saint (1)

Nicholas Ferrar was the founder of a religious community at Little Gidding, Huntingdonshire, England, which existed from 1626 to 1646. His family had been prominent in the affairs of the Virginia Company, but when that company was dissolved, he took deacon's orders and retired to the country.

At Little Gidding, his immediate family and a few friends and servants gave themselves wholly to religious observance. They restored the derelict church near the manor house, became responsible for services there, taught many of the local children, and looked after the health and well-being of the people of the neighborhood. A regular round of prayer according to the Book of Common Prayer was observed, along with the daily recital of the whole of the psalter. The members of the community became widely known for fasting, private prayer and meditation, and for writing stories and books illustrating themes of Christian faith and morality. The community also prepared "harmonies" of the gospels, one of which was presented to King Charles I by the Ferrar family.

The community did not long survive the death of Nicholas Ferrar. However, the memory of the religious life at Little Gidding was kept alive, principally through Izaak Walton's description in his *Life of George Herbert:* "He (Ferrar) and his family . . . did most of them keep Lent and all Ember-weeks strictly, both in fasting and using all those mortifications and prayers that the church hath appointed . . . and he and they did the like constantly on Fridays, and on the vigils or eves appointed to be fasted before the Saints' days; and this frugality and abstinence turned to the relief of the poor . . ."

The community became an important symbol for many Anglicans when religious orders began to be revived. Its life inspired T. S. Eliot, and he gave the title, "Little Gidding," to the last of his *Four Quartets,* one of the great religious poems of the twentieth century.

Nicholas Ferrar

Deacon, 1637

I Lord God, make us worthy of thy perfect love; that, with thy deacon Nicholas Ferrar and his household, we may rule ourselves according to thy Word, and serve thee with our whole heart; through Jesus Christ our Lord, who liveth and reigneth with thee and the Holy Ghost, one God, for ever and ever. *Amen.*

II Lord God, make us worthy of your perfect love; that, with your deacon Nicholas Ferrar and his household, we may rule ourselves according to your Word, and serve you with our whole heart; through Jesus Christ our Lord, who lives and reigns with you and the Holy Spirit, one God, for ever and ever. *Amen.*

Lessons and Psalm

Proverbs 1:20-33
Psalm 127
Galatians 6:7-10
Matthew 13:47-52

Preface of a Saint (1)

Episcopal military chaplains care for their flock of men, women, and children stationed in countries around the world, as well as at bases in the United States. In times of battle, chaplains often accompany their units—only without any weapons—in order to provide pastoral care, sacramental rites, and the comfort of prayer under extreme stress. They ably administer rites and logistical assistance in field hospitals and veterans centers, National Guard postings, and frequently a parish at home. Many Episcopal chaplains currently serve the Armed Forces of the United States.

The ministry of the Rev. Frederick "Ted" Howden, Jr., stands out among many heroic chaplaincies. He was twelve years old when his father was consecrated bishop of the Missionary District of New Mexico and Southwest Texas. His father ordained him deacon at St. Clement's Church in El Paso, Texas, on June 10, 1928, and priest, also at St. Clement's, on January 13, 1929. Ted Howden immediately began to serve several congregations in New Mexico, traveling great distances between them.

When World War II broke out, Howden held the rank of captain in the New Mexico State Guard, a unit predominantly made up of Hispanic, Latino, and Native Americans. He was the chaplain to the 200th Coast Artillery when it was federalized and sent to the Philippines in September 1941. He walked across the hills, from battery to battery, holding open-air services and distributing candy, soap, and cigarettes he had foraged for the troops.

When Bataan and Corregidor fell to Japanese forces in April and May 1942, Howden and his fellow soldiers were made prisoners of war and were forced to endure the Bataan Death March, during which some 18,000 died. During imprisonment in several prison camps, his heroism and faith were always apparent through the care he provided. Howden often gave his own food rations to others, insisting that they needed it more. He died of dysentery and starvation-induced pellagra on December 11, 1942, and was buried by his men in a small cemetery in the jungle of Mindanao, about a mile from the camp. His family would not learn of his fate until June 1943. After the war, in 1948, his remains were reinterred in Albuquerque, New Mexico.

Howden has been commemorated in the Diocese of the Rio Grande, particularly by veterans of the armed forces and their families who have faced physical, spiritual, and emotional harm; disabling injuries; and death itself while in the service of our country. Recalling his self-sacrifice, the Church honors all who answer our Lord's call to chaplaincy in the world's most dangerous places.

Frederick Howden, Jr.

Priest and Chaplain of the Armed Forces, 1942

I Almighty God, our sure defense: We give thee thanks for thy servant[s] Frederick Howden, [*N.*,] and all military chaplains who provided comfort and inspiration in time of battle; and, following the example of Jesus the Good Shepherd, laid down their lives in the service of others. Inspire and strengthen us, also, for the duties of life still before us, that we may be faithful to the end; through the same Jesus Christ, our Savior and Lord. *Amen.*

II Almighty God, our sure defense: We give you thanks for your servant[s] Frederick Howden, [*N.*,] and all military chaplains who provided comfort and inspiration in time of battle; and, following the example of Jesus the Good Shepherd, laid down their lives in the service of others. Inspire and strengthen us, also, for the duties of life still before us, that we may be faithful to the end; through the same Jesus Christ, our Savior and Lord. *Amen.*

Lessons and Psalm

Jeremiah 17:14-17
Psalm 18:1-6, 18-20
1 Corinthians 15:12-22
John 10:11-18

Preface of a Saint (2)

Francis de Sales served as the Roman Catholic bishop of Geneva from 1567 to 1622, but today he is primarily known for his writings on prayer and spiritual direction, particularly his work *Introduction to the Devout Life*.

As a young man, Francis studied for a political career, but he was deeply anxious for his salvation, prone to melancholy and despair, and was convinced that he has been predestined for damnation. In 1587, however, while a visitor at a church in Paris, he had a profound experience of the love of God. This sense of God's love and mercy would mark his writings on the spiritual life from that time forward. In response to this overwhelming sense of God's love, Francis changed his trajectory and resolved to become a priest.

In 1602 he became bishop of Geneva, although he was forced to remain in the parts of his diocese that were outside of the city, since Geneva itself was under Calvinist control. He wrote a number of books on the spiritual life which stressed the importance of love for God and neighbor rather than focusing on sin and penance, and which were notable in being directed toward laypeople. The influence of his *Introduction to the Devout Life* was not limited to Roman Catholic circles, but informed Protestant spiritual writers as well, including many Anglicans. In addition to his writing, Francis worked with Jane de Chantal in her foundation of a new religious order for women, the Congregation of the Visitation.

Jane de Chantal was a wealthy young widow with four small children. In her grief, she resolved never to remarry. She devoted herself instead to caring for the poor and the sick, to raising her children, and to managing her late husband's estates. Francis de Sales would become her spiritual director in 1604.

In 1610, Francis and Jane established the Congregation of the Visitation. Initially devoted to serving the poor and the sick, the order gradually evolved in a more contemplative direction. During Jane's 31 years in the community, she gave spiritual direction to a number of women and men in the form of letters, many of which have been preserved. Unusually, her order actively welcomed women as sisters who would not be considered by other orders because of their poor health or advanced age. When others questioned the wisdom of this decision, Jane merely replied, "What would you have me do? I rather like sick people myself. I'm on their side." By the time she died in 1641, the order had already grown to include 34 houses.

Francis de Sales
Bishop, 1622
and Jane de Chantal
Vowed Religious, 1641

I Most gracious God, who hast bidden us to act justly, love mercy, and walk humbly before thee; Grant that we, like thy servants Francis and Jane, may see and serve Christ in all people, and know him as the giver of all good things; through the same Jesus Christ our Lord, who liveth and reigneth with thee and the Holy Ghost, one God, now and for ever. *Amen.*

II Most gracious God, who has bidden us to act justly, love mercy, and walk humbly before you; Grant that we, like your servants Francis and Jane, may see and serve Christ in all people, and know him as the giver of all good things; through the same Jesus Christ our Lord, who lives and reigns with you and the Holy Spirit, one God, now and for ever. *Amen.*

Lessons and Psalm

Judges 6:11-24
Psalm 111
James 3:13-18
Mark 12:41-44

Preface of a Saint (3)

Lucy, or Lucia, was martyred at Syracuse, in Sicily, during the Diocletian persecution of 303–304. Her tomb can still be found in the catacombs of Syracuse. She was venerated soon after her death and her cult spread quickly throughout the church. She is among the saints and martyrs named in the Roman canon of the mass.

Most of the details of Lucy's life are obscure. In the tradition, she is remembered for her purity of life and her gentleness of spirit. Because her name means "light," she is sometimes thought of as the patron saint of those who suffer from diseases of the eyes.

In popular piety, Lucy is perhaps most revered because her feast day was for many centuries the shortest day of the year. (The reform of the calendar by Pope Gregory VIII in 1582 would shift the shortest day to December 21/22, depending upon the year.) It was historically on Lucy's day that the light began gradually to return and the days to lengthen. This was particularly powerful in northern Europe, where the days of winter were quite short. In Scandinavian countries, particularly Sweden, Lucy's day has long been a festival of light that is kept as both an ecclesiastical commemoration and a domestic observance.

In the domestic celebration of Lucia, a young girl in the family dresses in pure white (a symbol of Lucy's faith, purity, and martyrdom), wears a crown of lighted candles upon her head (a sign that on Lucy's day the light is returning), and serves her family special foods prepared especially for the day. In praise of her service, the young girl is called Lucy for the day.

Lucy of Syracuse

Martyr, 304

I Loving God, who for the salvation of all didst give Jesus Christ as light to a world in darkness: Illumine us, as thou didst thy daughter Lucy, with the light of Christ, that by the merits of his passion, we may be led to eternal life; through the same Jesus Christ, who with thee and the Holy Ghost liveth and reigneth, one God, for ever and ever. *Amen.*

II Loving God, for the salvation of all you gave Jesus Christ as light to a world in darkness: Illumine us, as you did your daughter Lucy, with the light of Christ, that by the merits of his passion, we may be led to eternal life; through the same Jesus Christ, who with you and the Holy Spirit lives and reigns, one God, for ever and ever. *Amen.*

Lessons and Psalm

Esther 4:9-16
Psalm 131
Revelation 19:5-8
John 1:9-14

Preface of a Saint (1)

The Carmelite theologian John of the Cross has been called "the poet's poet," "spirit of flame," and "celestial and divine."

John was born in 1542 at Fontiveros, near Avila, Spain. After his third birthday, his father died, leaving his mother and her children reduced to poverty. John received elementary education in an orphanage in Medina del Campo. By the age of seventeen, he had learned carpentry, tailoring, sculpturing, and painting through apprenticeships to local craftsmen.

After university studies with the Jesuits, John entered the Carmelite Order in Medina del Campo and completed his theological studies in Salamanca. In 1567, he was ordained to the priesthood and recruited by Teresa of Avila for the reformation of the Carmelite Order.

John became disillusioned with what he considered the laxity of the Carmelites and, in 1568, he opened a monastery of "Discalced" (strict observance) Carmelites, an act that met with sharp resistance from the General Chapter of the Calced Carmelites. John was seized, taken to Toledo, and imprisoned in the monastery. During nine months of great hardship, he comforted himself by writing poetry. It was while he was imprisoned that he composed the greater part of his luminous masterpiece, *The Spiritual Canticle,* as well as a number of shorter poems. His other major works include *The Ascent of Mount Carmel, The Living Flame of Love,* and *The Dark Night*. It is this latter work, *Noche obscura del alma,* that gave the English language the phrase "dark night of the soul."

After a severe illness, John died on December 14, 1591, in Ubeda, in southern Spain.

John of the Cross

Mystic and Monastic Reformer, 1591

I Judge eternal, throned in splendor, who didst give John of the Cross strength of purpose and faith that sustained him even through the dark night of the soul: Shed thy light on all who love thee, in unity with Jesus Christ our Savior; who with thee and the Holy Ghost liveth and reigneth, one God, for ever and ever. *Amen.*

II Judge eternal, throned in splendor, who gave John of the Cross strength of purpose and faith that sustained him even through the dark night of the soul: Shed your light on all who love you, in unity with Jesus Christ our Savior; who with you and the Holy Spirit lives and reigns, one God, for ever and ever. *Amen.*

Lessons and Psalm

1 Kings 19:1-9
Psalm 121
Colossians 2:4-6
John 16:12-22

Preface of God the Son

Georgia began to be Christianized in the fourth century. According to the *Church History* of Rufinus of Aquileia, the people of Georgia were drawn to the Gospel of Jesus Christ during the reign of the Emperor Constantine through the example of a woman named Nino, who was brought there as a captive from Cappadocia and sold as a slave.

The Georgian Prince Bakurius, from whom Rufinus heard the story, said that the captive woman first aroused the attention of the people through her piety and virtue. When asked, she replied that her way of life was an act of worship to Christ her God. Later, the mother of a young girl who had taken ill brought her to the captive woman, after having sought a remedy for her daughter's illness from all her other neighbors. Through the prayers of Nino, the little girl was healed.

The news of this miracle drew the attention of the queen, who was herself suffering from a grave illness. The queen was carried to the captive woman's cell and, through her prayers, she was likewise restored to health. At the queen's request, Nino told her of Christ Jesus, the Son of God, and when the queen expressed a desire to be baptized, the captive woman performed the sacrament herself.

After her conversion, the queen sought to convert her husband, but the king resisted. Later, while hunting, the king lost his way in the forest and a great darkness fell upon him, so that he could not see. Then the king remembered what he had heard about the captive woman's God and vowed to worship that God alone if he would save him. Immediately a light broke through the darkness and revealed the path home. The king then summoned Nino and was instructed in the Gospel by her. A magnificent church was erected and, at Nino's request, an envoy was sent to the emperor to request that priests be sent to Georgia to administer the Eucharist and to catechize the people.

Nino is known in the Orthodox tradition as Equal to the Apostles and Enlightener of Georgia. While many of the historical details remain sketchy, Georgia is highly unusual in its claim to have been evangelized by a female slave rather than by a famous apostle and evangelist, and the rough outlines of this tradition are therefore taken seriously by historians.

Nino's tomb in believed to be in the Bodbe Monastery, which is one of the major pilgrimage sites in Georgia. The Georgian church also uses a distinctive cross with drooping arms as a symbol of the cross that Nino is believed to have created to explain the gospel, by twisting a grapevine and tying it together with a strand of her hair.

Nino of Georgia

Missionary, c. 332

I Almighty God, who didst call thy servant Nino to be thine apostle to the people of Georgia, to bring those wandering in darkness to the true light and knowledge of thee; Grant us so to walk in that light, that we may come at last to the light of thine everlasting day; through Jesus Christ our Lord, who liveth and reigneth with thee and the Holy Ghost, one God, now and for ever. *Amen.*

II Almighty God, who called your servant Nino to be your apostle to the people of Georgia, to bring those wandering in darkness to the true light and knowledge of you; Grant us so to walk in that light, that we may come at last to the light of your everlasting day; through Jesus Christ our Lord, who lives and reigns with you and the Holy Spirit, one God, now and for ever. *Amen.*

Lessons and Psalm

2 Kings 5:1-14
Psalm 17:6-10
1 Corinthians 12:4-11
Luke 13:10-17

Preface of a Saint (3)

Dorothy Leigh Sayers is perhaps best known as a prolific fiction writer, but she was also a theological writer, linguist, translator, and passionate advocate of the truth of the Christian faith.

Dorothy was born in 1893 at Oxford to the chaplain of Christ Church. She would eventually graduate from Oxford in 1915 with honors. Although women were not awarded degrees at the time, she received her degree five years later when the policy changed. After graduation she became a copywriter at Benson's advertising and was highly successful in that business. During her time there she wrote her first novel, *Whose Body?* featuring a famous recurring character of hers, Lord Peter Wimsey.

In addition to fiction, however, Sayers also drew on her deep Christian faith and devotion to write about concerns facing the church. She began with *The Zeal for Thy House,* a play, and afterwards a BBC radio drama about the life of Jesus entitled *The Man Born to Be King.* She also took the church to task for its woeful neglect of dogma and doctrine, arguing in *Creed or Chaos* for the utmost importance of doctrine for Christian laity, and in the process cemented her place as a Christian apologist.

Writing on the centrality of dogma in Christianity, she wrote:

> It is not true at all that dogma is hopelessly irrelevant to the life and thought of the average man. What is true is that ministers of the Christian religion often assert that it is, present it for consideration as though it were, and, in fact, by their faulty exposition of it make it so. The central dogma of the Incarnation is that by which relevance stands or falls. If Christ were only man, then he is entirely irrelevant to any thought about God; if he is only God, then he is entirely irrelevant to any experience of human life. It is, in the strictest sense, necessary to the salvation of relevance that a man should believe rightly the Incarnation of Our Lord, Jesus Christ. Unless he believes rightly, there is not the faintest reason why he should believe at all. And in that case, it is wholly irrelevant to chatter about Christian principles.

She died in 1957 and is buried under the tower in St. Anne's Church in London.

Dorothy L. Sayers

Apologist and Spiritual Writer, 1957

I Almighty God, who didst strengthen thy servant Dorothy Sayers with eloquence to defend Christian teaching: Keep us, we pray, steadfast in thy true religion, that in constancy and peace we may always teach right doctrine, and teach doctrine rightly; through Jesus Christ our Lord, who liveth and reigneth with thee and the Holy Ghost, one God, now and for ever. *Amen.*

II Almighty God, who strengthened your servant Dorothy Sayers with eloquence to defend Christian teaching: Keep us, we pray, steadfast in your true religion, that in constancy and peace we may always teach right doctrine, and teach doctrine rightly; through Jesus Christ our Lord, who lives and reigns with you and the Holy Spirit, one God, now and for ever. *Amen.*

Lessons and Psalm

Judges 3:15-30
Psalm 19
1 Corinthians 12:4-11
John 21:1-9

Preface of God the Son

Katharina von Bora was born in 1499, the daughter of impoverished German nobles, and was educated at the Benedictine convent in Brehna. Instinctively devout, she initially felt deeply drawn to the monastic life, and as a teenager took vows at a Cistercian convent in Nimbschen.

As a young woman, however, Katharina became increasingly critical of many of the abuses that she perceived in the church, and became keenly interested in the movements of ecclesiastical reform. In 1523, she and 11 other sisters secretly contacted Martin Luther and asked for his help in escaping from the convent. Smuggled out in a fish wagon, they soon found that they had nowhere to go, because their families refused to take them back. Several of the Protestant reformers sheltered the women, and Katharina found a temporary home with the family of the famous painter Lucas Cranach.

Eventually all of the women found husbands within the new community of church reformers, but for Katharina no match was found. Most of her potential suitors found her intellect intimidating and her assertiveness off-putting. Eventually, she expressed a desire to wed Martin Luther himself, and rather to the surprise of most of his friends, he agreed.

Many within the early Lutheran community were opposed to Luther's marriage, fearing that it would open him to criticism that he had only left the monastic life because he did not want to fulfill his vow of celibacy, rather than because he was genuinely concerned about abuses within the church. But Luther came to believe that married life was itself a vocation from God, and also that clerical marriage gave women the opportunity to assist in the work of the Reformation as coworkers and colleagues.

Katharina therefore became an early model for the vocation of a pastor's spouse, assisting Martin in his ministry and providing hospitality to many, as well as raising six children and opening their home to a number of orphans. The family regularly hosted dozens of people at dinner, which would involve heated theological debates. Katharina was an active participant in these, knowing both the scriptures and Latin as well as many of the men, and Martin encouraged her contributions. He gave her a degree of authority that was unprecedented in that time, including allowing her to handle the publication of his works, and naming her as his sole heir upon his death. She died on December 20, 1552.

Katharina von Bora

Church Reformer, 1552

I Almighty God, who didst call thy servant Katharina von Bora from a cloister to work for the reform of thy church: Grant that, for the sake of thy glory and the welfare of thy church, we may go wherever thou dost call, and serve however thou dost will; through Jesus Christ, our only mediator and advocate. *Amen.*

II Almighty God, who called your servant Katharina von Bora from a cloister to work for the reform of your church: Grant that, for the sake of your glory and the welfare of your church, we may go wherever you should call, and serve however you should will; through Jesus Christ, our only mediator and advocate. *Amen.*

Lessons and Psalm

Isaiah 55:6-11
Psalm 46
Romans 3:21-28
John 15:1-11

Preface of Trinity Sunday

The Gospel according to John records several incidents in which Thomas appears, and from them we are able to gain some impression of the sort of man he was. When Jesus insisted on going to Judea, to visit his friends at Bethany, Thomas boldly declared, "Let us also go, that we may die with him" (John 11:16). At the Last Supper, he interrupted our Lord's discourse with the question, "Lord, we do not know where you are going; how can we know the way?" (John 14:5). And after Christ's resurrection, Thomas would not accept the account of the women and the other apostles, until Jesus himself appeared before him, showing him his wounds. This drew from him the first explicit acknowledgment of Christ's divinity, "My Lord and my God!" (John 20:28).

Thomas appears to have been a thoughtful if perhaps literal-minded man, inclined to skepticism; but he was a staunch friend when his loyalty was once given. The expression "Doubting Thomas," which has become established in English usage, is not entirely fair to Thomas. He did not refuse belief: he wanted to believe, but did not dare, without further evidence. Because of his goodwill, Jesus gave him a sign, although Jesus had refused a sign to the Pharisees. His Lord's rebuke was well deserved: "Blessed are those who have not seen and yet believe" (John 20:29). The sign did not create faith; it merely released the faith that was in Thomas already.

According to an early tradition mentioned by Eusebius and others, Thomas evangelized the Persians. Syrian Christians of India cherish a tradition that after his mission to Persia, he continued East and brought the Gospel to India. The site of his burial, in present-day Chennai, has been a shrine and place of Christian pilgrimage since antiquity.

Thomas' honest questioning and doubt, and Jesus' assuring response to him, have given many modern Christians courage to persist in faith, even when they are still doubting and questioning.

Saint Thomas the Apostle

I Everliving God, who didst strengthen thine apostle Thomas with sure and certain faith in thy Son's resurrection: Grant us so perfectly and without doubt to believe in Jesus Christ, our Lord and our God, that our faith may never be found wanting in thy sight; through him who liveth and reigneth with thee and the Holy Ghost, one God, now and for ever. *Amen.*

II Everliving God, who strengthened your apostle Thomas with firm and certain faith in your Son's resurrection: Grant us so perfectly and without doubt to believe in Jesus Christ, our Lord and our God, that our faith may never be found wanting in your sight; through him who lives and reigns with you and the Holy Spirit, one God, now and for ever. *Amen.*

Lessons and Psalm

Habakkuk 2:1-4
Psalm 126
Hebrews 10:35—11:1
John 20:24-29

Preface of Apostles and Ordinations

That Jesus was born is a fact both of history and revelation. The precise date of his birth, however, is not recorded in the Gospels, which are, after all, not biographies, and show little concern for those biographical details in which more modern Christians are interested. Such interest began to become prominent in the fourth century, together with the development of liturgical observances concerning the events of biblical history.

Scholars have offered various theories about how December 25 came to be selected as the date for the liturgical commemoration of the Nativity in the Western Church. An older scholarly view suggests that the date, coming as it does at the winter solstice, was already a sacred one, being observed by Roman pagans as the festival of the birth of the Unconquerable Sun (*dies natalis Solis Invicti*). This correspondence is noted by some early Christian writers themselves, who see it as a fitting parallel, but the pagan celebration was only established in the late third century, and the Christian observance of December 25 seems to have even earlier antecedents.

An alternative explanation calculates the date of Christmas based on the date of Passover and Easter. Many early Christian theologians, particularly in North Africa, calculated that the Crucifixion had taken place on the 14 of Nisan, which worked out to be March 25 on the Roman calendar. This date also became celebrated as the Feast of the Annunciation because of a widespread pious belief that Jesus died on the same date that he was conceived, showing how deeply interconnected all of the events of salvation history were. December 25, then, becomes the date of Christ's birth, because it is exactly nine months after the date of his conception. This method of calculating also explains the traditional dating in the Eastern church, which historically fixed the Nativity on January 6 rather than December 25. The Eastern church calculated the date of both Annunciation and Crucifixion using not the 14 of Nisan, but rather the 14 of Artemisios, the first spring month on the Greek calendar. This translates to April 6 on the Roman calendar, which is nine months before January 6.

The full title of the feast dates from the 1662 edition of the Book of Common Prayer. Prior to that revision, the day was known only as "Christmas Day." The word "Christmas," which can be traced to the twelfth century, is a contraction of "Christ's Mass."

The Nativity of Our Lord Jesus Christ

I O God, who makest us glad with the yearly remembrance of the birth of thy only Son Jesus Christ: Grant that as we joyfully receive him for our Redeemer, so we may with sure confidence behold him when he shall come to be our Judge; who liveth and reigneth with thee and the Holy Ghost, one God, world without end. *Amen.*

II O God, you make us glad by the yearly festival of the birth of your only Son Jesus Christ: Grant that we, who joyfully receive him as our Redeemer, may with sure confidence behold him when he comes to be our Judge; who lives and reigns with you and the Holy Spirit, one God, now and for ever. *Amen.*

One of the sets of Psalms and Lessons on page 579 is used.

Preface of the Incarnation

A Second Proper for Christmas Day

I O God, who hast caused this holy night to shine with the illumination of the true Light: Grant us, we beseech thee, that as we have known the mystery of that Light upon earth, so may we also perfectly enjoy him in heaven; where with thee and the Holy Ghost he liveth and reigneth, one God, in glory everlasting. *Amen.*

II O God, you have caused this holy night to shine with the brightness of the true Light: Grant that we, who have known the mystery of that Light on earth, may also enjoy him perfectly in heaven; where with you and the Holy Spirit he lives and reigns, one God, in glory everlasting. *Amen.*

One of the sets of Psalms and Lessons on the following page is used.

Preface of the Incarnation

A Third Proper for Christmas Day

I Almighty God, who hast given us thy only-begotten Son to take our nature upon him and at this time to be born of a pure virgin: Grant that we, being regenerate and made thy children by adoption and grace, may daily be renewed by thy Holy Ghost; through the same our Lord Jesus Christ, who liveth and reigneth with thee and the same Holy Ghost ever, one God, world without end. *Amen.*

II Almighty God, you have given your only-begotten Son to take our nature upon him, and to be born [this day] of a pure virgin: Grant that we, who have been born again and made your children by adoption and grace, may daily be renewed by your Holy Spirit; through our Lord Jesus Christ, to whom with you and the same Spirit be honor and glory, now and for ever. *Amen.*

Lessons and Psalm

I
Isaiah 9:2-4, 6-7
Psalm 96 *or* 96:1-4, 11-12
Titus 2:11-14
Luke 2:1-14 (15-20)

II
Isaiah 62:6-7, 10-12
Psalm 97 *or* 97:1-4, 11-12
Titus 3:4-7
Luke 2:(1-14) 15-20

III
Isaiah 52:7-10
Psalm 98 *or* 98:1-6
Hebrews 1:1-12
John 1:1-14

Preface of the Incarnation

Very probably a Hellenistic Jew, Stephen was one of the "seven men of good repute, full of the Spirit and of wisdom" (Acts 6:3), who were chosen by the apostles to relieve them of the administrative burden of "serving tables and caring for the widows." By this appointment to assist the apostles, Stephen, the first named of those the New Testament calls "The Seven," became the first to do what the church traditionally considers to be the work and ministry of a deacon.

It is apparent that Stephen's activities involved more than simply "serving tables," however, for the Acts of the Apostles speaks of his preaching and performing many miracles. These activities led him into conflict with some of the Jews, who accused him of blasphemy, and brought him before the Sanhedrin. His powerful sermon before the Council is recorded in the seventh chapter of Acts. According to this account, his denunciations of the Sanhedrin so enraged its members that, without a trial, they dragged him out of the city and stoned him to death. Stephen is traditionally regarded as the very first Christian martyr.

Saul, later called Paul, stood by, consenting to Stephen's death, but Stephen's example of steadfast faith in Jesus, and of intercession for his persecutors, was to find fruit in the mission and witness of Paul after his conversion. The Christian community in Jerusalem, taking fright at the hostility of the Judean authorities, was scattered, so that for the first time the Gospel of Christ began to spread beyond Jerusalem.

Saint Stephen, Deacon and Martyr

I We give thee thanks, O Lord of glory, for the example of the first martyr Stephen, who looked up to heaven and prayed for his persecutors to thy Son Jesus Christ, who standeth at thy right hand; where he liveth and reigneth with thee and the Holy Ghost, one God, in glory everlasting. *Amen.*

II We give you thanks, O Lord of glory, for the example of the first martyr Stephen, who looked up to heaven and prayed for his persecutors to your Son Jesus Christ, who stands at your right hand; where he lives and reigns with you and the Holy Spirit, one God, in glory everlasting. *Amen.*

Lessons and Psalm

Jeremiah 26:1-9, 12-15
Psalm 31 *or* Psalm 31:1-5
Acts 6:8—7:2a, 51c-60
Matthew 23:34-39

Preface of the Incarnation

John, the son of Zebedee, with his brother James, was called from being a fisherman to be a disciple and "fisher of men." With Peter and James, he became one of the inner group of three disciples whom Jesus chose to be with him at the raising of Jairus' daughter, at the Transfiguration, and in the garden of Gethsemane.

John and his brother James are recorded in the Gospel as being so hotheaded and impetuous that Jesus nicknamed them "Boanerges," which means, "sons of thunder." They also appear ambitious, in that they sought seats of honor at Jesus' right and left when he should come into his kingdom. Yet they were also faithful companions, willing, without knowing the cost, to share the cup Jesus was to drink. When the other disciples responded in anger to the audacity of the brothers in asking for this honor, Jesus explained that in his kingdom leadership and rule take the form of being a servant to all.

If, as is commonly held, John is to be identified with the "disciple whom Jesus loved," then he clearly enjoyed a very special relationship with his Master, reclining close to Jesus at the Last Supper, receiving the care of his mother at the cross, and being the first to understand the truth of the empty tomb.

The Acts of the Apostles records John's presence with Peter on several occasions: the healing of the lame man at the Beautiful Gate of the Temple, before the Sanhedrin, in prison, and on the mission to Samaria to lay hands upon the new converts that they might receive the Holy Spirit.

According to tradition, John later went to Asia Minor and settled at Ephesus. Under the Emperor Domitian, he was exiled to the island of Patmos, where he experienced the visions recounted in the Book of Revelation. Irenaeus, at the end of the second century, liked to recall how Polycarp, in his old age, had talked about the apostle whom he had known while growing up at Ephesus. It is probable that John died there. He alone of the Twelve is said to have lived to extreme old age and to have been spared a martyr's death.

Saint John, Apostle and Evangelist

I Shed upon thy church, we beseech thee, O Lord, the brightness of thy light; that we, being illumined by the teaching of thine apostle and evangelist John, may so walk in the light of thy truth, that we may at length attain to the fullness of life everlasting; through Jesus Christ our Lord, who liveth and reigneth with thee and the Holy Ghost, one God, for ever and ever. *Amen.*

II Shed upon your church, O Lord, the brightness of your light, that we, being illumined by the teaching of your apostle and evangelist John, may so walk in the light of your truth, that at length we may attain to the fullness of eternal life; through Jesus Christ our Lord, who lives and reigns with you and the Holy Spirit, one God, for ever and ever. *Amen.*

Lessons and Psalm

Exodus 33:18-23
Psalm 92 *or* 92:1-4, 11-14
1 John 1:1-9
John 21:19b-24

Preface of the Incarnation

Herod the Great, ruler of the Jews, appointed by the Romans in 40 BCE, kept the peace in Palestine for 37 years. His ruthless control, coupled with genuine ability, has been recorded by the Jewish historian Josephus, who describes him as "a man of great barbarity towards everyone." An Idumaean, married to the daughter of Hyrcanus, the last legal Hasmonean ruler, Herod was continually in fear of losing his throne. It is not surprising that the Magi's report of the birth of an infant King of the Jews (Matthew 2) would have caused him fear and anger. Although the event is not recorded in secular history, the story of the massacre of the Innocents would have been in keeping with what is known of Herod's character.

To protect himself against being supplanted by an infant king, Herod ordered the slaughter of all male children under two years of age in Bethlehem and the surrounding region. From antiquity, the church has consistently honored these innocent children as martyrs, even though they were quite obviously not Christians, because they were killed by one who was seeking to destroy Christ. Augustine of Hippo called them "buds, killed by the frost of persecution the moment they showed themselves."

Holy Innocents

I We remember this day, O God, the slaughter of the holy innocents of Bethlehem by the order of King Herod. Receive, we beseech thee, into the arms of thy mercy all innocent victims; and by thy great might frustrate the designs of evil tyrants and establish thy rule of justice, love, and peace; through Jesus Christ our Lord, who liveth and reigneth with thee, in the unity of the Holy Ghost, one God, for ever and ever. *Amen.*

II We remember today, O God, the slaughter of the holy innocents of Bethlehem by King Herod. Receive, we pray, into the arms of your mercy all innocent victims; and by your great might frustrate the designs of evil tyrants and establish your rule of justice, love, and peace; through Jesus Christ our Lord, who lives and reigns with you, in the unity of the Holy Spirit, one God, for ever and ever. *Amen.*

Lessons and Psalm

Jeremiah 31:15-17
Psalm 124
Revelation 21:1-7
Matthew 2:13-18

Preface of the Incarnation

Thomas Becket was born in London in 1118 to a wealthy Norman family and was educated in England and in France. He then became an administrator for Theobald, Archbishop of Canterbury. Later, he was sent to study law in Italy and France and, after being ordained as a deacon, he was appointed as Archdeacon of Canterbury. His administrative skills eventually brought him to the notice of King Henry II, who, to Thomas' surprise, appointed him as the Chancellor of England.

He and the King became intimate friends, and because of Becket's unquestioning loyalty and support of the King's interests in both church and state, Henry secured Thomas' election as Archbishop of Canterbury in 1162. Becket, foreseeing a break with his Royal Master, was reluctant to accept. As Archbishop he changed, as he tells us, "from a patron of play actors and a follower of hounds, to being a shepherd of souls." He also defended the interests of the church against those of his former friend and patron, the King. The struggle between the two became so bitter that Thomas sought exile at an abbey in France.

When he returned to England six years later, the fragile reconciliation between Henry and the Archbishop broke down. In a fit of rage, the King is alleged to have asked his courtiers, "Who will rid me of this meddlesome priest?" Four barons, taking Henry's words as an order, made their way to Canterbury, and, upon finding the archbishop in the cathedral on December 29, 1170, struck him down with their swords. Later, when the monks of Canterbury undressed Thomas' body to wash it and prepare it for burial, they discovered that under his episcopal robes their worldly and determined archbishop was wearing a hair shirt. While such a garment hardly proves that a person is a saint, it clearly indicates that Thomas was motivated in the exercise of his office by far more than political considerations. His final words to the four barons before receiving the fatal blow were, "Willingly I die for the name of Jesus and in the defense of the church."

Thomas Becket

Archbishop of Canterbury and Martyr, 1170

I O God, our strength and our salvation, who didst call thy servant Thomas Becket to be a shepherd of thy people and a defender of thy church; Keep thy household from all evil and raise up faithful pastors and leaders who are wise in the ways of the gospel; through Jesus Christ, the shepherd of our souls, who liveth and reigneth with thee and the Holy Ghost, one God, for ever and ever. *Amen.*

II O God, our strength and our salvation, you called your servant Thomas Becket to be a shepherd of your people and a defender of your church; Keep your household from all evil and raise up faithful pastors and leaders who are wise in the ways of the gospel; through Jesus Christ, the shepherd of our souls, who lives and reigns with you and the Holy Spirit, one God, for ever and ever. *Amen.*

Lessons and Psalm

Wisdom 6:1-8
Psalm 5:1-7
Romans 5:5-11
Luke 4:1-13

Preface of the Incarnation

Frances was born in a log cabin in Holmesville, Mississippi, in 1861, of African American and Native American descent. Raised by her grandparents, she later went to live with a brother in New Orleans, where she finished school and attended Straight College.

While she was still a young woman, Gaudet dedicated her life to prison reform. In 1894, she began holding prayer meetings for Black prisoners. She wrote letters for them, delivered messages, and found them clothing. Later, she extended this ministry to white prisoners as well. Her dedication to the imprisoned and to penal reform won her the respect of prison officials, city authorities, the governor of Louisiana, and the Prison Reform Association.

In 1900, she was a delegate to the international convention of the Women's Christian Temperance Union in Edinburgh, Scotland. Gaudet worked to rehabilitate young Black people arrested for misdemeanors or vagrancy, becoming the first woman to support young offenders in Louisiana. Her efforts helped to found the Juvenile Court.

Deeply committed to the provision of good education, she eventually purchased a farm and founded the Gaudet Normal and Industrial School. In time, it expanded to more than 105 acres, with numerous buildings, and also served as a boarding school for children with working mothers. Gaudet served as its principal until 1921, when she donated the institution to the Episcopal Diocese of Louisiana. Though it closed in 1950, the Gaudet Episcopal Home opened in the same location four years later to serve African American children aged four to sixteen.

Frances Joseph Gaudet

Educator and Social Reformer, 1934

I Merciful God, who didst raise up thy servant Frances Joseph Gaudet to be a champion of the oppressed: Grant that we, encouraged by her example, may advocate for all who are denied the fullness of life to which thou hast called all thy children; through Jesus Christ our Lord, who liveth and reigneth with thee and the Holy Ghost, one God, for ever and ever. *Amen.*

II Merciful God, who raised up thy servant Frances Joseph Gaudet to be a champion of the oppressed: Grant that we, encouraged by her example, may advocate for all who are denied the fullness of life to which you have called all your children; through Jesus Christ our Lord, who lives and reigns with you and the Holy Spirit, one God, for ever and ever. *Amen.*

Lessons and Psalm

Lamentations 3:26-36
Psalm 146
Acts 16:25-34
Luke 4:14-21

Preface of the Incarnation

The Commons

The Common of Saints

Concerning the Common of Saints

The festival of a saint is observed in accordance with the rules of precedence set forth in the Calendar of the Church Year, pages 3-6.

At the discretion of the Celebrant, and as appropriate, one of the following Commons may be used

a) at the commemoration of a saint listed in the Calendar, in place of the Proper for the Lesser Feasts appointed in this book
b) at the patronal festival or commemoration of a saint not listed in the Calendar.

Any of the sets of Lessons assigned to a given Common may be used with any of the Collects.

Common of a Martyr I

I O Almighty God, who didst give to thy servant *N.* boldness to confess the Name of our Savior Jesus Christ before the rulers of this world, and courage to die for this faith: Grant that we may always be ready to give a reason for the hope that is in us, and to suffer gladly for the sake of the same our Lord Jesus Christ; who liveth and reigneth with thee and the Holy Spirit, one God, for ever and ever. *Amen.*

II Almighty God, who gave to your servant *N.* boldness to confess the Name of our Savior Jesus Christ before the rulers of this world, and courage to die for this faith: Grant that we may always be ready to give a reason for the hope that is in us, and to suffer gladly for the sake of our Lord Jesus Christ; who lives and reigns with you and the Holy Spirit, one God, for ever and ever. *Amen.*

Lessons and Psalm

2 Esdras 2:42-48
Psalm 126 *or* 121
1 Peter 3:14-18, 22
Matthew 10:16-22

Preface of a Saint

Common of a Martyr II

I O Almighty God, by whose grace and power thy holy martyr *N.* triumphed over suffering and was faithful even unto death: Grant us, who now remember him with thanksgiving, to be so faithful in our witness to thee in this world, that we may receive with him the crown of life; through Jesus Christ our Lord, who liveth and reigneth with thee and the Holy Spirit, one God, for ever and ever. *Amen.*

II Almighty God, by whose grace and power your holy martyr *N.* triumphed over suffering and was faithful even to death: Grant us, who now remember *him* in thanksgiving, to be so faithful in our witness to you in this world, that we may receive with *him* the crown of life; through Jesus Christ our Lord, who lives and reigns with you and the Holy Spirit, one God, for ever and ever. *Amen.*

Lessons and Psalm

Ecclesiasticus 51:1-12
Psalm 116 *or* 116:1-8
Revelation 7:13-17
Luke 12:2-12

Preface of a Saint

Common of a Martyr III

I Almighty and everlasting God, who didst enkindle the flame of thy love in the heart of thy holy martyr *N.*: Grant to us, thy humble servants, a like faith and power of love, that we who rejoice in *her* triumph may profit by *her* example; through Jesus Christ our Lord, who liveth and reigneth with thee and the Holy Spirit, one God, for ever and ever. *Amen.*

II Almighty and everlasting God, who kindled the flame of your love in the heart of your holy martyr *N.*: Grant to us, your humble servants, a like faith and power of love, that we who rejoice in *her* triumph may profit by *her* example; through Jesus Christ our Lord, who lives and reigns with you and the Holy Spirit, one God, for ever and ever. *Amen.*

Lessons and Psalm

Jeremiah 15:15-21
Psalm 124 *or* 31:1-5
1 Peter 4:12-19
Mark 8:34-38

Preface of a Saint

Common of a Missionary I

I Almighty and everlasting God, we thank thee for thy servant *N.*, whom thou didst call to preach the Gospel to the people of _________ [or to the _________ people]. Raise up, we beseech thee, in this and every land evangelists and heralds of thy kingdom, that thy Church may proclaim the unsearchable riches of our Savior Jesus Christ; who liveth and reigneth with thee and the Holy Spirit, one God, now and for ever. *Amen.*

II Almighty and everlasting God, we thank you for your servant *N.*, whom you called to preach the Gospel to the people of _________ [or to the _________ people]. Raise up in this and every land evangelists and heralds of your kingdom, that your Church may proclaim the unsearchable riches of our Savior Jesus Christ; who lives and reigns with you and the Holy Spirit, one God, now and for ever. *Amen.*

Lessons and Psalm

Isaiah 52:7-10
Psalm 96 *or* 96:1-7
Acts 1:1-9
Luke 10:1-9

Preface of Pentecost

Common of a Missionary II

I Almighty God, who willest to be glorified in thy saints, and didst raise up thy servant *N.* to be a light in the world: Shine, we pray thee, in our hearts, that we also in our generation may show forth thy praise, who hast called us out of darkness into thy marvelous light; through Jesus Christ our Lord, who liveth and reigneth with thee and the Holy Spirit, one God, now and for ever. *Amen.*

II Almighty God, whose will it is to be glorified in your saints, and who raised up your servant *N.* to be a light in the world: Shine, we pray, in our hearts, that we also in our generation may show forth your praise, who called us out of darkness into your marvelous light; through Jesus Christ our Lord, who lives and reigns with you and the Holy Spirit, one God, now and for ever. *Amen.*

Lessons and Psalm

Isaiah 49:1-6
Psalm 98 *or* 98:1-4
Acts 17:22-31
Matthew 28:16-20

Preface of Pentecost

Common of a Pastor I

I O heavenly Father, Shepherd of thy people, we give thee thanks for thy servant *N.*, who was faithful in the care and nurture of thy flock; and we pray that, following *his* example and the teaching of *his* holy life, we may by thy grace grow into the stature of the fullness of our Lord and Savior Jesus Christ; who liveth and reigneth with thee and the Holy Spirit, one God, for ever and ever. *Amen.*

II Heavenly Father, Shepherd of your people, we thank you for your servant *N.*, who was faithful in the care and nurture of your flock; and we pray that, following *his* example and the teaching of *his* holy life, we may by your grace grow into the stature of the fullness of our Lord and Savior Jesus Christ; who lives and reigns with you and the Holy Spirit, one God, for ever and ever. *Amen.*

Lessons and Psalm

Ezekiel 34:11-16
Psalm 23
1 Peter 5:1-4
John 21:15-17

Preface of a Saint

Common of a Pastor II

I O God, our heavenly Father, who didst raise up thy faithful servant *N.* to be a [bishop and] pastor in thy Church and to feed thy flock: Give abundantly to all pastors the gifts of thy Holy Spirit, that they may minister in thy household as true servants of Christ and stewards of thy divine mysteries; through the same Jesus Christ our Lord, who liveth and reigneth with thee and the same Spirit, one God, for ever and ever. *Amen.*

II O God, our heavenly Father, who raised up your faithful servant *N.* to be a [bishop and] pastor in your Church and to feed your flock: Give abundantly to all pastors the gifts of your Holy Spirit, that they may minister in your household as true servants of Christ and stewards of your divine mysteries; through Jesus Christ our Lord, who lives and reigns with you and the Holy Spirit, one God, for ever and ever. *Amen.*

Lessons and Psalm

Acts 20:17-35
Psalm 84 *or* 84:7-11
Ephesians 3:14-21
Matthew 24:42-47

Preface of a Saint

Common of a Theologian and Teacher I

I O God, who by thy Holy Spirit dost give to some the word of wisdom, to others the word of knowledge, and to others the word of faith: We praise thy Name for the gifts of grace manifested in thy servant *N.*, and we pray that thy Church may never be destitute of such gifts; through Jesus Christ our Lord, who with thee and the same Spirit liveth and reigneth, one God, for ever and ever. *Amen.*

II O God, by your Holy Spirit you give to some the word of wisdom, to others the word of knowledge, and to others the word of faith: We praise your Name for the gifts of grace manifested in your servant *N.*, and we pray that your Church may never be destitute of such gifts; through Jesus Christ our Lord, who with you and the Holy Spirit lives and reigns, one God, for ever and ever. *Amen.*

Lessons and Psalm

Wisdom 7:7-14
Psalm 119:97-104
1 Corinthians 2:6-10, 13-16
John 17:18-23

Preface of a Saint, or of Trinity Sunday

Common of a Theologian and Teacher II

I O Almighty God, who didst give to thy servant *N.* special gifts of grace to understand and teach the truth as it is in Christ Jesus: Grant, we beseech thee, that by this teaching we may know thee, the one true God, and Jesus Christ whom thou hast sent; who liveth and reigneth with thee and the Holy Spirit, one God, for ever and ever. *Amen.*

II Almighty God, you gave to your servant *N.* special gifts of grace to understand and teach the truth as it is in Christ Jesus: Grant that by this teaching we may know you, the one true God, and Jesus Christ whom you have sent; who lives and reigns with you and the Holy Spirit, one God, for ever and ever. *Amen.*

Lessons and Psalm

Proverbs 3:1-7
Psalm 119:89-96
1 Corinthians 3:5-11
Matthew 13:47-52

Preface of a Saint, or of Trinity Sunday

Common of a Monastic I

I O God, whose blessed Son became poor that we through his poverty might be rich: Deliver us, we pray thee, from an inordinate love of this world, that, inspired by the devotion of thy servant *N.*, we may serve thee with singleness of heart, and attain to the riches of the age to come; through the same thy Son Jesus Christ our Lord, who liveth and reigneth with thee, in the unity of the Holy Spirit, one God, now and for ever. *Amen.*

II O God, whose blessed Son became poor that we through his poverty might be rich: Deliver us from an inordinate love of this world, that we, inspired by the devotion of your servant *N.*, may serve you with singleness of heart, and attain to the riches of the age to come; through Jesus Christ our Lord, who lives and reigns with you, in the unity of the Holy Spirit, one God, now and for ever. *Amen.*

Lessons and Psalm

Song of Songs 8:6-7
Psalm 34 *or* 34:1-8
Philippians 3:7-15
Luke 12:33-37 *or* Luke 9:57-62

Preface of a Saint

Common of a Monastic II

I O God, by whose grace thy servant *N.*, enkindled with the fire of thy love, became a burning and a shining light in thy Church: Grant that we also may be aflame with the spirit of love and discipline, and may ever walk before thee as children of light; through Jesus Christ our Lord, who with thee, in the unity of the Holy Spirit, liveth and reigneth, one God, now and for ever. *Amen.*

II O God, by whose grace your servant *N.*, kindled with the flame of your love, became a burning and a shining light in your Church: Grant that we also may be aflame with the spirit of love and discipline, and walk before you as children of light; through Jesus Christ our Lord, who lives and reigns with you, in the unity of the Holy Spirit, one God, now and for ever. *Amen.*

Lessons and Psalm

Acts 2:42-47a
Psalm 133 *or* 119:161-168
2 Corinthians 6:1-10
Matthew 6:24-33

Preface of a Saint

Common of a Saint I

I O Almighty God, who hast compassed us about with so great a cloud of witnesses: Grant that we, encouraged by the good example of thy servant *N.*, may persevere in running the race that is set before us, until at length, through thy mercy, we may with him attain to thine eternal joy; through Jesus Christ, the author and perfecter of our faith, who liveth and reigneth with thee and the Holy Spirit, one God, for ever and ever. *Amen.*

II Almighty God, you have surrounded us with a great cloud of witnesses: Grant that we, encouraged by the good example of your servant *N.*, may persevere in running the race that is set before us, until at last we may with him attain to your eternal joy; through Jesus Christ, the pioneer and perfecter of our faith, who lives and reigns with you and the Holy Spirit, one God, for ever and ever. *Amen.*

Lessons and Psalm

Micah 6:6-8
Psalm 15
Hebrews 12:1-2
Matthew 25:31-40

Preface of a Saint

Common of a Saint II

I O God, who hast brought us near to an innumerable company of angels and to the spirits of just men made perfect: Grant us during our earthly pilgrimage to abide in their fellowship, and in our heavenly country to become partakers of their joy; through Jesus Christ our Lord, who liveth and reigneth with thee and the Holy Spirit, one God, now and for ever. *Amen.*

II O God, you have brought us near to an innumerable company of angels, and to the spirits of just men made perfect: Grant us during our earthly pilgrimage to abide in their fellowship, and in our heavenly country to become partakers of their joy; through Jesus Christ our Lord, who lives and reigns with you and the Holy Spirit, one God, now and for ever. *Amen.*

Lessons and Psalm

Wisdom 3:1-9
Psalm 34 *or* 34:15-22
Philippians 4:4-9
Luke 6:17-23

Preface of a Saint

Common of a Saint III

I O Almighty God, who by thy Holy Spirit hast made us one with thy saints in heaven and on earth: Grant that in our earthly pilgrimage we may ever be supported by this fellowship of love and prayer, and may know ourselves to be surrounded by their witness to thy power and mercy. We ask this for the sake of Jesus Christ, in whom all our intercessions are acceptable through the Spirit, and who liveth and reigneth for ever and ever. *Amen.*

II Almighty God, by your Holy Spirit you have made us one with your saints in heaven and on earth: Grant that in our earthly pilgrimage we may always be supported by this fellowship of love and prayer, and know ourselves to be surrounded by their witness to your power and mercy. We ask this for the sake of Jesus Christ, in whom all our intercessions are acceptable through the Spirit, and who lives and reigns for ever and ever. *Amen.*

Lessons and Psalm

Ecclesiasticus 2:7-11
Psalm 1
1 Corinthians 1:26-31
Matthew 25:1-13

Preface of a Saint

New Commons for Various Occasions

Artists & Writers

I Eternal God, light of the world and Creator of all that is good and lovely: We bless thy name for inspiring [*N.* and] all those who, with images and words, hath filled us with desire and love for thee; through Jesus Christ our Savior, who with thee and the Holy Spirit liveth and reigneth, one God, for ever and ever. *Amen.*

II Eternal God, light of the world and Creator of all that is good and lovely: We bless your name for inspiring [*N.* and] all those who with images and words have filled us with desire and love for you; through Jesus Christ our Savior, who with you and the Holy Spirit lives and reigns, one God, for ever and ever. *Amen.*

Lessons and Psalm

1 Chronicles 29:14b-19
Psalm 90:14-17
1 Corinthians 3:1-3
John 21:15-17, 24-25

Preface

I Because in the beauty of holiness thou hast called us to worship thee; and hast given faithful artists and writers to illumine our prayer from age to age.

II Because in the beauty of holiness you call us to worship you, and you have given faithful artists and writers to illumine our prayer from age to age.

Common of the Blessed Virgin Mary, Godbearer

I Almighty God, by thy saving grace thou didst call Mary of Nazareth to be the mother of thine only Son: Inspire us by the same grace to follow her example of bearing God to the world. We pray through Jesus Christ her son our Savior. *Amen.*

II Almighty God, of your saving grace you called Mary of Nazareth to be the mother of your only begotten Son: Inspire us by the same grace to follow her example of bearing God to the world. We pray through Jesus Christ her son our Savior. *Amen.*

or

I Holy God, we magnify thy Name for calling the blessed Virgin Mary to bear thy Word of hope to the poor, the hungry, and those who have no voice: Give unto us thy grace and strength, that we might proclaim thy Good News in every age, with every tongue; through Jesus Christ our Savior, in the power of thy Holy Spirit. *Amen.*

II Holy God, we magnify your Name for calling the blessed Virgin Mary to bear your Word of hope to the poor, the hungry, and those who have no voice: Give us grace and strength to proclaim your Good News in every age, with every tongue; through Jesus Christ our Savior, in the power of your Holy Spirit. *Amen.*

Lessons and Psalm

Isaiah 43:9-13, 19a
Psalm 34:1-8
1 Corinthians 1:26-31
Luke 1:42-55

Preface

I Because even as blessed Mary didst consent to become God-bearer for the world, thou hast called us to bear thy Word to all whom our lives touch.

II Because as blessed Mary consented to become God-bearer for the world, you call us to bear your Word to all whom our lives touch.

Care of God's Creation

I Bountiful Creator, thou openest thy hand to satisfy the needs of every living creature: Make us continually thankful for thy loving providence, and grant that we, remembering the account we must one day give, may be faithful stewards of thine abundance, for the benefit of the whole creation; through Jesus Christ our Lord, through whom all things are made, who liveth and reigneth with thee and the Holy Spirit, one God, for ever and ever. *Amen.*

II Bountiful Creator, you open your hand to satisfy the needs of every living creature: Make us always thankful for your loving providence, and grant that we, remembering the account we must one day give, may be faithful stewards of your abundance, for the benefit of the whole creation; through Jesus Christ our Lord, through whom all things were made, and who lives and reigns with you and the Holy Spirit, one God, for ever and ever. *Amen.*

Lessons and Psalm

1 Kings 4:29-30, 33-34
Psalm 145:1-7, 22
Acts 17:24-31
John 1:1-5, 9-14

Preface

I For thou hast brought us into being and called us to care for the earth.

II Because you have brought us into being and called us to care for the earth.

Goodness of God's Creation

I God of creation, we thank thee for all that thou hast made and called good: Grant that we may rightly serve and conserve the earth, and live at peace with all thy creatures; through Jesus Christ, the firstborn of all creation, in whom thou art reconciling the whole world unto thyself. *Amen.*

II God of creation, we thank you for all that you have made and called good: Grant that we may rightly serve and conserve the earth, and live at peace with all your creatures; through Jesus Christ, the firstborn of all creation, in whom you are reconciling the whole world to yourself. *Amen.*

Lessons and Psalm

Job 14:7-9
Psalm 104:24-31
Romans 1:20-23
Mark 16:14-15

Preface

I Because in thy loving-kindness, thou hast brought the whole creation into being and blessed its goodness.

II *Instead of a Preface, Prayer D is recommended for use with this Proper.*

On the Occasion of a Disaster

I Compassionate God, whose Son Jesus wept at the grave of his friend Lazarus: Draw near to us in this time of sorrow and anguish, comfort those who mourn, strengthen those who are weary, encourage those in despair, and lead us all to fullness of life; through the same Jesus Christ, our Savior and Redeemer, who liveth and reigneth with thee, in the unity of the Holy Spirit, God for ever and ever. *Amen.*

II Compassionate God, whose Son Jesus wept at the grave of his friend Lazarus: Draw near to us in this time of sorrow and anguish, comfort those who mourn, strengthen those who are weary, encourage those in despair, and lead us all to fullness of life; through the same Jesus Christ, our Savior and Redeemer, who lives and reigns with you, in the unity of the Holy Spirit, God for ever and ever. *Amen.*

Lessons and Psalm

Job 14:7-13 *or* Jeremiah 31:15-20
Psalm 60:1-5 *or* 130 *or* 80:1-7 *or* 23
Romans 8:35-38 *or* Revelation 21:1-7 *or* Romans 8:18-25
Luke 6:20-26 *or* Mark 13:14-27

Preface of God the Son

or

Preface of the Commemoration of the Dead

On the Anniversary of a Disaster

I God of steadfast love, who didst lead thy people through the wilderness: Be with us as we remember [and grieve]. By thy grace, lead us, we pray, in the path of new life, in the company of thy saints and angels; through Jesus Christ, the Savior and Redeemer of the world. *Amen.*

II God of steadfast love, who led your people through the wilderness: Be with us as we remember [and grieve]. By your grace, lead us in the path of new life, in the company of your saints and angels; through Jesus Christ, the Savior and Redeemer of the world. *Amen.*

Lessons and Psalm

Job 14:7-13 *or* Jeremiah 31:15-20
Psalm 60:1-5 *or* 130 *or* 80:1-7 *or* 23
Romans 8:35-38 *or* Revelation 21:1-7 *or* Romans 8:18-25
Luke 6:20-26 *or* Mark 13:14-27

Preface of God the Son

or

Preface of the Commemoration of the Dead

Prophetic Witness in the Church

I Gracious Father, we pray for thy holy Catholic Church. Fill it with all truth, in all truth with all peace. Where it is corrupt, purify it; where it is in error, direct it; where in anything it is amiss, reform it. Where it is right, strengthen it; where it is in want, provide for it; where it is divided, reunite it; for the sake of Jesus Christ thy Son our Savior, who with thee and the Holy Spirit livest and reignest, one God, now and for ever. *Amen.*

II Gracious Father, we pray for your holy Catholic Church. Fill it with all truth, in all truth with all peace. Where it is corrupt, purify it; where it is in error, direct it; where in anything it is amiss, reform it. Where it is right, strengthen it; where it is in want, provide for it; where it is divided, reunite it; for the sake of Jesus Christ your Son our Savior, who with you and the Holy Spirit lives and reigns, one God, now and for ever. *Amen.*

Lessons and Psalm

Ezekiel 34:1-6, 20-22
Psalm 12:1-7
Acts 22:30—23:10
Matthew 21:12-16

Preface

I For thou dost cleanse and renew thy Church by the witness of thy saints, calling people in every age to holiness of life through the indwelling of thy Holy Spirit.

II For you cleanse and renew your Church by the witness of your saints, calling people in every age to holiness of life through the indwelling of your Holy Spirit.

Prophetic Witness in Society

I Almighty God, whose prophets hath taught us righteousness in the care of thy poor: By the guidance of thy Holy Spirit, grant that we may do justice, love mercy, and walk humbly in thy sight; through Jesus Christ, our Judge and Redeemer, who liveth and reigneth, with thee and the same Spirit ever one God. *Amen.*

II Almighty God, whose prophets taught us righteousness in the care of your poor: By the guidance of your Holy Spirit, grant that we may do justice, love mercy, and walk humbly in your sight; through Jesus Christ, our Judge and Redeemer, who lives and reigns with you and the same Spirit, one God, now and for ever. *Amen.*

Lessons and Psalm

Isaiah 55:11—56:1
Psalm 2:1-2, 10-12
Acts 14:14-17, 21-23
Mark 4:21-29

Preface

I Because in every age thou hast called brave souls to proclaim righteousness for the transformation of the world, that all may welcome the coming of thy holy reign.

II Because in every age you have called brave souls to proclaim righteousness for the transformation of the world, that all may welcome the coming of your holy reign.

Reconciliation and Forgiveness

I God of compassion, thou hast reconciled us in Jesus Christ who is our peace: Enable us to live as Jesus lived, breaking down walls of hostility and healing enmity. Give us grace to make peace with those from whom we are divided, that, forgiven and forgiving, we may ever be one in Christ; who with thee and the Holy Spirit reignest for ever, one holy and undivided Trinity. *Amen.*

II God of compassion, you have reconciled us in Jesus Christ who is our peace: Enable us to live as Jesus lived, breaking down walls of hostility and healing enmity. Give us grace to make peace with those from whom we are divided, that, forgiven and forgiving, we may ever be one in Christ; who with you and the Holy Spirit reigns for ever, one holy and undivided Trinity. *Amen.*

Lessons and Psalm

Genesis 8:12-17, 20-22
Psalm 51:1-17
Hebrews 4:12-16
Luke 23:32-43

Preface

I Because by the cross of our Lord Jesus Christ thou hast reconciled all things to thyself, not counting our sins against us and renewing our hearts to forgive as we have been forgiven.

II Because by the cross of our Lord Jesus Christ you have reconciled all things to yourself, not counting our sins against us and renewing our hearts to forgive as we have been forgiven.

Space Exploration

I Creator of the universe, whose dominion extends through the immensity of space: Guide and guard those who seek to fathom its mysteries [especially *N.N.*]. Save us from arrogance lest we forget that our achievements are grounded in thee, and, by the grace of thy Holy Spirit, protect our travels beyond the reaches of earth, that we may glory ever more in the wonder of thy creation; through Jesus Christ, thy Word, by whom all things came to be, who with thee and the Holy Spirit liveth and reigneth, one God, for ever and ever. *Amen.*

II Creator of the universe, your dominion extends through the immensity of space: Guide and guard those who seek to fathom its mysteries [especially *N.N.*]. Save us from arrogance lest we forget that our achievements are grounded in you, and, by the grace of your Holy Spirit, protect our travels beyond the reaches of earth, that we may glory ever more in the wonder of your creation; through Jesus Christ, your Word, by whom all things came to be, who with you and the Holy Spirit lives and reigns, one God, for ever and ever. *Amen.*

Lessons and Psalm

Job 38: 4-12, 16-18
Psalm 19:1-6 *or* Canticle 12
Revelation 1:7-8, 12-16
John 15:5-9

Preface of God the Father

or

Preface of the Epiphany

Scientists and Environmentalists

I God of grace and glory, thou didst create and sustain the universe in majesty and beauty: We thank you for [*N.* and] all in whom thou hast planted the desire to know thy creation and to explore thy work and wisdom. Lead us, like them, to understand better the wonder and mystery of creation; through Christ thine eternal Word, through whom all things were made. *Amen.*

II God of grace and glory, you create and sustain the universe in majesty and beauty: We thank you for [*N.* and] all in whom you have planted the desire to know your creation and to explore your work and wisdom. Lead us, like them, to understand better the wonder and mystery of creation; through Christ your eternal Word, through whom all things were made. *Amen.*

Lessons and Psalm

Genesis 2:9-20
Psalm 34:8-14
1 Corinthians 13:1-6
John 20:24-27

Preface

I Because, Holy God, mysterious and manifest, thou hast inspired searchers to know thee through thy creation, and revealest thy work, that thy people may rejoice in thy many gifts.

II Because, Holy God, mysterious and manifest, you inspire searchers to know you through your creation, and you reveal your work, so that your people may rejoice in your many gifts.

Principles of Revision

The qualifications and benchmarks for inclusion in the church calendar are as follows.

1. *Historicity:* Christianity is a radically historical religion, so in almost every instance it is not theological realities or spiritual movements but exemplary witness to the Gospel of Christ in lives actually lived that is commemorated in the Calendar.
2. *Christian Discipleship:* The death of the saints, precious in God's sight, is the ultimate witness to the power of the Resurrection. What is being commemorated is therefore the completion in death of a particular Christian's living out of the promises of baptism. Baptism is, therefore, a necessary prerequisite for inclusion in the Calendar.
3. *Significance:* Those commemorated should have been in their lifetime extraordinary, even heroic, servants of God and God's people for the sake, and after the example, of Jesus Christ. They may also be people whose creative work or whose manner of life has glorified God, enriched the life of the Church, or led others to a deeper understanding of God. In their varied ways, those commemorated have revealed Christ's presence in, and Lordship over, all of history; and continue to inspire us as we carry forward God's mission in the world. Commemoration thereby reminds us of our participation in the great cloud of witnesses: our own membership in a timeless community that surrounds and supports us, equipping us for ministry in the world and moving us toward maturity in Christ.

4. *Memorability:* The Calendar should include those who, through their devotion to Christ and their joyful and loving participation in the community of the faithful, deserve to be remembered by the Episcopal Church today. However, in order to celebrate the whole history of salvation, it is important also to include those "whose memory may have faded in the shifting fashions of public concern, but whose witness is deemed important to the life and mission of the Church" (Thomas Talley).

5. *Range of Inclusion:* The Calendar especially includes Episcopalians and other members of the Anglican Communion. Focusing above all on principles of Christian witness and discipleship, and honoring the movement of the Holy Spirit in the establishment of local observance, the Calendar seeks to represent the full breadth and depth of the Body of Christ.

6. *Local, Organic Observance:* Similarly, it should be the case that significant commemoration of a particular person already exists at the local and regional levels before that person is included in the Calendar.

7. *Perspective:* It should normatively be the case that a person be included in the Calendar only after two generations or fifty years have elapsed since that person's death. The passage of time permits the testing and flowering of their Christian witness. In any case, no fewer than two General Conventions shall pass after the person's death before any individual may be considered.

8. *Levels of Commemoration:* Principal Feasts, Sundays, and Major Holy Days have primacy of place in the Church's liturgical observance. It does not seem appropriate to distinguish between the various other commemorations by regarding some as having either a greater or a lesser claim on our observance of them. Each commemoration should be given equal weight as far as the provision of the liturgical propers is concerned (including the listing of three lessons).

9. *Distribution of Commemorations:* Normally, joint commemoration will arise through shared Christian witness or date of death. In some cases, unrelated commemorations will occur on the same date. In the observance of lesser feasts, the preference of the local community may be exercised.

Crafting Local Commemorations

History demonstrates that liturgical commemorations originate in the local community. Indeed, all proposed additions to the Calendar of the Church ought to begin as local commemorations. Included below is a process for developing such local observances, as well as some guiding questions that might help the local community through the process.

The Book of Common Prayer (pp. 13, 18, 195, and 246) permits memorials not listed in the Calendar, provides collects and readings for them (the Common of Saints), and recognizes the bishop's authority to set forth devotions for occasions for which no prayer or service has been provided by the Prayer Book. Although the Prayer Book does not require the bishop's permission to use the Common of Saints for memorials not included in the Calendar, it is appropriate that the bishop's consent be requested.

While these guidelines are general in nature, and not exhaustive in scope or situation, this process is suggested for initiating local, diocesan, or regional memorials.

1. *Establishment:* A congregation, diocese, or other community or organization establishes a commemoration for a specific person/occasion, on a specific day.
   - Who/what is being commemorated?
   - Why is this commemoration beneficial to the local community's liturgical life?
   - What would be lost if the commemoration were not observed?

(See the most recent set of criteria for inclusion in the Calendar of the Church ["Principles of Revision," pages 623-624]; and the set of Holy Days, Book of Common Prayer page 16, that take precedence on their dates.)

2. *Collects and Readings:* A collect and readings from the Common of Saints are chosen and used. Perhaps a new collect could be composed, and a new collection of readings assigned for use in the commemoration. The Standing Commission on Liturgy and Music and local diocesan liturgical bodies are available for consultation.
   - How might selections from Holy Scripture and the chosen, or new, collect communicate the reason for observing the commemoration?
   - What selections of Holy Scripture will help the congregation to better understand the commemoration?
   - What do we need to pray for in the collect to better understand the commemoration?

3. *Observance:* The congregation, diocese, province, or organization proceeds to annually observe the commemoration in their regular liturgical life.
   - How might you invite others to join the celebration?
   - Does it make sense to invite the local community? Nearby congregations? The diocese? The province?

4. *Evaluation:* The local community should engage in an ongoing evaluation of the commemoration. The evaluation should include conversation with members of the community and with participants in the observance. Earlier steps should be revisited if necessary.
   - How has your thinking in previous steps evolved through your observance of the commemoration?
   - What have you learned?
   - What feedback have you received?
   - What has surprised you as you've observed the commemoration?
   - To what extent has the local community embraced the observance?
   - Does anything need to change? How might the readings and collect need to be adapted?

5. *Wider Recognition:* Those interested in promoting a wider commemoration then begin to share the developed

materials with others, suggesting that they also adopt the commemoration. If at some time it is desired to propose it for optional observance by the wider Church, documented evidence of the spread and duration of local commemoration is essential to include in the proposal to the General Convention.

- Why should the commemoration be observed by the wider Church?
- What would the wider Church lose if it did not observe this commemoration?
- How would this commemoration strengthen or balance the Calendar of the Church?

(See the most recent set of criteria for inclusion in the Calendar of the Church ["Principles of Revision," pages 623-624].)

Some commemorations, perhaps many, will remain local, diocesan, or regional in character. This in no way reduces their importance to those who revere and seek to keep alive the memory of beloved and faithful witnesses to Christ. Regardless of local or Church-wide use, the Book of Common Prayer welcomes regular local commemorations in the liturgical life of the Church.

Index